COMPUTER SCIENCE WITH PASCAL
For Advanced Placement Students

COMPUTER SCIENCE WITH PASCAL
For Advanced Placement Students

STEVEN L. MANDELL ● COLLEEN J. MANDELL

WEST'S
Computer Education Series

WEST PUBLISHING COMPANY
St. Paul   New York   Los Angeles   San Francisco

COPYEDITING: Editing, Design, and Production
TEXT DESIGN: Adapted by Lucy Lesiak Design
COVER DESIGN: Editing, Design, and Production
COMPOSITOR: Better Graphics
ART AND TYPESETTING COORDINATION: The Quarasan Group.

TRS-80 is a trademark of the Radio Shack Division of Tandy Corporation. Apple is the registered trademark of Apple Computer, Inc. Commodore 64 is a trademark of Commodore Business Machines. IBM PC is a trademark of International Business Machines Corporation.

Disclaimer of Warranties and Limitation of Liabilities
The author has taken due care in preparing this book and the programs in it, including research, development, and testing to ascertain their effectiveness. The author and the publisher make no express or implied warranty of any kind with regard to these programs or the supplementary documentation in this book. In no event shall the author or the publisher be liable for incidental or consequential damages in connection with or arising out of the furnishing, performance, or use of any of these programs.

Library of Congress Cataloging in Publication Data

Mandell, Steven L.
    Computer science with PASCAL.

    Includes index.
    Summary: An introduction to computers and computer programming with emphasis on constructing programs with PASCAL.
    1. PASCAL (Computer program language)—Juvenile literature. 2. Electronic digital computers—Juvenile literature. [1. PASCAL (Computer program language) 2. Programming languages (Computers) 3. Computers] I. Mandell, Colleen J. II. Title.
    QA76.73.P2M3   1985   001.64'24   85-5354
    ISBN 0-314-89692-9
    3rd Reprint—1987

PHOTO CREDITS

1 Courtesy of Cullinet Software, Inc.; **5** National Center for Atmospheric Research/National Science Foundation; **7** (top) Courtesy of International Business Machines Corporation; (bottom) Courtesy of NCR Corporation; **8** (left) Courtesy of Apple Computer Inc.; (right) Courtesy of International Business Machines Corporation; **9** (left) Courtesy of Commodore Electronics Limited; (right) Courtesy of BASF Systems Corporation; **10** Courtesy of Philips; **12** Courtesy of Amdek Corporation; **19** Courtesy of International Business Machines; **25** Courtesy of Sperry Corporation; **41** Courtesy of Sperry Corporation; **61** Reproduced with permission of AT&T Corporate Archive; **81** Courtesy of International Business Machines Corporation; **107** Evans & Sutherland Computer Corporation; **127** U.S. Air Force Photo; **153** Courtesy of Westinghouse Electric Corporation; **171** Courtesy of Sperry Corporation; **199** Courtesy of Cubicomp Corporation; **213** Courtesy of International Business Machines Corporation; **233** Courtesy of Hewlett-Packard; **253** Courtesy of Ford Motor Company; **285** Courtesy of International Business Machines Corporation; **307** MINDSET Personal Computers; **329** Philips Scientific and Industrial Equipment Division; **348** Courtesy of International Business Machines Corporation; **365** Courtesy of National Semiconductor Corporation; **367** Courtesy of Norma Morris; **368** (top) Courtesy of National Semiconductor Corporation;

COMPUTER SCIENCE WITH PASCAL
For Advanced Placement Students

AUTHORS

Colleen J. Mandell, B.S., M.S., Ed. D.; Educator; Software Developer; Psychometrist; Associate Professor, College of Education, Bowling Green State University.

Steven L. Mandell, B.A., B.S.Ch.E., M.B.A., D.B.A., J.D.; Computer Book Author; Software Developer; Computer Lawyer; Associate Professor of Computer Systems, Bowling Green State University.

EDUCATIONAL CONSULTANT

Julie G. Fiscus, B.A., M.A.; Computer Educator

CONTENT SPECIALISTS

Susan K. Baumann, B.S.; Computer Educator; Computer Programmer

Robert A. Szymanski, B.S., M.B.A.; Computer Educator; Computer Programmer

Russ Thompson, B.S., M.B.A.; Computer Educator; Programmer Analyst

Dieter J. Zirkler, B.S., M.A.; Computer Educator; Mathematician; Psychologist

CRITICAL EVALUATORS FOR WEST'S COMPUTER EDUCATION SERIES

Bruce Don Bowen, Davis County School District, Data Processing Department, Layton, Utah; **Charles M. Bueler**, Assistant Superintendent for Instruction, Hannibal Public Schools, Hannibal, Missouri; **Dr. Tom Burnett**, Assistant to Superintendent for Computer Technology, Lincoln Public Schools, Lincoln, Nebraska; **Sharon Burrowes**, Wooster City Schools, Wooster, Ohio; **Bruce B. Burt**, West Chester School District, West Chester, Pennsylvania; **Vincent Cirello**, East

Meadow High School, Curriculum Center, East Meadow, New York; **Don M. Cochran**, Bartlesville High School, Bartlesville, Oklahoma; **Dr. George E. Cooke**, Assistant Superintendent, Indiana Area School District, Indiana, Pennsylvania; **Carolyn Cox**, Virginia Beach City Public Schools, Office of Curriculum and Staff Development, Virginia Beach, Virginia; **Joseph Crupie**, North Hills High School, Pittsburgh, Pennsylvania; **Charles R. Deupree**, Ionia Public Schools, Ionia, Michigan; **Dr. Helen Ditzhazy**, Assistant Superintendent, Jackson Public Schools, Jackson, Michigan; **Dr. John H. Emhuff**, Assistant Superintendent, Instruction, Mt. Vernon, Indiana; **Ms. Carol Haynes**, Prospect School, Learning Center Director, Hinsdale, Illinois; **Ken Hendrickson**, Oak Park Elementary School, Newbury Park, California; **Dr. Sandra Howe**, Kalamazoo Public Schools, Kalamazoo, Michigan; **Monica J. Ilas**, Media Specialist for Lakewood Public Schools, Lakewood, Ohio; **Doris Kassera**, Media Specialist, Eau Claire Elementary Schools, Eau Claire, Wisconsin; **Colvin Kindschi**, Oak Park Elementary School, Newbury Park, California; **Douglas Krugger**, Computer Operations Center, School District of the City of Erie, Erie, Pennsylvania; **Mary E. Larnard**, Newburyport High School, Newburyport, Massachusetts; **Wally Leech**, The Media Center, Greater Johnstown School District, Johnstown, Pennsylvania; **Letitia Martin**, Indian Hills Elementary School, North Little Rock, Arkansas; **Marilyn Mathis**, Murfreesboro City Schools, Murfreesboro, Tennessee; **Dr. Judith K. Meyers**, Lakewood City Schools, Coordinator Media Services, Lakewood, Ohio; **Mark A. Mitrovich**, Principal, Clarkston High School, Clarkston, Washington; **Willis Parks**, Coordinator of Computer Education, North Canton City Schools, North Canton, Ohio; **Bette Pereira**, Harrison High School, Harrison, Ohio; **Bruce Raskin**, Mathematics-Microcomputer Department Chairman, Miami Springs Junior High School, Pembroke Pines, Florida; **Gary R. Reichelt**, Clackamas Community College, Portland, Oregon; **Lynda M. Reynen**, Computer Science Director, Ft. Pierce Central High School, Ft. Pierce, Florida; **Leon Roland**, Computer Coordinator, Billings Public Schools, Billings, Montana; **Richard Sheets**, Computer Specialist, Mesa Public School District #4, Mesa, Arizona; **Charlotte Shepperd**, Seguin High School, Seguin, Texas; **W. Richard Smith**, Clovis West High School, Fresno, California; **John R. Speckien**, Director of Curriculum Development, Boulder Valley School District, Boulder, Colorado; **Raymond J. Tombari**, Braintree High School, Braintree, Massachusetts; **Joanne Troutner**, Computer Coordinator & Media Specialist, Tippecanoe School District, Lafayette, Indiana; **Jan Van Dam**, Computer Curriculum Coordinator, Rochester Community Schools, Rochester, Michigan; **A. Thomas Vincent**, Coordinator of Vocational Education, Gallup McKinley County Public Schools, Gallup, New Mexico; **Richard Weisenhoff**, Howard County Public Schools, Elliott City, Maryland.

REVIEWERS FOR *COMPUTER SCIENCE WITH PASCAL FOR ADVANCED PLACEMENT STUDENTS*

Robert Baker
Narbonne High School
Manhattan Beach, California

Kathleen Beard
Upland High School
Upland, California

Sharon Burrowes
Wooster City Schools
Wooster, Ohio

Don M. Cochran
Bartlesville High School
Bartlesville, Oklahoma

Steven T. Cottrell
Woods Cross High School
Bountiful, Utah

Michael Owens
Director of Curriculum &
    Instruction
College Station Independent
    School District
College Station, Texas

Naomi R. Salaman
Boulder High School
Boulder, Colorado

Richard A. Silvius
Northampton Area Senior High
    School
Northampton, Pennsylvania

W. Richard Smith
Clovis West High School
Fresno, California

Jan Van Dam
Computer Curriculum Coordi-
    nator
Rochester Community Schools
Rochester, Michigan

A NOTE ON THE READING LEVEL

The reading level of **Computer Science with Pascal for Advanced Placement Students** has been checked and verified to fall within the tenth through twelfth grade span. Nine samples of approximately 100-150 words were checked. The following indexes were used: Estimated Dale, Fog Index, Flesch Grade Level, Smog Index, and the Frye.

Edward D. Fiscus, Ph.D.
Associate Professor and Chair
Department of Special Education
College of Education
Bowling Green State University
Bowling Green, Ohio

Preface

WEST'S COMPUTER EDUCATION SERIES

The computer revolution has excited the education profession more than any other technological advancement. It is clear that students must be able to master computer skills if they are to survive in a technology-based world. The goal of West's Computer Education Series is to provide the necessary learning packages to support the classroom teacher in accomplishing the objectives of the computer curriculum.

Before embarking on West's Computer Education Series, great care was taken to plan the overall concept of a fully integrated series as well as to assess the particular requirements for each individual text. An extensive survey of computer educators was done across the country in the very early stages of development. After the basic plans for the series were established, many teachers and computer coordinators were asked to comment on the general scope of the series and the specific content for each of the texts. The manuscripts were read and evaluated by many computer educators, and student and teacher feedback was obtained through field testing. Computer professionals were then assigned the task of technically verifying all of the material. Many changes and refinements were incorporated throughout the development of each text, and great care was taken to maintain the integrity of the series each step along the way. The result of this very careful development and review process is a product the authors and the publisher are proud and confident to present to the educational community.

Three additional factors were given top priority during this project: Reading level, pedagogical design, and teacher materials. Students must be presented material at the appropriate reading level if educational objectives are to be accomplished. Grade spans have been kept to a maximum of three years, thus enabling a close targeting of both level and relevancy of examples. The pedagogical design of each book was carefully developed based upon grade level and subject matter. Additionally, the series was developed with an overall pedagogical plan, making it very easy for the teacher and the students to move from one text to the next. We have employed outlines, learning objectives, vocabulary lists, learning checks, summary points, tests, glossaries and other devices appropriate to specific titles to enhance the educational process for the student.

The teachers' manuals that accompany each text in West's Computer Education Series are complete, thorough and easy to use for teachers at any level of computer expertise. The manuals offer an extensive package of materials to assist the teacher in reinforcing the concepts introduced in the texts.

ABOUT THIS TEXT

Computer Science with Pascal for Advanced Placement Students is designed to prepare students to take the College Entrance Examination Board's Advanced Placement Computer Science Test. This textbook provides thorough coverage of all areas emphasized on the examination such as algorithm development, programming methodology, and data structures.

The programming language used on the examination is Pascal as originally defined by Jensen and Wirth. This textbook presents structured problem solving through UCSD Pascal because of its popularity in high schools. Differences between UCSD Pascal and the original definition of the language are indicated in the text. All programs have been run through both Apple and IBM machine implementations: Apple II Pascal and the UCSD p-System.

Each chapter contains standard pedagogical devices: A chapter outline, learning objectives, and introduction provide a framework for helping the student to focus on the chapter content. Advanced Placement Chapter Highlights for each chapter are highlighted after the learning objectives. This is a list of topics that appear in the chapter and are also covered in the Advanced Placement Computer Science Examination. Numerous sample computer programs are included to permit the student to make a smooth transition from the abstraction of language rule to the concrete design of program instructions. Learning checks with inverted answers are included as a means of self-testing before proceeding to a subsequent section. Summary points and a vocabulary list are used to reinforce the most important concepts presented in the chapter. Finally, a chapter test and programming problems allow the teacher and students an opportunity to evaluate their level of mastery of the material.

The teacher's manual to support this book is divided into three parts: Classroom Administration, Test Bank, and Additional Teacher Materials. In the administration section a standard format is used for each chapter to assist the teacher: Summary, Objectives, Vocabulary, Outline, Learning Activities, Answers to Chapter Test, Solutions to Programming Problems in Text, and Additional Programming Problems with Solutions. The test bank section includes by chapter approximately 750 true/false and multiple choice questions with the associated answer key. The final section of the teacher's manual includes blackline masters for transparencies and student study sheets as well as a resource list and expanded glossary.

TO THE STUDENT

The goal of this textbook is to prepare you to pass the Advanced Placement Computer Science Examination given by the College Entrance Examination Board. This examination is intended to test your understanding of programming methodology, algorithms, and data structures. Therefore, the authors of this text have placed considerable emphasis on these areas. You will also learn the Pascal programming language which is used on the Advanced Placement Examination. In developing this text, a number of features were included to help you recognize important ideas and remember the material easier.

Chapter Outline

Each chapter begins with an outline that gives you an overall picture of what is in the chapter and prepares you to read more effectively.

Learning Objectives

This list tells you specifically what you will achieve by studying and understanding each chapter.

Advanced Placement Chapter Highlights

The topics covered in the chapter which also appears on the Advanced Placement Computer Science Examination are listed to help you prepare for the exam.

Learning Checks

You will find questions following each section within the chapter which are intended to help you check your progress. When you are able to answer the Learning Check questions correctly, you are ready to go on to the next section.

Sample Computer Programs

The many sample computer programs will help you understand the concepts explained and learn to write your own programs.

Summary Points

A point-by-point summary at the end of each chapter restates the important chapter ideas to make studying and remembering easier.

Vocabulary List

A list of the important new terms and concepts with their definitions is included at the end of each chapter as another study aid.

Chapter Test

Taking the chapter test will let you check how much of the chapter material you remember and understand.

Programming Problems

By completing the programming problems after each chapter you can build your programming skills.

ACKNOWLEDGMENTS

Many individuals have been involved in the development of the material for West's Computer Education Series. These professionals have provided invaluable assistance for the completion of a series of this magnitude: Greg Allgair, Kim Girnus, John Gregor, Steve Hoffman, Craig Howarth, Rhonda Raifsnider, and Jeff Sanborn on student material; Mike Costarella, Margaret Gallito, Sara Hosler, Gloria Pfeif, and Jennifer Urbank on instructor material; Norma Morris and Donna Pulschen on manuscript development; Shannan Benschoter, Linda Cupp, Charles Drake, Lisa Evans, Janet Lowery, Sally Oates, Valerie Pocock, Brian Sooy, Candace Streeter, Nancy Thompson, and Michelle Westlund on manuscript production; and Meredith Flynn and Kathy Whitacre on photographs.

The production management of all of the books in the series is a tribute to the many talents of Marta Fahrenz. The educational surveys and teacher communications were designed and maintained by editor Carole Grumney, a very special person. Debora Wohlford, sales manager for elementary/high school texts, has been extremely important in market research and in helping to shape the scope of the series. One final acknowledgment goes to our publisher and valued friend, Clyde Perlee, Jr., without whose support the project would never even have been attempted.

Contents

CHAPTER 2   PROGRAMMING METHODOLOGY   25

CHAPTER 3 SIMPLE DATA TYPES AND PARTS OF A PASCAL PROGRAM 41

CHAPTER 4 READING AND WRITING DATA 61

CHAPTER 5   INTRODUCTION TO PASCAL STATEMENTS   81

CHAPTER 6   DECISION STRUCTURES AND COMPOUND STATEMENTS   107

CHAPTER 7   LOOPS   127

CHAPTER 8   PROGRAMMING STYLE, DEBUGGING AND TESTING   153

CHAPTER 11   ARRAYS   213

CHAPTER 12   RECORDS AND SETS   233

CHAPTER 15   POINTER VARIABLES AND LINKED LISTS   307

CHAPTER 16   STACKS, QUEUES, AND TREES   329

CHAPTER 17   NUMERICAL ALGORITHMS   349

CHAPTER 18   APPLICATIONS OF COMPUTING   367

CHAPTER 19   SOCIAL IMPLICATIONS OF COMPUTING   385

APPENDIX A IDENTIFIERS   396

APPENDIX B SYNTAX DIAGRAMS   397

APPENDIX C PASCAL RESERVED WORDS   402

APPENDIX D PASCAL STANDARD IDENTIFIERS   403

COMPUTER SCIENCE
WITH PASCAL
For Advanced
Placement Students

CHAPTER 1

Introduction to Computers and Computer Programming

CHAPTER OUTLINE

LEARNING OBJECTIVES

INTRODUCTION

WHAT CAN COMPUTERS DO?
  Speed • Accuracy • Memory

TYPES OF COMPUTERS
  Supercomputers • Mainframes • Minicomputers
  • Microcomputers

      LEARNING CHECK 1-1

HARDWARE
  Input Devices • Central Processing Unit • Output Devices

      LEARNING CHECK 1-2

SOFTWARE
  System Programs • Application Programs • Is It Okay to Copy
  Someone Else's Software?

1

LEARNING OBJECTIVES

After studying this chapter, you should be able to:

1. Explain the three functions of computers.
2. List the three things that make computers especially useful.
3. Name the four basic types of computers and briefly describe each one.
4. List some advantages and disadvantages of each type of computer.
5. Define hardware and software.
6. Name the three components of a computer system.
7. Explain the purpose of each component.
8. Name and describe the three parts of the central processing unit.
9. Explain what system programs are.
10. Describe the purpose of such system programs as the supervisor program, the job control program, the input/output management system, the language translation program, library programs, and utility programs.
11. Define application programs.
12. Explain the difference between batch and interactive processing.
13. Discuss the three levels of computer programming languages.
14. Describe how a compiler works and how it differs from an interpreter.
15. Give a brief history of the programming language Pascal.
16. Explain the concept of a structured programming language.

INTRODUCTION

Computers are tools people use to solve problems. There are many different types of computers in existence, differing mainly in how fast they can process data and how much data they can store. This chapter will discuss the four basic types of computer systems. The **hardware**, or physical parts that make up a computer system and **software**, or programs a computer runs, will be covered. An overview of programming languages will conclude the chapter.

ADVANCED PLACEMENT CHAPTER HIGHLIGHTS

The following topics from the Advanced Placement Computer Science Exam are covered in this chapter:

major hardware components
system software
operating systems
language translation programs
batch and interactive processing
levels of programming languages

WHAT CAN COMPUTERS DO?

A computer is a machine whose functions fall into three categories:

1. Arithmetic—addition, subtraction, multiplication, and division.
2. Logic—The comparison of different values. For example, computers can determine that the number 13 is less than 182.
3. Storage and retrieval of information.

These functions may seem simple enough for humans to perform and in fact they are. What distinguishes these human abilities from those of a computer's is the speed and accuracy with which the function can be accomplished. For instance, a computer can correctly solve thousands of calculations in a fraction of a second, whereas it would take even the fastest person days or weeks to do the same.

Speed

The speed of computer processing is measured in very small fractional units of a second (see Figure 1-1). Although a difference of just one-billionth of a second seems insignificant, it can be important when the computer must complete numerous tasks, each involving many functions.

3

FRACTION OF A SECOND	SYMBOL	REPRESENTATION
Millisecond	ms	one-thousandth
Microsecond	μs	one-millionth
Nanosecond	ns	one-billionth
Picosecond	ps	one-trillionth

Figure 1-1   UNITS OF COMPUTER SPEED

Accuracy

The accuracy of computers is probably an even more important feature than speed. Even though a computer could do a great deal of work very quickly, it would be of little value to anyone if the results were not reliably accurate.

How can we be certain the computer produces correct results all the time? The basic functions of computers are made possible through special instructions wired into their electronic circuitry. The circuitry allows the computer to perform hundreds of thousands of these functions at very high speeds without human intervention. In order to make certain that the computer is operating correctly and providing accurate results, self-checking capabilities are built into the circuitry. In this way, the accuracy of internal operations can be monitored. For example, the circuitry would make sure that when the computer saw an addition sign (+), it would always add and not subtract sometimes or multiply other times.

Memory

In addition to being very fast and accurate, computers also can store large amounts of information. The area where this information is stored is known as memory. A computer must know the exact location in memory where each piece of information is kept and then be able to retrieve the required information at a very high speed. The ability of computers to store large quantities of information in a small amount of space and retrieve specific information as required is another major advantage because of the potential for saving valuable time and storage space.

The combination of speed, accuracy, and memory are what makes computers so useful.

TYPES OF COMPUTERS

Computers today come in various sizes and shapes, ranging from tiny hand-held devices to some that are several feet in height and diameter. Over the years, computers have become smaller and smaller, yet, they have also become increasingly powerful.

Computers can be grouped into four categories: supercomputers, mainframes, minicomputers, and microcomputers. Generally, these four types differ in price, amount of memory, speed, and processing capabilities. These differences are becoming less and less distinct as technology continues to advance, providing greater processing capabilities at lower prices.

Supercomputers

The most powerful machines available today are called **supercomputers**. They are the largest, fastest, and most expensive computers, and there are less than 60 in operation. Only two families of supercomputers are currently available for sale: the CRAY 1, developed by Cray Research, and the CYBER 205, developed by Control Data Corporation (see Figure 1-2).

Both the CRAY 1 and the CYBER 205 can perform processing operations extremely fast. To even be considered a supercomputer, a machine must have the capability of performing at least 10 million arithmetic operations per second. Supercomputers can solve the com-

Figure 1-2 THE CRAY 1

plex calculations required for such applications as weather forecasting, top secret weapons research, and petroleum and engineering research.

Mainframes

For most business applications, the extremely high speed processing capabilities of a supercomputer are not necessary. An alternative system such as a **mainframe** is adequate. Mainframes can be further subdivided into small, medium, and large systems. Most mainframes are manufactured as a "family" of computers. For example, the IBM System 370 (see Figure 1-3) consists of several different mainframe models, varying in size and capabilities.

Most medium-sized and large companies use mainframe computers. Usually, a mainframe is placed at a central location, concentrating the majority of processing in one area. Terminals at other locations can then be connected to the mainframe.

In comparison with supercomputers, the fastest mainframe can perform only about 1 million arithmetic operations per second. With the continuing advancement of computer technology, it can be expected that future mainframe computers will perform even faster, become smaller, and continue to decline in cost.

Minicomputers

Minicomputers are lower-priced, general-purpose systems that can perform many of the same functions as some mainframes (see Figure 1-4). They are typically used in "turnkey" systems. The term "turnkey" indicates that these systems are generally small in size and very easy to install. They can be plugged into a standard electrical outlet and they do not require special air-conditioning equipment like large systems. Minicomputers usually have smaller memories than mainframes.

When minicomputers were first developed, they were used for such specialized tasks as controlling manufacturing processes. Their uses have expanded greatly since then. Also, the speed of processing of minicomputers is fast approaching that of mainframes; in the near future, the distinction between the two will probably blur.

Microcomputers

The **microcomputer** is currently the smallest and least costly type of computer. Because of the low cost of microcomputers and the flexibility of available software packages, their popularity has risen tremendously in the past few years.

In the mid-1970s, when microcomputers were first introduced, they were primarily used for playing games. Since that time, numerous software packages have been developed for a wide variety of applications, not only in business but also in medicine, education, and just

Figure 1-3 IBM SYSTEM 370

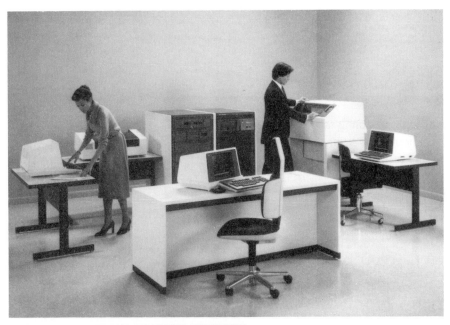

Figure 1-4 MINICOMPUTER SYSTEM

IBM Personal Computer

Apple IIe

Figure 1-5 TWO POPULAR MAKES OF MICROCOMPUTERS

about any other area imaginable. Figure 1-5 illustrates two popular microcomputers available today.

LEARNING CHECK 1-1

1. What three basic functions can computers perform?
2. Name three reasons computers are very useful to people.
3. What is a supercomputer?
4. What is meant by a turnkey system?
5. How long is a nanosecond?

Answers:

1. Arithmetic; logical comparisons; storage and retrieval of information. 2. They are fast, accurate, and can store large amounts of information that is easily retrieved. 3. It is an extremely fast, large computer capable of performing at least 10 million arithmetic operations a second. 4. A system that is very easy to install and requires no special air-conditioning or physical environment. 5. A nanosecond is a billionth of a second.

HARDWARE

Hardware is the actual physical components of a computer system. The components of a computer system are basically the same, regardless of whether it is a microcomputer or a large mainframe. These basic parts are:

8

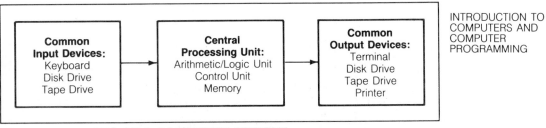

Figure 1-6 PARTS OF A COMPUTER SYSTEM

1. Input devices.
2. Central processing unit.
3. Output devices.

The parts of a computer system are shown in Figure 1-6.

Input Devices

Input is the **data** that are put into the computer so that the computer can process them. Data are the facts that the computer uses to obtain results. Some commonly used input devices are:

1. Keyboards.
2. Disk drives.
3. Tape drives.
4. Cassette recorders.

With microcomputers, the keyboard and the disk drive are the most commonly used input devices. The user can enter data to the computer by typing them at the keyboard or by having the computer read them from a diskette. Sometimes a diskette is called a floppy disk because it is made of soft plastic that is flexible. Figure 1-7 shows a disk

Figure 1-7 FLOPPY DISKETTE WITH DISK DRIVE

drive and a floppy disk. Cassette recorders may also be used with microcomputers to store information on cassette tapes.

Larger computer systems also use disk drives to input data, but these disk drives are much larger and more complex than the ones used with microcomputers. They read information from hard magnetic disks. These disks are magnetized with a material such as iron oxide. Several magnetic disks are generally grouped together to form disk packs. Tape drives are also used to input information in large computer systems. Tape drives are used to read information that has been stored on magnetic tape.

Central Processing Unit

The central processing unit (CPU) is the heart of the computer. In a microcomputer, the CPU is on a single silicon chip. This silicon chip is called the **microprocessor**. A microprocessor is shown in Figure 1-8. The CPU is made up of three main parts:

1. Control unit.
2. Arithmetic/logic unit.
3. Main memory.

Control Unit

As its name implies, the control unit is in control of the activities of the CPU. The control unit does not process or store any data, but directs the operations of the other parts of the computer. Instructions given to

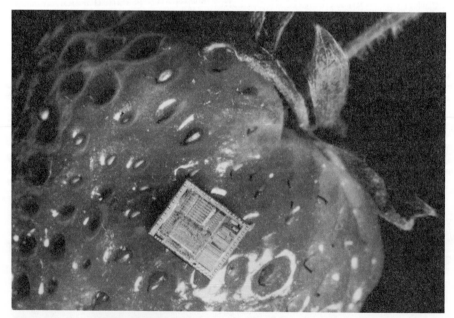

Figure 1-8 MICROPROCESSOR

the computer by the user are interpreted by the control unit, which sends out signals to circuits to execute the instructions. The appropriate input devices are directed to send the necessary data to the computer. The control unit also keeps track of which parts of the program have already been executed and which ones are left to be done. Finally, it controls the execution of specific instructions, collects the output, and sends the output to the designated output device, for example a display screen. The control unit uses system programs to perform these functions. System programs will be discussed later in this chapter.

Arithmetic/Logic Unit

The arithmetic/logic unit (ALU) is the part of the computer that performs arithmetic computations and logical operations. A logic statement makes a comparison and then does something based on the result. For example, "If today is Friday, then go to track practice after school; if not, don't." This is not exactly the type of logic statement a computer would work with, but the idea is the same. The computer would work with a logic statement more like this: "If this is the end of the input data, then make the calculations and print the results; if not, read more of the input data." Arithmetic and logic statements are the only type of instructions that the ALU can execute.

Main Memory

Main memory is the storage area where the computer keeps information. This storage area holds instructions, data, and the intermediate and final results of processing. Main memory is made up of a large number of storage locations, each of which can hold a small amount of information.

Output Devices

Output is the results that come from the computer after it has finished processing input. Some commonly used output devices are:

1. A display screen (console or monitor).
2. A printer.
3. A disk drive.
4. A tape drive.

Printing output to the display screen gives the user the program results in a quick, readable way. Output that is printed to the screen is called **soft copy** output. This is because output displayed on the screen is not going to be there permanently. When the screen changes, it is gone. Often a printer is used to create a permanent copy of output. Output printed on paper is called **hard copy**. A typical printer is shown in Figure 1-9. Storing information on a floppy disk, cassette tape, magnetic tape, or magnetic disk allows it to be used by the computer again. Each of these methods is useful, depending on the circumstances.

11

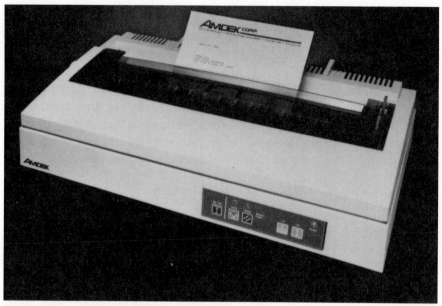

Figure 1-9 DAISY WHEEL PRINTER

🖐LEARNING CHECK 1-2

1. What are some commonly used input devices?
2. What input devices are generally used with microcomputers?
3. Name the three parts of a central processing unit.
4. What is the difference between soft-copy and hard-copy output?
5. What is the CPU of a microcomputer called?

Answers:

1. keyboard; disk drive; tape drive   2. keyboard; disk drive   3. control unit; arithmetic/logic unit; main memory   4. Soft-copy output is printed to the screen; hard copy output is printed on paper and can be saved for later use.   5. the microprocessor

SOFTWARE

At present, computers must be given instructions called programs that will direct them step by step in solving a problem. **Programs** and series of programs are also known as software. People who write programs are called **programmers**. Some programs direct the computer in its own internal operations. These are called **system programs**. Other programs are written to solve users' problems. They are **application programs**.

System Programs

System programs directly affect the operation of the computer. They are designed to help the computer system run quickly and efficiently by coordinating the operation of the circuitry.

In early computer systems, human operators watched over computer operations, decided the order in which programs were run, and prepared the necessary input and output devices needed by a program. But as the processing speeds of the CPUs increased, the speed of the human operators stayed the same. Time delays and errors caused by human operators became a serious problem.

In the 1960s, **operating systems** were developed to overcome this problem. An operating system is a set of system programs that allows a computer to manage its own operations and run at its own speed. It coordinates the computer's activities so that all the parts of the computer will be used efficiently.

Since computers vary in the size of their main memory, in the number of instructions they can perform, and in the methods used to code and store information, operating system programs also vary among different computers. An operating system that will work with one type of computer generally will not work on another.

The operating system works through several programs: a supervisor program, a job control program, an input/output management system, a language translation program, library programs, and utility programs.

Supervisor Program

The **supervisor program** (also called monitor or executive), is the major component of the operating system. It coordinates the activities of all other parts of the operating system. When the computer is first turned on, the supervisor program is the first program to be used. The supervisor schedules the order of input and output operations. It also sends messages to the computer operator if an error occurs or if the computer requires additional direction.

Job Control Program

A job is a unit of work to be processed by the CPU. Job control commands are used to identify the beginning of a job, the specific program to be executed, the work to be done, and the input/output devices required. The **job control program** translates the job control commands written by a programmer into machine language. **Machine language**, the language the computer understands, will be discussed later in this chapter.

Input/Output Management System

When a user-written program requests information to be transferred into or out of main memory, the **input/output (I/O) management system** oversees and coordinates these processes. Input and output

13

devices are assigned to specific programs and information is moved between the devices and memory locations.

Language Translation Programs

A computer can only understand machine language. In order for it to use an English-like program such as those written in Pascal, it must have a **language translation program**. This program translates the English-like program into machine language. Language translation programs will be discussed in more detail later in this chapter.

Library Programs

Library programs are programs, or routines, whether written by the user or supplied by the manufacturer, that are frequently used in other programs. To avoid rewriting these routines each time they are needed, they are stored in a system library and called into main memory when needed. They are then linked together with other programs to perform specific tasks.

Utility Programs

Utility programs perform specialized functions. For example, a utility program can transfer data from a tape to a disk, to another tape, or to a printer. Another utility program might sort data into a particular sequence for easier handling by the computer.

Application Programs

While system programs meet the computer's needs, application programs meet the user's needs. Application programs are the programs that solve a specific problem on the computer. In your school, for example, an application program might average and print your grades. In business, application programs calculate payrolls, perform the accounting for income and expenses, and provide reports for managers.

Is It Okay to Copy Someone Else's Software?

Many people in the computer industry—including young programmers—lose a great deal of money because of illegal copying. The software authors and publishers invest huge amounts of time and effort to produce good programs. Any copying really means money has been "stolen" from the developers of software. It also means hard work goes uncompensated.

Some people who copy software state that television viewers videotape copyrighted television programs. They argue that the United States Supreme Court's "Betamax decision" made that kind of copying legal. Shouldn't the same kind of ruling apply to software? No! There are clear differences between videotaping a television program and copying a piece of software. Home taping of television shows does not affect the market value of the show. Copying software does affect the profits that publishers and authors receive for producing a program.

Other people believe that software prices are too high. They object to being called pirates because of their software copying. They insist they are not selling any programs to make a profit. They only want to *save* money. Software companies have raised their prices to make up for profits lost because of illegal copying.

Another reason given for copying disks is that people do not want to spend a lot of money for a program that might turn out to be useless. But today that excuse is gone. Generally, software is better than it once was. Most computer magazines review software so that the buyer will have more knowledge about a program.

Software companies have tried to protect disks against copying with specific disk formats. If a disk is copy-protected, software buyers cannot make a backup copy in case something happens to the original disk despite the fact that the copyright law permits it.

Laws exist that protect copyrighted material. Law-making bodies, such as the U.S. Congress, will be updating copyright laws to match developments in technology. Most of the current cases about copyrights concern the "big-time pirates" who copy thousands of disks to sell for profit. Yet even the seemingly innocent copying for friends can eat into the profits of software authors.

LEARNING CHECK 1-3

1. What is software?
2. Describe why library programs are useful.
3. Explain what is meant by the operating system of a computer.
4. What is the major component of the operating system and what is its purpose?
5. The supervisor program of the operating system is also called the _____ or _____ program.

Answers:

1. A computer program or a series of programs.   2. Since they consist of commonly used programs or routines that are already written, library programs can save time for the programmer.   3. The operating system is a set of system programs that allows a computer to manage its own operations and run at its own speed.   4. The supervisor program is the major component of the operating system. It coordinates the activities of the other parts of the operating system.   5. monitor, executive

BATCH AND INTERACTIVE PROCESSING

A computer can execute programs in two basic ways: by **batch** or **interactive processing**.

In batch processing, the user does not interact or "speak" with the computer once the program has begun execution. Your school may compile, average, and print grades and attendance in a batch process. The computer will go through all the students, generally by grade, class, and last name, to process the data. A utility company may use batch processing to generate all the bills for one month. Batch processing is slow; programs and data may "wait in line" until it is their "turn" to be processed. Still, batch processing can make good use of computer time. The programs are executed in an efficient manner. Also, they can be run at times when the system is less busy, such as at night.

By contrast, communicating with the computer through an input device such as a terminal keyboard involves direct or online interaction with the computer. Using the electronic teller at a bank is a kind of interactive processing. Playing education or entertainment games is also interactive. During interactive processing, programs are translated and executed and the results returned to the terminal in a matter of seconds.

LEVELS OF LANGUAGES

To date, more than 200 programming languages have been developed. Less than ten of these languages have been used to write the majority of software in existence today. Some languages seem to closely resemble English, whereas others use strange combinations of numbers and letters. The closer a programming language is to the language a computer understands, the more machine-like it will appear. Likewise, the closer a programming language represents our way of speaking, the more like English it will seem.

According to the degree of programmer orientation (or closeness to our way of speaking), programming languages can be categorized in one of three levels: machine, low-level, or high-level languages.

Machine Language

Although there are many different languages in which programs can be written, the only language a computer can really understand is machine language, also known as binary representation.

Data represented in binary form are stored within the computer as a series of "on" and "off" states of electricity, representing binary digits. Each number or letter of a word is represented by a unique combination of binary digits, also called **bits**. An "on" bit indicates the presence of an electric current, whereas an "off" bit indicates its absence. A programmer writing instructions for a program in machine language can specify an "on" bit with the number 1 and an "off" bit with the number 0. As you can imagine, it is a long and tedious process to convert every character to a string of ones and zeros when you are programming in machine language (see Figure 1-10).

(a) HIGH-LEVEL LANGUAGE (Pascal)

C := A + B;

(b) MACHINE LANGUAGE (MOS-TECH 6502 MACHINE LANGUAGE)

1010	0000	0000	0000	0000	1101
1010	1101	0000	1110	0000	1101
0111	1001	0110	0000	0000	1100
1101	1000				
1000	1101	0011	1111	0000	1100

**Figure 1-10   A HIGH-LEVEL STATEMENT AND ITS MACHINE
LANGUAGE EQUIVALENT**

Low-Level Languages

To make programming easier, other languages have been developed.
One such language is called **assembler language**; it is referred to as a
low-level language. Instead of representing instructions as different
combinations of ones and zeroes, special symbolic words known as
mnemonics (nih-MON-iks) are used. For example, the mnemonic GET
or PUT could be written in an assembler program, and the computer
would know which operational steps it should perform. Figure 1-11
shows an assembler program.

To write a program in assembler language, the programmer must
know not only the specific type of computer that will execute the
program, but also how that computer operates. The program is tailored
very closely to the characteristics of a specific machine. An assembler
program then must be written for each type of computer that is to use
the program.

High-Level Languages

Although it is much simpler to write a program in assembler language
than machine language, considerable knowledge of the internal opera-

LABEL	OP CODE	OPERANDS A AND B	REMARKS
OVERTIME	AP	OVRTME,FORTY	CALCULATE OVERTIME PAY
	MP	OVRTME,WKRATE	
	AP	GROSS,WKRATE	
	SP	WKHRS,FORTY	
	MP	WKHRS,ONEHLF	
	MP	GROSS,WKHRS	
	MVN	GROSS+5(1),GROSS+6	
	ZAP	GROSS(7),GROSS(6)	
	AP	GROSS,OVERTIME	

Figure 1-11   SAMPLE ASSEMBLER PROGRAM

tions of the computer is still required. To make programming even easier, other languages have been developed that resemble English even more closely. These languages do not require programmers to understand the technical details of internal computer operations. Because these languages are strongly oriented toward the programmer, rather than the computer, they are termed **high-level languages**. One of the main advantages of high-level languages is that programs written in them can usually be run on a variety of computers with minimal changes.

There are many different languages that are classified as high-level languages. A few of the most popular are COBOL, BASIC, FORTRAN, and Pascal. This book will teach the programming language Pascal.

COMPILING AND EXECUTING A PROGRAM

As mentioned above, when a program is entered to the computer it must be translated into machine language before the computer can execute it. The program that is entered to the computer is called the **source program**. It has this name because this program is the source for the computer's translation.

The translation is performed by either an **interpreter** or a **compiler**. The difference between an interpreter and a compiler is that the compiler creates an **object program** that contains the entire source program in machine language. This object program is then loaded in the computer's memory and the computer is able to execute it.

With an interpreter, on the other hand, the source program is translated into machine language and executed one statement at a time. This approach saves space in the computer's memory. However, it can also be very inefficient. Program statements that are used more than once must be translated each time they are executed.

In UCSD Pascal, a Pascal program is first translated into p-code. This p-code is the "machine language" version of the program which is actually executed. Figure 1-12 illustrates this process.

Once a program is translated the computer is able to **execute** it. When a program is executed, the computer reads the object program from the beginning to the end and does what the program statements tell it to do.

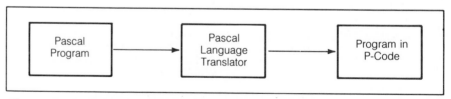

Figure 1-12 TRANSLATING A PASCAL PROGRAM

PASCAL

Pascal is considered to be one of the best general-purpose computer programming languages. A general-purpose language is one that can be used to write many different types of programs.

Pascal is a **structured programming language**. Structured programming languages have two characteristics:

1. They can be broken down into small, fairly independent subprograms.
2. They allow the programmer to control in a concise manner whether or not certain statements will be executed and how many times statements will be executed.

These two characteristics make Pascal programs easy to write and understand.

Pascal is a fairly new programming language. It was designed by Professor Niklaus Wirth of Switzerland in 1969 and 1970. Professor Wirth named the language after Blaise Pascal, a 17th century mathematician and philosopher. Pascal was only 19 when he invented a mechanical adding machine. He invented the adding machine to help his father, who was a tax collector and had to do a lot of arithmetic by hand. A picture of the adding machine is shown in Figure 1-13.

The programming language Pascal has a capital letter only at the beginning of the word. Some programming language names are written in all capital letters. This is because these names are **acronyms**, or words whose letters each stand for another word. For example, BASIC

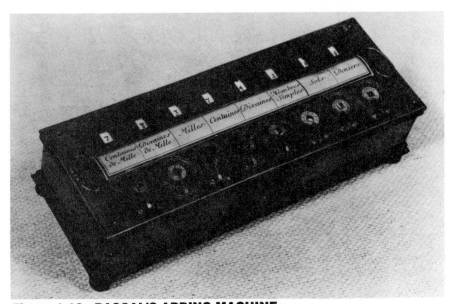

Figure 1-13 PASCAL'S ADDING MACHINE

stands for *Beginners' All-Purpose Symbolic Instruction Code*. Since Pascal is named after a person and is not an acronym, only the first letter of the word is capitalized.

One purpose of this book is to help students prepare for the Advanced Placement Computer Science Examination.

This textbook is mainly intended for students who are using the **UCSD Pascal compiler**. The UCSD Pascal compiler was designed at the University of California at San Diego. It is the Pascal compiler that is most widely used with microcomputers.

The Advanced Placement Computer Science Examination is based on the original definition of Pascal as established by Niklaus Wirth. UCSD Pascal is basically a superset of Wirth's Pascal. This means that UCSD Pascal includes virtually everything that was in the original language but also has some extra features. These extra features have been added to make programming in Pascal easier and more pleasant.

Whenever a feature is introduced in this book that is not part of the original definition of Pascal, it will be so noted. Such topics will not be covered on the advanced placement test.

LEARNING CHECK 1-4

1. Briefly explain the difference between batch and interactive processing.
2. List the three levels of programming languages.
3. What is a source program?
4. What is an object program?
5. Give two characteristics of structured programming languages.

Answers:

1. In batch processing, jobs are saved and executed all at once without user intervention. In interactive processing, the user communicates with the computer while the program is being executed. 2. Machine language, low-level language, high-level language. 3. A program that will be translated into machine language before execution. 4. The program that results when a compiler translates a source program into machine language. 5. They can be broken down into small, fairly independent subprograms. They allow the programmer to control, in a concise manner, whether or not certain statements will be executed and how many times statements will be executed.

SUMMARY POINTS

- Computers can basically perform only three functions:
  1. Arithmetic.
  2. Logical operations.
  3. Storage and retrieval of information.

  The combination of speed, accuracy, and memory is what makes them so useful.

- There are four main types of computers: supercomputers, mainframes, minicomputers, and microcomputers.
- Hardware is the term used to refer to the physical parts of a computer system. A computer system consists of three major components: input devices, the central processing unit, and output devices.
- Software is a program or series of programs. System programs are programs designed to help the computer system run quickly and efficiently by coordinating its operations. Application programs are written to meet a specific user need.
- Batch processing is a processing method in which a group of items are collected and then processed by the computer in a continuous stream without human intervention. Interactive processing allows the user to communicate with the computer while the program is being executed.
- Machine language is the only language the computer understands. All other programming languages must be translated into machine language. Low-level languages such as assembler language use mnemonics or symbolic words to give instructions. High-level languages such as Pascal are more like English than assembler languages. The programmer does not have to understand the inner workings of the computer to use high-level languages.
- Pascal is a general-purpose structured programming language. It was designed by Niklaus Wirth in 1969 and 1970. The UCSD Pascal compiler is the Pascal compiler most widely available for microcomputers and is the basis of the version of Pascal used in this book.
- Any differences between UCSD Pascal and the original language designed by Niklaus Wirth will be noted.

VOCABULARY LIST

Acronym A word whose letters each stand for another word.

Application program A program designed to meet a particular user need.

Arithmetic/logic unit The part of the CPU which performs arithmetic and does logical operations.

Assembler language A symbolic programming language that uses abbreviations rather than 0s and 1s; an assembler program translates an assembler language program into machine language.

Batch processing A method of processing in which jobs are collected and forwarded to the computer in a group and processed in a continuous stream.

Bit The smallest unit of information that can be represented in binary notation; a 0 or 1 for off or on as an electrical impulse; short for *BI*nary digi*T*.

Central processing unit (CPU) The part of the computer that does the work. The CPU also directs the order in which operations are done and has a memory.

Compiler A program that translates an entire source program into machine language. The resulting program is the object program.

Control unit The part of the CPU which determines the order in which computer operations will be performed.

Data Facts that the computer uses as input.

Execute To read and carry out the instructions in a program.

Hard copy Output that is printed on paper.

Hardware The actual physical components of a computer system.

High-level language An English-like programming language that must be translated into machine code before execution.

Input Data that are put into a computer to be processed.

Input devices Equipment such as a keyboard, disk drive, or cassette recorder used to enter data into a computer.

Input/output (I/O) management system A part of the operating system that controls and coordinates the CPU while receiving input, executing programs in storage, and regulating output.

Interactive processing Processing in which the user can communicate with the computer while the program is being executed.

Interpreter A program that translates a source program into machine language one line at a time.

Job control program A program that translates into machine language the job control statements written by a programmer to indicate what the computer should do during a program.

Language translation program The instructions that translate the English-like programs written by programmers into machine-executable code.

Library program A user-written or manufacturer-supplied program or subroutine that is frequently used in other programs.

Low-level language A programming language, such as assembler language, that is close to machine language.

Machine language The language a program must be in for a computer to be able to execute the program. It must be written in binary code.

Main memory Storage area where the computer keeps information.

Mainframe A large computer, often used in business, to which many terminals can be attached.

Microcomputer A small digital computer with most of the capabilities of larger computers; the center of the computer is the microprocessor.

Microprocessor A single silicon chip in a microcomputer, on which the CPU is located.

Minicomputer A generally lower-priced, general-purpose system that can perform many of the same functions as a mainframe.

Mnemonics A symbolic name or memory aid; used in assembly language and in high-level computer languages.

Object program The program that results when a compiler translates a source program into machine language.

Operating system A collection of programs that permit a computer to manage itself and avoid idle CPU time.

Output Results the computer obtains after processing input.

Output devices Equipment such as a screen, disk drive, cassette recorder, or printer used to store, display, or print out information.

Program A list of instructions that a computer uses to solve a specific problem.

Programmer A person who writes programs.

Soft copy Output displayed on the monitor screen.

Software A program or a series of programs.

Source program A program that must be translated into machine language before it can be executed.

Structured programming language A language that allows a large problem to be broken down methodically into smaller units. It also allows the programmer to easily control the order in which a program will be executed. This approach leads to programs that are logical and easy to understand.

Supercomputer An extremely large, powerful computer capable of performing at least 10 million arithmetic operations per second.

Supervisor program The major component of an operating system; it coordinates the activities of all other parts of the operating system.

System program A program written to coordinate the operation of computer circuitry and to help the computer run quickly and efficiently.

UCSD Pascal compiler The compiler most widely used for Pascal on microcomputers.

Utility program A part of the operating system that can perform functions such as sorting, merging, and transferring data from one input or output device to another.

CHAPTER TEST

VOCABULARY

Match each term from the numbered column with the best description from the lettered column.

1. Library program

2. Application program

3. Supervisor program

4. Output devices

5. Input/output management system

6. Software

7. Source program

8. Soft copy

9. Batch processing

10. UCSD Pascal compiler

a. A method of processing data and executing programs in which items are collected and forwarded to the computer in a group and processed in a continuous stream.

b. A program designed to meet a particular user need.

c. A user-written or manufacturer-supplied program or subroutine that is frequently used in other programs.

d. Processing in which the user can communicate with the computer while the program is being executed.

e. A program or a series of programs.

f. The compiler most widely used for Pascal on microcomputers.

g. Programming that allows a large problem to be broken down methodically into smaller units. It also allows the programmer to concisely control the order in which a program will be executed. This leads to programs that are logical and easy to understand.

h. A program written to coordinate the operation of computer circuitry and to help the computer run quickly and efficiently.

i. A part of the operating system that controls and coordinates the CPU while receiving input, executing programs in storage, and regulating output.

j. The major component of an operating system; it coordinates the activities of all other parts of the operating system.

11. Structured programming language

12. System program

13. Interactive processing

14. Supercomputer

15. Job control program

k. A program that must be translated into machine code before it can be executed.

l. A program that translates into machine language the job control statements written by a programmer to indicate what the computer should do during a program.

m. An extremely large, powerful computer capable of performing at least 10 million arithmetical operations per second.

n. Output displayed on the monitor.

o. Equipment such as a monitor, disk drive, cassette recorder or printer used to store or print out information.

QUESTIONS

1. How are computers able to consistently process data accurately?
2. List the four categories of computers and give a brief description of each.
3. What are the input devices with the computer system you are using? What are the output devices?
4. What is the difference between computer hardware and computer software?
5. Name and describe the purpose of each of the three parts of the central processing unit.
6. In what ways are operating systems beneficial to users?
7. Why is it still difficult to use assembler language, even though it has advantages over machine language?
8. Does your computer use batch or interactive processing or both? Which processing method do you prefer? Why?
9. Explain the difference between a system program and an application program.

CHAPTER 2

Programming Methodology

CHAPTER OUTLINE

LEARNING OBJECTIVES

INTRODUCTION

STEPS IN PROBLEM SOLVING
Understanding the Problem • Developing a Solution • Sample
Problem

LEARNING CHECK 2-1

TOP-DOWN PROGRAM DESIGN
Modularization • Stepwise Refinement • Top-Down versus Bottom-Up
Program Design

FLOWCHARTS

PSEUDOCODE

LEARNING CHECK 2-2

SUMMARY POINTS

VOCABULARY LIST

CHAPTER TEST
Vocabulary • Questions

LEARNING OBJECTIVES

After studying this chapter, you should be able to:

1. List the six steps in developing a program.
2. Explain what is meant by understanding the problem.
3. Define the term "algorithm."
4. Develop algorithms for simple problems.
5. Define top-down program design.
6. Explain how stepwise refinement is used in top-down programming.
7. Explain the difference between top-down and bottom-up programming design.
8. List four advantages of top-down programming.
9. Draw flowcharts for simple problems.
10. Explain the differences between a single-alternative decision step and a double-alternative decision step.
11. Pseudocode simple programs.
12. Explain what is meant by a loop.

ADVANCED PLACEMENT CHAPTER HIGHLIGHTS

The following topics from the Advanced Placement Computer Science Exam are covered in this chapter:

designing a problem solution
defining the problem in terms of needed input, processing, and
    output
modularization
top-down and bottom-up methodologies
stepwise refinement of modules

INTRODUCTION

People who are good programmers are also good problem solvers. Writing a program is a way of solving a problem using a computer. This chapter will examine solving problems in a systematic way. The steps in reaching a solution to a problem will be explained. Flowcharting and pseudocoding will also be introduced as two ways of representing a solution to a programming problem.

STEPS IN PROBLEM SOLVING

People solve problems every day. Most problems have a number of solutions. There is often more than one way to arrive at the correct

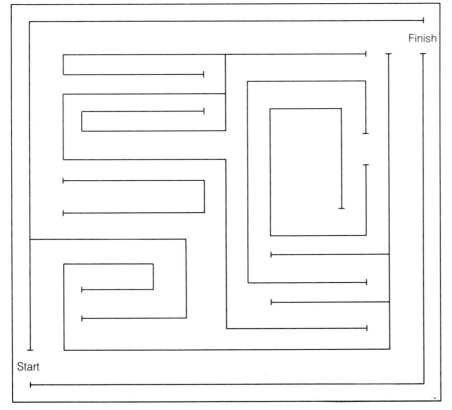

Finish

Start

Figure 2-1   A MAZE

answer to a problem. Figure 2-1 shows a maze. There are many ways of traveling from the start to the finish of this maze, but one way is considerably shorter than the others. By stopping for a minute and looking ahead, the most direct route can easily be found. Programming problems generally are not this easy to solve, but a little time spent studying a programming problem can save considerable time and trouble later.

There are some basic steps that can help the programmer develop a program in an efficient way:

1. Understanding the problem.
2. Developing a solution to the problem.
3. Writing the program.
4. Typing the program and having the computer run it.
5. Correcting any errors in the program.
6. Testing the program.

In this chapter, the first two steps will be discussed in detail.

Understanding the Problem

It is impossible to arrive somewhere if it is not clear where you are going. To write a program it is necessary to know what results are

27

required. This means the programmer must have a clear idea of what the output should be. When the programmer decides what kinds of results are desired, then it can be determined what information will be needed to obtain those results. Put another way, the programmer can then decide what kind of input is necessary in order to obtain the correct ouput.

To take a simple example, if a program is needed to convert inches into yards, the output will be given in yards. The input will be the number of inches to be changed into yards and also the number of inches there are in one yard. The programmer now has all of the information necessary to solve the problem.

Developing a Solution

Once the necessary input and output are determined, it is time to write down the steps needed to arrive at the correct results from the input. A list of the sequence of steps needed to solve a problem is called an **algorithm**. An algorithm must list every step necessary to obtain the correct results from the input. Remember that the computer cannot tell if a step is left out; it depends on the programmer to tell it everything.

Sample Problem

Solving programming problems is like many jobs people do every day. A good example is making a pizza. The desired output is a pizza that tastes good. First, the exact type of pizza must be determined. In this example, the desired output will be a pepperoni and cheese pizza. Once the type of pizza to be made has been decided, it will be apparent what ingredients will be needed. For a pepperoni pizza the input would look something like this:

Dough	*Toppings*
flour	sauce
water	cheese
yeast	pepperoni
salt	

The needed input and output are shown in Figure 2-2. Next, the steps in making the pizza must be listed. The major steps could look like this:

1. Preheat oven.
2. Prepare dough.
3. Put sauce and toppings on pizza.
4. Cook the pizza.

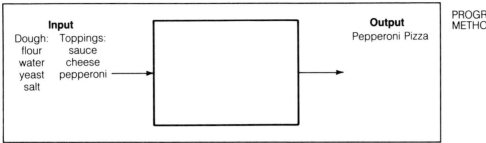

Figure 2-2 INPUT AND OUTPUT FOR MAKING A PIZZA

These steps are a basic algorithm for solving the problem of making a pizza. This algorithm will need to be further refined by breaking each of these steps into many smaller steps. For example, step 2 could be broken down like this:

1. Read the recipe for dough.
2. Assemble the ingredients.
3. Measure each ingredient.
4. Mix the ingredients.
5. Let the dough rise.
6. Grease the pan.
7. Spread the dough in the pan.

Even some of these steps could be broken down further. Step 3 could contain many substeps. Figure 2-3 shows how making a pizza could be broken down into many smaller jobs. In Figure 2-3 only step 2, preparing the dough, has been broken down further. Of course, each of the steps could be broken down.

LEARNING CHECK 2-1

1. What are the six steps necessary in developing a program?
2. What is meant by understanding the problem?
3. What is an algorithm?
4. Write an algorithm for a task you have performed, such as making a bed, building a shop project, or cleaning your bedroom.

Answers:

1. Understanding the problem; developing a solution to the problem; writing the program; typing the program into the computer and running it; correcting any errors in the program; and testing the program.   2. The programmer must know exactly what results the program is expected to yield. Then the programmer can determine the needed input.   3. The sequence of steps needed to solve a problem.

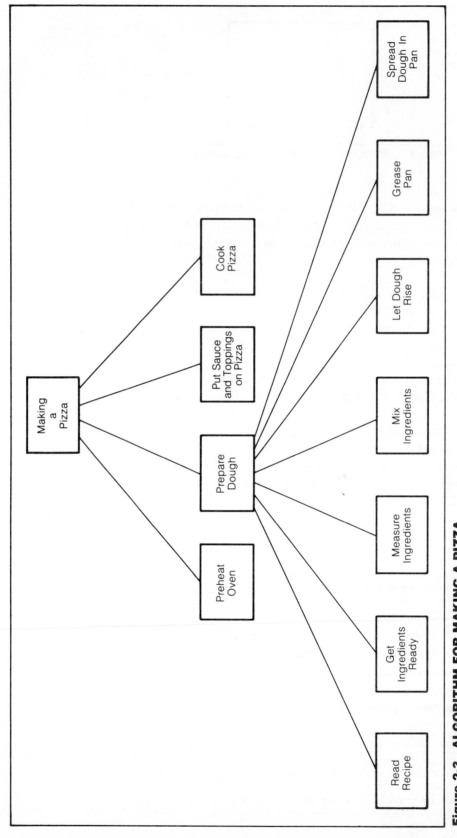

Figure 2-3 ALGORITHM FOR MAKING A PIZZA

As has already been mentioned, a structured programming language like Pascal has two basic characteristics:

1. It allows a large program to be broken down into **subprograms** or **modules**.
2. It allows the programmer to control, in a concise way, whether or not statements will be executed and how many times statements will be executed.

It is this first characteristic of structured programming that will be discussed next.

Modularization

In many ways, writing a program is similar to making a pizza. A small program can probably be written all at once. A large program is much easier to write if it has been broken down into many subprograms or modules. Modules are fairly independent subprograms that are usually written to perform a specific task. The process of breaking a program down into modules is called **modularization**.

Developing a solution to a large problem can be difficult because of the large amount of detail involved. This is where **top-down program design** becomes very helpful. Top-down design proceeds from the general to the specific. This allows the programmer to deal with the major problems first and worry about the specific details later. For example, in making a pizza, the first question was not how much flour needed to be used in the dough. This question would not be taken up until the subtask of making the dough was actually undertaken.

Stepwise Refinement

The process used in top-down design is called **stepwise refinement**. Stepwise refinement is the process of gradually breaking a program down into simpler and simpler subprograms.

Top-down design helps the programmer keep in mind an overall view of the problem. It also increases the chance of the programmer realizing early in the programming process whether or not a particular solution will work. This approach can save time, and it also helps write programs that are efficient and logical.

Top-Down versus Bottom-Up Program Design

The opposite of top-down design is **bottom-up program design**, which refers to the process of starting at the lowest level and working upwards to the general program structure. For example, the programmer might start with a piece of the actual code and then work it into the program as a whole. The program is then being built from the bottom up.

FLOWCHARTS

One way of visually representing the steps in a program is to use a **flowchart**. Flowcharts use symbols that have specific meanings. Figure 2-4 shows some of the symbols used in a flowchart. The flowchart for a program adding three numbers together is illustrated in Figure 2-5. Arrows are drawn between the symbols to show the direction of flow of the program. The first symbol represents the beginning of the program. The second symbol is an input step: the three numbers are read to the computer. Next is the processing step. Processing steps are where the work of the program is actually done. In this case, it is where the three numbers are added together. The last symbol is the stop step, showing where the program ends.

In a flowchart, a **decision step** is represented by the diamond-shaped symbol. A decision step is used when the computer is making a comparison. What would happen if a program was to read a letter and only print the letter if it was a consonant? The steps in solving such a problem would look like this:

1. Read letter.
2. Compare letter to list of consonants.
3. If letter is a consonant, print it.

The flowchart for this program is shown in Figure 2-6. This is a **single-alternative decision step**. Action is taken only if the letter is a consonant. If the letter is a vowel, nothing happens.

A **double-alternative decision step** is one where one action is taken if the step is true and another if it is false. An example would be a

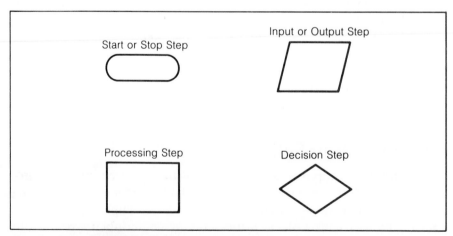

Figure 2-4   FLOWCHARTING SYMBOLS

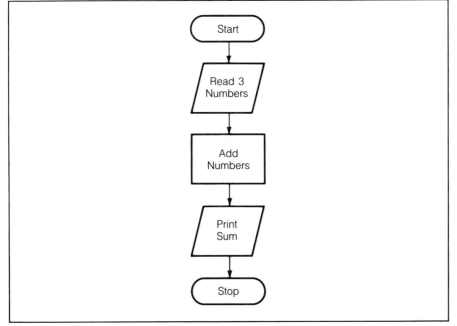

Figure 2-5 FLOWCHART FOR FINDING SUM

program that reads in two numbers and then prints the larger of the two. The algorithm would look like this:

1. Read two numbers.
2. Compare the two numbers.
3. If the first is larger, print it.
4. If the first is not larger, print the second.

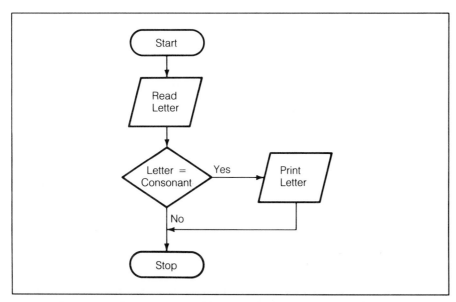

**Figure 2-6 FLOWCHART SHOWING SINGLE-ALTERNATIVE
DECISION STEP**

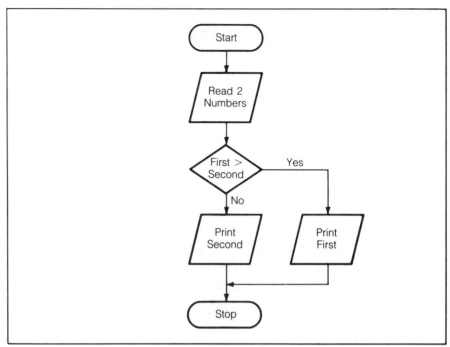

Figure 2-7 FLOWCHART SHOWING DOUBLE-ALTERNATIVE DECISION STEP

A flowchart for this program is shown in Figure 2-7. In this flowchart, the "Yes" route is taken if the first number is larger than the second. Otherwise the "No" route is taken.

Loops can also be represented by using flowcharts. A loop allows a particular part of a program to be repeated as many times as needed. Consider the following program:

1. Read 20 numbers.
2. Add the numbers together.
3. Print the total.

Such a program could easily be written by using a loop. The flowchart is shown in Figure 2-8. The name Count is used to keep track of the number of times the loop has been executed. When the loop has been executed 20 times, Total will be printed. Notice that before the loop is entered Total is set to zero, so that the first number read can be added to Total.

Flowcharting makes the logic of a program easy to follow. It helps the programmer to visualize how a program will be written.

PSEUDOCODE

Pseudocode is a narrative description of a program's logic. While a flowchart only presents the logic of a program, pseudocode often

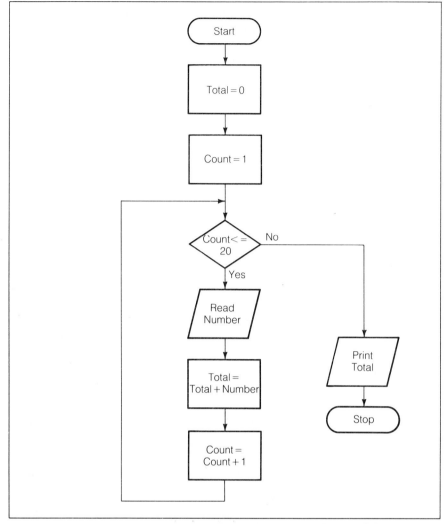

Figure 2-8 FLOWCHART DEMONSTRATING USE OF A LOOP

resembles an actual program. Pseudocode uses English statements to express a program's actions. Pseudocode is often more useful than a flowchart in developing a program. Pseudocode is more like an actual computer program than a flowchart.

Pseudocode can be used to represent simple and complex Pascal programs. Remember how a flowchart was used to represent a program that read three numbers, added them together, and printed the sum (see Figure 2-5)? The pseudocode below represents the same program.

Start

    Read X, Y, Z
    SUM = X + Y + Z
    Print SUM

Stop

35

The single-alternative decision step requires the program to ask one question. In pseudocode, the question looks like this:

```
If (an expression is true) then
    statement(s)
```

The statement or statements directly under the If statement are only executed if the expression is true. People often use this type of logic to make decisions. For example, if you like pizza and go to a restaurant, you might decide:

```
If (this restaurant has pizza) then
    order pizza
```

In a double-alternative decision step, one action is taken if the expression is true and another if it is false. Pseudocode for a double-alternative decision step is illustrated below.

```
If (an expression is true) then
    statement(s)
Else
    statement(s)
```

The statement or statements directly below the Else statement are only executed if the expression is false. The pseudocode below describes a program that reads two numbers and prints the larger of the two numbers. Compare this program to the flowchart in Figure 2-7.

```
Start
    Read X and Y
    If X > Y then
        print X
    Else
        print Y
Stop
```

Loops can also be represented in pseudocode. Look at the general form of this loop in pseudocode:

```
While (an expression is true) do
        statement(s)
End loop
```

This loop will be executed as long as the expression following the While statement is true. Notice that the words "End loop" mark where the loop stops. Here is the pseudocode for the program that is flowcharted in Figure 2-8:

Start

    TOTAL = 0
    COUNT = 1
    While COUNT <= 20 do
      Read NUMBER
      TOTAL = TOTAL + NUMBER
      COUNT = COUNT + 1
    End loop
    Print TOTAL

Stop

Pseudocode lets the programmer concentrate on a program's logic rather than the syntax, or grammatical rules, of a programming language. You can often avoid many painful hours spent fixing programs by constructing and checking pseudocode versions of the programs before writing the actual program. Solutions written in pseudocode can easily be translated into any high-level programming language.

✒ LEARNING CHECK 2-2

1. Think of a job you have done. Break it down into smaller jobs, following the example in Figure 2-3.
2. Write down every step needed to evaluate this expression:

$$\frac{14 + 8 - 12}{2} + \frac{6}{3}$$

3. What is pseudocode?
4. Explain the difference between top-down and bottom-up program design.

Answers:

1. Run dishwasher.   1. Load dishes. 2. Put in soap. 3. Start dishwasher. 4. After dishwasher is done, unload dishwasher.   2. a. 14 + 8 = 22 b. 22 − 12 = 10 c. 10 ÷ 2 = 5 d. 6 ÷ 3 = 2 e. 5 + 2 = 7   3. Pseudocode is a narrative description of a program's logic.   4. In top-down design the programmer works from the general to the specific, whereas in bottom-up design the programmer works from the specific to the general.

SUMMARY POINTS

- This chapter has discussed ways of developing programs. It is important to develop a program in a logical way. This will make writing a program progress quickly, and there will be less chance of error. Before a program can be written, it is important to understand what its purpose is. Then the needed input and output can be determined. The steps needed to solve the problem should be listed. Such a list is called an algorithm.

- Large programs can be broken down into more manageable subprograms through the process of modularization. Since Pascal is a structured programming language, the programmer can write subprograms that work together to solve a large problem.
- Flowcharting is a way of visually representing a program. Each symbol represents a step in solving the problem.
- Pseudocode lists the steps of a program in English. The program can then easily be translated into a programming language.
- Top-down design uses stepwise refinement to break a large program down into smaller and smaller modules.

VOCABULARY LIST

Algorithm A sequence of steps used to solve a problem.

Bottom-up program design A method of designing a program where the programmer works from the specific to the general.

Decision step A step in solving a problem where a comparison is made. The step that will be done next depends on the results of the comparison.

Double-alternative decision step A decision step in which one step follows if the comparison made in the decision step is true and another if it is false.

Flowchart A method of visually representing the steps in solving a problem.

Loop A control statement that allows a series of instructions to be executed repeatedly as long as specified conditions are constant.

Module A fairly independent part of a larger program that is designed to perform a specific job.

Modularization The process of breaking a program down into modules.

Pseudocode Program statements written briefly in English, not in a programming language; a verbal description of the programming logic.

Single-alternative decision step A decision step in which a subsequent step is performed only if the comparison made in the decision step is true. If the comparison is false, no action is taken.

Stepwise refinement The process of breaking a large program down into smaller and smaller subprograms, used in top-down programming design.

Subprogram A part of a larger program that performs a specific job.

Top-down program design A method of designing a program that works from the general to the specific by using stepwise refinement.

CHAPTER TEST

VOCABULARY

Match each term from the numbered column with the best description from the lettered column.

1. Pseudocode

a. A decision step in which one step follows if the comparison made in the decision step is true and another if it is false.

2. Data

 b. A narrative description of a program's logic.

3. Flowchart

 c. Programming that allows a large problem to be methodically broken down into smaller units. It also allows the programmer to control the order in which a program will be executed. This leads to programs that are logical and easy to understand.

4. Stepwise refinement

 d. To read and carry out the instructions in a program.

5. Top-down programming

 e. A part of a larger program that performs a specific job.

6. Subprogram

 f. The facts the computer uses to obtain results.

7. Algorithm

 g. A sequence of steps used to solve a problem.

8. Double-alternative decision step

 h. A method of program design that works from the general to the specific.

9. Program

 i. A decision step in which a subsequent step is performed only if the comparison made in the decision step is true. If the comparison is false, nothing happens.

10. Execute

 j. A method of visually representing the steps in solving a problem.

11. Single-alternative decision step

 k. A list of instructions for a computer to use to solve a specific problem.

12. Structured programming language

 l. The process of breaking a large program down into smaller and smaller subprograms.

QUESTIONS

1. Think of a job you have performed. What input was needed? What was the result? What steps were necessary? Be as specific as possible.
2. Write an algorithm to solve the following problem. George has $10.00. He wants to go to the movies. It costs $3.00 to get into the show. Popcorn will cost him $.80. After the movie, he would like to go to the bookstore and buy some paperbacks. If he buys two paperbacks at $1.75 each, how much money will he have left? There will be a 5 percent sales tax on the books.
3. List the four flowcharting symbols mentioned in this chapter and tell what each represents.
4. Write a flowchart for a program that will read in two names and print the name that comes first alphabetically. Write the pseudocode for this program.

5. Write the pseudocode for a program that will read the scores on ten tests. Use a loop to do this. The grades will be assigned on the following basis:

A—90 points or better
B—82 points or better
C—74 points or better
D—60 points or better
F—less than 60 points

Print the correct grade for each score.

CHAPTER 3

Simple Data Types and Parts of a Pascal Program

CHAPTER OUTLINE

LEARNING OBJECTIVES

INTRODUCTION

DATA

VARIABLES

CONSTANTS

IDENTIFIERS

RESERVED WORDS

SIMPLE DATA TYPES
INTEGER • REAL • CHAR • STRING • BOOLEAN •
LONG INTEGER

LEARNING CHECK 3-1

PARTS OF A PASCAL PROGRAM
Program Heading • Constant Declarations • Variable Declarations
• The Body of the Program

41

LEARNING CHECK 3-2

PROGRAM FIND_MILES

PUNCTUATION

COMMENTS

LEARNING CHECK 3-3

SUMMARY POINTS

VOCABULARY LIST

CHAPTER TEST
 Vocabulary • Questions

LEARNING OBJECTIVES

After studying this chapter, you should be able to:

1. Write valid Pascal identifiers.
2. Describe the difference between a program variable and a program constant.
3. Write Pascal variable declaration statements.
4. Write Pascal constant declaration statements.
5. Identify the six simple data types discussed in this chapter and describe the characteristics of each.
6. Identify the basic parts of a Pascal program.
7. Be able to use the semicolon correctly in simple Pascal programs.

ADVANCED PLACEMENT CHAPTER HIGHLIGHTS

The following topics from the Advanced Placement Computer Science Exam are covered in this chapter:

 simple data types
  real numbers
  integers
  character data
  logical (BOOLEAN) data
 basic structure of a Pascal program
  program heading
  declaration statements

INTRODUCTION

The rules for writing programs in Pascal are very specific. This chapter will cover some of the rules for giving names to values stored in the computer and for using different types of data in a program. The basic parts of a Pascal program will be explained. At the end of the chapter this material will be used to write a simple Pascal program.

DATA

Computer programs use data, which are the facts given to the computer so that it can produce the desired results. To write a Pascal program converting feet to miles, the computer needs to know two things before it can find the answer. First, the computer needs to know the formula for converting feet to miles. Second, the computer needs to know the number of feet to be changed to miles. At that point, the computer would have all the data needed to find the answer. Here is the pseudocode for this program:

```
Start
    Read FEET
    MILES = FEET / FEET-IN-A-MILE
    Print MILES
Stop
```

The flowchart is shown in Figure 3-1.

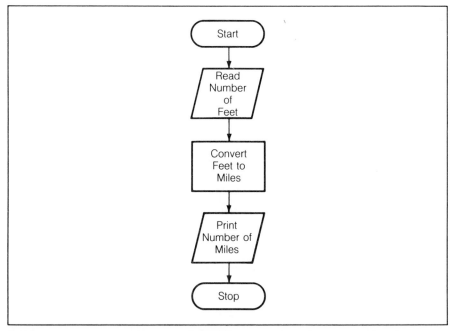

Figure 3-1   FLOWCHART FOR PROGRAM TO CONVERT FEET INTO MILES

VARIABLES

When the CPU stores programs, data, and output, it does not do so randomly. It uses a systematic method to assign a location to each data item and instruction. Each location has an address so that the CPU can find the item's location in memory when it needs to use the item. In order to process data, the CPU needs to first locate each instruction and piece of data.

Computer storage can be compared with a long row of mailboxes. Each mailbox is a specific location with its own number and address. Each can hold one item of information. Since each location in storage has a different address, stored program instructions can locate particular items by giving their addresses. One of the most important things about Pascal is that the programmer may assign names to these locations. Then it is not necessary to know where the computer is storing these values. These names are called **variable names** (or **variables** for short). The value stored in a variable may change during program execution. It is a good idea to choose variable names that describe what each variable represents, or **descriptive variable names**. In the example above, two variable names will be needed. FEET would be a good choice to stand for the number of feet to be changed to miles. This is an example of an **input variable**, a value that is entered to the computer to obtain the needed results. The result could be given the variable name MILES. This is an **output variable**, the result the computer gives. The result MILES will change depending on the value of the input variable FEET.

CONSTANTS

One more data value is needed in the example above. It is the number of feet in a mile. This is called a **constant**. Constants, like variables, are used to represent storage locations. The value stored in a constant remains the same throughout the program. The number of feet in a mile

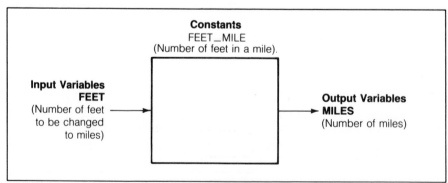

Figure 3-2 DATA TABLE FOR PROGRAM TO CONVERT FEET INTO MILES

is a value that will not change. To stand for 5280 (the number of feet in a mile), the constant name FEET_MILE could be used. Figure 3-2 is a data table. It shows the variables and constants used in this example.

IDENTIFIERS

There are some rules in Pascal for making variable names. All variables must be **valid** Pascal **identifiers**. An identifier must always start with a letter of the alphabet. The rest of the identifier can be made up of any combination of letters and numbers. Identifiers are valid if they meet these rules. Here are some examples of valid Pascal identifiers:

```
GRADE_POINT
NUM1346
MONTH10
```

Note the use of the underline character in the first example. It is the only character that can be used in an identifier other than a letter or a number. Although the underline character may be used in most versions of Pascal, including UCSD Pascal, it is not allowed in the original definition of the language. The UCSD Pascal compiler ignores the underline character. This means it sees the identifiers MILESRUN and MILES_RUN as identical. The underline character is used to separate words to make them easier for people to understand. Another way of constructing easy-to-read identifiers is to use a combination of small and capital letters:

```
NumItems
InchesLong
SalesTax
```

The UCSD compiler treats capital and small letters as if they were the same. Because of this, the compiler would treat the four variable names below as if they were all exactly the same:

```
YEARSOLD    YearsOld    yearsold    YEARS_OLD
```

The programmer should pick variable names that are easy to understand. The easier the variables are to understand, the easier it will be for other people to follow your program. See if you can tell why the variable names listed below are invalid:

```
1_MILE        (begins with a number)
YEARS OLD     (has a blank space)
SALES#        (has a character that is not allowed)
```

In addition to variables, identifiers must be used to represent constants and such routines as procedures and functions, which will be discussed

45

later. These names can be as long as the programmer desires. But the UCSD Pascal compiler will only look at the first eight characters in the identifier. For example, both these variables are valid:

MONTH_NUM   MONTH_NUM11

but they will be treated by the compiler as if they were identical, since the first eight characters in each are the same.

RESERVED WORDS

In Pascal there are certain **reserved words**. These words have a specific meaning to the compiler, and so they cannot be used as variable or constant names. The following is a list of some common reserved words:

AND	ELSE	IF	RECORD
ARRAY	END	NOT	THEN
BEGIN	FILE	OF	TO
CONST	FOR	OR	TYPE
DO	FUNCTION	PROCEDURE	VAR
DOWNTO	GOTO	PROGRAM	WHILE

Predefined or **standard identifiers**, like reserved words, have a specific meaning to the compiler. They should not be redefined by the programmer. A complete listing of reserved words and predefined identifiers for your compiler is given in the compiler documentation.

SIMPLE DATA TYPES

All variables in a Pascal program must be assigned a data type. The data type assigned to a particular variable depends on what kind of values that variable will contain. The data types covered in the following sections are INTEGER, REAL, CHAR, STRING, BOOLEAN, and LONG INTEGER. Pascal also allows the programmer to make new data types. These are called user-defined data types and will be covered in Chapter 10.

All of these are referred to as **simple** (or **primitive**) **data types**. This is because their components, or parts, cannot be broken down into smaller parts. Later in this book, linear and nonlinear data types will be introduced. Both of these data types can be broken down into smaller components.

INTEGER

An **integer** is a whole number or its opposite. It never has a decimal point and can be either positive or negative. If there is no sign in front of the number, it is assumed that the number is positive. Here are some examples:

$$-2532 \quad +48 \quad 7 \quad -10 \quad 0$$

What is wrong with these examples?

25.48   (decimal point)
+4,687   (comma)
387*   (character other than a digit)

Notice that a comma cannot be used to separate large numbers. The data type INTEGER is used to store integers.

REAL

The data type REAL is used for storing real numbers. Any numbers with a decimal point is real. For example:

$$2567.0 \quad 0.6 \quad -385.0 \quad +467.1121$$

In Pascal, all real numbers must have at least one digit on either side of the decimal point. As in data type INTEGER, the plus sign may or may not be included. What is incorrect in these examples?

−.65   (no digit on left side of decimal point)
100   (no decimal point)
+487.   (no digit on right side of decimal point)

CHAR

Data type CHAR is any single character on the keyboard. The character must be enclosed in single quotation marks. Some examples are as follows:

$$\text{'*'} \quad \text{'B'} \quad \text{'2'} \quad \text{'%'} \quad \text{'Y'}$$

What is wrong with these examples of CHAR data?

'0   (missing right quotation mark)
'22'   (more than one character inside quotation marks)
%   (quotation marks missing)
"A"   (cannot use double quotation marks)

STRING

STRING is a data type that can store character strings. Any characters on the keyboard may be used. The entire string is enclosed in single quotation marks:

```
'12448 CLOVERDALE RD.'
'What are you doing today?'
'          '
'578-42-8856'
```

Below are two incorrect examples.

```
'Uriah Heep          (missing right quotation mark)
"DOUBLE CHEESE"      (used double quotation marks)
```

What if a string looked like this:

```
'DON'T SIT UNDER THE APPLE TREE.'
```

The compiler would see the single quotation mark in DON'T as the end of the string. This problem can be avoided by using two single quotation marks:

```
'DON''T SIT UNDER THE APPLE TREE.'
```

When this line is printed, it will have only a single quotation mark:

```
DON'T SIT UNDER THE APPLE TREE.
```

Data type STRING is not a part of the original definition of Pascal. Many Pascal compilers do not allow STRING variables. If your compiler does not allow the use of data type STRING you will need to refer to Appendix G for the proper method of handling strings of characters. The STRING data type has been included in UCSD Pascal because it makes handling strings of characters easy.

BOOLEAN

The data type BOOLEAN is probably the most difficult for the beginner to understand. A BOOLEAN variable can be true or false. These are the only two choices. For example, if the variable CORRECT is a BOOLEAN variable, it must be equal to either true or false. It may help to think of a BOOLEAN variable as a switch: the switch is either turned on or off.

LONG INTEGER

In UCSD Pascal, a variable of data type INTEGER may not be greater than 32,767 or less than $-32,767$. If it is possible that the value of an integer variable may be larger or smaller than these numbers, the variable should be declared as data type LONG INTEGER. Data type LONG INTEGER may contain any integer up to 36 digits in length.

Since many other Pascal compilers allow very large integers to be assigned to data type INTEGER, they do not require the additional data type LONG INTEGER.

1. Which of the following are valid variable names?

   a. TOP20

   b. AMOUNT$

   c. GameScore

   d. GRATEFUL_DEAD

   e. BEGIN

   f. 1st

   g. Look Out

   h. SALES%

   i. outer

   j. CHEVY1957

2. How many different ways can the variable name top_10 be written? List at least five. Will the compiler see all of these names as being the same?

3. Which data type is each of the following?

   a. FALSE

   b. -1.28

   c. 4678

   d. '$'

   e. 'STOP THAT CAR'

   f. 0.689

   g. '379-50-5466'

   h. 'Marvin K. Mooney'

   i. TRUE

   j. '4'

   k. 0

   l. '45,122'

4. Are these numbers valid or invalid as data type INTEGER?

   a. 785

   b. 000

   c. -437820

   d. 687*

   e. .486

   f. +155

   g. 6

5. What is a simple data type?

Answers:

1. a, c, d, i, j   2. TOP_10, top10, Top10, top_10, TOP10; yes

3. a. BOOLEAN
   b. REAL
   c. INTEGER
   d. CHAR
   e. STRING
   f. REAL
   g. STRING
   h. STRING
   i. BOOLEAN
   j. CHAR
   k. INTEGER
   l. STRING

4. valid: a, b, f, g   5. A data type that cannot be broken down into smaller parts.

PARTS OF A PASCAL PROGRAM

Just like any other language, Pascal has rules that must be followed. **Syntax rules** explain how the parts of a language should be put together. Syntax also involves spelling and punctuation. The rules of English are present whether you are aware of them or not. For example, sentences are capitalized and end with a punctuation mark. Complete sentences need a subject and a verb and words must be spelled correctly. To students, these rules are automatic because they have been speaking and writing the English language for years. The syntax rules in

49

```
PROGRAM program_name;

CONST
    constant_name = value;

VAR

    variable_name : data_type;

BEGIN

    statement1;
    statement2;
            •
            •
            •
            •
    last_statement*

END.
```
* In UCSD Pascal, the semicolon between last_statement and END is optional.

Figure 3-3   BASIC STRUCTURE OF A PASCAL PROGRAM

Pascal may seem complex or awkward in the beginning, but with practice they will become second nature.

The general structure of a Pascal program is shown in Figure 3-3. The following sections will cover the basic syntax rules of the Pascal language.

Program Heading

Every program must have a name. The name is given in the first line of the program, which is called the **program heading**. The program heading begins with the reserved word PROGRAM, followed by the name of the program. The format for the program heading is shown in Figure 3-4. Any valid Pascal identifier may be used as a program name. It is best to pick one that describes what the program does. For example, for the program converting feet to miles, the name FIND_MILES might be chosen. The following are examples of valid program headings:

```
PROGRAM AREA;
PROGRAM FindNum;
PROGRAM STARTER1;
```

Notice that all program headings end with a semicolon. Listed below are some invalid headings.

```
PROGRAM 1ST;          (program name begins with a number)
PROGRAM AVE GRADE;    (space in program name)
PROGRAM COMPUTE       (no semicolon at the end)
PROGRM SOCCER;        (PROGRAM is misspelled)
```

```
┌─────────────────────────┐
│  PROGRAM program_name;  │
└─────────────────────────┘
```

Figure 3-4   FORMAT FOR THE PROGRAM HEADING

Constant Declarations

The **constant declaration statement** starts with the reserved word
CONST. It goes after the program heading, but before the variable
declarations. A constant can be any of the six data types REAL, IN-
TEGER, LONG INTEGER, CHAR, STRING, or BOOLEAN or it can be a
user-defined data type. In the sample program FIND_MILES, the constant declaration would be stated as:

```
CONST
    FEET_MILES = 5280.0;
```

Notice that instead of giving a data type after the equal sign, the actual
number was written. The value cannot be changed during the running
of the program. Other examples of constant declarations are as follows:

```
CONST
    PI = 3.14;
    SPEED = 55;
    FLAG = FALSE;
    NAME = 'GEORGE';
    PERCENT = '%';
```

Figure 3-5 shows the format for the constant declaration statement.

Variable Declarations

In Pascal, all variables must be declared by data type before they can be
used in the body of the program. This is done in the **variable declaration statement**. After this statement comes the reserved word BEGIN,
signaling the beginning of the body of the program.

The variable declaration starts with the reserved word VAR. This is
followed by any variable names and their data types. Each variable
declaration statement ends with a semicolon. Figure 3-6 shows the
format of a variable declaration statement.

```
┌──────────────────────────────┐
│  CONST                        │
│      constant_name = value;   │
└──────────────────────────────┘
```

**Figure 3-5   FORMAT FOR THE CONSTANT DECLARATION
STATEMENT**

51

```
VAR
    variable_name : data_type;
    variable_name : data_type;*

*All variable names of the same type may be
listed together and separated by commas.
```

Figure 3-6   FORMAT FOR THE VARIABLE DECLARATION STATEMENT

Here is one way of writing a variable declaration:

```
VAR
    FEET    : REAL;
    MILES   : REAL;
    COUNT   : INTEGER;
    ID_NUM  : INTEGER;
```

It could also have been written:

```
VAR
    MILES, FEET    : REAL;
    COUNT, ID_NUM  : INTEGER;
```

In the second example, all of the variables of the same type are placed on a single line. This procedure saves space and makes it easier to tell which variables are of the same data type. Notice that each variable is separated by a comma. The spaces around the colons and the commas are not necessary, but they make the program easier to read. The whole VAR declaration statement could have been written on one line:

```
VAR FEET,MILES : REAL;  COUNT, ID_NUM : INTEGER;
```

Putting different parts of the declaration statement on separate lines makes the program easier to follow. Whichever style is chosen, it is a good idea to remain consistent throughout the program.

The format for declaring an integer to be of data type LONG INTEGER is:

```
VAR
    LARGENUM : INTEGER[N];
```

where N is any positive digit up to 36. The N indicates the number of digits that will be allowed in this integer. For example, for the declaration statement:

```
VAR
    BIGGIE : INTEGER[8];
```

the largest value that could be stored in BIGGIE is 99999999.

A string declaration could look like this:

```
NAME : STRING;
```

The length of this string will be the number of characters assigned to the string. It is also possible to state the maximum number of characters to be allowed in a string:

```
NAME : STRING[35];
```

This string may have up to 35 characters. The number in brackets after the word STRING may be as large as 255. This allows a string to be up to 255 characters long. Here are a few examples:

```
TITLE : STRING[95];

NATION : STRING[38];
```

TITLE may have up to 95 characters, while NATION may have up to 38. If no length is specified for a string in its declaration statement, the string may contain up to 80 characters.

The Body of the Program

After the declaration statement comes the reserved word BEGIN. The next part of the program is where the work of the program is done. This is called the body of the program. Any needed processing is completed within the body. It can be as long as necessary. The reserved word END completes the program. The program always ends with a period.

LEARNING CHECK 3-2

1. Which of the following program headings are correct?
   a. `PROGRAM SEARCH;`
   b. `PROGRAM TELL ME;`
   c. `PROGRAM PhoneBill`
   d. `AVERAGE;`
   e. `PROGRAM FIND_SQUARE;`
   f. `PROGRAM 70PERCENT;`
2. What is the main difference between a constant and a variable?
3. Which of these constant declaration statements are correct? What data type is each?
   a. `X = 4.35`
   b. `SCORE : 4;`
   c. `PRINT = 'THE CORRECT ANSWER IS:';`
   d. `FLAG = TRUE;`

PROGRAM FIND_MILES

Figure 3-7 shows the Pascal program that will find the answer to the problem that has been discussed in this chapter. Note that the constant FEET_MILES is declared to be a real number. For now, it is a good idea to make all the values in a computation the same data type. Since FEET and MILES are both data type REAL, FEET_MILES was made real too. Notice the output in Figure 3-7. The value for FEET entered was 52800.0. The answer printed to the monitor was

THERE ARE 1.00000E1 MILES IN 5.28000E4 FEET.

The result, 1.00000E1, is written in **exponential notation** or **scientific notation**. The number after the letter E (in this case 1) indicates the number of places to shift the decimal point. If the number has a plus sign in front of it (or no sign), the decimal point is shifted to the right. For a minus sign, the decimal point is shifted to the left. The answer could be written as the real number 10.0. Listed on the next page are a few more examples.

```
PROGRAM FIND_MILES;
(*  FIND THE NUMBER OF MILES IN A GIVEN NUMBER OF FEET *)

CONST
   FEET_MILES = 5280.0;

VAR
   FEET, MILES : REAL;

BEGIN

   WRITELN ('HOW MANY FEET ARE TO BE CHANGED INTO MILES? ');
   READ (FEET);
   MILES := FEET / FEET_MILES;
   WRITELN ('THERE ARE ', MILES, ' MILES IN ', FEET, ' FEET.')

END.   (*  FIND_MILES *)


Running ...
HOW MANY FEET ARE TO BE CHANGED INTO MILES?
52800.0
THERE ARE   1.00000E1 MILES IN   5.28000E4 FEET.
```

Figure 3-7 PROGRAM FIND_MILES

2.68930E4	26893.0
1.68000E-1	0.168
4.20000E4	42000.0

Chapter 4 will explain how real numbers can be formatted so that they are printed in regular decimal form.

Locate the body of the program in Figure 3-7. The body is the part between the reserved words BEGIN and END. The first statement starts with the word WRITELN. This causes the computer to write the sentence inside the parentheses to the monitor. The READLN statement reads in the number that is typed at the keyboard by the user. The statement

```
MILES := FEET / FEET_MILES;
```

actually calculates the number of miles. Each of these types of statements will be discussed in detail later.

PUNCTUATION

One of the most confusing aspects of Pascal for the beginner is where to put a semicolon. A semicolon is used to separate Pascal statements. According to the original definition of Pascal, no semicolon is to be used before the reserved word END. Some Pascal compilers do not permit a semicolon to be placed before the END. In UCSD Pascal, a semicolon may or may not be used before the reserved word END. There are no punctuation marks after the reserved words CONST and VAR. A period is always used at the end of the program. Look at the punctuation in the program in Figure 3-4 again. Notice that a semicolon was not used before the word END.

COMMENTS

Comments are used to explain to people what is going on in a program. Comments have no meaning to the computer. In Pascal, all comments must be enclosed in parentheses and asterisks:

```
(* This is a comment *)
```

or braces:

```
{ Here is another one }
```

55

In this book, parentheses and asterisks will be used because not all keyboards have braces.

Comments may be used anywhere in a program. After the program heading, it is a good idea to describe what the entire program does. Comments should also be used within the program to explain what each section does. Comments may continue for as many lines as desired.

The comments in a program are called the **program documentation**. Well-documented programs not only make it easier for the programmer but for anyone else trying to understand the program. Comments are particularly useful if a program needs to be changed in the future. It is important to form the habit of documenting programs as they are written.

LEARNING CHECK 3-3

1. Which data types are each of the following constants?

   a.   NUM = 0;
   b.   OFF = FALSE;
   c.   STAR = '*';
   d.   DIVISOR = -61.77;
   e.   SPACES = '   ';

2. Write these real numbers in exponential notation.

   a. 0.06788
   b. +455.56
   c. 8000.0
   d. -123.1

3. Discuss the difference between an input variable and an output variable.

Answers:

1. a. INTEGER
   b. BOOLEAN
   c. CHAR
   d. REAL
   e. STRING

2. a. 6.788000E-2 b. 4.555560E2 c. 8.000000E3 d. -1.231000E2   3. Input variables are the data we enter to the computer. The results the computer returns to us are the output variables.

SUMMARY POINTS

- This chapter has discussed the use of variable and constant names to represent storage locations. The value stored in a variable may change when a program is executed, but the value of a constant must remain the same. These names must be valid Pascal identifiers, which means that they must start with a letter and may contain any letter or number or the underline character, but no other characters.

- Six data types were discussed. They were INTEGER, REAL, CHAR, STRING, BOOLEAN, and LONG INTEGER.
- The basic parts of a Pascal program are the program heading, the constant declaration statement, the variable declaration statement, and the body of the program.
- Proper punctuation of a Pascal program is critical. Semicolons are used to separate Pascal statements. Although originally Pascal did not permit the use of a semicolon before the reserved word END, in UCSD Pascal a semicolon is optional before an END.

VOCABULARY LIST

Comments Statements in a computer program that explain to people what is being done in the program. They are ignored by the computer.

Constant An identifier whose value may not change during program execution.

Constant declaration statement The statement that tells the compiler the specified value to be associated with a constant.

Descriptive variable name A variable name that explains what the variable represents. For example, the variable AVE could be used to represent the average of a group of numbers.

Exponential notation The representation of a real number with only one digit to the left of the decimal point, multiplied by a power of ten. For example, 153.25 would be represented in exponential notation as 1.53250E2.

Identifier A name chosen by the programmer to represent a variable, constant, or other routine in a Pascal program.

Input variable A value that is entered to the computer to obtain a needed result.

Integer A whole number or its opposite.

Output variable Information the computer returns as the result of processing input.

Predefined identifiers Words that have a specific meaning to the Pascal compiler. They may not be redefined by the programmer.

Primitive data type See **Simple data type**.

Program documentation A written description of a program and what it accomplishes.

Program heading The first statement in a Pascal program. It contains the reserved word PROGRAM, followed by the program name.

Reserved words Words that have a specific meaning to the Pascal compiler. They may not be redefined by the programmer.

Scientific notation See **Exponential notation**.

Simple data type A data type that cannot be broken down into smaller components.

Standard identifier See **Predefined identifier**.

Syntax rules Conventions that explain how the parts of a language should be put together.

Valid Correct, follows the rules.

Variable A name chosen by the programmer to represent a storage location. The value in the storage location may change during program execution.

Variable declaration statement The statement that tells the compiler the variable names that will be used to represent storage locations.

Variable name See **Variable**.

CHAPTER TEST

VOCABULARY

Match each term from the numbered column with the best description from the lettered column.

1. Storage locations

    a. The set of rules of a programming language that control how a program can be written.

2. Variable name

    b. Words that have a specific meaning to the Pascal compiler. They may not be redefined by the programmer.

3. Syntax rules

    c. A variable name that explains what the variable represents. For example, the variable AVE could be used to represent the average of a group of numbers.

4. Reserved words

    d. A name chosen by the programmer to represent a storage location. The value of the storage location may change during program execution.

5. Simple data types

    e. The first statement in a Pascal program. It contains the name of the program.

6. Program heading

    f. Information the computer returns as the result of processing input.

7. Identifier

    g. Correct; follows the rules.

8. Integer

    h. Statements in a computer program that explain what is being done in the program. They are ignored by the computer.

9. Comments

    i. A name that is given to a variable, constant, program, function, or procedure.

10. Valid

    j. The part of the computer where information can be kept; the memory.

11. Input variable

12. Descriptive variable name

    k. A whole number or its opposite.

    l. A value that is entered to the computer to obtain the needed result.

13. Output

    m. Data types that cannot be broken down into smaller components.

QUESTIONS

1. Coach Kramer wants to find out the batting average for each member of her girls' softball team. Coach Kramer figures batting averages this way:

$$\frac{\text{Number of hits}}{\text{Number of times at bat } - \text{ number of walks}}$$

   a. Write the pseudocode for a program to find a batting average.
   b. Make a flowchart for this problem. Be sure to choose descriptive variable names.
   c. Write a program heading and variable declaration statement that would be appropriate for this problem.

2. Are these valid real numbers? If not, change them so they will be.

   a. $+367.0$
   b. $-.7896$
   c. $1,487.735$
   d. $\$485.20$
   e. -6.0
   f. 0.248
   g. 67%
   h. 419

3. Write the following declaration statements a different way. Try to make them as easy to read as possible.

   a.
   ```
   VAR PERCENT : REAL;
        SALE_PRICE : REAL;
        NUM : INTEGER;
        DATE : INTEGER;
   ```

   b.
   ```
   CONST LENGTH = 25.00;
   ```

   c.
   ```
   VAR
        CHECK:BOOLEAN;
        SCORE:INTEGER;
        INNING:INTEGER;
        NUM:INTEGER;
   ```

4. Write the variable and constant declaration statements for a program that finds the average of three real numbers, X, Y, and Z. Write a descriptive program heading for this program.

5. Rewrite the variable declaration statement shown below so it is more readable.

   ```
   VAR GALLON,DISTANCE,TIME:REAL;    COUNT:INTEGER;
   ```

6. Insert the necessary punctuation marks in this program.

```
PROGRAM MILEAGE

VAR
    MILES   GALLONS   MPG   REAL

BEGIN

    WRITELN ('HOW MANY MILES DID YOU DRIVE?')
    READLN (MILES)
    WRITELN ('HOW MANY GALLONS OF GAS DID YOU USE?')
    READLN (GALLONS)
    MPG := MILES / GALLONS
    WRITELN ('YOU GOT  ', MPG, ' MILES PER GALLON OF GAS.')

END
```

CHAPTER 4

Reading and Writing Data

CHAPTER OUTLINE

LEARNING OBJECTIVES

After studying this chapter, you should be able to:

1. Explain the purpose of the WRITE and WRITELN statements.
2. Explain the difference beween the WRITE and WRITELN statements in writing to the screen.
3. Use WRITE and WRITELN statements to write prompts to the screen.
4. Use the WRITE and WRITELN statements to output program results to the screen.
5. Explain the purpose of the READ and READLN statements.
6. Explain the difference between the READ and READLN statements in reading from the keyboard.
7. Use READ and READLN statements to read data that have been entered at the keyboard.
8. Format output of real numbers and integers.
9. Format output of strings.

ADVANCED PLACEMENT CHAPTER HIGHLIGHTS

The following topics from the Advanced Placement Computer Science Exam are covered in this chapter:

input and output
monitor input and output

INTRODUCTION

In Chapter 3, a simple program for changing feet to miles was presented. In order for the program to work, there had to be a way to let the computer know the number of feet to be changed to miles. The number of feet was the input data. These data had to be entered to the computer and the results of the calculation needed to be output in readable form.

In this chapter various ways of entering data to the computer at the keyboard will be presented. Also, ways of printing results to the monitor screen will be explained.

THE WRITE AND WRITELN STATEMENTS

The WRITE and WRITELN statements are used to display output on the monitor screen. In most programs WRITE statements have two basic purposes:

1. To print a prompt for the user.
2. To print the results after a program has been run.

WRITING PROMPTS

When a program reaches a place where the user is supposed to enter some data, a **prompt** should be printed to the screen. A prompt is a sentence that tells the user that the computer is ready for data to be entered. It prompts the user to respond. It should also tell the user what type of data are expected. When the user sees a prompt on the screen, it is a signal to enter the data.

In the FIND_MILES program, the prompt looked like this:

```
WRITELN ('HOW MANY FEET ARE TO BE CHANGED INTO MILES?');
```

This instruction tells the program user to enter the number of feet to be changed to miles. The general form of the WRITE statement is as follows:

WRITE (output);

Whatever is to be printed to the screen must be in parentheses. If it is of data type CHAR or STRING it must be enclosed in single quotation marks. The syntax for this statement is shown in Figure 4-1.

In the FIND_MILES program, the prompt used the word WRITELN instead of WRITE. WRITELN is read "write line". A WRITELN command looks like this:

WRITELN (output);

There is a difference between the WRITE and WRITELN statements. After the computer executes a WRITE statement, the **cursor** remains at the end of the line, wherever the printing stopped. The cursor is the little box that indicates where printing will appear on the screen. The user can then enter data starting at this spot. In a WRITELN statement, after printing to the screen, the cursor returns to the beginning of the next line. The WRITELN statement includes a carriage return, just like the carriage return on a typewriter.

WRITE AND WRITELN STATEMENTS
WRITE (output); WRITELN (output);

Figure 4-1   SYNTAX FOR WRITE AND WRITELN STATEMENTS

63

```
PROGRAM HELLO1;
(* PRINTS MESSAGE TO THE MONITOR USING WRITE STATEMENTS *)

BEGIN

    WRITE ('HI ');
    WRITE ('THERE ');
    WRITE ('HOW ARE ');
    WRITE ('YOU DOING?');
    WRITELN

END.   (* HELLO1 *)



Running . . .
HI THERE HOW ARE YOU DOING?


PROGRAM HELLO2;
(* PRINTS MESSAGE TO THE MONITOR USING WRITELN STATEMENTS *)

BEGIN

    WRITELN ('HI');
    WRITELN ('THERE');
    WRITELN ('HOW ARE');
    WRITELN ('YOU DOING?');
    WRITELN

END.   (* HELLO2 *)



Running . . .
HI
THERE
HOW ARE
YOU DOING?
```

Figure 4-2 TWO HELLO PROGRAMS

Figure 4-2 contains two short programs that show the differences
between the WRITE and WRITELN statements. Notice that the output
for the two programs is different. In the first program, WRITE statements are used. When this program is executed, all of these strings will
print on the same line. Any number of WRITE statements can be used. If
there is room, everything will print on the same line.

In the first statement in Program HELLO1

```
WRITE ('HI ');
```

there is a space between HI and the quotation mark. If spaces had not
been left at the end of each string, the output would have looked like
this:

```
HITHEREHOW AREYOU DOING?
```

The computer only leaves spaces where the programmer tells it to.

Spaces appear in the strings HOW ARE and YOU DOING? because the strings were typed in with spaces.

In the program HELLO1, the last statement is WRITELN. The WRITELN statement is used alone to return to the beginning of the next line. If there had been be no WRITELN statement, the cursor would have remained on the same line as the printing. It would wait right after the last character printed, in this case a question mark. WRITELN statements alone can be used to leave blank lines on the screen. This helps to space the output so that it is more readable. For example, if the output is to be double-spaced, the command

```
WRITELN;
```

can be placed between each output statement.

THE READ AND READLN STATEMENTS

After the user enters data, the computer has to read those data. Also needed is a way of assigning the data to variables. We do this by using a READ or a READLN statement. As shown in Figure 4-3, these two statements are written this way:

> READ (variable1, variable2, . . .);
> READLN (variable1, variable2, . . .);

The READ or READLN statements tell the computer to stop and wait until the user enters the data at the keyboard. Next, the computer takes the value entered and assigns it to the variable name in parentheses. The value entered must be of the same data type as the variable. This means if NUM has been declared to be of data type REAL, the data entered must be of type REAL. If there was a READ statement like this in the program:

```
READ (NUM);
```

a correct response would be to enter something like:

```
14.75
```

```
┌─────────────────────────────────────────┐
│ READ AND READLN STATEMENTS               │
├─────────────────────────────────────────┤
│ READ (variable1, variable2, . . . );     │
│ READLN (variable1, variable2, . . . );   │
└─────────────────────────────────────────┘
```

Figure 4-3 SYNTAX FOR READ AND READLN STATEMENTS   **65**

If we entered

B

program execution would stop because of the mismatch in data types. When you are typing CHAR or STRING data at the keyboard, it is not necessary to put quotation marks around the data.

Even though data types should match, Pascal will allow an IN-TEGER value to be assigned to a variable that has been declared to be data type REAL. The compiler will convert the whole number to a real number by adding a decimal point and a zero.

Just as in the WRITELN statement, the READLN statement includes a carriage return. This means that if a READLN statement is used, the user must hit the return key after entering the data. When a READ statement is used, the data are read as soon as they are entered and a space is typed. It is possible to have a number of variables in one READ or READLN statement. Each variable name must be separated by a comma.

In Figure 4-4, program ADD1 adds four integers together. The first time the program is run, all four integers are placed on one line. The program reads them and adds them together. The numbers are separated by spaces. The number of spaces does not matter. The second time the program is run, three numbers are typed on one line and the fourth on the next. The computer will keep reading until it finds four numbers, even if it has to go on to the next line. The third time the program is run, every number is on a separate line and the number does not necessarily start at the left margin. The computer again simply keeps looking until it finds the numbers.

A READ statement could also have been used in program ADD1. It would have worked the same way, except that the user would not have to hit the return key after entering the last data item. Instead, the user could just type a space. With a READLN statement, the return key must be hit after the last data item is entered. After the data are read, the cursor returns to the beginning of the next line.

In program ADD2 (Figure 4-5), four integers are again added together. In this program, four READ statements are used, one for each integer. The first time the program is run, all four values are typed on one line. Many values can be read on one line by using a separate READ statement for each value. In a READ statement, the cursor remains on the same line after reading a data value. If there are no more values on that line, the computer will look for values on the following line. In program ADD2, the four READ statements could have been replaced with one:

```
READ (NUM1, NUM2, NUM3, NUM4);
```

Figure 4-6 illustrates an important difference between the READ and READLN statements. Program ADD3 has four separate READLN

```
        PROGRAM ADD1;
        (* THIS PROGRAM ADDS FOUR INTEGERS TOGETHER *)

        VAR
            NUM1, NUM2, NUM3, NUM4, SUM : INTEGER;

        BEGIN

            WRITELN ('TYPE IN THE FOUR NUMBERS TO BE ADDED TOGETHER: ');
            READLN (NUM1, NUM2, NUM3, NUM4);
            SUM := NUM1 + NUM2 + NUM3 + NUM4;
            WRITELN ('THE SUM OF ', NUM1, ', ', NUM2, ', ', NUM3, ' AND ',
            NUM4, ' IS ', SUM)

        END.    (* ADD1 *)


        Running . . .
        TYPE IN THE FOUR NUMBERS TO BE ADDED TOGETHER:
        4 8 103 15
        THE SUM OF 4, 8, 103 AND 15 IS 130


        Running . . .
        TYPE IN THE FOUR NUMBERS TO BE ADDED TOGETHER:
        4 8 103
        15
        THE SUM OF 4, 8, 103 AND 15 IS 130


        Running . . .
        TYPE IN THE FOUR NUMBERS TO BE ADDED TOGETHER:
            4
        8
                103
        15
        THE SUM OF 4, 8, 103 AND 15 IS 130
```

Figure 4-4 PROGRAM ADD1

statements. The first time the program is run, each integer is entered on a separate line. The program works as expected. The second time the program is run, not all of the integers are typed on a separate line. Note the output for this program. The computer has added together the first number on each line. Any other number on the same line is ignored. Since there is only one variable in each READLN statement, the computer reads a value to that variable and then goes to the beginning of the next line. The reason for this is that a READLN statement is being used. This is important to remember when you are using READ and READLN statements. It is important that no necessary data be skipped over.

The READ statement behaves differently when data are read from files rather than from the keyboard. This difference will be discussed later in this book.

String data should be entered only by using a READLN statement,

```
PROGRAM ADD2;
(* THIS PROGRAM ADDS FOUR INTEGERS TOGETHER *)

VAR
    NUM1, NUM2, NUM3, NUM4, SUM : INTEGER;

BEGIN

    WRITELN ('TYPE IN THE FOUR NUMBERS TO BE ADDED TOGETHER: ');
    READ (NUM1);
    READ (NUM2);
    READ (NUM3);
    READ (NUM4);
    READLN;
    SUM := NUM1 + NUM2 + NUM3 + NUM4;
    WRITELN ('THE SUM OF ', NUM1, ', ', NUM2, ', ', NUM3, ' AND ',
    NUM4, ' IS ', SUM)

END.    (* ADD2 *)



Running ...
TYPE IN THE FOUR NUMBERS TO BE ADDED TOGETHER:
8   17   108   3
THE SUM OF 8, 17, 108 AND 3 IS 136



Running ...
TYPE IN THE FOUR NUMBERS TO BE ADDED TOGETHER:
8
17
108
3
THE SUM OF 8, 17, 108 AND 3 IS 136
```

Figure 4-5   PROGRAM ADD2

since the compiler cannot tell where the string ends. When a READLN
statement is used to read in a string, everything on that line is assigned
to the variable.

LEARNING CHECK 4-1

1. Explain the difference between a WRITE statement and a WRITELN statement.
2. What two things should a prompt tell the user?
3. What two things does a READ statement do?
4. Why do we need to have a READ or READLN statement after a prompt?

Answers:

1. The WRITELN statement includes a carriage return, while the WRITE statement does not. When information is printed to the screen by a WRITELN statement, the cursor returns to the beginning of the next line.   2. It should tell the user at what point data are to be entered and what type of data are to be entered.   3. It reads the data and it assigns the data value to the corresponding variable in parentheses.   4. If a READ or READLN statement is not present, the computer will not be able to read the data value entered and assign it to a variable.

```
PROGRAM ADD3;
(* THIS PROGRAM ADDS FOUR INTEGERS TOGETHER *)

VAR
    NUM1, NUM2, NUM3, NUM4, SUM : INTEGER;

BEGIN

    WRITELN ('TYPE IN THE FOUR NUMBERS TO BE ADDED TOGETHER: ');
    READLN (NUM1);
    READLN (NUM2);
    READLN (NUM3);
    READLN (NUM4);
    SUM := NUM1 + NUM2 + NUM3 + NUM4;
    WRITELN ('THE SUM OF ', NUM1, ', ', NUM2, ', ', NUM3, ' AND ',
    NUM4, ' IS ', SUM)

END.   (* ADD3 *)


Running . . .
TYPE IN THE FOUR NUMBERS TO BE ADDED TOGETHER:
19
46
2
12
THE SUM OF 19, 46, 2 AND 12 IS 79


Running . . .
TYPE IN THE FOUR NUMBERS TO BE ADDED TOGETHER:
19 146
9
103 12
44
THE SUM OF 19, 9, 103 AND 44 IS 175
```

Figure 4-6   PROGRAM ADD3

WRITING OUTPUT

After a program has determined a result, the user needs to be able to
see that result. One way to see the result is to have it printed to the
monitor screen. In the program adding four integers together, the
statement that printed the result looked like the line below:

```
WRITELN ('THE SUM OF ', NUM1, ', ', NUM2, ', ', NUM3, ' AND ',
NUM4, ' IS ', SUM)
```

This is a rather complicated WRITELN statement. There are a number
of parts to it. Each part is separated by a comma. The character strings
are enclosed in quotes. They will be printed to the monitor screen
exactly as they appear. Note the first string:

```
'THE SUM OF ',
```

There is a space after the word OF. If the space was omitted, OF could run into the value of NUM1 when the line was printed. The variables NUM1, NUM2, NUM3, NUM4, and SUM are not in quotes. It is not the variable name NUM1 that we want to print, but rather the value stored in NUM1. Notice the comma in quotes between the variables. This places a comma between each number. The word AND was put before the last number so that it would be printed before the last number was printed.

Spending a little extra time on writing output statements like this can make a program's results much more understandable. It is important to remember to always place character strings in single quotation marks and to separate each part of the output line with commas.

FORMATTING OUTPUT

Output is **formatted** to make it more readable. Formatting means controlling the way in which the output will be printed. A sample program that explains this idea would be one that read six integers and printed them in columns. The integers will be called A, B, C, D, E, and F. Each column is to be ten spaces wide. The WRITELN statement would be written as below.

```
WRITELN (A:10, B:10, C:10, D:10, E:10, F:10);
```

Each variable name is followed by a colon and the number of spaces in that column. A WRITELN statement could also be used to set up a heading for these columns. It could look like this:

```
WRITELN ('A':10, 'B':10, 'C':10, 'D':10, 'E':10, 'F':10);
```

Figure 4-7 illustrates formatting integer output with column headings. Formatting can be helpful when results need to be printed in columns or in a table.

Formatting Real Numbers

In Chapter 3 the answer to the FIND_MILES program was written in exponential notation. The WRITELN statement looked like this:

```
WRITELN ('THERE ARE ', MILES, ' MILES IN ', FEET, ' FEET.')
```

When 52800.0 was entered as the number of feet to be changed to miles, the result was printed this way:

```
THERE ARE 1.00000E1 MILES IN 5.28000E4 FEET.
```

```
PROGRAM COLUMNS;
(* THIS PROGRAM PRINTS SIX INTEGERS IN COLUMNS EACH TEN SPACES WIDE *)

VAR
    A, B, C, D, E, F : INTEGER;

BEGIN

    WRITE ('TYPE IN THE 6 INTEGERS: ');
    READLN (A, B, C, D, E, F);
    WRITELN ('A':10, 'B':10, 'C':10, 'D':10, 'E':10, 'F':10);
    WRITELN (A:10, B:10, C:10, D:10, E:10, F:10)

END.    (* COLUMNS *)



Running . . .
TYPE IN THE 6 INTEGERS: 11 689 4 121 8 1093
          A         B         C         D         E         F
         11       689         4       121         8      1093
```

Figure 4-7 PROGRAM COLUMNS

Often it is preferable to have the result printed in regular decimal form. To do this, the WRITELN statement needs to be written like the statement below:

```
WRITELN ('THERE ARE ', MILES:8:2,' MILES IN ',
FEET:8:2, ' FEET.');
```

Now the output will look like this:

```
THERE ARE   10.00 MILES IN  52800.00 FEET.
```

To format a real number, the variable name is written, followed by a colon. The first number after the colon is the total length or number of characters in the number, including the decimal point and the plus or minus sign. Even if there is no plus or minus sign, a space should be allowed for one. The total length of this number is seven:

```
-785.43
```

Be sure to make the length large enough. If the length is larger than the actual number, blank spaces will be included at the beginning of the number.

This first number, showing the total length, is followed by a colon and then a second number. This second number indicates how many digits are to be printed after the decimal point. In the FIND_MILES example, two decimal places were chosen. The UCSD compiler will round the result off to two decimal places.

71

The following example further explains this idea. Suppose the result of a program is 3748.69812. If a WRITE statement is written like this:

```
WRITE (NUM:8:2);
```

the compiler will round off the result to two decimal places. The result would be printed as

```
3748.70
```

Additional examples appear below.

Unformatted Result	WRITE Statement	Result Printed As
1.48958E2	WRITE (NUM:7:2);	148.96
1.77424E1	WRITE (NUM:8:4);	17.7424
+2.68394E1	WRITE (NUM:6:2);	+26.84
−3.18367E1	WRITE (NUM:7:3);	−31.837

Figure 4-8 shows a program that prints the real number 68.2135 using different formats. Study each format.

1. `WRITELN (R);`
   This is unformatted. The result is in exponential notation.

```
PROGRAM PRINTR;
(* THIS PROGRAM READS A REAL NUMBER AND PRINTS IT USING DIFFERENT
FORMATS *)

VAR
    R : REAL;

BEGIN

    WRITE ('TYPE IN A REAL NUMBER: ');
    READLN (R);
    WRITELN (R);
    WRITELN (R:8:4);
    WRITELN (R:6:2);
    WRITELN (R:3:2);
    WRITELN (R:11:2)

END.    (* PRINTR *)



Running . . .
TYPE IN A REAL NUMBER: 68.2135
  6.82135E1
  68.2135
  68.21
  68.21
      68.21
```

Figure 4-8   PROGRAM PRINTR

2. `WRITELN (R:8:4);`

This prints the number as entered. Notice that there is a blank space at the beginning of the line. If there is no sign, the computer leaves a blank where the sign would have been.

3. `WRITELN (R:6:2);`

This statement prints the number with only two decimal places. The compiler has rounded the answer off to two decimal places.

4. `WRITELN (R:3:2);`

The length in this format statement is only three. This is too short for this number. Notice the number as printed has a length of six: 68.21. Because of a protective device built into the compiler, the number printed with two decimal places even though the length number used was too small.

5. `WRITELN (R:11:2);`

In this example, the length is longer than the number. Notice the spaces at the beginning of the line. This happened because the compiler placed the number so that the last digit would be in the 11th position on the line. The number is **right-justified**. When a number is right-justified, any blanks will be on the left side of the number. The symbol ƀ will be used to represent a blank in the examples below, which show various outputs for the number 14.73:

Program Statement	*Output*
`WRITELN (NUM:6:2);`	ƀ14.73
`WRITELN (NUM:8:2);`	ƀƀƀ14.73
`WRITELN (NUM:11:2);`	ƀƀƀƀƀƀ14.73

Formatting Integers

Integers can also be formatted. Figure 4-9 shows how this is done. The variable name is followed by a colon and then the length of the number. The statement WRITELN (I:2); shows that the compiler will not let part of the number be cut off. It still printed the entire number although the number is three digits long. In the last WRITELN statement, the number is right-justified. All of the blanks are on the left.

Formatting Strings

String data may be formatted. If they are not formatted, they are printed in a field of exactly the same length as the string. For example, the size of the field for the statement.

```
WRITELN ('THIS IS A STRING.');
```

would be 17 spaces.

```
PROGRAM PRINTI;
(* THIS PROGRAM READS AN INTEGER VALUE AND PRINTS IT USING DIFFERENT
FORMATS *)

VAR
    I : INTEGER;

BEGIN

    WRITE ('TYPE IN AN INTEGER: ');
    READLN (I);
    WRITELN (I);
    WRITELN (I:3);
    WRITELN (I:2);
    WRITELN (I:8)

END.    (* PRINTI *)



Running . . .
TYPE IN AN INTEGER: 105
105
105
105
      105
```

Figure 4-9 PROGRAM PRINTI

In Figure 4-10, our string is formatted four different ways.

1. WRITELN ('THIS IS A STRING.');
This is unformatted. The string is printed in a field that is the same length as the string.

```
PROGRAM PRINTS;
(* THIS PROGRAM PRINTS A STRING USING DIFFERENT FORMATS *)

BEGIN

    WRITELN ('THIS IS A STRING.');
    WRITELN ('THIS IS A STRING.':17);
    WRITELN ('THIS IS A STRING.':22);
    WRITELN ('THIS IS A STRING.':10)

END.    (* PRINTS *)



Running . . .
THIS IS A STRING.
THIS IS A STRING.
     THIS IS A STRING.
THIS IS A
```

Figure 4-10 PROGRAM PRINTS

2. WRITELN ('THIS IS A STRING.':17);
The formatted size is the same as the length of the string. This will have the same effect as the first statement.

3. WRITELN ('THIS IS A STRING.':22);
This string will be right-justified. There will be five blank spaces on the left.

4. WRITELN ('THIS IS A STRING.':10);
In this example the field is smaller than the length of the string. This string will be **truncated** on the right.

Note in this last example that string formats work differently than whole and real numbers. The compiler will not allow part of a number to be cut off (except for rounding off decimal places). With strings, however, we can cut off part of a string by placing it in a field that is too short. It is important to be careful when you are formatting strings.

PROGRAM CIRCLE

A practice program follows that combines a number of commands learned in this chapter. In the program, the user will be prompted to enter the diameter of a circle. From this information, the program will calculate:

1. The radius of the circle (diameter/2).
2. The circumference of the circle ($\pi \times$ diameter).
3. The area of the circle ($\pi \times$ radius^2).

This information will be printed in columns that are each 15 spaces wide. Figure 4-11 shows program CIRCLE. First the diameter is entered and assigned to the variable DIAMETER. From this information, the radius, circumference, and area are calculated. This information is written with one WRITELN statement. Each value will be rounded off to two decimal places and each real number will be right-justified in a field containing 15 spaces. Notice that headings were also written for this information, in the statement:

```
WRITELN ('DIAMETER':15, 'RADIUS':15,
    'CIRCUMFERENCE':15, 'AREA':15);
```

Each of these labels will be placed in fields 15 spaces wide so that each label will print above the correct number. It is important to label results so that the user can easily understand them.

75

```
PROGRAM CIRCLE;
(* THIS PROGRAM READS THE DIAMETER OF A CIRCLE IN INCHES.  FROM THESE
DATA THE RADIUS, CIRCUMFERENCE, AND AREA OF THE CIRCLE ARE THEN COMPUTED. *)

CONST
    PI = 3.14;

VAR
    DIAMETER, RADIUS, CIRCUM, AREA : REAL;

BEGIN

    WRITE ('WHAT IS THE DIAMETER OF THE CIRCLE IN INCHES? ');
    READLN (DIAMETER);
    RADIUS := DIAMETER / 2;
    CIRCUM := DIAMETER * PI;
    AREA := PI * RADIUS * RADIUS;
    WRITELN ('DIAMETER':15, 'RADIUS':15, 'CIRCUMFERENCE':15, 'AREA':15);
    WRITELN (DIAMETER:15:2, RADIUS:15:2, CIRCUM:15:2, AREA:15:2)

END.   (* CIRCLE *)



Running . . .
WHAT IS THE DIAMETER OF THE CIRCLE IN INCHES? 10.0
        DIAMETER           RADIUS  CIRCUMFERENCE              AREA
          10.00              5.00           31.40            78.50
```

Figure 4-11 PROGRAM CIRCLE

LEARNING CHECK 4-2

1. Consider the number −28.3765. How will this number be output to the screen with each of the formats below? Be sure to indicate any blank spaces by using a ƀ.

   a. NUM:5:1
   b. NUM:7:3
   c. NUM:2:2
   d. NUM:11:2
   e. NUM:6:2

2. Write a WRITELN statement that will print eight integers in columns six spaces wide.
3. Explain what right-justified means.

Answers:

1. a. −28.4 b. −28.377 c. −28.38 d. ƀƀƀƀ−28.38 e. −28.38   2. WRITELN (I1:6, I2:6, I3:6, I4:6, I5:6, I6:6, I7:6, I8:6);   3. Right-justified means that the values will line up at the right margin. Any blank spaces will be on the left side.

SUMMARY POINTS

● Chapter 4 has examined how the user can enter data at the keyboard. The program can then process these data as needed. By using WRITE or

WRITELN statements, prompts can be printed to the screen. A prompt tells the user to enter data. READ and READLN statements can be used to assign values to variables.

- The WRITE and WRITELN statements are also used to print results on the screen. Formatting is used to line items up in columns and to round off real numbers to the number of decimal places desired. Formatting makes program output easier to read.

VOCABULARY LIST

Cursor A box that indicates where printing will next appear on the screen.
Format To control the way in which output will be printed.
Prompt A statement printed to the monitor that tells the user to enter data.

Right-justified Lined up on the right side of the field, so that any blank spaces will be on the left side of the field.
Truncate To cut off part of a value. For example, if 17.23 was truncated at the decimal point the result would be 17.

CHAPTER TEST

VOCABULARY

Match each term from the numbered column with the best description from the lettered column.

1. Constant

2. Right-justified

3. Variable declaration statement

4. Format

5. Truncate

6. Prompt

7. Exponential notation

8. Program documentation

a. A sentence printed to the monitor that tells the user to enter data.

b. To control the way in which output will be printed.

c. The written description of a program and what it accomplishes.

d. A Pascal statement that declares a variable name and its data type.

e. A box that indicates where typed material will appear on the screen.

f. A name chosen by the programmer to represent a storage location. The value of the storage location may not change during program execution.

g. Lined up on the right side of the field, so that any blank spaces will be on the left side of the field.

h. Rules that explain how the parts of a language should be put together.

77

9. Syntax rules

i. The representation of a real number with only one digit to the left of the decimal point, multiplied by a power of ten.

10. Cursor

j. A Pascal statement that defines a program constant.

11. Constant declaration statement

k. To cut off.

QUESTIONS

1. Why can't a READ statement be used to read a string?
2. The numbers below are in exponential notation. How would they print if they were formatted by the statement NUM:7:2?

   a. 2.57834E2
   b. −3.16289E1
   c. 9.97384E2
   d. +1.24765E1
   e. 4.00000E2

3. Where will the cursor be located after each of these statements is executed?

   a. `WRITELN ('TYPE IN A LETTER.');`
   b. `WRITE ('WHAT IS THE SECOND NUMBER?');`
   c. `WRITE ('WHAT IS YOUR AGE?');`
   d. `WRITELN ('ENTER ACCOUNT NUMBER.');`

4. How will these strings be printed? Be sure to indicate any blanks with a ƀ.

   a. `WRITELN ('THERE IS A MONKEY IN THE TREE.':15);`
   b. `WRITELN ('LOOK DOWN HERE.':15);`
   c. `WRITELN ('WHAT IS YOUR MIDDLE NAME?':30);`
   d. `WRITELN ('ANSWER THE DOOR.');`
   e. `WRITELN ('MARY HAD A LITTLE LAMB.':10);`

5. Look at this program segment, and then tell what the values of X, Y, and Z will be in each part below if the data are entered as shown.

   ```
   READ (X);
   READ (Y);
   READ (Z);
   ```

a.			b.	c.	
4	16	10	16	109	
108	7		81	63	70
32			1182	2871	532

6. Look at the following program segment, and then tell what the values of A, B, and C will be in each part below if the data are entered as stated.

   ```
   READLN (A);
   READLN (B);
   READLN (C);
   ```

a.			b.	
77	32	0	44	
188			18	97
16	2871		100	82

7. Below is another program segment. What will the values of L, M, and N be, given the data below?

```
READLN (L, M, N);
```

a. 4   15   82
   91   0
   12
b. 66
   77   18

8. What is formatting? Why do programmers format output?
9. What will these program statements print to the monitor? (Be sure to indicate blanks.)

```
WRITE ('THAT''S');
WRITE (' ALL');
WRITELN;
WRITELN;
WRITELN ('FOLKS!');
```

PROGRAMMING PROBLEMS

1. Look at the two programs in Figure 4-1. Can you write a program that places each of the words 'HI THERE HOW ARE YOU DOING?' on a separate line?
2. Write a program that prints the following:
      first line: your name
      second line: your age
      third line: blank
      fourth line: your address
3. Write a program that reads five real numbers. Print each number in a field seven characters long so that it has two decimal places.
4. Read four integers. Print them so they are in columns each ten spaces wide. Add headings for the columns. Here is a sample of how the output might look:

FIRST	SECOND	THIRD	FOURTH
5	16	101	10

Leave a blank line between the header and the integers.

CHAPTER 5

Introduction to Pascal Statements

CHAPTER OUTLINE

LEARNING OBJECTIVES

INTRODUCTION

ASSIGNMENT STATEMENTS

> **LEARNING CHECK 5-1**

ARITHMETIC OPERATORS
   Addition • Subtraction • Multiplication • Division • DIV and MOD
   • Unary Plus and Minus

> **LEARNING CHECK 5-2**

ORDER OF OPERATIONS

ALGEBRAIC EQUATIONS

> **LEARNING CHECK 5-3**

IF/THEN STATEMENTS

IF/THEN/ELSE STATEMENTS

> **LEARNING CHECK 5-4**

SUMMARY POINTS

VOCABULARY LIST

LEARNING OBJECTIVES

After studying this chapter, you should be able to:

1. Define and explain the purpose of an assignment statement.
2. Write valid Pascal assignment statements.
3. Define the terms: arithmetic operator, relational operator, operand, expression, and control statement.
4. Name the six arithmetic operators and explain the function of each.
5. Write statements using the unary plus and minus signs.
6. Write assignment statements using the six arithmetic operators.
7. List the order of operations in Pascal.
8. Write statements using parentheses to control the order in which operations will be done.
9. Write program segments using IF/THEN and IF/THEN/ELSE control statements.
10. Explain the meaning of each of the relational operators.
11. Explain the purpose of a control statement.

ADVANCED PLACEMENT CHAPTER HIGHLIGHTS

The following topics from the Advanced Placement Computer Science Exam are covered in this chapter:

expressions and assignments
  operators and operator precedence
  assignment statements
control statements
  single-alternative decision statements
  double-alternative decision statements

INTRODUCTION

In Chapter 3, the different data types were explained. In this chapter, you will learn how to assign values to variables. Arithmetic operations in Pascal are also presented. In the conclusion of the chapter, two Pascal statements are introduced that allow the programmer to determine whether or not a certain part of a program will be executed.

Computer programs solve problems for us. In the program converting feet to miles in Chapter 3, a way was needed to make a new variable, which was called MILES, to hold the result of the calculation FEET / FEET_MILE. This was done by using an **assignment statement**. The general format is shown in Figure 5-1. The assignment statement in the FIND_MILES program is:

MILES := FEET / FEET_MILE;

The result of the computation FEET / FEET_MILE is assigned to the variable MILES. This statement should be read "MILES is assigned the value of FEET divided by FEET_MILE." The symbol := should not be thought of as an equal sign. As many assignment statements as are necessary may be used in a program. The general form of an assignment statement is:

variable := expression

An **expression** can consist of a variable, a constant, or any valid combination of variables, constants, or operators. An **operator** is a symbol that stands for a process, like a plus or minus sign. In this case, the symbol := stands for the process of assignment, or storing the result of the expression on the right side of the statement in the variable on the left side of the statement.

We can write a program to find the average of three integers in two steps. The sum of the three numbers is found and this sum is then divided by three (the number of items being averaged). The first assignment statement could be written:

SUM := A + B + C;

The sum of A + B + C is now stored in the variable SUM. The second step could look like this:

AVE := SUM / 3;

Figure 5-2 shows the data table for this program. What type of number will AVE be? Since AVE is likely to be a real number, AVE will have to be declared to be of data type REAL. Figure 5-3 gives the complete program for this problem.

variable := expression;

Figure 5-1 SYNTAX FOR THE ASSIGNMENT STATEMENT

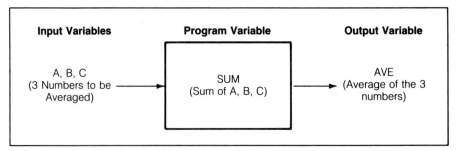

Figure 5-2 DATA TABLE FOR PROGRAM AVERAGE

An assignment statement does not always have to have an arithmetic operation. It can be used to move a value from one variable to another:

```
TEMP := SUM;
```

After this statement is executed, the value of TEMP is the same as the value of SUM. The value of SUM remains the same. This type of statement can often be useful.

An assignment can be used to find the opposite of a number:

```
A := -A;
```

Suppose the beginning value of A is −105. The value of −A will then be 105. This value, 105, will then be stored in A. This statement has the

```
PROGRAM AVERAGE;
(* FINDS THE AVERAGE OF 3 NUMBERS *)

VAR
    SUM, A, B, C : INTEGER;
    AVE         : REAL;

BEGIN

    WRITE ('WHAT ARE THE 3 NUMBERS? ');
    READLN (A, B, C);
    SUM := (A + B + C);
    AVE := SUM / 3;
    WRITELN ('THE AVERAGE IS ', AVE:7:2)

END.   (* AVERAGE *)


Running . . .
WHAT ARE THE 3 NUMBERS? 4 12 26
THE AVERAGE IS    14.00
```

Figure 5-3 PROGRAM AVERAGE

same effect as multiplying A by −1. Here is another assignment statement:

```
SUM := SUM + 1;
```

This statement increases the value of SUM by one. Such a statement is useful if it is necessary to count how many there are of a certain item.

It is not necessary to have a variable name on the right side of an assignment statement. If COUNT is declared to be of data type INTEGER, this statement would be valid:

```
COUNT := 10;
```

On the other hand, the statement

```
COUNT := 1.5;
```

is not valid because 1.5 is a real number and cannot be assigned to COUNT, since COUNT has been declared to be of data type INTEGER. For the same reason this statement is invalid:

```
COUNT := COUNT + 2.75;
```

If COUNT has been declared to be of data type REAL, this would be a valid assignment statement:

```
COUNT := 14;
```

The compiler can convert the integer number into a real number.

Assignment statements can also be used with STRING and CHAR data. Here is a program segment:

```
PROGRAM ASSIGN;

VAR
    STAR : CHAR;
    NAME, NEWNAME : STRING;

BEGIN

    STAR := '*';
    NAME := 'JONATHAN DAVID';
```

The value of STAR is now *. The variable NAME now contains the value JONATHAN DAVID. Remember that with CHAR and STRING data the value assigned to the variable must be enclosed in single quotes. Since the variables NAME and NEWNAME are both of the same data type (STRING), an assignment statement could be written like this:

```
NEWNAME := NAME;
```

NAME is not enclosed in quotation marks because it is a variable name, not a character string. Now both NAME and NEWNAME contain the character string JONATHAN DAVID. The following statement would be invalid:

```
STAR := NEWNAME;
```

The data type CHAR may contain only one character.

The data type BOOLEAN can be assigned only one of two values: true or false. If ANSWER is declared to be of type BOOLEAN the assignment statement could look like this:

```
ANSWER := TRUE;
```

or like this:

```
ANSWER := FALSE;
```

In all these examples of assignment statements, the computer determines the value of the expression on the right side of the assignment statement. This result is then assigned to the variable on the left side of the assignment statement.

◣ LEARNING CHECK 5-1

1. Explain why the compiler can convert an integer to a real number. Why cannot a real number be converted to an integer?
2. Assume all the variables below have been declared as data type REAL. Which of these assignment statements are valid?

   a. `PERCENT := 0.75;`
   b. `COST = -14.85;`
   c. `NUM := 51;`
   d. `FIRST := LAST;`
   e. `HEIGHT := HEIGHT - 4.51;`
   f. `SCORE + 1 := SCORE;`
   g. `451 := HEIGHT * WIDTH;`
   h. `SIZE := LENGTH / 12;`

3. Given the following declaration statement, which of the assignment statements below are valid?

   ```
   VAR
       SCORE, NUM, TOTAL : INTEGER;
   ```

   a. `SCORE := 1.5;`
   b. `TOTAL := SCORE * NUM;`
   c. `NUM := NUM + 1;`
   d. `SCORE := NUM / TOTAL;`
   e. `NUM * 2 := TOTAL;`
   f. `TOTAL := SCORE - NUM;`

ARITHMETIC OPERATORS

There are six **arithmetic operators** in Pascal. An arithmetic operator is a symbol that stands for a particular arithmetic process, such as addition or subtraction. The first four arithmetic operators are familiar to us:

+ addition
− subtraction
* multiplication
/ division

The symbols and their meanings are listed in Figure 5-4. Each of them will be examined individually.

Addition

In addition, the value of the first **operand** is added to the value of the second operand. An operand is a value upon which an arithmetic operation is performed. In this example

$$14 + 12$$

the operands are 14 and 12. The arithmetic operator is the plus sign. Integers can be added together. The result will always be an integer.

```
A := 1 + 4;
```

Although the value of the expression above will always be an integer, variable A may be declared to be of data type INTEGER or of data type REAL. The compiler will convert the integer to a real number. Figure 5-5 lists two programs that show this. In both programs, X and Y are

Arithmetic Operator	Meaning	Example
+	addition	A + B
−	subtraction	A − B
*	multiplication	A * B
/	division	A / B

Figure 5-4   ARITHMETIC OPERATORS

87

```
PROGRAM TOT1;
(* ADD TWO INTEGERS TOGETHER AND PLACE THE RESULT IN AN INTEGER VARIABLE *)

VAR
    X, Y, SUM : INTEGER;

BEGIN

    WRITE ('TYPE IN THE TWO NUMBERS TO BE ADDED TOGETHER: ');
    READLN (X, Y);
    SUM := X + Y;
    WRITELN ('THE SUM IS ', SUM)

END.   (* TOT1 *)




Running . . .
TYPE IN THE TWO NUMBERS TO BE ADDED TOGETHER: 456 61
THE SUM IS 517




PROGRAM TOT2;
(* ADD TWO INTEGERS TOGETHER AND PLACE THE RESULT IN AN REAL VARIABLE *)

VAR
    X, Y : INTEGER;
    SUM    : REAL;

BEGIN

    WRITE ('TYPE IN THE TWO NUMBERS TO BE ADDED TOGETHER: ');
    READLN (X, Y);
    SUM := X + Y;
    WRITELN ('THE SUM IS ', SUM:7:2)

END.   (* TOT2 *)




Running . . .
TYPE IN THE TWO NUMBERS TO BE ADDED TOGETHER: 456 61
THE SUM IS  517.00
```

Figure 5-5 PROGRAMS TOT1 AND TOT2

integers that are added together. In TOT1 the result, SUM, is an integer. In TOT2 the result has been assigned to a variable of data type REAL. Therefore, the result has been converted to a real number.

When two real numbers are added together, the result must always be of data type REAL. Here are some examples of addition with variables of data type REAL:

```
POINT := 100.00 + TEXT1;

DIAMETER := 35.75 + 0.68;

DISTANCE1 := DISTANCE1 + 5.0;
```

An integer and a real number may be added together. The result must always be placed in a real variable.

Subtraction

In subtraction, the value of the second operand is subtracted from the value of the first operand. The rules concerning the use of INTEGER and REAL data types are the same as for addition. Look at these examples:

Statement	Data Type
`COUNT := COUNT - 1;`	INTEGER
`YARDS := 108 - 16;`	INTEGER
`COST := PRICE - 1.85;`	REAL
`BILL := 486.85 - 115.23;`	REAL

Multiplication

The Pascal operator for multiplication is the asterisk (*). It is the only sign that may be used for multiplication. In multiplication, the value of the first operand is multiplied by the value of the second operand. The result of two integers being multiplied together will always be an integer. As in subtraction and addition, this result may be placed in a variable of either data type INTEGER or REAL. The result of two real numbers being multiplied together will always be of data type REAL. Some examples:

Statement	Data Type
`SQUARE := 4 * 4;`	INTEGER
`SCORE := TD * 6;`	INTEGER
`AREA := HEIGHT * 12.34;`	REAL

Division

In Pascal, the arithmetic operator for division is the slash sign (/). The first operand is divided by the second operand.

The result of one integer being divided by another must always be assigned to a REAL variable. This is because the result will usually be a real number. Two real numbers may be divided by each other. Again, the result will be a real number. In these examples all of the variables on the left side of the assignment statement have been declared to be of data type REAL:

```
PERCENT := SUM / 80.5;
FRACTION := 10 / 3;
HEIGHT := FEET / 36;
```

89

As in arithmetic, division by zero is not allowed. Thus the statement below is not valid:

```
NUM := SCORE / 0;
```

DIV and MOD

The two arithmetic operators DIV and MOD can be used with integers only. The result will always be an integer. The DIV operation truncates the result of a division problem to the integer value. Below are some examples.

$$
\begin{array}{r}
4 \text{ quotient} \\
6\overline{)27} \\
\underline{24} \\
3 \text{ remainder}
\end{array}
$$

In the statement below, A is of data type INTEGER:

```
A := 27 DIV 6;
```

The value of A will be 4. There is never a decimal point in the result of a DIV operation. Here's another example:

```
X := 105 DIV 12;
```

The division problem looks like this:

$$
\begin{array}{r}
8 \text{ quotient} \\
12\overline{)105} \\
\underline{96} \\
9 \text{ remainder}
\end{array}
$$

The value of X will be 8.

Here's the same problem using the MOD operator:

```
REM := 105 MOD 12;
```

The result of the MOD operation is the remainder from the DIV operation. The value of REM is 9. REM is assigned the value of the remainder. REM must also be declared to be data type INTEGER. Look at the problems below and see if you agree with the answers given.

Problem	Answer
8 DIV 3	2
8 MOD 3	2
140 DIV 12	11
140 MOD 12	8
160 DIV 8	20
160 MOD 8	0

```
LARGE := − 14 / ( +A);
MIDDLE := Z + 16 * ( − 104);
A := B DIV ( − C);
```

Figure 5-6 CORRECT USE OF UNARY PLUS AND MINUS SIGNS

As in regular division, the divisor in a DIV or MOD operation may not be equal to zero. Both of these statements are invalid:

```
A DIV 0
B MOD 0
```

The MOD function may not be used with LONG INTEGER values.

Unary Plus and Minus

The **unary plus** and **minus** signs are used alone with a number. The plus sign leaves the number unchanged whereas the minus sign results in the opposite of the number. For example:

$$-47 \qquad +83 \qquad -Y \qquad -Z \qquad -0.365$$

If there is no sign, it is assumed that the number is positive. In writing arithmetic expressions, two arithmetic operators may not be next to each other. For example, this would be an invalid expression:

```
A := X + -Y + Z;
```

Instead, the expression must be written this way:

```
A := X + (-Y) + Z;
```

The parentheses separate the $-Y$ from the addition sign. Look at Figure 5-6 for some examples.

LEARNING CHECK 5-2

1. Explain why the result of dividing two integers must be assigned to a variable of data type REAL.
2. Write an assignment statement that will square B and place the result in variable X.
3. Which of these DIV and MOD expressions are valid:

   a. `12.5 DIV 6`
   b. `10 DIV 0`
   c. `12 MOD 8`
   d. `205 MOD 0.5`

4. Add parentheses to these expressions so that they are valid Pascal expressions:

    a. −148 / −14
    b. 68 * +ZERO
    c. 18 + −16 + +28
    d. +A / −B + C * −D

5. Assume X has been declared as data type INTEGER. Tell what the value assigned to X will be in each case.

    a. X := 100 MOD 3;
    b. X := 92 DIV 8;
    c. X := 14 MOD 13;
    d. X := X MOD 1;

Answers:

ORDER OF OPERATIONS

In Pascal, arithmetic expressions can be written that have many operations in them. Here is an example:

$$4 * 18 + 20 / 5 - 3$$

In this expression, several steps need to be performed to find the answer. To determine how to solve this problem, it is necessary to have an **order of operations**. This states the order in which the arithmetic will be done. The order of operations, as shown in Figure 5-7, specifies that multiplication and division are done before addition and subtraction. Any operations that are on the same level are done from left to right. In the expression above, 4 * 18 and 20 / 5 are both at the same level. First, 4 is multiplied by 18, since we are moving from left to right. Then 20 will be divided by 5. After all of the multiplication and division are done, then the addition and subtraction are completed. It will be done from left to right since addition and subtraction are both on the same level. The steps for the expression above will be:

1. $4 * 18 = 72$
2. $20 / 5 = 4$
3. $72 + 4 = 76$
4. $76 - 3 = 73$

The value of this expression will be 73.

1. Evaluate anything in parentheses.
2. *, /, DIV, and MOD are evaluated before + and −
3. Arithmetic operators at the same level (such as * and DIV) are evaluated left to right

Figure 5-7 ORDER OF OPERATIONS

In the example above, what if it was necessary to subtract three from five before doing the rest of the problem? The order in which arithmetic operations are done can be controlled by using parentheses. The expression above could be written:

$$4 * 18 + 20 / (5 - 3)$$

In this case the steps would be:

1. $5 - 3 = 2$
2. $4 * 18 = 72$
3. $20 / 2 = 10$
4. $72 + 10 = 82$

The value of the expression would be 82. Any expressions in parentheses are always evaluated first. If two sets of parentheses are nested (one inside the other) the innermost one will be evaluated first:

$$1500 / (10 * (14 - 4))$$

The steps in evaluating this expression are:

1. $14 - 4 = 10$
2. $10 * 10 = 100$
3. $1500 / 100 = 15$

The result is 15. Below is the same problem with no parentheses:

$$1500 / 10 * 14 - 4$$

The steps would be:

1. $1500 / 10 = 150$
2. $150 * 14 = 2100$
3. $2100 - 4 = 2096$

Obviously, a very different answer is obtained. If you have any doubts about how an expression you have written will be evaluated, always use parentheses. This way you will know exactly how the arithmetic will be done. Adding parentheses when they are not necessary will not hurt anything. It also can make a program easier to understand.

ALGEBRAIC EQUATIONS

Algebraic expressions often look like this:

$$\frac{A * B}{N - 1} * \frac{X + Y^2}{N + 1}$$

How would such an expression be written in Pascal? Parentheses are needed to control the order in which the arithmetic is done. The left fraction would be written:

```
(A * B) / (N - 1)
```

It is not necessary to put A * B in parentheses but it might help clarify the expression. The right fraction would look like:

```
(X + Y * Y) / (N + 1)
```

Notice that Y is multiplied by itself to square it. Next the two sides are multiplied together:

```
(A * B / (N - 1)) * ((X + Y * Y) / (N + 1))
```

Parentheses enclose each entire term. All of the operations in each term must be performed before the two sides are multiplied together. Be careful when you are using parentheses inside other sets of parentheses. It is very easy to leave one off or put it in the wrong place, resulting in an error when your program is run.

LEARNING CHECK 5-3

1. Use this program segment to write Pascal statements for the problems below and then answer the questions.

```
PROGRAM COMPUTE;

VAR
    NUM1, NUM2, A, B, C : REAL;

BEGIN

    A := 15.0;
    B := 3.0;
    C := 27.0;
```

a. Subract A from B. Then multiply the result by two. Assign this value to the variable NUM1. What will the value of NUM1 be?

b. Divide C by B. Then divide the result by two. Assign the result to NUM2. What will the value of NUM2 be?

c. Add A and C together. Divide this result by B. Assign the result to A. What will the value of A be?

d. Subtract B from C. Square the result. Then assign the result to NUM1. Figure out what the value of NUM1 will be.

2. Evaluate the following expressions:

   a. 4 − 6 / 2
   b. 6.5. + 8.5 − 4.3
   c. 18 + (−16) / 4
   d. 280 / 7 ∗ 6
   e. 73.5 / 2.5 ∗ 16.75
   f. 73.5 / (2.5 ∗ 16.75)
   g. 6 − 15 DIV 4
   h. 85 MOD 3 − 18
   i. 85 MOD (3 − 18)
   j. (16 + 32) / 2
   k. 38 ∗ 20 − 8

Answers:

1. a.   NUM1 := (B − A) ∗ 2;
         NUM1 = −24.0

   b.   NUM2 := (C / B) / 2;   (first set of parentheses is optional)
         NUM2 = 4.5

   c.   A := (A + C) / B;
         A = 14.0

   d.   NUM1 := (C − B) ∗ (C − B);
         NUM1 = 576.0

2. a. 1.0 b. 10.7 c. 14.0 d. 240.0 e. 492.45 f. 1.76 (rounded to two decimal places) g. 3 h. −17 i. 10 (Although the quotient is negative, the remainder will be positive because the dividend is positive.) j. 24.0 k. 752

IF/THEN STATEMENTS

In real life, people are constantly making decisions. Many decisions are based on a particular situation. You start making decisions when you awaken in the morning. Some of the decisions might be: is there time for a shower and breakfast? If it is raining outside, wear a raincoat, otherwise wear a regular coat. If you do not feel well, should you stay in bed?

In order to be useful, computer programs also need to allow for decisions. Computer programs do this by evaluating conditions. For example, is variable A larger than zero? If so, something may be done to A that will not occur if it is less than or equal to zero. Decisions can be coded by using an IF/THEN statement. The IF/THEN statement tests to see if a given condition is true. It looks like this:

IF condition THEN
expression;

```
┌─────────────────────────────┐
│     IF/THEN STATEMENT       │
├─────────────────────────────┤
│     IF condition THEN       │
│         expression;         │
└─────────────────────────────┘
```

Figure 5-8 SYNTAX FOR THE IF/THEN STATEMENT

If the condition is true, the next part of the statement is executed. If the condition is false, the program goes on to the following statement. The syntax for this statement is illustrated in Figure 5-8. The IF/THEN statement is one Pascal statement. It has a semicolon only at the end of the statement, so there is no semicolon after THEN. We could write the statement all on one line:

IF condition THEN expression;

Putting it on two lines and indenting the second one makes the program logic easier to follow.

Comparisons are frequently used with IF/THEN statements, by using **relational operators**. Relational operators are operators that compare one operand with another. The relational operators in Pascal are listed in Figure 5-9. The same operators are used in mathematics, although some of the symbols are slightly different.

Below is an example of an IF/THEN statement:

```
IF Z = Y THEN
   Z := Z + 10;
```

This is read "If Z is equal to Y then assign the value of Z plus ten to A." In this example, Z will be increased by ten only if Z is equal to Y. This statement could be changed to the opposite:

```
IF Z <> Y THEN
   Z := Z + 10;
```

In this case, the value of Z will be increased by ten only if it is *not* equal

Operator	Meaning	Example
=	equals	X = Y
<>	does not equal	X <> Y
>	greater than	X > Y
>=	greater than or equal to	X >= Y
<	less than	X < Y
<=	less than or equal to	X <= Y

Figure 5-9 RELATIONAL OPERATORS

to Y. If Z is equal to Y, the program will simply skip to the next statement.

Relational operators may also be used with character and string data. Look at the expressions below and how they are evaluated.

Expression	Evaluates as
'A' < 'D'	true
'JIMINY' < 'JIMI'	false
'PARTRIDGE' = 'PARTRIDGE'	true
'P' <> 'Q'	true

Now we will write a program using an IF/THEN statement. The local record store is having a sale. All of the albums are marked down to $5. If you buy six or more albums, you get 10 percent off the total price. The flowchart for this program is illustrated in Figure 5-10. First, the number of albums to be bought needs to be read. This number will be multiplied by the price per album, $5. Now it will need to be deter-

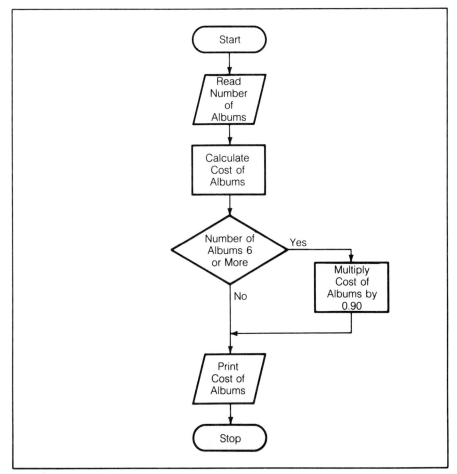

Figure 5-10 FLOWCHART FOR PRICE1

```
PROGRAM PRICE1;
(* FIND THE TOTAL COST OF THE RECORD ALBUMS.  THE ALBUMS ARE $5.00 EACH.
IF 6 OR MORE ARE BOUGHT, THERE IS A 10% DISCOUNT *)

VAR
   ALBUMS : INTEGER;
   COST   : REAL;

BEGIN

   WRITE ('HOW MANY ALBUMS ARE BEING BOUGHT? ');
   READLN (ALBUMS);
   COST := ALBUMS * 5.00;

   IF ALBUMS >= 6 THEN
      COST := COST * 0.90;

   WRITELN ('THE COST OF THE ALBUMS IS $', COST:6:2)

END.   (* PRICE1 *)



Running . . .
HOW MANY ALBUMS ARE BEING BOUGHT? 7
THE COST OF THE ALBUMS IS $ 31.50


Running . . .
HOW MANY ALBUMS ARE BEING BOUGHT? 4
THE COST OF THE ALBUMS IS $ 20.00
```

Figure 5-11 PROGRAM PRICE1

mined if the number of albums being bought is greater than or equal to
six. If it is, the price charged will be only 90 percent of the total (100%
− 10% = 90%). For this problem, the IF/THEN statement could be:

```
IF ALBUMS >= 6 THEN
   COST := COST * 0.90;
```

It also could be written as:

```
IF ALBUMS > 5 THEN
   COST := COST * 0.90;
```

Either way, 10 percent is taken from the total price if six or more
albums are being purchased. Figure 5-11 contains the complete program.

IF/THEN/ELSE STATEMENTS

The IF/THEN statement is called a single-alternative IF statement. This
is because there is only one choice. The comparison is either true or
false. If the expression is false, nothing is done. Suppose the discount on
the records is a little different. Consider this pricing scheme:

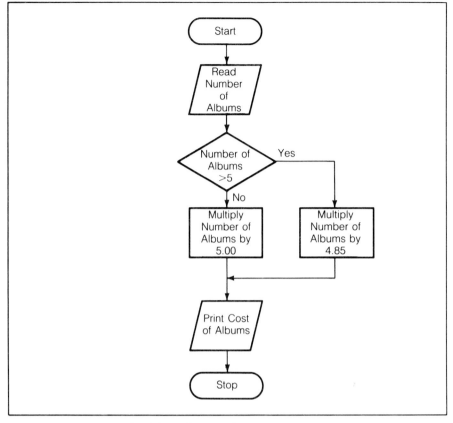

Figure 5-12   FLOWCHART FOR PRICE2

- one to five albums—$5.00 each
- six or more albums—$4.85 each

Look at the flowchart for this problem in Figure 5-12. The easiest way to write this program would be to use a double-alternative IF statement. The syntax for this statement is illustrated in Figure 5-13. It looks like this:

```
IF condition THEN
    expression1
ELSE
    expression2;
```

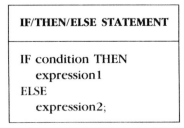

IF/THEN/ELSE STATEMENT

```
IF condition THEN
    expression1
ELSE
    expression2;
```

Figure 5-13   SYNTAX FOR THE IF/THEN/ELSE STATEMENT   **99**

In this case, if the stated condition is true, the expression following that condition is executed. If it is not true, the expression following ELSE is executed. One or the other of the expressions will always be executed. Notice that there is a semicolon only at the very end of the statement. The IF/THEN/ELSE statement is a single Pascal statement. For the problem computing the cost of the albums the IF/THEN/ELSE statement could look like this:

```
IF ALBUMS <= 5 THEN
    COST := ALBUMS * 5.00
ELSE
    COST := ALBUMS * 4.85;
```

This statement could be changed around and still produce the same results:

```
IF ALBUMS > 5 THEN
    COST := ALBUMS * 4.85
ELSE
    COST := ALBUMS * 5.00;
```

Figure 5-14 is the complete program for this problem.

```
PROGRAM PRICE2;
(* FIND THE TOTAL COST OF THE RECORD ALBUMS.  IF 1-5 ALBUMS ARE BOUGHT,
THE PRICE IS $5.00 EACH.  IF 6 OR MORE ALBUMS ARE BOUGHT, THEY ARE
$4.85 EACH  *)

VAR
    ALBUMS : INTEGER;
    COST   : REAL;

BEGIN

    WRITE ('HOW MANY ALBUMS ARE BEING BOUGHT? ');
    READLN (ALBUMS);

    IF ALBUMS > 5 THEN
       COST := ALBUMS * 4.85
    ELSE
       COST := ALBUMS * 5.00;

    WRITELN ('THE COST OF THE ALBUMS IS $', COST:6:2)

END.   (* PRICE2 *)



Running . . .
HOW MANY ALBUMS ARE BEING BOUGHT? 6
THE COST OF THE ALBUMS IS $ 29.10


Running . . .
HOW MANY ALBUMS ARE BEING BOUGHT? 5
THE COST OF THE ALBUMS IS $ 25.00
```

Figure 5-14 PROGRAM PRICE2

The IF/THEN and IF/THEN/ELSE statements are called **control statements**. A control statement allows the programmer to determine whether or not a statement (or group of statements) will be executed and how many times. In the IF/THEN and IF/THEN/ELSE statements, a condition is evaluated. What is done next depends on the result of that evaluation. There are other control statements in Pascal that will be introduced later in this book.

In expressions containing both arithmetic ($+$, $-$, $*$, $/$, DIV, and MOD) and relational operators, the arithmetic operations are always performed first. Consider this expression:

```
IF  A  *  B  =  C  THEN
```

First, the value of A $*$ B is found and then this value is compared to C. Listed below is a program segment:

```
VAR
      A, B, C, LARGEST, SMALLEST : INTEGER;

BEGIN

      A := 4;
      B := 10;
      C := 6;
```

Study the expressions below to see if you agree with how they evaluate.

Expression	*Evaluation*
IF A > B THEN	false (4 is not greater than 10)
IF A + C = B THEN	true (4 + 6 = 10)
IF C <= B * 2 THEN	true (6 is less than or equal to 10 $*$ 2)
IF 10 < B THEN	false (10 is not less than 10)

LEARNING CHECK 5-4

1. The program shown in Figure 5-2 has two assignment statements:

```
SUM := A + B + C;
AVE := SUM / 3;
```

Write these two statements as one, using parentheses.
2. Write a Pascal assignment statement to represent each equation.

a. $X = \dfrac{Y2}{2}$

b. $A = Y + Z \times 3$

c. $B = \dfrac{X + 10}{4 \times 8} + 2$

d. $Z = 12 + (-A) - \dfrac{A + B}{X}$

3. Given the following program segment, tell whether the expressions below will evaluate as true or false.

```
PROGRAM ONE;

VAR
    I, J, K : INTEGER;
    ANSWER, MORE : BOOLEAN;
    ADDRESS : STRING;

BEGIN

    I := 10;
    J := 12;
    K := 0;
    ANSWER := TRUE;
    MORE := FALSE;
    ADDRESS := '101 S. Main';
```

a. I >= J
b. ANSWER <> MORE
c. K < I
d. ADDRESS = '101 S. MAIN'
e. J = 12
f. MORE = TRUE
g. J = K + I

Answers:

SUMMARY POINTS

- A number of valuable features of Pascal have been reviewed in this chapter. Assignment statements are used to assign values to variables. The value of an arithmetic expression is found by following the order of operations, which determines the order in which arithmetic operations are done. This order can be changed by using parentheses.
- The IF/THEN and IF/THEN/ELSE statements are control statements that test a condition. If the condition tested is true, the next part of the statement is executed. Otherwise, this step is skipped. IF/THEN/ELSE statements provide one option if the condition is true, another if it is false. In this way, the programmer can control whether or not a certain step will be executed. Control statements will be important in virtually every Pascal program.

VOCABULARY LIST

Arithmetic operator A symbol that stands for an arithmetic process, such as addition or subtraction.

Assignment statement A statement that allows a value to be stored in a variable.

Control statement A statement that allows the programmer to determine whether or not a statement (or a group of statements) will be executed and how many times.

Expression Any valid combination of variable(s), constant(s), operator(s), and parentheses.

Operand A value on which an arithmetic operation is performed.

Operator A symbol that stands for a process.

Order of operations The sequence in which expressions are evaluated.

Relational operators Operators that compare one operand with another.

Unary minus sign A symbol (−) used alone with a number that gives the opposite of the number.

Unary plus sign A symbol (+) used alone with a number that leaves the number unchanged.

CHAPTER TEST

VOCABULARY

Match each term from the numbered column with the best description from the lettered column.

1. Unary minus sign

2. Operator

3. Relational operators
4. Unary plus sign

5. Operand

6. Arithmetic operator

7. Assignment statement

8. Expression

a. A statement that allows a value to be stored in a variable.

b. Operators that compare one operand with another.

c. A symbol that stands for a process.

d. A symbol used alone with a number that gives the opposite of the number.

e. A variable, constant, or any valid combination of variables, constants, and operators.

f. A value on which an operation is performed.

g. A symbol used alone with a number that leaves the number unchanged.

h. A symbol that stands for an arithmetic process, such as addition or subtraction.

QUESTIONS

1. Explain in your own words what an assignment statement does.
2. What is the value of each expression listed below? What data type will the result be?

   a. 10 / 4
   b. 14 + 18 + 32
   c. 5 DIV 2
   d. 5 MOD 2
   e. 16.5 * 18.3
   f. 414 - 318
   g. 162 DIV 11
   h. 162 MOD 11
   i. 162 / 11

3. List each of the relational operators and tell what each one does.
4. What is the difference between an IF/THEN statement and an IF/THEN/ELSE statement? Give appropriate examples of each.
5. Given the program segment below, determine what output will be generated by the control statements that follow.

```
PROGRAM EX;

VAR

    FLOWER : STRING;
    QUANTITY, MANY : INTEGER;

BEGIN

    QUANTITY := 2 * 8;
    FLOWER := 'ZINNIA';
    MANY := QUANTITY - 3;
```

```
a.  IF FLOWER > 'ZINNIA' THEN
        WRITELN ('THIS IS THE RIGHT FLOWER.')
    ELSE
        WRITELN ('KEEP LOOKING.');
```

```
b.  IF MANY = 12 THEN
        WRITELN ('MANY IS A DOZEN.');
```

```
c.  IF QUANTITY >= 16 THEN
        WRITELN ('THERE ARE ENOUGH.')
    ELSE
        WRITELN (FLOWER);
```

PROGRAMMING PROBLEMS

1. Write a program that finds the result of the following equation:

$$\frac{16.8 - 8.0}{3.3} + \frac{7.0 + 2}{12.5 \times 2}$$

2. Sally wants to buy a new outfit. The items she would like to buy are:

- sweater—$35.00
- skirt—$28.50
- blouse—$22.95
- bracelet—$12.25

The clothing store is having a sale next Tuesday. Everything except for jewelry will be 15 percent off. Write a program to tell Sally how much the items listed above would cost now. Also figure out how much the items would cost if Sally waited until they were on sale. Both amounts should be printed at the end of the program.

3. Write a program that will determine the cost of a movie ticket. The customer's age is entered at the keyboard. If the age is 12 or less, the cost of the ticket is $2. If the customer's age is 13 or more, the cost is $3.50. Write the cost of the ticket to the monitor with appropriate labeling.

4. WJCR 1414 Radio is giving $140 to the 14th person to call in. Billie needs the money for her new ten-speed bike. She has figured that each call takes 6.4 seconds to be answered after it begins ringing at the radio station. It then takes 12.8 seconds for the radio station to answer the phone and tally the call. It will take her 5.8 seconds to dial the call. Write a program that Billie can use to determine how many seconds she should wait before calling the radio station.

5. Write a program that will print an integer only if it is even. (Hint: think about how the MOD operator could be used to do this.)

6. Steve Hoffman has a carpet cleaning business. Write a program for him to determine how much to bill a customer. He charges:

1. $1.00 per square yard for normal carpets.
2. $1.20 per square yard for extra-dirty carpets.
3. $0.05 extra per square yard if the carpet is to be deodorized.
4. $0.25 extra per square yard if the carpet is to be treated with carpet shield protector.

Allow Steve to enter the length and width of a room in feet and have the program compute the number of square yards. Assume the rooms are rectangular. Use prompts to find out if the carpet is extra-dirty or if it needs to be deodorized or treated with carpet shield protector. Print the amount of the bill to the monitor.

CHAPTER 6

Decision Structures and Compound Statements

CHAPTER OUTLINE

LEARNING OBJECTIVES

INTRODUCTION

COMPOUND STATEMENTS

PROGRAM SEWING

NESTED IF/THEN/ELSE STATEMENTS

LEARNING CHECK 6-1

PROGRAM PIZZA

ELSE IF STATEMENTS

PROGRAM WEEK

CASE STATEMENTS

LEARNING CHECK 6-2

SUMMARY POINTS

VOCABULARY LIST

LEARNING OBJECTIVES

After studying this chapter, you should be able to:

1. Define a compound statement.
2. Write compound IF/THEN/ELSE statements.
3. Explain how nested IF/THEN/ELSE statements work.
4. Write correctly nested IF/THEN/ELSE statements.
5. Write ELSE IF control statements.
6. Write CASE statements.
7. Determine which control statement is the most appropriate for a given programming problem.

ADVANCED PLACEMENT CHAPTER HIGHLIGHTS

The following topics from the Advanced Placement Computer Science Exam are covered in this chapter:

  compound statements
  conditional control statements

INTRODUCTION

Control statements are an important part of computer programs. Control statements allow the programmer to determine two things:

1. Whether or not a particular section of a program will be executed.
2. How many times a section of a program will be executed.

The last part of Chapter 5 introduced the IF/THEN and IF/THEN/ELSE statements. Such control statements, which determine whether a particular part of a program will be executed, are called **decision structures**. They make a decision based on how an expression evaluates. This chapter introduces more decision structures. Each decision structure is particularly useful in certain situations.

COMPOUND STATEMENTS

So far the programs in this book have contained simple Pascal statements. What if it was necessary to write an IF/THEN statement that did more than one thing? Below is an IF/THEN statement that checks to see if an integer is positive. If the number is positive, it will be squared. The IF/THEN statement looks like this:

```
IF X >= 0 THEN
    X := X * X;
```

Think about how this result could be printed only if X is a positive number. We could accomplish this by using two separate IF/THEN statements:

```
IF X >= 0 THEN
    X := X * X;
IF X >= 0 THEN
    WRITELN (X);
```

This would give the desired result. A simpler way would be to write a **compound statement**. In this case, the compound statement would look like this:

```
IF X >= 0 THEN
    BEGIN
        X := X * X;
        WRITELN (X)
    END;
```

The general syntax for the compound IF/THEN statement is shown in Figure 6-1.

A program based on this example is presented in Figure 6-2. Notice that the final value of X is printed only if X is a positive number. If X is

---

COMPOUND IF/THEN STATEMENT

IF condition THEN
  BEGIN
    statement1;
    statement2;
      .
      .
      .
    last ___ statement
  END;

Figure 6-1   SYNTAX FOR COMPOUND IF/THEN STATEMENT

```
PROGRAM SQUARE;
(* THIS PROGRAM SQUARES A NUMBER IF IT IS POSITIVE.  THE RESULT IS
THEN PRINTED ONLY IF IT IS A POSITIVE NUMBER *)

VAR
   X : INTEGER;

BEGIN

   WRITE ('TYPE IN AN INTEGER. ');
   READLN (X);

   (* DETERMINE IF X IS POSITIVE *)
   IF X >= 0 THEN
      BEGIN
         X := X * X;
         WRITELN (X)
      END

END.   (* SQUARE *)


Running . . .
TYPE IN AN INTEGER. 6
36
```

Figure 6-2   PROGRAM SQUARE

zero or negative, nothing is done. A compound statement must always start with the reserved word BEGIN and conclude with the reserved word END. A compound statement can contain any number of individual statements. The compound statement above is made of two simple statements:

$$X := X * X;$$

and

$$WRITELN (X)$$

No semicolon appears after the second statement. This is because it is followed by END, which marks the conclusion of the compound statement. No semicolon is needed before END, although in UCSD Pascal one may be used if desired.

Remember that the body of a Pascal program starts with BEGIN and finishes with END. The body of a Pascal program is thus one compound statement. It is possible to have many compound statements in a program. Some compound statements may be within others. Each compound statement must have its own BEGIN and END. Otherwise the compiler cannot tell where each one starts and finishes. Program SEWING in the following section will demonstrate the use of compound statements.

PROGRAM SEWING

The purpose of the program SEWING is to tell students how much fabric they will need to complete a home economics project. Each student has a choice of making an apron or a vest. Aprons take 2.0 yards of fabric and vests take 1.25 yards. The flowchart for this program is in Figure 6-3. First, the student is asked to enter the name of the item to be made. It must be an apron or a vest. An IF/THEN/ELSE statement is used to determine which item has been chosen. The amount of fabric needed is assigned to the variable YARDS. The amount is then printed for the student to read. This program is shown in Figure 6-4. There are two compound statements in this program. The first compound statement follows the expression IF ITEM = 'APRON' THEN. This compound statement is made up of two simple statements:

```
YARDS := 2.0;
WRITELN ('YOU WILL NEED ', YARDS:7:2, ' YARDS OF FABRIC FOR YOU APRON.')
```

Be careful not to put a semicolon after the reserved word END that occurs before the ELSE portion of an IF/THEN/ELSE statement. Re-

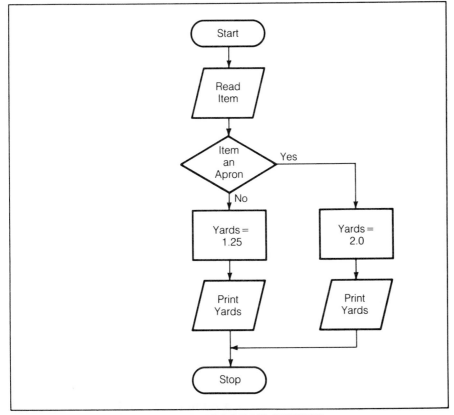

Figure 6-3 FLOWCHART FOR PROGRAM SEWING

```
PROGRAM SEWING;
(* THIS PROGRAM TELLS HOME ECONOMICS STUDENTS HOW MUCH FABRIC THEY WILL
NEED FOR THEIR SEWING PROJECT.  THE PROJECTS TAKE:
     1. APRON : 2.0 YARDS
     2. VEST : 1.25 YARDS *)

 VAR
     ITEM  : STRING;
     YARDS : REAL;

 BEGIN

     WRITELN ('WHICH PROJECT ARE YOU MAKING, AN APRON OR A VEST?');
     READLN (ITEM);

     (* COMPUTE AMOUNT OF FABRIC NEEDED FOR THE ITEM *)
     IF ITEM = 'APRON' THEN
        BEGIN
            YARDS := 2.0;
            WRITELN ('YOU WILL NEED ', YARDS:7:2, ' YARDS FOR YOUR APRON.')
        END
     ELSE
        BEGIN
            YARDS := 1.25;
            WRITELN ('YOU WILL NEED ', YARDS:7:2, ' YARDS FOR YOUR VEST.')
        END

     END.   (* SEWING *)


Running . . .
WHICH PROJECT ARE YOU MAKING, AN APRON OR A VEST?
APRON
YOU WILL NEED    2.00 YARDS FOR YOUR APRON.


Running . . .
WHICH PROJECT ARE YOU MAKING, AN APRON OR A VEST?
VEST
YOU WILL NEED    1.25 YARDS FOR YOUR VEST.
```

Figure 6-4 PROGRAM SEWING

member that IF/THEN/ELSE is all one statement. When the prompt, WHICH PROJECT ARE YOU MAKING, AN ARON OR A VEST?, is printed to the monitor, the user must type APRON in capital letters in order for the expression IF ITEM = 'APRON' to evaluate as true. Any other response will cause the ELSE portion of the statement to be executed.

NESTED IF/THEN/ELSE STATEMENTS

It is possible to have one IF/THEN/ELSE statement inside of another. Sometimes this is necessary when a number of conditions need to be checked. For example, consider a program to find the largest of three numbers. The flowchart for this problem is shown in Figure 6-5. The

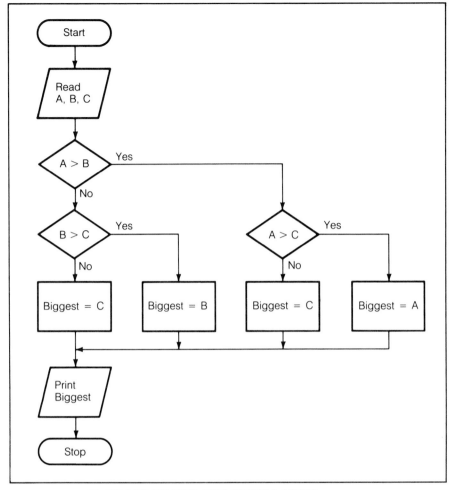

Figure 6-5 FLOWCHART FOR PROGRAM LARGE

numbers need to be compared with one another in an orderly way to
determine the largest number. One way is to use **nested statements**.
Look at program LARGE in Figure 6-6. First A is compared with B. If A is
larger than B, then A is compared to C. If A is larger than C, the value of
A is assigned to the variable BIGGEST. Otherwise, C is assigned to
BIGGEST. The ELSE portion of the program is executed only if B is
larger than A. In that case B is compared to C and the larger of the two
is assigned to the variable BIGGEST. Notice that there is one IF/THEN/
ELSE nested within the IF/THEN part of the statement and there is
another complete IF/THEN/ELSE statement nested within the ELSE part.
The inner IF/THEN/ELSE must be nested completely within one portion
of the outer IF/THEN/ELSE. It may not overlap like this:

```
IF A > B THEN
   IF A > C THEN
      BIGGEST := A
   ELSE
ELSE
   BIGGEST := B;
```

113

```
PROGRAM LARGE;
(* THIS PROGRAM READS THREE REAL NUMBERS AND PRINTS THE LARGEST
OF THE THREE *)

VAR
   A, B, C, BIGGEST : REAL;

BEGIN

   WRITE ('TYPE IN THE THREE REAL NUMBERS: ');
   READLN (A, B, C);

   (* DETERMINE WHICH IS THE LARGEST NUMBER *)
   IF A > B THEN
      IF A > C THEN
         BIGGEST := A
      ELSE
         BIGGEST := C
   ELSE
      IF B > C THEN
         BIGGEST := B
      ELSE
         BIGGEST := C;

   WRITELN ('THE LARGEST OF THE THREE NUMBERS ', A:7:2, ', ', B:7:2, ',',
   ' AND ', C:7:2, ' IS ', BIGGEST:8:2)

END.   (* LARGE *)


Running . . .
TYPE IN THE THREE REAL NUMBERS: 6.90 123.80 34.60
THE LARGEST OF THE THREE NUMBERS    6.90,   123.80, AND    34.60 IS    123.80
```

Figure 6-6   PROGRAM LARGE

Logically, this makes no sense and such a program would not execute properly.

How does the compiler know which ELSE goes with which IF/THEN? It starts from the innermost IF/THEN and matches it to the ELSE that is closest to it. It works from the inside out, matching each IF/THEN with the corresponding ELSE. Figure 6-7 shows three nested IF/

```
IF condition THEN
   IF condition THEN
      IF condition THEN
         statement1
      ELSE
         statement2
   ELSE
      statement3
ELSE
   last__statement;
```

Figure 6-7   NESTED IF/THEN/ELSE STATEMENTS

THEN/ELSE statements. Each IF/THEN is bracketed with its matching ELSE. Carefully indenting each IF/THEN helps to make the matching ELSE easier to locate. They should both start in the same column. In the next section, a program will be written that combines a number of the items introduced so far in this chapter.

LEARNING CHECK 6-1

1. What is a compound statement?
2. Why is the body of a Pascal program a compound statement?
3. What is a nested IF/THEN/ELSE statement?
4. Look at program LARGE in Figure 6-6. Suppose that the values of A and B are equal and are larger than C. Which one will be printed, A or B?

Answers:

1. A compound statement is a sequence of statements (possibly including other compound statements) bracketed by the words BEGIN and END. 2. The body of a Pascal program is a single compound statement because it starts with BEGIN and finishes with END. 3. A nested IF/THEN/ELSE statement is an IF/THEN/ELSE statement that is contained inside another IF/THEN/ELSE statement. It must be entirely inside either the IF/THEN or the ELSE portion of the outer statement. 4. The value of B would be printed.

PROGRAM PIZZA

Smiley's Pizza Pub needs a program to compute the cost of pizzas for its customers. Pizzas come in three sizes:

9-inch—$3.50
12-inch—$4.75
16-inch—$6.50

If the customer wants a thick-crusted pizza, it costs 50 cents extra regardless of the size of the pizza. Each extra topping costs:

9-inch—$.40
12-inch—$.55
16-inch—$.75

First the cost of the basic pizza will be determined. This amount depends on the size of the pizza. It could be found by writing a series of IF/THEN statements:

```
IF SIZE = 9 THEN
    COST := 3.50;
IF SIZE = 12 THEN
    COST := 4.75;
IF SIZE = 16 THEN
    COST := 6.50;
```

Here three single-alternative IF statements have been used. Each pizza will fall into one of these categories since these are the only sizes of pizza available. The same result could be achieved by using nested IF/THEN/ELSE statements:

```
IF SIZE = 9 THEN
    COST := 3.50
ELSE
    IF SIZE = 12 THEN
        COST := 4.75
    ELSE
        COST := 6.50;
```

It is important that a semicolon be placed only at the end of this entire statement.

ELSE IF STATEMENTS

A simpler way of writing this program would be to use an ELSE IF statement. It would look like this:

```
IF SIZE = 9 THEN
    COST := 3.50
ELSE IF SIZE = 12 THEN
    COST := 4.75
ELSE IF SIZE = 16 THEN
    COST := 6.50;
```

Figure 6-8 diagrams the syntax of the ELSE IF statement. Again, note that there is only one semicolon. Figure 6-9 shows the flowchart for the PIZZA program. Each ELSE IF is executed only if the condition stated is true; otherwise the program goes on to the next ELSE IF. If none of the stated conditions are true, then none of the statements following the

---

ELSE IF STATEMENT

IF condition1 THEN
   statement1
ELSE IF condition2 THEN
   statement2;
     .
     .
     .
ELSE
   last ___ statement;

Note: The final ELSE and the statement following it are optional.

Figure 6-8 SYNTAX FOR ELSE IF STATEMENT

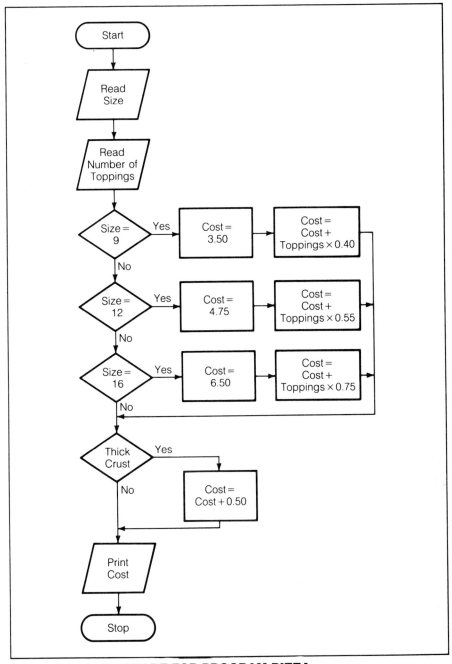

Figure 6-9 FLOWCHART FOR PROGRAM PIZZA

conditions will be executed. Nothing will be changed. If the programmer would like something to be done even if none of the conditions is
true, an ELSE clause can be used. The ELSE will always be executed if
none of the conditions above it is true. An appropriate ELSE for the
PIZZA program would be:

```
ELSE
      WRITELN ('NO PIZZA IS AVAILABLE IN THAT SIZE.')
```

```
PROGRAM PIZZA;
(* THIS PROGRAM COMPUTES THE COST OF PIZZAS FOR SMILEY'S PIZZA
PARLOR.  THE COST OF A PIZZA IS:
      9 INCH - $3.50
     12 INCH - $4.75
     16 INCH - $6.50
EACH EXTRA TOPPING COSTS:
      9 INCH - $0.40
     12 INCH - $0.55
     16 INCH - $0.75
PIZZAS WITH A THICK CRUST ARE $0.50 EXTRA, REGARDLESS OF THE SIZE.

THE VARIABLES USED ARE:
    COST      - THE COST OF EACH PIZZA
    SIZE      - THE SIZE OF EACH PIZZA
    TOPPINGS - NUMBER OF TOPPINGS DESIRED ON THE PIZZA
    CRUST     - WHETHER OF NOT A THICK CRUST IS DESIRED *)

VAR
    COST : REAL;
    SIZE, TOPPINGS : INTEGER;
    CRUST : STRING;

BEGIN


    WRITELN ('WHAT SIZE PIZZA DO YOU WANT?');
    WRITELN ('THE CHOICES ARE : 9, 12, OR 16 INCHES');
    READLN (SIZE);

    WRITELN ('HOW MANY TOPPINGS WOULD YOU LIKE?');
    WRITELN ('TYPE IN A WHOLE NUMBER UP TO 6.');
    READLN (TOPPINGS);

    (* DETERMINE COST OF PIZZA WITH DESIRED NUMBER OF TOPPINGS *)
    IF SIZE = 9 THEN
        BEGIN
           COST := 3.50;
           COST := COST + (TOPPINGS * 0.40)
        END
    ELSE IF SIZE = 12 THEN
        BEGIN
           COST := 4.75;
           COST := COST + (TOPPINGS * 0.55)
        END

    ELSE IF SIZE = 16 THEN
        BEGIN
           COST := 6.50;
           COST := COST + (TOPPINGS * 0.75)
        END;

    (* ADD $0.50 IF THICK-CRUSTED *)
    WRITELN ('DO YOU WANT A THICK CRUST?');
    WRITELN ('ANSWER YES OR NO.');
    READLN (CRUST);

    IF CRUST = 'YES' THEN
        COST := COST + 0.50;

    (* PRINT OUT TOTAL COST OF PIZZA *)
    WRITELN ('THE COST OF YOUR PIZZA IS $', COST:7:2)

END.   (* PIZZA *)
```

Figure 6-10 PROGRAM PIZZA

(continued next page)

```
Running . . .
WHAT SIZE PIZZA DO YOU WANT?
THE CHOICES ARE : 9, 12, OR 16 INCHES
12
HOW MANY TOPPINGS WOULD YOU LIKE?
TYPE IN A WHOLE NUMBER UP TO 6.
2
DO YOU WANT A THICK CRUST?
ANSWER YES OR NO.
YES
THE COST OF YOUR PIZZA IS $    6.35
```

Figure 6-10   PROGRAM PIZZA (continued)

If the user typed 14 for the pizza size, that message would be printed to the monitor.

It would be necessary to return to the beginning of the program to allow the user to reenter the size of the pizza correctly, a technique that will be covered later in the book. This kind of checking for incorrect data is one of the signs of a well-written program. Spend some time studying program PIZZA in Figure 6-10.

PROGRAM WEEK

When the user is asked to type data at the keyboard, it is best to make entering the data as easy as possible. One way of doing this is to use codes that represent something else. An example would be assigning a number to represent each day of the week:

1—Sunday
2—Monday
3—Tuesday
4—Wednesday
5—Thursday
6—Friday
7—Saturday

It is much simpler for the user to type a 5 than to type THURSDAY. There is less chance of a typing error, and time is saved.

The programmer will probably need to assign the corresponding day to a variable so that the day of the week and not a number will be printed. This can be done by using ELSE IF statements. In the program in Figure 6-11, the variable D has been declared to be of data type INTEGER and DAY of data type STRING. The program reads in an integer and assigns it to variable D. The corresponding value is assigned to the variable DAY.

```
PROGRAM WEEK1;
(* THIS PROGRAM TRANSLATES A CODE NUMBER INTO A DAY OF THE WEEK.  THE
CODES AND THEIR CORRESPONDING DAYS ARE:
        1 - SUNDAY
        2 - MONDAY
        3 - TUESDAY
        4 - WEDNESDAY
        5 - THURSDAY
        6 - FRIDAY
        7 - SATURDAY      *)

VAR
    D   : INTEGER;   (* INTEGER CODE FOR DAY OF WEEK *)
    DAY : STRING;  (* STRING CONTAINING NAME OF DAY OF WEEK *)

BEGIN

    WRITELN ('WHAT IS THE CODE FOR THE DAY?');
    WRITELN ('ENTER AN INTEGER 1-7');
    READLN (D);

    (* ASSIGN CORRESPONDING DAY *)
    IF D = 1 THEN
      DAY := 'SUNDAY'
    ELSE IF D = 2 THEN
        DAY := 'MONDAY'
    ELSE IF D = 3 THEN
        DAY := 'TUESDAY'
    ELSE IF D = 4 THEN
        DAY := 'WEDNESDAY'
    ELSE IF D = 5 THEN
        DAY := 'THURSDAY'
    ELSE IF D = 6 THEN
        DAY := 'FRIDAY'
    ELSE IF D = 7 THEN
        DAY := 'SATURDAY';

    WRITELN ('THE DAY IS ', DAY, '.')

END.   (* WEEK1 *)


Running . . .
WHAT IS THE CODE FOR THE DAY?
ENTER AN INTEGER 1-7
3
THE DAY IS TUESDAY.
```

Figure 6-11 PROGRAM WEEK1

CASE STATEMENTS

Program WEEK could also be written with a CASE statement. The CASE statement checks each label; when the value of the expression matches the label, the statement following the colon is executed. The CASE statement for this program would be:

```
CASE D OF
    1 : DAY := 'SUNDAY';
    2 : DAY := 'MONDAY';
    3 : DAY := 'TUESDAY';
    4 : DAY := 'WEDNESDAY';
    5 : DAY := 'THURSDAY';
    6 : DAY := 'FRIDAY';
    7 : DAY := 'SATURDAY'
END;    (* CASE *)
```

The syntax for the CASE statement is diagrammed in Figure 6-12. Figure 6-13 shows another version of program WEEK, this time using the CASE statement. The value used as a label in the CASE statement may be of type INTEGER, BOOLEAN, CHAR, or user-defined (discussed in Chapter 10).

Notice that each line in a CASE statement is followed by a semicolon. Also the CASE statement ends with the word END, even though there is no BEGIN. Case statements are handy in many situations. The example below shows how an appropriate message can be printed depending on the value of the variable GRADE. The variable GRADE has been declared to be of data type CHAR.

```
CASE GRADE OF
    'A' : WRITELN ('ALL RIGHT!');
    'B' : WRITELN ('GOOD JOB.');
    'C' : WRITELN ('NOT BAD.');
    'D', 'F' : WRITELN ('TRY HARDER NEXT TIME.')
END;    (* CASE *)
```

More than one label may be listed on a line. An example of this is the statement

```
    'D', 'F' : WRITELN ('TRY HARDER NEXT TIME.')
```

This statement will be executed if the value of GRADE is either D or F.

CASE STATEMENT

CASE expression OF
    label1 : statement1;
    label2 : statement2;
          .
          .
          .
    last_label : last_statement
END;

Note: In UCSD Pascal, a semicolon may or may not be used before the END.

Figure 6-12 SYNTAX FOR THE CASE STATEMENT

```
        PROGRAM WEEK2;
        (* THIS PROGRAM TRANSLATES A NUMBER CODE INTO A DAY OF THE WEEK.  THE
        CODES WITH THEIR CORRESPONDING DAYS OF THE WEEK ARE:
              1 - SUNDAY
              2 - MONDAY
              3 - TUESDAY
              4 - WEDNESDAY
              5 - THURSDAY
              6 - FRIDAY
              7 - SATURDAY      *)

        VAR
           D   : INTEGER;  (* INTEGER CODE REPRESENTING DAY OF WEEK *)
           DAY : STRING;   (* STRING CONTAINING DAY OF THE WEEK *)

        BEGIN

           WRITELN ('WHAT IS THE CODE FOR THE DAY?');
           WRITELN ('ENTER AN INTEGER 1-7.');
           READLN (D);

           (* ASSIGN CORRESPONDING DAY *)
           CASE D OF
              1 : DAY := 'SUNDAY';
              2 : DAY := 'MONDAY';
              3 : DAY := 'TUESDAY';
              4 : DAY := 'WEDNESDAY';
              5 : DAY := 'THURSDAY';
              6 : DAY := 'FRIDAY';
              7 : DAY := 'SATURDAY'

           END;   (* CASE *)

           WRITELN ('THE DAY IS ', DAY, '.')

         END.  (* WEEK2 *)



        Running . . .
        WHAT IS THE CODE FOR THE DAY?
        ENTER AN INTEGER 1-7.
        5
        THE DAY IS THURSDAY.
```

Figure 6-13 PROGRAM WEEK2

LEARNING CHECK 6-2

1. Consider the program segment below:

```
IF OUNCES = 40 THEN
   SIZE := 'JUMBO'
ELSE IF OUNCES = 25 THEN
   SIZE := 'LARGE'
ELSE IF OUNCES = 18 THEN
   SIZE := 'REGULAR'
ELSE
   WRITELN ('THIS PRODUCT DOES NOT COME IN ', OUNCES, ' OUNCE SIZE.');
```

What will the value of SIZE be if OUNCES is equal to each of the values below?

a. 18
b. 40
c. 20
d. 50
e. 25

2. How does the compiler determine which IF/THEN goes with which ELSE when there are nested IF/THEN/ELSE statements?
3. List two examples of programming problems where the CASE statement would be useful.
4. List four decision structures.

Answers:

1. a. REGULAR b. JUMBO c. value of SIZE is undefined; computer will print: THIS PRODUCT DOES NOT COME IN 20 OUNCE SIZE. d. value of SIZE is undefined; computer will print: THIS PRODUCT DOES NOT COME IN 50 OUNCE SIZE. e. LARGE   2. The compiler starts with the innermost IF/THEN and matches it to the closest ELSE; then it works from the inside out, matching each IF/THEN with the corresponding ELSE.   3. The CASE statement could be used to assign the name of the month if the month has been enterd as a number; it also could be used to assign a price to an item if the item has been given a price code.   4. IF/THEN, IF/THEN/ELSE, ELSE IF, CASE

SUMMARY POINTS

- In this chapter, compound statements were explained. Compound statements start with BEGIN and conclude with END. They can contain any number of statements including other compound statements.
- Nested IF/THEN/ELSE statements allow the programmer to check for a number of conditions. It is very important to make sure that the nesting is done properly. Indenting each set of IF/THEN/ELSE statements makes it easier to check for correct nesting.
- An ELSE IF statement can be used to check for a number of conditions without confusion. Each ELSE IF is executed only if the condition being checked is true. The CASE statement is used to compare a variable to a list of labels. If the variable matches one of the labels, the statement following that label is executed.
- One of the best features of Pascal is its wide variety of convenient control statements. There is a control statement for practically every purpose.
- The control statements in this chapter are called decision structures. They allow the programmer to determine whether or not a certain part of the program will be executed. Control statements that allow the programmer to repeat sections of a program as many times as desired will be introduced in the next chapter.

VOCABULARY LIST

Compound statement   A series of statements that starts with BEGIN and concludes with END.

Decision structure   A control statement used to determine whether or not a statement or statements in a program will be executed.

Nested statement   A statement that is contained within another statement.

CHAPTER TEST

VOCABULARY

Match each term from the numbered column with the best description from the lettered column.

1. Nested statement

2. Order of operations

3. Decision structure

4. Compound statement

5. Control statement

a. A statement that is contained within another statement.

b. A statement that allows the programmer to determine whether or not a statement (or a group of statements) will be executed and how many times the statement will be executed.

c. A series of statements that starts with BEGIN and concludes with END.

d. The sequence in which expressions are evaluated.

e. A control statement that determines whether or not a portion of a program will be executed.

QUESTIONS

1. Rewrite the following segment, using one compound statement instead of three IF/THEN statements:

```
IF LETTER = 'A' THEN
    VOWELS := VOWELS + 1;
IF LETTER = 'A' THEN
    CONT := TRUE;
IF LETTER = 'A' THEN
    WRITELN ('THIS LETTER IS A VOWEL.');
```

2. Rewrite the following program segment so that it is properly indented. Bracket the IF/THEN/ELSE statements that go together.

```
IF INCHES > 64 THEN
IF INCHES > 72 THEN
IF INCHES > 76 THEN
HEIGHT := 'HUGE'
ELSE
HEIGHT := 'TALL'
ELSE
HEIGHT := 'AVERAGE'
ELSE
HEIGHT := 'SHORT';
```

3. Rewrite the program segment in question 2 using ELSE IF statements.

4. Write a CASE statement that will assign a color when a code letter is used. The code table is listed below:

```
R       RED
G       GREEN
B       BROWN
O       ORANGE
W       WHITE
P       PURPLE
Y       YELLOW
```

5. Consider the following program segment:

```
CASE KIND OF
    1 : FISH := 'BASS';
    2 : FISH := 'CARP';
  3,4 : FISH := 'TROUT';
    5 : FISH := 'PERCH';
  6,7 : FISH := 'WALLEYE'
END;
WRITELN (FISH);
```

What will be printed for each of the assignment statements below?

```
KIND := 1 + 5;
KIND := 2 * 2;
KIND := 1;
KIND := 7;
```

PROGRAMMING PROBLEMS

1. Mr. Hasselschwartz, the librarian, would like a program to calculate library fines. Fines are charged on the following basis:

general books
    paperbacks: $.15/day
    other general books: $.20/day
magazines: $.25/day
reference books
    encyclopedias: $.50/day
    other reference books: .35/day

Write a program to calculate fines using nested IF/THEN/ELSE statements. Use prompts to ask the user to enter the type of book and the number of days it is overdue. Print the amount of the fine to the monitor screen.

2. Write a program that reads the length and width of a rectangle or a square. The length and width will be entered in inches. Then determine if the figure is a square. If it is a square, print the area of the square. If it is a rectangle, print the perimeter of the rectangle. Print the results with appropriate labels.

3. Pat Nabel's father will only allow her to make $10.00 worth of long-distance phone calls a month. She would like a program to figure out the cost of each of her calls. Below is a code number for each type of call Pat makes and the cost of each per minute.

Code	To	Cost per Minute
1	her grandmother in Santa Clara	.22
2	her brother in Pittsburgh	.14
3	her boyfriend in Hamburg	.73

Use a CASE statement to assign the cost per minute depending on the code number entered. Also read in the length of the phone call in minutes. Then assign the appropriate charge. The output should be formatted like this:

THE COST OF THIS CALL IS $2.83

4. Mickey Koth likes to go on cross-country bike trips. She needs a way of calculating the amount of time a particular bike trip will take. The distance she can travel in an hour depends on the weather conditions. They are as follows:

E: excellent conditions; 25 miles per hour
G: good conditions; 20 miles per hour
P: poor conditions; 13 miles per hour

Write a program that will allow Mickey to enter the distance in miles and then type a code (E, G, P) for the weather conditions. The amount of time the trip will take her should then be printed in hours.

5. Steve Cavanaugh works for Uptown Lumber Company on weekends and evenings. He is paid $3.60 an hour, except when he works more than 15 hours a week. Then he is paid $3.75 an hour for every hour over 15. State income tax is taken out of his weekly check as follows:

6% of his income if he makes $50.00 or less a week
7% of his income if he makes more than $50.00 a week

Write a program that will calculate how much Steve's weekly paycheck will be. Write it so that Steve can type in the number of hours he works in a given week. The amount of his paycheck will be printed so that he can read it.

6. Write a program that will calculate what coins could be given out in change. The amount of money will always be less than a dollar. For example, if the amount of change entered is:

43

the computer should print:

QUARTERS	DIMES	NICKELS	PENNIES
1	1	1	3

CHAPTER 7

Loops

CHAPTER OUTLINE

LEARNING OBJECTIVES

After studying this chapter, you should be able to:

1. Explain what is meant by a loop.
2. Write a loop using the REPEAT/UNTIL control statement.
3. Write a loop using the WHILE control statement.
4. List two differences between the REPEAT/UNTIL loop and the WHILE loop.
5. Write programs using the FOR loop.
6. List three things done automatically by the FOR loop.
7. Write programs that check input data to make certain a program will be able to use it.
8. Explain why GOTO statements should not be used in Pascal programs unless there is no alternative.
9. List the three BOOLEAN operators and explain the purpose of each.
10. Use BOOLEAN operators in programs.
11. Evaluate expressions using BOOLEAN operators.
12. Explain what is meant by a scalar data type.

ADVANCED PLACEMENT CHAPTER HIGHLIGHTS

The following topics from the Advanced Placement Computer Science Exam are covered in this chapter:

control statements
   loops
BOOLEAN expressions and operations

INTRODUCTION

In Chapter 4, a program was written that calculated the radius, circumference, and area of a circle. It probably would have been faster to figure the results by hand than to write this program. But suppose it was necessary to calculate those values for a thousand circles. In such a situation, computers can really save time. The computer can easily do the same job over and over again.

This chapter will introduce a new type of control statement, called a loop. Loops allow the programmer to repeat a particular section of a program as many times as needed. A loop contains a series of instructions that will be executed repeatedly as long as specified conditions are not changed. This means that each time through a loop a condition will be evaluated. The condition must evaluate as true or false. How this

---

REPEAT/UNTIL LOOP

REPEAT
   statement1;
     .
     .
     .
   last_statement
UNTIL condition;
Note: In UCSD Pascal, a semicolon before the UNTIL is optional.

Figure 7-1 SYNTAX FOR REPEAT/UNTIL LOOP

condition evaluates will determine whether the loop will be executed. In this chapter, three types of loops will be explained.

THE REPEAT/UNTIL LOOP

The first type of loop control statement that will be examined is the REPEAT/UNTIL loop. The syntax for the REPEAT/UNTIL loop is shown in Figure 7-1. The loop starts with the word REPEAT. Every statement between the REPEAT and the UNTIL is executed. These statements are the loop body. The condition following the word UNTIL is then evaluated. If the condition evaluates as false, the program goes back up to REPEAT and executes the sequence of statements again. If the condition evaluates as true, control transfers to the statement following the UNTIL and the loop is not executed again. Figure 7-2 shows how the REPEAT/UNTIL loop is represented in a flowchart.

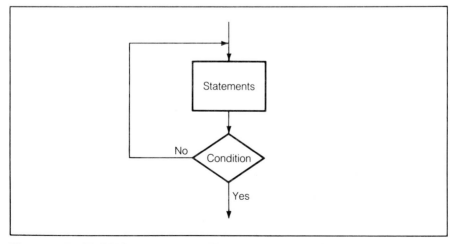

Figure 7-2 FLOWCHART FOR REPEAT/UNTIL LOOP

Study the program segment below.

```
NUM := 2;
REPEAT
    NUM := NUM + 1
UNTIL NUM = 4;
```

This loop will be executed twice. Going into the loop the first time, the value of NUM will be two. The statement NUM := NUM + 1 is executed, making the value of NUM three. The condition NUM = 4 will evaluate as false since three is not equal to four. The loop is executed again, adding one more to NUM. Since NUM = 4 is now true, the loop will not be executed again. Instead, the statement following the loop will be executed. In the next section, a complete program will illustrate the use of the REPEAT/UNTIL statement.

Program FACTORIAL1

The purpose of the program that follows is to calculate the factorial of a positive integer. The general formula for calculating a factorial is

$$N * (N-1) * (N-2) * \ldots * 1$$

Six factorial would be

$$6 * 5 * 4 * 3 * 2 * 1 = 720$$

In mathematics, this quantity would be written as 6!, which is read "six factorial." The factorial of one is one.

The flowchart for program FACTORIAL1 is represented in Figure 7-3. Study the complete program in Figure 7-4. First, the value of N is entered at the keyboard and read. This value is assigned to the variable TEMP. This step is included so the original value of N can be printed in the WRITELN statement at the end of the program. Since the value of N will be changed during program execution, it is important to store the original value in another variable. In this case, TEMP has been used for this purpose. The variable name TEMP stands for temporary. TEMP is used to temporarily hold the value of N.

Next, an IF/THEN/ELSE statement is used to determine whether the value of N is one. If N is equal to one, the value of FACT is set to one. If N is not equal to one, the ELSE portion of the IF/THEN/ELSE statement is executed. FACT is set to the value of N before the loop starts. In the loop, N is first decreased by one, and then FACT is multiplied by this new value of N. This value of N is then compared to one. As long as N is not equal to one, the loop will be executed. Once the value of N is equal to one, the statement after the loop will be executed. Suppose the integer five is used for the value of N. Trace through the program and see if you agree with the values below. The values listed are the values of N and FACT at the end of each repetition of the loop.

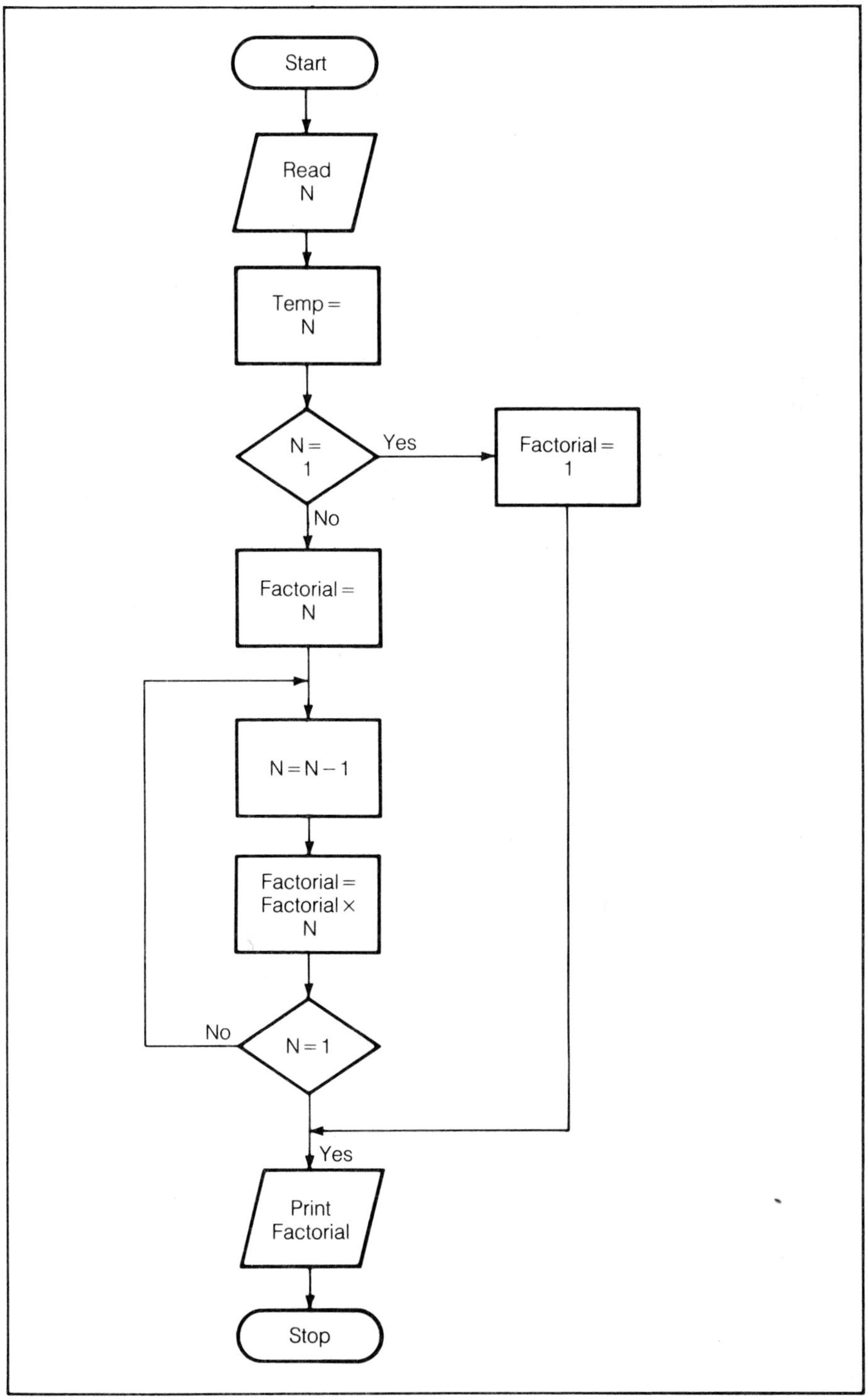

Figure 7-3 FLOWCHART FOR PROGRAM FACTORIAL1

```
PROGRAM FACTORIAL1;
(* THIS PROGRAM COMPUTES THE FACTORIAL OF A POSITIVE INTEGER *)

VAR
    N, TEMP : INTEGER;
    FACT : INTEGER[10];

BEGIN

    WRITE ('WHAT IS THE INTEGER? ');
    READLN (N);
    TEMP := N;

(* IF N = 1, FACTORIAL = 1 *)
    IF N = 1 THEN
        FACT := 1
    ELSE
(* LOOP TO COMPUTE FACTORIAL *)
        BEGIN
            FACT := N;
            REPEAT
                N := N - 1;
                FACT := FACT * N
            UNTIL N = 1
        END;    (* ELSE *)

    WRITELN (TEMP, ' FACTORIAL IS ', FACT)


    Running . . .
    WHAT IS THE INTEGER? 8
    8 FACTORIAL IS 40320
```

Figure 7-4   PROGRAM FACTORIAL1

Number of Times Through the Loop	N	FACT
1	4	20
2	3	60
3	2	120
4	1	120

Why was the factorial of one not set in the REPEAT/UNTIL loop like the other factorials? The program segment below shows what would happen in the loop if the value assigned to N was one:

```
    FACT := N;              (FACT is assigned the value of one)

    REPEAT
        N := N - 1;         (N := 0)
        FACT := FACT * N     (FACT := 0)
```

The statement

```
FACT := FACT * N
```

would assign zero to FACT. But the factorial of one is one. So by using the loop, the program would have obtained an incorrect result for the factorial of one. There is another serious problem with using one for the value of N in this loop. What will this condition evaluate as at the end of the loop?

```
UNTIL N = 1
```

The condition will evaluate as false because N is now equal to zero. The next time through the loop the value of N will be -1. The value of N will never be one. Instead, it will become a smaller and smaller negative number. This loop will never stop. This is called an **infinite loop**. It is important that the programmer be careful not to let this happen in writing programs. Careful testing of possible data values can help avoid this problem.

Notice that FACT has been declared to be of data type LONG INTEGER. This is because factorials become large numbers very quickly. For example, eight factorial is 40320. The data type INTEGER cannot contain an integer larger than 32767. The declaration

```
FACT : INTEGER[10];
```

allows FACT to contain an integer up to 9,999,999,999.

LEARNING CHECK 7-1

1. Why are loops useful in computer programs?
2. Describe a job you do that involves repeating a task over and over again until a certain condition is met.
3. How many times will the loop in the following program segment be executed? What will the value of I be at the end of the loop each time through?

```
PROGRAM EX1;

VAR
    I : INTEGER;

BEGIN

    I := 1;
    REPEAT
        I := I + 1;
        WRITELN (I)
    UNTIL I >= 10;
```

THE WHILE LOOP

The WHILE loop is similar to the REPEAT/UNTIL loop. The syntax for the WHILE loop is shown in Figure 7-5. If a WHILE loop contains more than a single statement, it must have a BEGIN and an END. In the WHILE loop, a condition is tested before the body of the loop is executed. A flowchart of a WHILE loop is shown in Figure 7-6. The program segment below shows how a WHILE loop might be used in a program.

```
COUNT := 1;

WHILE COUNT < 16 DO
    BEGIN
        READLN (CLASS);
        WRITELN (CLASS);
        COUNT := COUNT + 1
    END;
```

WHILE LOOP

WHILE condition DO
  BEGIN
    statement1;
       .
       .
       .
    last_statement
END;

Note: In UCSD Pascal, a semicolon before END is optional.

134   **Figure 7-5 SYNTAX FOR WHILE LOOP**

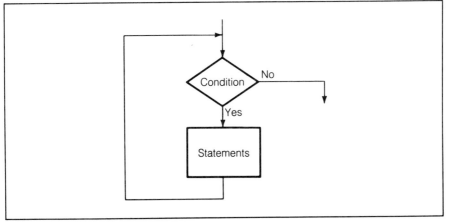

Figure 7-6 FLOWCHART FOR WHILE LOOP

This program segment could be used to read and write a list of classes. The value of COUNT is set to one before the loop is entered. This is called **initializing** the variable. The value of COUNT was initialized to one. If the value of COUNT had not been initialized, the statement COUNT := COUNT + 1 would be meaningless. It is impossible for the computer to increase the value of a variable if the original value of the variable has not been set. COUNT is called a **loop control variable**, because COUNT is used to control how many times the loop will be executed. Each time through the loop the value of COUNT is increased by one until the condition COUNT < 16 is false. Then the program will skip down to the statement following the END. The loop in the example above will be executed 15 times. It could be used to read and write a list of 15 classes. If the variable COUNT had been initialized to 16 rather than one, the first time the expression

```
WHILE COUNT < 16 DO
```

was evaluated, it would be false and the loop would not have been executed at all.

Note the difference between the WHILE and the REPEAT/UNTIL loop. Since the condition in the REPEAT/UNTIL loop is evaluated at the end of the loop, the REPEAT/UNTIL loop will always be executed at least once. Another difference is that the WHILE loop is executed while a condition is true, whereas the REPEAT/UNTIL loop is executed until a condition is true—in other words, as long as it is false.

Program FIVES

A WHILE loop will now be used to count by fives. The flowchart for this program is presented in Figure 7-7. The variable COUNT is initialized to five. Then the condition COUNT <= FINAL is evaluated. If it is true, the loop is executed. The value of COUNT is printed. Then five is added

135

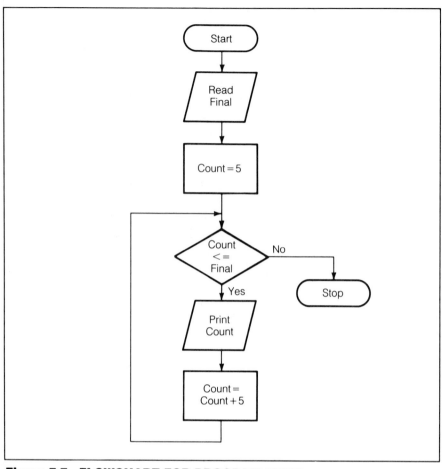

Figure 7-7   FLOWCHART FOR PROGRAM FIVES

to COUNT. The loop then branches back to the condition COUNT <= FINAL. The loop will be executed until COUNT is not less than or equal to FINAL. Then the program stops. Figure 7-8 shows the complete program. What if the value of FINAL is not a multiple of five—will this program still work? For example, if the value of FINAL is set to 18, the last time through the loop the value of COUNT will be 20 and value of FINAL will be 18. The expression being evaluated will look like this:

```
WHILE 20 <= 18 DO
```

The condition will be false and the loop will not be executed again. The program will stop. Trace through the loop to make sure that you understand this point.

THE FOR LOOP

The FOR loop is a third useful loop control statement. The syntax is shown in Figure 7-9. This loop could be used in a program segment like this:

```
FOR I := 1 TO 7 DO
    WRITELN ('WE ARE ON LOOP ', I);
```

This loop will be repeated seven times. Notice that no BEGIN or END is needed in the example above. This is a single statement. If there was more than one statement in the loop, then a BEGIN and an END would be needed. In this example of the FOR loop, three steps have been done automatically:

1. I has been initialized to 1.

```
PROGRAM FIVES;
(* THIS PROGRAM COUNTS BY FIVES FROM FIVE TO THE VALUE OF FINAL *)

VAR
    COUNT, FINAL : INTEGER;

BEGIN

    WRITELN ('HOW FAR DO YOU WANT TO COUNT BY FIVES?');
    WRITELN ('TYPE IN AN INTEGER.');
    READLN (FINAL);
    COUNT := 5;

    (* LOOP TO ADD FIVE TO COUNT UNTIL VALUE OF FINAL IS REACHED *)
    WHILE COUNT <= FINAL DO
        BEGIN
            WRITELN (COUNT);
            COUNT := COUNT + 5
        END    (* WHILE *)

END.  (* FIVES *)



Running . . .
HOW FAR DO YOU WANT TO COUNT BY FIVES?
TYPE IN AN INTEGER.
45
5
10
15
20
25
30
35
40
45



Running . . .
HOW FAR DO YOU WANT TO COUNT BY FIVES?
TYPE IN AN INTEGER.
28
5
10
15
20
25
```

Figure 7-8 PROGRAM FIVES

FOR LOOP USING "TO" FORMAT

FOR loop_control_variable := beginning_value TO end_value DO
  BEGIN
    statement1;
      .
      .
      .

    last_statement
  END;

FOR LOOP USING "DOWNTO" FORMAT

For loop_control_variable := beginning_value DOWNTO end_value
DO
  BEGIN
    statement1;
      .
      .
      .

    last_statement
  END;

Note: The value of the loop control variable may not be changed in the loop body. In UCSD Pascal, a semicolon before the END is optional.

Figure 7-9 SYNTAX OF FOR LOOP

2. Each time through the loop the expression I <= 7 is evaluated. If it evaluates as true, the loop will be executed.

3. One is added to the value of I each time through the loop.

In a FOR loop, the loop control variable may not be changed in the body of the loop.

In Figure 7-10 there are four examples of FOR loops. Program EX1 shows the example above and what the results are when the program is run.

The loop control variable does not have to start at one. This loop would also be executed seven times:

```
FOR I := 27 TO 33 DO
    WRITELN ('WE ARE ON LOOP ', I);
```

The loop control variable may also be of data type CHAR. The loop

```
FOR LETTER := 'A' TO 'G' DO
    WRITELN (LETTER);
```

will again be executed seven times. Programs EX2 and EX3 in Figure 7-10 show these two programs. Any expression that evaluates as data type INTEGER or CHAR may be used as a loop control variable. This is because these are **scalar data types**. A scalar data type is a data type where all of the values may be listed. Sometimes these are called **ordinal data types**. For example, it is possible to list the integral values between 16 and 105 or the character letter values between G and Z. REAL and STRING are not scalar data types. How could all of the values between 10.8 and 47.65 be listed? They are infinite. Likewise, if NAME is of data type STRING, an expression such as

```
FOR NAME := MARY TO SARAH DO
```

```
PROGRAM EX1;

VAR
    I : INTEGER;

BEGIN

  FOR I := 1 TO 7 DO
      WRITELN ('WE ARE ON LOOP ', I)

END.  (* EX1 *)
```

Running . . .
```
WE ARE ON LOOP 1
WE ARE ON LOOP 2
WE ARE ON LOOP 3
WE ARE ON LOOP 4
WE ARE ON LOOP 5
WE ARE ON LOOP 6
WE ARE ON LOOP 7
```

```
PROGRAM EX2;

VAR
    I : INTEGER;

BEGIN

    FOR I := 27 TO 33 DO
        WRITELN ('WE ARE ON LOOP ',I)

END.  (* EX2 *)
```

Running . . .
```
WE ARE ON LOOP 27
WE ARE ON LOOP 28
WE ARE ON LOOP 29
WE ARE ON LOOP 30
WE ARE ON LOOP 31
WE ARE ON LOOP 32
WE ARE ON LOOP 33
```

Figure 7-10 PROGRAMS ILLUSTRATING USE OF FOR LOOPS

(continued next page)

139

```
PROGRAM EX3;

VAR
    LETTER : CHAR;

BEGIN

    FOR LETTER := 'A' TO 'G' DO
        WRITELN (LETTER)
END.   (* EX3 *)
```

Running . . .

```
A
B
C
D
E
F
G
```

```
PROGRAM EX4;

VAR
    I : INTEGER;

BEGIN

    FOR I := 7 DOWNTO 1 DO
        WRITELN ('WE ARE ON LOOP ', I)

END.   (* EX 4 *)
```

Running . . .

```
WE ARE ON LOOP 7
WE ARE ON LOOP 6
WE ARE ON LOOP 5
WE ARE ON LOOP 4
WE ARE ON LOOP 3
WE ARE ON LOOP 2
WE ARE ON LOOP 1
```

Figure 7-10 PROGRAMS ILLUSTRATING USE OF FOR LOOPS (continued)

is meaningless. Later on in this book another scalar data type will be studied, the user-defined scalar data type.

The data type BOOLEAN is also a scalar data type. Its values are true and false. But, since it only has two values, it is not generally useful as a loop control variable in a FOR loop.

Expressions may be used in the FOR loop as long as they evaluate as a scalar data type. For example,

```
FOR X := (2 * 10) TO (200 - 50) DO
    WRITELN (X);
```

is a valid FOR loop. It would be the same as writing

```
FOR X := 20 TO 150 DO
    WRITELN (X);
```

There is another way of writing a FOR loop. Its syntax is illustrated at the bottom of Figure 7-9. It looks like this:

```
FOR I := 7 DOWNTO 1 DO
    WRITELN ('WE ARE ON LOOP ', I);
```

The value of I is initialized to 7. Each time through this loop the value of I will be decreased by one. The loop will be executed as long as the expression $I >= 1$ evaluates as true. Program EX4 in Figure 7-10 contains this program and its output.

LEARNING CHECK 7-2

1. What is the difference between the FOR/TO and the FOR/DOWNTO loops?
2. Name three things that are done automatically in the FOR loop.
3. How many times will the WHILE loop below be executed? What will the value of Y be at the end of each loop execution? What will the value of X be?

```
Y := 0;
X := Y;

WHILE Y < 11 DO
    BEGIN
        Y := Y + X;
        X := X + 1;
        WRITELN (X, Y)
    END
```

Answers:

X	Y
1	0
2	1
3	3
4	6
5	10

1. In the FOR/TO loop the loop control variable is increased by one each time through the loop whereas with the FOR/DOWNTO loop it is decreased by one.   2. a. Initialize the loop control variable.   b. Evaluate the condition in the FOR statement; if it evaluates as true, the loop will be executed again.   c. Increase (or decrease in the case of DOWNTO) the loop control variable by one each time through the loop.   3. The WHILE loop will be executed five times.

CHECKING FOR INCORRECT DATA

It is important that the programmer check to make certain that the data typed at the keyboard by the user can be used by the program. The factorial problem shown earlier in this chapter is a good example. Suppose the user had entered an integer that was less than one. The program would have been caught in an infinite loop. This is one kind of error the programmer needs to check for so that the user can reenter the data without terminating program execution or losing earlier entries.

```
PROGRAM FACTORIAL2;
(* THIS PROGRAM COMPUTES THE FACTORIAL OF A POSITIVE INTEGER *)

VAR
   N, TEMP : INTEGER;
   FACT : INTEGER[10];

BEGIN

   WRITE ('WHAT IS THE INTEGER? ');
   READLN (N);

   (* LOOP TO MAKE CERTAIN N IS GREATER THAN ZERO *)
   WHILE N < 1 DO
      BEGIN
         WRITELN ('THE INTEGER MUST BE GREATER THAN ZERO.');
         WRITELN ('PLEASE TYPE IN THE INTEGER.');
         READLN (N)
      END;   (* WHILE *)

   TEMP := N;

(* IF N = 1, FACTORIAL = 1 *)
   IF N = 1 THEN
      FACT := 1
   ELSE
   (* LOOP TO COMPUTE FACTORIAL *)
      BEGIN
         FACT := N;

         REPEAT
            N := N - 1;
            FACT := FACT * N
         UNTIL N = 1
      END;   (* ELSE *)

   WRITELN (TEMP, ' FACTORIAL IS ', FACT)

END.   (* FACTORIAL2 *)


   Running . . .
WHAT IS THE INTEGER? -14
THE INTEGER MUST BE GREATER THAN ZERO.
PLEASE TYPE IN THE INTEGER.
7
7 FACTORIAL IS 5040
```

Figure 7-11 PROGRAM FACTORIAL2

Figure 7-11 shows how the factorial program could be rewritten to check for incorrect data. A WHILE loop has been used for this purpose. This is an example of an excellent use for a WHILE loop. If the value of N is less than one, the loop will be executed. The loop prints an error message telling the user that N must be greater than zero. The user is then asked to reenter N. If this time, the value of N entered is greater than zero, the program will go on to the next statement following the loop. If N is still incorrect, the loop will be repeated.

A REPEAT/UNTIL loop would not have worked well here. Remember that the REPEAT/UNTIL loop is always executed at least once. In this case, the loop should not be executed at all if the value of N is greater than zero. A REPEAT/UNTIL loop is useful when a loop must be executed at least once.

A FOR loop also would not be useful for the type of error checking that was done in the factorial problem. It is not possible to know whether or not the loop will be executed or how many times the loop will be executed. The FOR loop is useful when it can be determined before execution how many times a loop should be executed.

THE GOTO STATEMENT

The GOTO statement allows program execution to branch to another part of a program. Here is an example:

```
12: WRITELN ('TYPE IN A NEGATIVE NUMBER.');
READ (X);
IF X >= 0 THEN
    GOTO 12;
```

The program will branch back up to the statement

```
12: WRITELN ('TYPE IN A NEGATIVE NUMBER.');
```

if X is greater than or equal to zero. The 12 is a label. It marks the statement so that the computer will know where to branch to. A label may be any integer up to 9999. It must be declared in a label declaration statement, like this:

```
LABEL 12;
```

The GOTO statement is not a structured programming statement. It is always better to use a structured control statement rather than the GOTO statement. In the example above, it would be much better to write the program segment this way:

```
REPEAT
    WRITELN ('TYPE IN A NEGATIVE NUMBER.');
    READLN (X)
UNTIL X < 0;
```

143

GOTO statements often cause program errors. They make the logic of a program much harder to follow. None of the programs in this book require the use of the GOTO statement. It is recommended that it not be used in writing Pascal programs unless absolutely necessary.

BOOLEAN OPERATORS

So far, the arithmetic operators (+, −, *, /, DIV and MOD) and the relational operators (=, <>, <, >, <=, >=) have been covered. Now a third type of operator will be discussed. These are the BOOLEAN operators. The BOOLEAN operators are used for BOOLEAN expressions only. Remember that BOOLEAN expressions are expressions that evaluate as true or false. The three BOOLEAN operators are NOT, AND, and OR.

NOT is a unary operator; it is used with a BOOLEAN expression. For example, if the variable A was of data type INTEGER, the expression

```
WHILE NOT (A > 0) DO
```

would evaluate as true if A > 0 was false. If A was equal to one, the expression

```
WHILE NOT (A > 0) DO
```

would evaluate as false.

The operator AND is used to combine two BOOLEAN expressions. For example, the expression

```
IF (HEIGHT > 72) AND (WEIGHT > 150) THEN
```

will evaluate as true only if HEIGHT > 72 and WEIGHT > 150 are both true. Both of these expressions must be true for the entire expression to be true.

The OR operator is also used to combine two BOOLEAN expressions. In this case, only one of the expressions needs to evaluate as true for the entire expression to evaluate as true. In the expression

```
IF (HEIGHT > 72) OR (WEIGHT > 150) THEN
```

if either HEIGHT > 72 *or* WEIGHT > 150 is true, the entire expression will also evaluate as true. Not all Pascal compilers require the use of parentheses when you are using relational operators with BOOLEAN expressions, but some do. It is a good idea to always use parentheses with BOOLEAN operators, if for no other reason than to make the

program logic easy to understand. The BOOLEAN operators are evaluated in this order:

```
NOT
AND
OR
```

Figure 7-12 shows the order in which all types of operators will be evaluated.

An expression using NOT will be evaluated first, then AND, and last OR. Here is an example of a BOOLEAN expression:

```
NOT (10 < 12) OR (10 * 3 = 30)
```

This expression would be evaluated in this order:

1. Expressions in parentheses are evaluated left to right.
   (10 < 12) evaluates as true.
   (10 * 3 = 30) evaluates as true (30 = 30).
2. NOT is evaluated before OR.
   NOT (TRUE) evaluates as false.
   (FALSE) OR (TRUE) evaluates as true.

Thus the expression

```
NOT (10 < 12) OR (10 * 3 = 30)
```

evaluates as true. When you are evaluating a complex BOOLEAN expression such as the one just done, it is important to be careful to perform each step in the correct order. Breaking the expression down into small parts makes it simpler.

The programmer can use parentheses to change the order in which the expression will be evaluated, just as parentheses are used with arithmetic and relational operators. If the programmer wanted the OR operation to be evaluated before the NOT, the expression could be written:

```
NOT ((10 < 12) OR (10 * 3 = 30))
```

NOT   AND, *, /, DIV, MOD   OR, +, −   <, <=, =, <>, >=, >
Operators on the same level are evaluated from left to right.

Figure 7-12 ORDER OF OPERATIONS

The steps to evaluate this expression would be:

1. NOT ((TRUE) OR (TRUE)).
2. NOT (TRUE) = FALSE.

This expression would evaluate as false. The parentheses have changed the entire meaning of the expression.

We will now write a program that uses BOOLEAN operators. This program will be used to write the appropriate activity for a given day. It is shown in Figure 7-13. Two questions are asked of the user:

```
IS TODAY A SCHOOLDAY?
```

and

```
IS TODAY SUNNY?
```

There are four different combinations of answers to these questions:

```
SCHOOLDAY AND SUNNY
SCHOOLDAY AND NOT SUNNY
NOT SCHOOLDAY AND SUNNY
NOT SCHOOLDAY AND NOT SUNNY
```

Each of these conditions is tested for. A different sentence is printed depending on which of the conditions is true. Look at the expression

```
IF SCHOOLDAY AND SUNNY THEN
```

You may wonder why this expression isn't written

```
IF SCHOOLDAY = TRUE AND SUNNY = TRUE THEN
```

This is because the variables SCHOOLDAY and SUNNY already have the value of true or false.

Study the BOOLEAN expressions below and make certain that you understand how each is evaluated.

Expression	Evaluates as
NOT (1 * 4 = 5)	TRUE
(18 < 16) OR (7 + 2 = 9)	TRUE
(18 < 16) AND (7 + 2 = 9)	FALSE
(2 + 8 <= 11) AND (17 * 2 = 34)	TRUE
NOT (12 > 8 - 2)	FALSE

```
PROGRAM ACTIVITY;
(* THIS PROGRAM DETERMINES WHAT ACTIVITY WILL BE DONE ON A PARTICULAR DAY. *)

VAR
    ANSW1, ANSW2 : STRING;
    SCHOOLDAY, SUNNY : BOOLEAN;

BEGIN

    WRITELN ('IS TODAY A SCHOOLDAY?');
    WRITELN ('TYPE IN YES OR NO.');
    READLN (ANSW1);

    IF ANSW1 = 'YES' THEN
        SCHOOLDAY := TRUE
    ELSE
        SCHOOLDAY := FALSE;

    WRITELN ('IS TODAY SUNNY?');
    WRITELN ('TYPE IN YES OR NO.');
    READLN (ANSW2);

    IF ANSW2 = 'YES' THEN
        SUNNY := TRUE
    ELSE
        SUNNY := FALSE;

    IF SCHOOLDAY AND SUNNY THEN
        WRITELN ('GO TO SCHOOL TODAY.');

    IF SCHOOLDAY AND NOT SUNNY THEN
        WRITELN ('WEAR RAINCOAT TO SCHOOL TODAY.');

    IF NOT SCHOOLDAY AND NOT SUNNY THEN
        WRITELN ('WATCH TV TODAY.');

    IF NOT SCHOOLDAY AND SUNNY THEN
        WRITELN ('PLAY BALL TODAY!')

END.  (* ACTIVITY *)
```

Running . . .
```
IS TODAY A SCHOOLDAY?
TYPE IN YES OR NO.
YES
IS TODAY SUNNY?
TYPE IN YES OR NO.
NO
WEAR RAINCOAT TO SCHOOL TODAY.
```

Running . . .
```
IS TODAY A SCHOOLDAY?
TYPE IN YES OR NO.
NO
IS TODAY SUNNY?
TYPE IN YES OR NO.
YES
PLAY BALL TODAY!
```

Figure 7-13 PROGRAM ACTIVITY

1. What is a BOOLEAN operator? What are the three BOOLEAN operators? In what order are they evaluated?
2. What is an infinite loop?
3. What is a scalar data type? What are the three scalar data types that have been covered so far?

Answers:

BOOLEAN
CHAR
INTEGER
are:

1. A BOOLEAN operator is an operator used with a BOOLEAN expression. The BOOLEAN operators are NOT, AND, and OR.   2. An infinite loop is a loop in which the condition controlling loop repetition will never contain the value needed to stop the loop.   3. A scalar data type is a data type whose values can be listed. The three scalar data types studied so far

---

SUMMARY POINTS

- This chapter introduced a new type of control statement, the loop. The loop allows the programmer to repeat a series of instructions as many times as is needed. There are three basic types of loops: the REPEAT/UNTIL loop, the WHILE loop, and the FOR loop.
- In the WHILE loop, a condition is evaluated at the beginning of the loop. While that condition is true, the loop is executed.
- In a REPEAT/UNTIL loop, the condition is evaluated at the end of the loop. Until that condition becomes true, the loop is repeated.
- The FOR loop is useful when it can be determined before program execution how many times a loop is to be executed.
- Checking to make sure that data the user enters will work with a particular program is very important. If the data are not correct for the program, an error message should be printed to the monitor and the user should be prompted to reenter the data.
- The BOOLEAN operators are NOT, AND, and OR. They are used with BOOLEAN expressions; that is, expressions that evaluate as true or false.

VOCABULARY LIST

Infinite loop A loop in which the condition controlling loop repetition will never contain the value needed to stop the loop.

Initialize To set a variable to a starting value.

Loop control variable A variable whose value is used to control the repetition of a loop.

Ordinal data type See **Scalar data type**.

Scalar data type A data type where all of the values of that data type may be listed. INTEGER, CHAR, and BOOLEAN are all scalar data types, as is the user-defined data type.

VOCABULARY

Match each term from the numbered column with the best description from the lettered column.

1. Initialize

    a. A control statement that allows a series of instructions to be executed repeatedly as long as specified conditions are constant.

2. Loop

    b. To set a variable to a starting value.

3. Infinite loop

    c. A step in solving a problem where a comparison is made. The step that will be done next depends on the results of that comparison.

4. Loop control variable

    d. A loop in which the condition controlling loop repetition will never contain the value needed to stop the loop.

5. Decision step

    e. A variable whose value is used to control the repetition of a loop.

QUESTIONS

1. Explain how a REPEAT/UNTIL loop works.
2. How many times will the loop below be executed? What will the value of NUM be at the end of the loop each time through?

```
PROGRAM EX2;

VAR
    NUM : INTEGER;

BEGIN

    NUM := 12;

    REPEAT
        NUM := NUM - 2;
        WRITELN (NUM)
    UNTIL NUM < 0;
```

3. How is a WHILE loop different from a REPEAT/UNTIL loop?

4. Rewrite the program below using a WHILE loop instead of the RE-PEAT/UNTIL loop.

```
PROGRAM EXAMPLE;

VAR
    COUNT : INTEGER;
    NAME  : STRING;

BEGIN

    COUNT := 1;

    REPEAT
        WRITELN ('TYPE IN A NAME.');
        READLN (NAME);
        COUNT := COUNT + 1
    UNTIL COUNT >= 8

END.
```

5. Rewrite the program in question 4 using a FOR loop.
6. Why is it important to design programs that make sure the user has entered data that will work with the program?
7. Using the following program segment, evaluate the BOOLEAN expressions below.

```
VAR
    ANSWER : BOOLEAN;
    X, Y, Z : INTEGER;

BEGIN

    ANSWER := TRUE;
    X := 4;
    Y := 3;
    Z := 12;
```

a. NOT ANSWER
b. (X * Y = Z) AND (X = 4)
c. (X + Z = 10) OR (4 * 4 = 10)
d. ANSWER AND (X + Y * 10 = 14)

PROGRAMMING PROBLEMS

1. Write a program that uses a FOR loop to read five numbers and print the largest of the five. Then rewrite your program using a WHILE loop.
2. Write a program that reads an integer I and calculates $I + (I - 1) + (I - 2) + \ldots + 1$. For example, if the integer read was six, the calculation would look like this:

$$6 + 5 + 4 + 3 + 2 + 1 = 21$$

Use an appropriate type of loop to do this problem. Print the result to the monitor.

3. Write a program that will read the number of miles run by a person each day for a week (seven days). Use a FOR loop to allow the user to input the number of miles run on day 1, 2, and so on. Then calculate and print to the monitor the total number of miles run per week and the average number of miles run per day.

4. Write a program that allows a grocer to take inventory. The program should ask the user what the inventory number of the current item is (for instance, 1 = cheese, 2 = lettuce, 3 = steak) and the amount of each item. Use a REPEAT/UNTIL loop to allow the grocer to enter a new item. (HINT: Use a CASE statement to tell the program that item number 1 means cheese or item number 2 means lettuce, etc.) The program should output to the monitor screen the total number and value (in dollars and cents) of each item in stock. For example, the output could look like this:

ITEM	NUMBER	VALUE
CHEESE	4	$50.10
LETTUCE	20	$20.00
STEAK	15	$75.00

5. Write a program that simulates a burglar alarm. Use a loop to continually read a variable that indicates whether the alarm should be set off. Allow the user to enter an integer from 10 to 50 to control the length of time the alarm should run. Use the statement WRITELN (CHR(7)); to cause the monitor to beep.

CHAPTER 8

Programming Style, Debugging, and Testing

CHAPTER OUTLINE

LEARNING CHECK 8-5

SUMMARY POINTS

VOCABULARY LIST

CHAPTER TEST
  Vocabulary • Questions

PROGRAMMING PROBLEMS

LEARNING OBJECTIVES

After studying this chapter, you should be able to:

1. Explain what good programming style is and why it is important.
2. List three characteristics of a program with good style.
3. Write good beginning program documentation and good documentation within the body of the program.
4. List the two places in a program where indentation can make a program easier to understand.
5. Use spacing and blank lines to make programs easier to follow.
6. Explain why it is important to use meaningful variable names.
7. Define syntax, run-time, and logic errors.
8. Debug programs containing syntax, run-time, and logic errors.
9. Describe two program testing methods.
10. Describe boundary cases, the null case, and illegal cases.
11. Describe the program proof construct.
12. Describe and use program tracing and hand simulation.

ADVANCED PLACEMENT CHAPTER HIGHLIGHTS

The following topics from the Advanced Placement Computer Science Exam are covered in this chapter:

program annotation
  comments
    indentation and formatting
  debugging and testing

INTRODUCTION

This chapter covers three topics: (1) programming style, (2) debugging a program, and (3) testing a program. **Programming style** refers to the way in which a program is written to make it easier for people to read and understand. **Debugging** refers to finding and correcting program errors. **Program testing** is the systematic process of checking a program to see if the program contains any errors.

PROGRAMMING STYLE

The style of a program has nothing to do with the actual Pascal statements. The compiler can execute a program that has poor style just as easily as a program that has good style.

The following statements are true of a program with good style:

1. The program is well documented.
2. Indentation and blank spaces have been used to make the program easier to read and understand.
3. Variables have been given meaningful names.

Each of these three points will be discussed in this chapter.

Documentation

Documentation is the use of comments to explain what is being done in a computer program. These comments are used to make the program easier for people to understand. The comments mean nothing to the compiler. Comments must be enclosed like this:

```
(* A COMMENT *)
```

or like this:

```
{ANOTHER COMMENT}
```

The enclosing symbols tell the compiler to ignore what falls between them. When writing comments, the programmer should try to make them as brief and clear as possible. Documentation appears in two basic places in a program:

1. After the program heading (beginning documentation)
2. Within the body of the program.

Beginning Documentation

After the program heading comes the documentation that explains the program as a whole. The purpose of the program is stated here. This is where any input the program needs is described. For example, a comment like:

```
(* THE USER ENTERS AN INTEGER AT THE KEYBOARD. *)
```

```
PROGRAM MEAL;
(* THIS PROGRAM CALCULATES THE COST OF A PURCHASE AT A FAST-FOOD
RESTAURANT.  THE USER ENTERS AN INTEGER AT THE KEYBOARD THAT
REPRESENTS THE COST OF A SPECIFIC ITEM.  THE USER THEN ENTERS
HOW MANY OF THAT ITEM ARE DESIRED.  THE COST OF THE ITEM
IS THEN CALCULATED.  THE USER IS THEN ALLOWED TO ENTER ANOTHER
ITEM.  WHEN THE USER IS DONE ENTERING AN ORDER, THE TOAL COST OF
THE ORDER IS PRINTED TO THE MONITOR.

THE CODE USED TO ENTER FOOD ITEMS IS AS FOLLOWS:

    CODE NUMBER      ITEM               COST OF ITEM
    ---------------------------------------------------------------

        1            HAMBURGER          $0.75
        2            CHEESEBURGER       $0.90
        3            FRENCH FRIES       $0.55
        4            FRUIT PIE          $0.60
        5            DRINK              $0.50

        6    USED TO INDICATE END OF THE ORDER.
    ---------------------------------------------------------------

MAJOR VARIABLES USED:
    FOOD     - CODE NUMBER TO INDICATE A PARTICULAR ITEM.
    COST     - COST OF AN ITEM.
    NUMBER   - HOW MANY OF A PARTICULAR ITEM ARE DESIRED.
    TOTCOST  - THE TOTAL COST OF AN ORDER.
    -----------------------------------------------------------  *)

VAR
    FOOD, NUMBER   : INTEGER;
    COST, TOTCOST : REAL;

BEGIN

    (* INITIALIZE TOTAL COST TO ZERO *)
    TOTCOST := 0;

    (* READ IN CODE NUMBER OF FIRST ITEM *)
    WRITELN ('ENTER CODE NUMBER FOR FOOD ITEM.');
    WRITELN ('IF ORDER IS COMPLETE, TYPE IN THE NUMBER 6.');
    READLN (FOOD);

    (* LOOP TO READ IN EACH FOOD ITEM AND ASSIGN COST *)
    WHILE FOOD <> 6 DO
        BEGIN
            (* INITIALIZE COST OF AN ITEM TO ZERO *)
            COST := 0.0;

            (* LOOP TO ALLOW USER TO REENTER CODE NUMBER IF AN
            INCORRECT NUMBER HAS BEEN ENTERED. *)
            WHILE (FOOD < 1) OR (FOOD > 6) DO
                BEGIN
                    WRITELN ('CODE NUMBER MUST BE BETWEEN 1 AND 6.');
                    WRITELN ('PLEASE REENTER CODE NUMBER.');
                    READLN (FOOD)
                END;   (* WHILE *)
```

Figure 8-1   A WELL-DOCUMENTED PROGRAM   *(continued next page)*

explains the type of data that must be typed at the keyboard. The output produced by the program should also be explained here. All of the input in programs so far in this book has been read from the keyboard and all of the output has been printed to the monitor screen. Later on, this will not necessarily be true. For example, input may come from a diskette and output may go to a printer. As programs become more complex, it is important to state exactly where input comes from and where output will be going. This is very important to people who are not familiar with the program but who want to understand it.

It is also important for the major variables to be listed at the beginning of a program and the purpose of each variable to be explained. Study the program in Figure 8-1. This program calculates the cost of an order at a fast-food restaurant. Each of the variables used in this program has been listed in the beginning documentation. Follow-

```
(* CASE STATEMENT TO ASSIGN APPROPRIATE COST TO EACH FOOD
ITEM *)
CASE FOOD OF
    1 : COST := 0.75;
    2 : COST := 0.90;
    3 : COST := 0.55;
    4 : COST := 0.60;
    5 : COST := 0.50
END;    (* CASE *)

(* DETERMINE HOW MANY OF A PARTICULAR ITEM ARE DESIRED
AND COMPUTE TOTAL COST *)
WRITELN ('HOW MANY OF THIS ITEM ARE DESIRED.');
READLN (NUMBER);
COST := COST * NUMBER;
TOTCOST := TOTCOST + COST;

(* READ IN CODE NUMBER OF NEXT ITEM *)
WRITELN ('ENTER CODE NUMBER FOR FOOD ITEM.');
WRITELN ('IF ORDER IS COMPLETE, TYPE IN THE NUMBER 6.');
READLN (FOOD)

END;    (* WHILE *)

(* PRINT TOTAL COST OF THE ORDER TO THE MONITOR *)
WRITELN ('THE TOTAL COST OF THIS ORDER IS $ ', TOTCOST:7:2)

END. (* MEAL *)
```

Running . . .

```
ENTER CODE NUMBER FOR FOOD ITEM.
IF ORDER IS COMPLETE, TYPE IN THE NUMBER 6.
2
HOW MANY OF THIS ITEM ARE DESIRED.
4
ENTER CODE NUMBER FOR FOOD ITEM.
IF ORDER IS COMPLETE, TYPE IN THE NUMBER 6.
4
HOW MANY OF THIS ITEM ARE DESIRED.
2
ENTER CODE NUMBER FOR FOOD ITEM.
IF ORDER IS COMPLETE, TYPE IN THE NUMBER 6.
3
HOW MANY OF THIS ITEM ARE DESIRED.
3
ENTER CODE NUMBER FOR FOOD ITEM.
IF ORDER IS COMPLETE, TYPE IN THE NUMBER 6.
6
THE TOTAL COST OF THIS ORDER IS $    6.45
```

Figure 8-1   A WELL-DOCUMENTED PROGRAM (continued)

ing the variable name, a brief explanation of each variable's purpose is given. This is especially helpful to people unfamiliar with the program.

Beginning documentation may include any codes that are used in the program. In the sample program there is a table that lists each food item, its code number, and the cost of that item. These code numbers are used in the CASE statement in the body of the program.

Documentation within the Program Body

Documentation within the program body involves comments that are placed inside the program itself. These comments are usually brief, no more than a few lines in length. Comments should be placed before control statements, explaining the purpose of each one. Look at the comment before the second WHILE loop in PROGRAM MEAL. It explains the purpose of the loop:

```
(* LOOP TO ALLOW USER TO REENTER CODE NUMBER IF AN INCORRECT NUMBER HAS
BEEN ENTERED. *)
```

This comment briefly explains what the loop does. The loop checks to make sure the code number is valid. The comment also explains that the loop allows the user to reenter a code number if an invalid number has been entered.

It is a good idea to also have comments before READ and WRITE statements unless the meaning of the statement is absolutely clear. Comments following the reserved word END can help in matching up an END with its BEGIN. For example:

```
WHILE FOOD <> 6 DO
   BEGIN
      statement;
          .
          .
          .
   END   (* WHILE *)
```

Comments within the body of a program may be placed on separate lines like this:

```
(* CASE STATEMENT TO ASSIGN APPROPRIATE COST TO EACH FOOD ITEM *)
```

or after a Pascal statement, like this:

```
READLN (NUM);   (* READ NUMBER OF ITEMS *)
```

LEARNING CHECK 8-1

1. What should be included in beginning program documentation?
2. What should be included in documentation in the program body?
3. What three things are true of a program with good style?

Answers

Indentation and Spacing

Imagine an essay written for an English class that had no paragraphs, margins, or blank lines. The essay would be a sheet of paper filled with sentence after sentence. It probably would not be easy to read or understand. Certainly it would not be enjoyable to read and would not receive a good grade. A programmer should attempt to make a program as easy to read as a well-written English essay. Although the use of indentation and spacing make no difference to the computer, they can make following a program much more pleasant for humans.

Indentation

Indentation refers to blank spaces left at the beginning of Pascal statements. There are two places where indentation helps to make a program more readable:

1. To separate a control statement from the rest of a program.
2. To separate a compound statement from the rest of the program.

An IF/THEN/ELSE statement could be written this way:

```
IF X <> Y THEN SUM := SUM + X
ELSE WRITELN (X, ' IS A DUPLICATE NUMBER.');
```

It also could be written like this:

```
IF X <> Y THEN
SUM := SUM + X
ELSE
WRITELN (X, ' IS A DUPLICATE NUMBER.');
```

But in this book it will be written this way:

```
IF X <> Y THEN
    SUM := SUM + X
ELSE
    WRITELN (X, ' IS A DUPLICATE NUMBER.');
```

All three of these examples would be treated the same by the compiler. It is easiest to read and follow the logic of the program in the last example. The same is true for indenting compound statements. Indentation makes it easy to see which statements are a part of the compound statement. In program MEAL, this program segment is indented twice.

```
WHILE (FOOD < 1) OR (FOOD > 6) DO
    BEGIN
      WRITELN ('CODE NUMBER MUST BE BETWEEN 1 AND 6.');
      WRITELN ('PLEASE REENTER CODE NUMBER.');
      READLN (FOOD)

    END;  (* WHILE *)
```

The first indentation is to set off the WHILE loop statements. The second indentation shows that the statements between the BEGIN and the END are all part of a compound statement.

Spacing

Spaces are left in Pascal statements to make the statements more readable. As far as the compiler is concerned, it is not necessary to leave

159

spaces between variables and operators. The examples on the left side of the table below have no spaces around the operators or after the word READLN. The right side shows these same statements with spaces. This is a matter of personal preference. Generally, leaving spaces helps to separate each part of the statement and make it more readable.

Without Space	*With Spaces*
| ```
READLN(X,Y,Z);
COST:=COST+(COST*PERCENT);
WHILE(COUNT<>100)OR(X*Y>10)DO
``` | ```
READLN (X, Y, Z);
COST := COST + (COST * PERCENT);
WHILE (COUNT <> 100) OR (X * Y > 10) DO
``` |

Blank Lines

Blank lines can be used to separate different sections of the program. It is a good idea to use blank lines around control statements. A blank line before and after a loop makes it easy to see where the loop begins and ends. In program MEAL, blank lines have been used to separate sections of the program.

Using Meaningful Names

Meaningful names should be used to represent variables and constants in Pascal programs. In program MEAL, the variable name TOTCOST is a meaningful name. It stands for the two words "total cost." It is easy to figure out that this variable represents the total cost of the meal. Names in Pascal programs should be chosen to describe the variables that the names represent.

Sometimes it is not possible to find a meaningful name, as in the case of a loop control variable. Then it is usually best to choose a simple name such as I (for integer) or COUNT.

Meaningful names are particularly useful in helping people other than the programmer understand a program.

⩗LEARNING CHECK 8-2

1. Why are program statements indented?
2. Name two types of statements that may be indented to set them apart from the rest of the program.
3. Give three examples of meaningful variable names used in a program in this book.

Answers:

1. Program statements are indented to set those statements apart from the rest of the program. 2. compound statements, statements within control statements 3. MPG—miles per gallon; YARDS—yards of fabric; SIZE—size of a pizza.

Computer programming is a complex process. Programmers from novices to experts find **program errors** or **bugs** in their programs. Different types of program errors can occur in a program. Each type of program error affects the compiler and the program differently. Program testing is a systematic process of checking a program to see if it contains any program errors. Debugging is the process of locating and correcting program errors. Program testing and debugging are important in the development of all software.

Program Errors

Three types of program errors can occur in a program. They are **syntax** (also called **compile-time**), **run-time**, and **logic errors**. The compiler will react differently to each type of program error. Each type of program error usually requires the programmer to use different debugging techniques to locate and correct the error.

Syntax errors are violations of the grammatical rules of a programming language. In Pascal, syntax errors result from a failure to follow the rules of Pascal. Syntax errors are the most common program error for beginning programmers. They are usually due to typographical errors. A common syntax error is the absence of a semicolon to separate two Pascal statements. Figure 8-2 lists some other common syntax errors and shows the error message generated.

Syntax errors are, fortunately, easy to locate and correct. Syntax errors are discovered when a program is compiled. The Pascal compiler will report each syntax error found in the program. Any syntax error in a Pascal program is serious. A program cannot be executed until all syntax errors are corrected.

Run-time errors cause abnormal program behavior during the execution of a program. The end result of many run-time errors is that a

```
                                          Error
                                          Message
PROGRAM COUNT;
   CONST MILE   :   5280               '=' expected
   VAR
      I      : INTEGER
      SUM    : REAL;                   ';' expected (possibly
                                       on line above)
   BEGIN
      WRITE(MILES RUN TODAY: ;         ')' expected
      READLN (TODAY);                  Undeclared identifier
      I := TODAY;                      Undeclared identifier
      SUM = I * MILE                   ':=' expected
      WRITELN ('FEET RUN: ',SUM)       ')' expected (Integer
      WRITELN ('MILES RUN:',I:3:2);    expected)
                                       unexpected end of
                                       input
```

Figure 8-2   PROGRAM COUNT

161

> 1. Division by zero.
> 2. Using a variable in a program before assigning a value to it.
> 3. Assigning a value to a variable that is larger than the specified bounds of the variable.

Figure 8-3 COMMON RUN-TIME ERORS

program will not be completely executed by the computer. Some common run-time errors are listed in Figure 8-3.

Run-time errors are more difficult to locate and correct than syntax errors. Run-time errors are sometimes noted by the compiler. However, compilers' reactions to run-time errors vary considerably. Run-time errors can be caused directly by the coding of a program or indirectly by input to a program.

Logic errors are flaws in a program's algorithms, formulas, or logic. Programs with logic errors will often compile, execute, and output data. However, the output will usually be incorrect. Error messages will not appear if a logic error occurs in a program. These facts make logic errors difficult to locate and correct.

A common logic error is the incorrect translation of a formula into Pascal. For example, the average of any two numbers is the sum of the two numbers divided by 2. A logic error would occur if this formula was translated into the following Pascal statement:

$$AVE := X + Y / 2;$$

This formula would add one number to ½ the other number. So, this formula would calculate the average of four and two as five, instead of the correct answer, three.

⚡LEARNING CHECK 8-3

1. Describe syntax, run-time, and logic errors.
2. When are syntax, run-time, and logic errors normally discovered?
3. What is the type of error in this program segment?

```
PROGRAM TEMP;

CONST
   CONVERSION = 0;

VAR
   FAHR, CELS : REAL;

BEGIN

   WRITE ('PLEASE ENTER TEMPERATURE: ');
   READLN (FAHR);
   IF FAHR > 32 THEN
      CELS := FAHR / CONVERSION
   ELSE
      CELS := FAHR + (2/3) FAHR;
```

4. What type of error is present in this program segment?

```
FOR I := 1 TO 10 DO
   BEGIN
       SUM := SUM + 1;
       PROD := SUM * I
   END;

IF SUM > 1000 THEN
      WRITELN ('GOAL REACHED');
ELSE
      WRITELN ('GOAL NOT REACHED');
```

Answers:

1. A syntax error is a violation of the grammatical rules of a programming language. A run-time error causes abnormal program behavior during execution. A logic error is a flaw in a program's algorithms, formulas, or logic.   2. Syntax errors are discovered during compilation. Run-time errors are discovered during execution. Logic errors are discovered during output of a program.   3. Run-time; division by zero is not allowed.   4. Syntax; a semicolon should not precede ELSE.

Program Testing

Program testing is a way of checking the correctness of a program. Programs are tested to see if they contain any errors. Program testing is an important step in the development of a program. Software developers spend between 30 and 80 percent of their time testing their programs.

A program can be tested in different ways. Most program testing methods use sets of input data to check if the program reacts correctly. A **complete testing approach** would test all possible paths of logic in a program. This approach only works with small programs. The number of possible paths in moderate to large programs is so large that the complete testing approach is not practical.

Selective program testing is normally used to verify programs. Selective program testing checks three special cases: **boundary cases**, the **null case**, and **illegal cases**.

The boundary cases are the data sets that fall at the very extremes of the legal range of data. A common programming error is the "off-by-one" error. This error occurs when boundary or termination conditions are not handled correctly. For example, the loop in Figure 8-4 is supposed to execute N times. Actually it only executes N − 1 times.

```
WHILE LOOP < N DO
   BEGIN
       WRITELN ('THIS LOOP SHOULD GO N TIMES');
       WRITELN ('IT REALLY GOES N - 1 TIMES');
       WRITELN ('LOOK AT THE TEST IN THE WHILE');
       WRITELN ('FOR THE REASON (HINT: < )');
       LOOP := LOOP + 1

   END
```

Figure 8-4 THE OFF-BY-ONE ERROR

The null case occurs when a table holds no elements, a file is empty, or a variable does not contain a value. Test data that represent these cases should be run with your programs. The illegal cases are those data that violate the specifications of your program. Entering data larger then the specified size of an input variable or entering data that are meaningless can cause some programs to "crash," or terminate execution.

Large programs should be tested in chunks or modules. It is far easier to test the reactions of a 25-to-30-line segment than a program of 300 lines. These methods do not ensure that a tested program is error-free. Program testing can only help reduce the number of errors in the final program.

Program proofs have been suggested as a better way of program testing. The **program proof concept** uses program statements to prove mathematical theorems about program behavior. The values of variables before and after program statements are stated in algebraic formulas. The formulas are then used to prove the correctness of a program. The idea of program correctness has not been sufficiently developed enough for use with large programs.

LEARNING CHECK 8-4

1. Why are programs tested?
2. What are the differences between complete and selective testing?
3. What is the program proof concept?

Answers:

1. Programs are tested to reduce the number of errors that they contain.   2. Complete testing tests all logical paths in a program. Selective testing only tests the boundary cases, the null cases, and illegal cases.   3. The program proof concept is a method of program testing in which program statements are used to prove mathematical theorems about a program's behavior.

Debugging

Debugging program errors is an important part of the programming process. Even expert programmers write programs that contain bugs. Average professional programmers spend more than 25 percent of their time debugging programs. This section will present a few techniques that can help you reduce your debugging time.

Syntax errors are normally caught by the compiler. Most Pascal

```
100  IF TEXT <> 'TRUE' THEN
200    WRITELN ('FALSE');
300  ELSE
400    WRITELN ('TRUE');
```

Figure 8-5 COMPILER COMPLEXITIES

```
WRITE   ('HOW MANY HOURS DID YOU RUN: ');
READLN (TIME);
WRITE   ('HOW MANY MILES DID YOU RUN: ');
READLN (DISTANCE);
SPEED := DISTANCE / TIME;
WRITELN ('YOUR SPEED WAS : ',  SPEED);
```

Figure 8-6   A POSSIBLE RUN-TIME ERROR

compilers will list the location and the type of error. A good debugging strategy for syntax errors is to debug a program top-down. An early syntax error can cause the compiler to flag other correct statements. Often, the compiler may flag a statement that is correct. For example, the compiler flags line 300 and 400 in Figure 8-5. Actually, line 200 is incorrect.

There should be no semicolon following statements directly before an ELSE. Syntax errors can best be avoided by careful attention to program detail and careful typing. You can easily decrease your debugging time by reducing the number of syntax errors in your programs.

Run-time errors will often cause a program to crash. Some Pascal compilers will note the location and type of error. Many compilers do not, which can make debugging run-time errors difficult.

A good strategy for locating run-time errors is to use WRITELN statements to print values of important variables. This technique is called **program tracing**. This allows you to follow the execution of a program.

The best way to prevent run-time errors is to use **defensive programming**. Defensive programming means that a program is written so that program errors are trapped by the program. Run-time errors are often caused by illegal input. For example, the program segment in Figure 8-6 calculates and prints how fast a jogger ran. The user must input the number of hours run.

If the user typed 0, a "division by zero" error would occur. One defensive programming technique is to test all user input. A WHILE loop can be used to test the user's input. Figure 8-7 demonstrates how a

```
WRITE   ('HOW MANY HOURS DID YOU RUN: ');
READLN (TIME);
WHILE TIME <= 0 DO
    BEGIN
        WRITELN ('YOU MUST INPUT GREATER THAN ZERO HOURS.');
        WRITE ('PLEASE ENTER THE HOURS RUN: ');
        READLN (TIME);
        WRITELN
    END;
WRITE ('HOW MANY MILES DID YOU RUN: ');
READLN (DISTANCE);
SPEED := DISTANCE / TIME;
WRITELN ('YOUR SPEED WAS: ', SPEED);
```

Figure 8-7   DEFENSIVE PROGRAMMING

```
WRITE ('ENTER FIRST NUMBER: ');
READLN (X);
WRITELN;
WRITE ('ENTER SECOND NUMBER: ')'
READLN (Y);
AVERAGE := X + Y / 2
WRITELN ('THE AVERAGE OF  ',X, ' AND ',Y, ' IS ',AVERAGE);
```

Figure 8-8 A LOGIC ERROR

WHILE loop could be used to test the number of hours input by the user. Defensive programming requires extra effort in coding a program, but it can save you time locating and correcting program errors.

Logic errors can often go unnoticed in a program. Logic errors are usually caught by some error in a program's output. Most Pascal compilers cannot flag logic errors. So, locating logic errors can be difficult.

Program tracing is a good method of locating logic errors. The WRITELN statements allow the program logic to be followed. Errors in algorithms or formulas can then be easier to find. If a program uses procedures or functions, WRITELN statements should be inserted before and after the procedures or functions are called. Program tracing is often used with hand simulation of a program. **Hand simulation** means that the programmer pretends to be the computer. The programmer reads through the program and performs all the operations normally done by the computer. Figure 8-8 illustrates a program segment that calculates the average of two numbers. If $X = 10$ and $Y = 30$, the segment calculates and prints the value 25. If you calculate the average by hand, you obtain the value 20. In this way, program tracing and hand simulation can help you identify logic errors.

LEARNING CHECK 8-5

1. How should one debug syntax errors? Why?
2. What is program tracing?
3. What is hand simulation of a program?

Answers:

1. Syntax errors should be debugged using a top-down approach. Early syntax errors can cause the compiler to flag later statements as syntax errors, even though they are correct.   2. Program tracing is a debugging technique used to locate run-time and syntax errors. WRITELN statements are inserted into the program. The values of key variables are then printed.   3. Hand simulation of a program is the process of hand executing a program. The programmer pretends to be the computer.

SUMMARY POINTS

- Good programming style refers to writing a program so that it is easy as possible for humans to read and understand. Programs that have good style are well documented and use indentation and blank spaces to make the program easier to follow. Also, meaningful names are used to identify variables and constants.

- Documentation should be used both at the beginning of a program and within the body of a program. The documentation at the beginning should contain a general description of the program. The documentation in the body of the program should be used to explain specific sections of the program.

- Control statements and compound statements should be indented to set them apart from the rest of the program. Using blank spaces around operators makes statements easier to read. Blank lines, like indentation, are used to separate a section of a program from the rest of the program.

- It is important to use meaningful names for Pascal variables and constants. This makes it easier to remember what a particular variable represents.

- Computer programs are written not just for the computer. They are also written for people. Using good programming style makes it easier for people to understand and use a program.

- Most programmers find program errors in the majority of their programs.

- Program testing is a systematic method of checking for errors in a program. Two methods of program testing are the complete testing approach and the selective testing approach. The complete testing approach is only practical for very small programs. The selective testing approach checks three special cases: boundary cases, the null case, and illegal cases.

- Three types of program errors are syntax, run-time, and logic errors. Syntax errors are violations of the grammatical rules of a programming language. Run-time errors cause abnormal program behavior during execution. They will often cause a program to stop executing. Logic errors are flaws in a program's algorithms, formulas, or logic. Logic errors often cause incorrect program output.

- Syntax errors are normally caught by the compiler. It prints the location and type of error. Syntax errors can be avoided by careful attention to program detail. Run-time errors will often cause a program to crash. Program tracing is a good technique for locating and correcting run-time errors. Logic errors are difficult to locate. Program tracing and hand simulation are two techniques used to locate and correct logic errors.

VOCABULARY LIST

Boundary case Data that fall at the very extremes of the legal range.

Bug An error in a program that causes it to behave in an incorrect manner.

Compile-time error See **Syntax error**.

Complete testing approach A method of program testing that tests all paths of logic in a program.

Debugging The process of locating and correcting program errors.

Defensive programming A method of programming that stresses the anticipation of input errors and the protection of a program from possible errors.

Hand simulation The process of the programmer performing all operations in a program normally performed by the computer.

Illegal case Data that violate the specifications or logic of a program.

Logic error A flaw in the algorithms, formulas, or logic of a program.

Null case Occurs when a table holds no elements, a file is empty, or a variable contains no value.

Program error A flaw or error in a program that causes the program not to run properly; a syntax, run-time, or logic error.

Program proof concept A method of program testing that uses program statements to prove mathematical theorems about program behavior.

Program testing A systematic process of testing a program to see if it contains any program errors.

Program tracing A method of locating program errors by using WRITELN statements.

Programming style The way in which a program is written—whether it is easy for people to read and understand.

Run-time error A program error that causes abnormal program behavior during execution.

Selective testing approach A method of program testing that tests the boundary, null, and illegal cases.

Syntax error A violation of the grammatical rules of a programming language.

CHAPTER TEST

VOCABULARY

Match each term from the numbered column with the best description from the lettered column.

1. Programming style

2. Program testing

3. Run-time errors

4. Syntax errors

5. Boundary case

a. Flaws in a program's algorithms, formulas, or logic that cause incorrect program output.

b. Flaws in a program that often cause the program to stop running early.

c. A debugging technique that can be used to find run-time and logic errors. WRITE and WRITELN statements are inserted into a program to allow the programmer to examine the variable values and follow the program logic.

d. The process of finding and correcting program errors.

e. The anticipation of potential program errors and the inclusion of program statements that keep track of the variable values and flag program errors.

6. Hand simulation

    f. A debugging technique where the programmer pretends to be the computer. The programmer performs, by hand, all the operations normally done by the computer in a program.

7. Defensive programming

    g. The way in which a program is written; whether it is easy for people to read and understand.

8. Logic errors

    h. Violations of the grammatical rules of a programming language.

9. Program proof concept

    i. A method of program testing that uses program statements to prove mathematical theorems about program behavior.

10. Program tracing

    j. Data that fall at the very extremes of the legal range.

QUESTIONS

1. What is good programming style?
2. Rewrite the following Pascal statements, using blank spaces to make them more readable:
   a. `WRITELN('THE SUM OF ',X,Y,Z,'IS',SUM);`
   b. `PERCENT:=(NUM1+NUM2+NUM3)/TOTAL;`
   c. `SCORE:=10*12+50*10;`
3. Why should meaningful variable names be used in programs?
4. List a few common run-time errors.
5. What is defensive programming? How can it save the programmer time?
6. Use defensive programming to protect this program segment from user input of zero or negative numbers.

```
WRITE  ('PLEASE ENTER YOUR DEPOSIT:');

READLN (DEPOSIT);

BALANCEN := BALANCEP + DEPOSIT;

WRITELN ('YOUR NEW BALANCE IS: ', BALANCEN);
```

PROGRAMMING PROBLEMS

1. The Tuesday evening bowling league would like a program to compute the average bowling score of each of its players. The program should read each bowler's name and the scores of her last five games. The average of these five should then be calculated. The output should be similar to this:

```
SALLY DOE HAS AN AVERAGE SCORE OF 173.5
```

The program must be well documented and use meaningful variable names.

169

2. Write a program that will read the length and width of a rectangle from the keyboard. The length and width should be given in inches. The program should then calculate the perimeter and area of the rectangle. These results should be printed to the monitor. The program must be well documented and use meaningful variable names.

3. Write a program that will read a list of ten last names. The program should determine which of the names comes first and which of the names comes last alphabetically. The output should be similar to this:

```
THE NAME WHICH COMES FIRST ALPHABETICALLY IS ABBOT.
THE NAME WHICH COMES LAST ALPHABETICALLY IS WYNMANN.
```

4. Write a program to compute an individual's typing speed. The program should read the following information from the keyboard:

   a. Name.
   b. Number of words typed.
   c. Number of minutes spent typing.
   d. Number of errors.

   The formula for calculating words typed per minute is:

   $$\text{WPM} = \frac{\text{number of words typed} - (\text{number of errors} * 5)}{\text{number of minutes spent typing}}$$

   Print the number of words typed per minute to the monitor. Use meaningful variable names. Document the program thoroughly.

5. The following program contains several syntax errors. Debug and compile the program.

```
PROGRAM MPG;

VAR
    DIST : REAL;
    GALLONS = REAL;
    MPG   : REAL;

BEGIN

    WRITE ('HOW MANY MILES WILL YOU TRAVEL?);
    READLN (DIST);
    WRITELN;
    WRITE ('WHAT IS THE MPG RATING OF YOUR CAR?");
    READLN (MPG);
    GALLONS = DIST / MPG;
    WRITELN;
    WRITELN ('YOU WILL NEED ' GALLONS ' TO TRAVEL '; DIS:7:2, ' MILES.')

END
```

CHAPTER 9

Functions and Procedures

CHAPTER OUTLINE

CHAPTER TEST
Vocabulary • Questions
PROGRAMMING PROBLEMS

LEARNING OBJECTIVES

After studying this chapter, you should be able to:

1. Call a function or procedure.
2. Pass parameters between the calling program and the subprogram.
3. Identify the need for a function or procedure.
4. Identify the need for a variable parameter by a procedure.
5. Trace a nested block structure.
6. Identify the scope of any variable declared in a program.
7. Distinguish between global and local variables.
8. Recognize and describe any misuses of functions and procedures.
9. Document a function or procedure properly.

ADVANCED PLACEMENT CHAPTER HIGHLIGHTS

The following topics from the Advanced Placement Computer Science Exam are covered in this chapter:

subprograms
    functions
    procedures
    parameters
        actual and formal parameters
        value and variable parameters
scope of identifiers
    global identifiers
    local identifiers
    the scope block

INTRODUCTION

An important characteristic of structured programming languages is that they allow large programs to be broken down into relatively independent subprograms. There are two types of subprograms in

Pascal—functions and procedures. Writing a function or a procedure is very similar to writing a complete Pascal program. This chapter will examine the rules for writing functions and procedures. Using functions and procedures reduces a large, complex program to a form that is more simple to write and understand.

FUNCTIONS

A **function** is a subprogram that is used to determine a single value. Figure 9-1 shows the format of a function. A function begins with a **function heading**, which usually contains three parts. The first part is the reserved word FUNCTION followed by the name of the function, which may be any valid Pascal identifier and should describe the function's purpose.

The second part of the function heading contains the formal **parameter** list. Parameters are used to pass values between the subprogram and the program calling the subprogram. A **formal parameter** is a variable that represents a value which will be passed to the function or procedure from the calling program. The type of each formal parameter is also listed in the function heading. If there are no parameters to be passed to the function, the formal parameter list and parentheses are omitted.

The final part of the function heading is a colon followed by the data type of the function. The data type must be a standard data type (INTEGER, REAL, CHAR, or BOOLEAN) or a user-defined scalar or subrange data type (user-defined scalar and subrange data types are discussed in Chapter 10).

	Name of Part of the Function
FUNCTION function_name (formal parameter list) : data type;	(function heading)

VAR
    variable_name : data type;
    variable_name : data type;
	(local variable declarations)

BEGIN
    statement1:
        •
        •
    last_statement
 	
END;
	(body of the function)

Figure 9-1 FORMAT FOR FUNCTIONS

Here are some examples of function headings:

```
FUNCTION SAME (X, Y, Z : CHAR; NUM : INTEGER) : BOOLEAN;

FUNCTION CODE (LETTER : CHAR) : CHAR;

FUNCTION CODE (NUM2 : REAL) : REAL;

FUNCTION CALC : REAL;
```

In the first function heading, function SAME is of data type BOOLEAN. It has four formal parameters: X, Y, Z, and NUM. The variables X, Y, and Z are of data type CHAR; NUM is of data type INTEGER. Notice that if there is more than one parameter of the same type, these parameters may be declared together. Declaration statements are separated by semicolons. When a function is executed these formal parameters will be replaced by actual values.

Look at the last function heading:

```
FUNCTION CALC : REAL;
```

This is an example of a function that has no parameters. The formal parameter list and parentheses have been omitted.

The remainder of the function format consists of the **local variable** declarations and the function body. Any identifiers that are declared in the local variable declaration section are defined only during the execution of the function. The function body describes the data manipulation to be performed by the function.

Below is a function that converts a Celsius temperature to the corresponding Farenheit temperature:

```
FUNCTION FTEMP (CTEMP : REAL) : REAL;
    BEGIN
        FTEMP := 1.8 * CTEMP + 32.0
    END;  (* FTEMP *)
```

The name of this function is FTEMP and the data type is REAL. The only parameter in this function is CTEMP, which is also of data type REAL. Note that there is only one statement in the body of this function. The body of a function must always contain at least one statement that assigns a value to the function. In this example the statement

```
FTEMP := 1.8 * CTEMP + 32.0
```

is used to assign a value to FTEMP. Also notice that the reserved word END is followed by a semicolon and not a period as it is at the end of the main program.

Variable : = function_name (actual parameter list):

Figure 9-2 FORMAT FOR A FUNCTION CALL

Function Calls

Function FTEMP can be executed by using a **function call**. A function call, illustrated in Figure 9-2, is an expression that causes the function to be executed. A function may be called from the main program, a procedure, or another function; in this chapter, all of the examples will be of functions being called from a main program. The following would be valid function calls for FTEMP:

```
FAHREN  := FTEMP (48.5);

IF TEMP < 0 THEN FAHREN := FTEMP (X + 2);

FAHREN := FTEMP (CELSIUS);
```

In the function calls listed above, the result of FTEMP will be assigned to FAHREN. FAHREN must be declared to be of the same data type as FTEMP, in this case, REAL.

The parameters in the function call are referred to as the **actual parameters**. The actual parameters are the values that will replace the variable names in the formal parameter list when the function is executed. The first actual parameter is associated with the first formal parameter, the second actual parameter with the second formal parameter, and so on. There must be the same number of actual parameters as there are formal parameters. In function calls, the actual parameters must be listed in parentheses. If there is more than one actual parameter, they must be separated by commas. The actual parameters may be any valid expression, but the expression must evaluate to the same data type as the corresponding formal parameter in the function. The only exception to this rule is that an integer may be assigned to a formal parameter that is of data type REAL.

Look at the last function call listed above:

```
FAHREN := FTEMP (CELSIUS);
```

The variable CELSIUS is an actual parameter. Since the formal parameter CTEMP is of data REAL, CELSIUS must be declared to be of data type REAL (or INTEGER). CELSIUS must have a value assigned to it before the function FTEMP is called. The value of CELSIUS will be substituted for the formal parameter CTEMP. Figure 9-3 shows how this substitution takes place when the function is called.

Any functions or procedures in a program are placed at the beginning of the program, after the declaration statements. The short program that contains function FTEMP is illustrated in Figure 9-4. In this

175

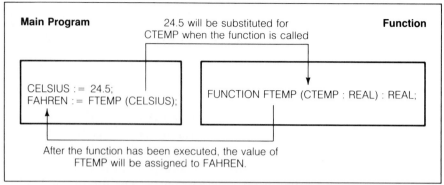

Figure 9-3 ACTUAL AND FORMAL PARAMETERS

example, it would have been easier to simply place the statement converting the temperature in the main program. But when functions become long and complex, it is easier to write them separately from the rest of the program. Also, this function can be called from the main program as many times as needed.

For example, a Celsius temperature conversion may have been necessary near the beginning of a program and again later on in the same program. Functions aid the programmer by eliminating repetitious statements. Below is a chart containing more examples of function headings and calls. The chart illustrates how the actual parameters will be passed to the formal parameters when the function is called.

FUNCTION CALL   FUNCTION HEADING

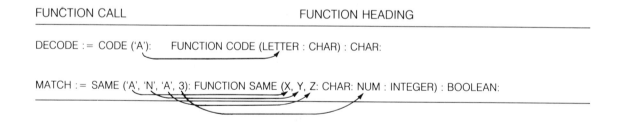

LEARNING CHECK 9-1

1. Which of the following function headings are correctly formatted?
   a. FUNCTION SUM (X, Y : REAL) : REAL;
   b. FUNCTION FIND (A, B, C; NUM : INTEGER) : BOOLEAN;
   c. FUNCTION DOUBLE : REAL;
   d. LARGE (ITEM1, ITEM2, ITEM3, : CHAR; COUNT : INTEGER);
2. Write a function call that would be valid for each of the function headings below.
   a. FUNCTION LETTER (CODE1, CODE2, CODE3 : CHAR) : CHAR;
   b. FUNCTION PAYCHECK (HOUR, RATE, TAX : REAL) : REAL;
   c. FUNCTION SIZE (OUNCES : REAL) : STRING;

```
PROGRAM CONVERT;
(* THIS PROGRAM READS A CELSIUS TEMPERATURE AND CALLS FUNCTION F_TEMP
WHICH CONVERTS THE TEMPERATURE TO FAHRENHEIT.  THIS RESULT IS THEN PRINTED
TO THE MONITOR.                                                          *)

VAR
    CELSIUS, FAHREN : REAL;
    PRINT : INTERACTIVE;

(***********************************************************************)
FUNCTION F_TEMP (C_TEMP : REAL) : REAL;
(* THIS FUNCTION CONVERTS A TEMPERATURE FROM CELSIUS TO FAHRENHEIT. *)

BEGIN  (* F_TEMP *)

   F_TEMP := 1.8 * C_TEMP + 32.0

END;  (* F_TEMP *)
(***********************************************************************)

BEGIN   (* CONVERT *)

   WRITE ('WHAT IS THE CELSIUS TEMPERATURE TO BE CONVERTED? ');
   READLN (CELSIUS);
   FAHREN := F_TEMP (CELSIUS);
   WRITELN ('THE TEMPERATURE IN FAHRENHEIT IS ', FAHREN:7:2)

END.   (* CONVERT *)




PROGRAM CONVERT;
(* THIS PROGRAM READS A CELSIUS TEMPERATURE AND CALLS FUNCTION F_TEMP
WHICH CONVERTS THE TEMPERATURE TO FAHRENHEIT.  THIS RESULT IS THEN PRINTED
TO THE MONITOR.                                                          *)

VAR
    CELSIUS, FAHREN : REAL;

(***********************************************************************)
FUNCTION F_TEMP (C_TEMP : REAL) : REAL;
(* THIS FUNCTION CONVERTS A TEMPERATURE FROM CELSIUS TO FAHRENHEIT. *)

BEGIN  (* F_TEMP *)

   F_TEMP := 1.8 * C_TEMP + 32.0

END;  (* F_TEMP *)
(***********************************************************************)

BEGIN   (* CONVERT *)

   WRITE ('WHAT IS THE CELSIUS TEMPERATURE TO BE CONVERTED? ');
   READLN (CELSIUS);
   FAHREN := F_TEMP (CELSIUS);
   WRITELN ('THE TEMPERATURE IN FAHRENHEIT IS ', FAHREN:7:2)

END.   (* CONVERT *)



Running . . .

WHAT IS THE CELSIUS TEMPERATURE TO BE CONVERTED?  24.50
THE TEMPERATURE IN FAHRENHEIT IS   76.10
```

Figure 9-4 PROGRAM CONVERT

3. Consider the following function heading:

```
FUNCTION TOTAL (SUBTOT1, SUBTOT2, SUBTOT3, TAX : REAL) : REAL;
```

Tell what value will be substituted for each of the formal variables above given the function calls below.

a. TOTCOST := TOTAL (105.06, 140.00, 1785.00, 0.05);

b. AMOUNT := TOTAL (1084.55, 77.66, 1054, 0.10);

4. The END statement that signifies the completion of the function is followed by a _____.

5. The actual parameters that are passed to the function are represented in the _____ by the _____.

Answers:

PROCEDURES

A function is a subprogram that is used to determine one value and return this value to the calling program. A **procedure** is a subprogram that is used to perform a specific task and may return several values. An example of a specific task would be adding sales tax to the price of an item. A procedure doesn't have to return any values to the calling program, but may be used to simply read or write data. The format for a procedure is shown in Figure 9-5. The **procedure heading** has two parts. The first part is the reserved word PROCEDURE and the name of the procedure. The name may be any valid Pascal identifier and should describe the purpose of the procedure.

The second part of the procedure heading is the formal parameter list. The formal parameter list is written in the same way as for a function. If there are no parameters, the formal parameter list and parentheses should be omitted. Notice that the procedure has no data type. This is because the procedure name will not return a value to the calling program. A function requires a data type since the function is assigned a value. The purpose of the procedure name is only to identify the procedure so that it may be referenced by the calling program. If the procedure is to return any values to the calling program, these values must be represented by variables in the formal parameter list.

The remainder of the procedure format consists of the local variable declarations and the procedure body. Any identifiers that are declared in the local variable declaration section are defined only during the execution of the procedure. The procedure body describes

PROCEDURE	Name of Part of the Procedure
PROCEDURE procedure_name (formal parameter list);	(procedure heading)

VAR
   variable_name : data type;
   variable_name : data type;
	(local variable declarations)

BEGIN
   statement1;
     •
     •
     •
   last_statement
 	
END;
	(body of the procedure)

Figure 9-5   FORMAT FOR PROCEDURES

the data manipulation to be performed by the procedure. The formal parameters represent the actual parameters in this data manipulation.

Procedures, like functions, are useful for two basic reasons:

1. The subprogram may be called any number of times. This means that if the same operations need to be repeated in a program, using a subprogram to do these operations will make the program shorter.
2. Procedures help to break down a large, complex program into more manageable subprograms. Since each subprogram has a specific task, the program logic is easier to follow.

Procedure Calls

Procedures, like functions, may be called from a main program, another procedure, or a function. The **procedure call** contains the name of the procedure and the actual parameter list. The format of the procedure call is shown in Figure 9-6. The first actual parameter is associated with the first formal parameter, the second actual parameter with the second formal parameter, and so on. Actual parameters are separated by commas and there must be the same number of actual parameters and formal parameters. The value of the corresponding actual parameter at the time of the call is assigned to each formal parameter that is a value

Procedure_name (actual parameter list):

Figure 9-6   FORMAT FOR A PROCEDURE CALL

179

parameter. Each actual parameter corresponding to a variable formal parameter must be a variable. Value and variable parameters will be discussed in the next section. For variable parameters the data type of each actual parameter and its corresponding formal parameter must be the same. For value parameters, each actual parameter must be "assignment compatible" with its corresponding formal parameter. The following are some examples of procedure calls:

```
AMOUNT (X, 109.98, PRICE);

ANSWER (AVE1, AVE2, AVE3, GRADE);
```

Sample Program

The next program will calculate and print statistics for members of a basketball team. This program is shown in Figure 9-7. Procedure STATS is used to print each player's statistics. The name, total points scored, average points per game, and highest number of points scored in one game are printed for each player, as well as headings for this information. No calculations are performed in the procedure and no results are passed back to the main program.

VALUE AND VARIABLE PARAMETERS

All of the parameters used in subprograms in this chapter have been **value parameters**. Value parameters work in only one direction. They pass values to subprograms but no value is passed back to the calling program. A local variable for the procedure is initialized to the value of the corresponding actual parameter when the procedure is called. This local variable is manipulated by the procedure and any changes in the value of this local variable will not be reflected in the value of the actual parameter. The value is not changed in the calling program. Program TOTAL1 in Figure 9-8 demonstrates this feature. In procedure SUM, the total of three numbers is assigned to variable X, which is then printed. After SUM has been executed, the values of A, B, and C are printed. The value of A is the same as it was before SUM was called. Although the value of the formal parameter X was changed in procedure SUM, this new value was not returned to the main program.

Value parameters protect variables from being accidentally changed. If the programmer needs to pass a parameter to a procedure but does not want the value of that parameter to be changed in the calling program, a value parameter should be used.

What if this new value of X calculated in procedure SUM needed to be returned to the main program? In this case, X would be declared as a **variable parameter**. A variable parameter is a two-way parameter. It returns its value to the calling program. Variable parameters are always preceded by VAR in the formal parameter list. Figure 9-9 contains the same program as Figure 9-8, except that X is now a variable parameter.

```
PROGRAM B_BALL;
(* THIS PROGRAM COMPUTES THE STATISTICS FOR A PLAYER ON A BASKETBALL
TEAM.  THE PLAYER'S NAME AND THE NUMBER OF POINTS SCORED IN EACH GAME
BY THAT PLAYER ARE ENTERED AT THE KEYBOARD. THE TOTAL NUMBER OF
POINTS SCORED AND THE AVERAGE NUMBER OF POINTS SCORED PER GAME
ARE CALCULATED.  THE MOST NUMBER OF POINTS SCORED IN A SINGLE
GAME IS DETERMINED.  PROCEDURE STATS IS THEN CALLED TO PRINT
THESE RESULTS. *)

VAR
   NAME : STRING;
   AVE : REAL;
   POINTS, HIGH, TOT, I : INTEGER;

(*********************************************************************)
PROCEDURE STATS (PL_NAME : STRING;  PL_AVE : REAL; PL_TOT, PL_HIGH : INTEGER);
(* THIS PROCEDURE PRINTS OUT THE STATISTICS FOR AN INDIVIDUAL
PLAYER *)

BEGIN

   WRITELN;
   WRITELN ('PLAYER''S':20, 'TOTAL':10, 'AVE PER':10, 'MOST POINTS' :15);
   WRITELN ('NAME':17, 'POINTS':13, 'GAME':10, 'IN ONE GAME':15);
   WRITELN ('_____');
   WRITELN (PL_NAME:20, PL_TOT:10, PL_AVE:10:2, PL_HIGH:15);

END;   (* STATS *)
(*********************************************************************)

BEGIN   (* B_BALL *)

   HIGH := 0;
   TOT := 0;
   WRITELN ('ENTER PLAYER''S NAME');
   READLN (NAME);
   WRITELN ('ENTER NUMBER OF POINTS MADE IN EACH OF THE 8 GAMES');

   (* LOOP TO READ SCORE FOR EACH GAME AND DETERMINE TOTAL POINTS
   SCORED AND MOST POINTS SCORED IN A SINGLE GAME *)
   FOR I := 1 TO 8 DO
      BEGIN
         READ (POINTS);
         TOT := POINTS + TOT;
         IF POINTS > HIGH THEN
            HIGH := POINTS
      END;   (* FOR *)

   (* DETERMINE AVERAGE POINTS SCORED PER GAME *)
   AVE := TOT / 8;

   (* CALL PROCEDURE STATS TO PRINT RESULTS *)
   STATS (NAME, AVE, TOT, HIGH);

END.   (* B_BALL *)


Running . . .
ENTER PLAYER'S NAME
GINNY ELLING
ENTER NUMBER OF POINTS MADE IN EACH OF THE 8 GAMES
 3 2 5 0 6 2 8 3
            PLAYER'S      TOTAL     AVE PER     MOST POINTS
            NAME          POINTS    GAME        IN ONE GAME
_____
         GINNY ELLING       29       3.63              8
```

Figure 9-7 PROGRAM B_BALL

```
PROGRAM TOTAL1;
(* THIS PROGRAM DEMONSTRATES THAT WHEN A VALUE PARAMETER IS CHANGED
IN A SUBPROGRAM THAT NEW VALUE IS NOT RETURNED TO THE CALLING
PROGRAM.  THIS PROGRAM READS THREE NUMBERS ENTERED AT THE KEYBOARD
AND CALLS PROCEDURE SUM TO ADD THE THREE NUMBERS TOGETHER.  ALTHOUGH THE
VALUE OF VARIABLE X IS  CHANGED IN PROCEDURE SUM, THIS RESULT
IS NOT RETURNED TO THE CALLING PROGRAM. *)

VAR
   A, B, C : REAL;

(***************************************************************************)
PROCEDURE SUM (X, Y, Z : REAL);
(* THIS PROCEDURE ADDS X, Y, AND Z TOGETHER AND PUTS THE SUM IN
VARIABLE X *)

BEGIN   (* SUM *)

   X := X + Y + Z;
   WRITELN ('THE TOTAL IS ', X:7:2)

END;   (* SUM *)
(***************************************************************************)

BEGIN   (* TOTAL1 *)

   WRITELN ('TYPE IN THE 3 NUMBERS TO BE ADDED TOGETHER.');
   READ (A, B, C);
   WRITELN;
   SUM (A, B, C);
   WRITELN (' A= ',A:6:2, ' B= ',B:6:2, ' C= ',C:6:2)

END.   (* TOTAL1 *)



Running . . .
TYPE IN THE 3 NUMBERS TO BE ADDED TOGETHER.
 45.88 719.03 19.66
THE TOTAL IS  784.57
 A=  45.88 B=  719.03 C=  19.66
```

Figure 9-8 A PROGRAM USING VALUE PARAMETERS

Notice that the new value of X has been returned to the calling program.

If a parameter is a variable parameter, it must be listed as a variable name in the procedure call. If the actual parameter is a constant and the corresponding formal parameter is a variable parameter, the procedure would try to change the value of the constant if the value of the formal parameter was changed inside the procedure. Also, the actual parameter may not be an expression if the corresponding formal parameter is a variable parameter. It is impossible to assign a value to an expression. Because of this, only value parameters may be expressions.

Variable parameters should not be used with functions. Functions are used to return a single value and that value will be assigned to the function name. If more than one value needs to be returned to the calling program, it is necessary to use a procedure.

```
PROGRAM TOTAL2;
(* THIS PROGRAM DEMONSTRATES THAT WHEN A VARIABLE PARAMETER IS CHANGED
IN A SUBPROGRAM THAT NEW VALUE IS RETURNED TO THE CALLING
PROGRAM.  THIS PROGRAM READS THREE NUMBERS ENTERED AT THE KEYBOARD
AND CALLS PROCEDURE SUM TO ADD THE THREE NUMBERS TOGETHER.  THE VALUE OF
THE VARIABLE X IS CHANGED IN PROCEDURE SUM.  THIS NEW VALUE IS RETURNED
TO THE MAIN PROGRAM.  *)

VAR
    A, B, C : REAL;

(**********************************************************************)
PROCEDURE SUM (VAR X : REAL; Y, Z : REAL);
(* THIS PROCEDURE ADDS X, Y, AND Z TOGETHER AND PUTS THE SUM IN
VARIABLE X *)

BEGIN    (* SUM *)

   X := X + Y + Z;
   WRITELN ('THE TOTAL IS ', X:7:2)

END;    (* SUM *)
(**********************************************************************)

BEGIN    (* TOTAL2 *)

   WRITELN ('TYPE IN THE 3 NUMBERS TO BE ADDED TOGETHER.');
   READ (A, B, C);
   WRITELN;
   SUM (A, B, C);
   WRITELN (' A= ',A:6:2, ' B= ',B:6:2, ' C= ',C:6:2)

END.    (* TOTAL2 *)



Running . . .

TYPE IN THE 3 NUMBERS TO BE ADDED TOGETHER.
 45.88 719.03 19.66
THE TOTAL IS  784.57
 A=  784.57 B=  719.03 C=  19.66
```

Figure 9-9   A PROGRAM USING VARIABLE PARAMETERS

PROGRAM ART

The program in Figure 9-10 determines art supplies needed for an art class. Each student is allowed to make one project: a ceramic vase, a water color, or a series of charcoal sketches. The name of the project and the number of students making that project are entered at the keyboard. After all the data are entered, the supplies needed are printed to the monitor.

The program branches to one of three procedures, depending on which project has been chosen. The parameters passed depend on the materials needed for that project. The variable NUM is passed to let the procedure know how many of a particular project are to be made. NUM is a value parameter, so its value remains unchanged. The art supplies are variable parameters. The new values of these supplies need to be

183

```
PROGRAM ART;
(* THIS PROGRAM DETERMINES THE QUANTITY OF SUPPLIES NEEDED FOR AN ART CLASS.
EACH STUDENT IS ALLOWED TO MAKE ONE PROJECT.  THE PROJECTS AND THE
SUPPLIES NEEDED FOR EACH ARE LISTED BELOW:

NAME OF PROJECT                 SUPPLIES NEEDED
1.  VASE                        0.5 POUNDS OF CLAY
                                5 OUNCES OF GLAZE
                                1 BRUSH

2.  WATER_COLOR                 1 BOX WATER COLORS
                                1 CANVAS
                                1 BRUSH

3.  SKETCHES                    4 PIECES OF CHARCOAL
                                8 PIECES OF NEWSPRINT

THE NAME AND QUANTITY OF EACH PROJECT TO BE MADE ARE ENTERED AT THE
KEYBOARD.  WHEN ALL THE DATA ARE ENTERED, THE AMOUNT OF SUPPLIES
NEEDED IS PRINTED TO THE MONITOR.  *)

VAR
    NUM, PAINTS, CANVAS, CHARCOAL, PAPER, BRUSH : INTEGER;
    CLAY, GLAZE : REAL;
    PROJECT : STRING;
    ANSWER : CHAR;

(*******************************************************************)

PROCEDURE PROJECT1 (NUM:INTEGER; VAR CLAY, GLAZE:REAL; VAR BRUSH:INTEGER);
(* THIS PROCEDURE DETERMINES THE QUANTITY OF SUPPLIES NEEDED TO MAKE
CERAMIC VASES FOR AN ART CLASS *)

BEGIN   (* PROJECT1 *)

    CLAY := CLAY + NUM * 0.5;
    GLAZE := GLAZE + NUM * 5.0;
    BRUSH := BRUSH + NUM

END;   (* PROJECT1 *)

(*******************************************************************)

PROCEDURE PROJECT2 (NUM : INTEGER; VAR PAINTS, CANVAS, BRUSH : INTEGER);
(* THIS PROCEDURE DETERMINES THE QUANTITY OF SUPPLIES NEEDED TO MAKE
WATER COLOR PAINTINGS FOR AN ART CLASS *)

BEGIN   (* PROJECT2 *)

    PAINTS := PAINTS + NUM;
    CANVAS := CANVAS + NUM;
    BRUSH := BRUSH + NUM

END;   (* PROJECT2 *)

(*******************************************************************)
```

Figure 9-10   PROGRAM ART

(continued next page)

```
PROCEDURE PROJECT3 (NUM : INTEGER; VAR CHARCOAL, PAPER : INTEGER);
(* THIS PROCEDURE DETERMINES THE QUANTITY OF SUPPLIES NEEDED TO MAKE
SKETCHES FOR AN ART CLASS *)

BEGIN   (* PROJECT3 *)

    CHARCOAL := CHARCOAL + 4 * NUM;
    PAPER := PAPER + 8 * NUM

END;   (* PROJECT3 *)

(**********************************************************************)

BEGIN   (* ART *)

    CLAY := 0.0;
    GLAZE := 0.0;
    PAINTS := 0;
    CANVAS := 0;
    CHARCOAL := 0;
    PAPER := 0;
    BRUSH := 0;

    (* LOOP TO ALLOW TYPE AND QUANTITY OF PROJECTS TO BE ENTERED *)
    REPEAT

        WRITELN ('WHICH OF THE THREE PROJECTS IS TO BE MADE?');
        WRITE ('ENTER ONE OF THE FOLLOWNG:  VASE, WATER_COLOR, SKETCHES: ');
        READLN (PROJECT);
        WRITE ('HOW MANY OF THIS PROJECT ARE TO BE MADE? ');
        READLN (NUM);

        (* DETERMINE WHICH PROJECT IS TO BE MADE AND CALL APPROPRIATE
        SUBROUTINE *)
        IF PROJECT = 'VASE' THEN
            PROJECT1 (NUM, CLAY, GLAZE, BRUSH)
        ELSE IF PROJECT = 'WATER_COLOR' THEN
            PROJECT2 (NUM, PAINTS, CANVAS, BRUSH)
        ELSE IF PROJECT = 'SKETCHES' THEN
            PROJECT3 (NUM, CHARCOAL, PAPER);

        (* DETERMINE IF THERE ARE MORE PROJECTS TO BE ENTERED *)
        WRITELN ('ARE THERE MORE SUPPLIES TO BE ORDERED?');
        WRITELN ('IF THERE ARE, TYPE IN A Y AND HIT THE RETURN KEY.');
        WRITE ('IF YOU ARE DONE, JUST HIT THE RETURN KEY. ');
        READLN (ANSWER);

    UNTIL ANSWER <> 'Y';

    (* PRINT QUANTITIES OF ART SUPPLIES NEEDED TO THE MONITOR *)
    WRITELN;
    WRITELN;
    WRITELN ('THE FOLLOWING ART SUPPLIES WILL BE NEEDED:');
    WRITELN('_____');
    WRITELN;
    WRITELN (CLAY:7:2, ' POUNDS OF CLAY');
    WRITELN (GLAZE:7:2, ' OUNCES OF GLAZE');
    WRITELN (PAINTS:7, ' SETS OF WATERCOLORS');
    WRITELN (CANVAS:7, ' CANVASES');
    WRITELN (CHARCOAL:7, ' PIECES OF CHARCOAL');
    WRITELN (PAPER:7, ' SHEETS OF NEWSPRINT');
    WRITELN (BRUSH:7, ' BRUSHES')

END.   (* ART *)
```

Figure 9-10 PROGRAM ART (continued)

```
Running . . .
WHICH OF THE THREE PROJECTS IS TO BE MADE?
ENTER ONE OF THE FOLLOWING:  VASE, WATER_COLOR, SKETCHES:   VASE
HOW MANY OF THIS PROJECT ARE TO BE MADE?   14
ARE THERE MORE SUPPLIES TO BE ORDERED?
IF THERE ARE, TYPE IN A Y AND HIT THE RETURN KEY.
IF YOU ARE DONE, JUST HIT THE RETURN KEY.   Y
WHICH OF THE THREE PROJECTS IS TO BE MADE?
ENTER ONE OF THE FOLLOWING:  VASE, WATER_COLOR, SKETCHES:   WATER_COLOR
HOW MANY OF THIS PROJECT ARE TO BE MADE?   9
ARE THERE MORE SUPPLIES TO BE ORDERED?
IF THERE ARE, TYPE IN A Y AND HIT THE RETURN KEY.
IF YOU ARE DONE, JUST HIT THE RETURN KEY.   Y
WHICH OF THE THREE PROJECTS IS TO BE MADE?
ENTER ONE OF THE FOLLOWING:  VASE, WATER_COLOR, SKETCHES:   SKETCHES
HOW MANY OF THIS PROJECT ARE TO BE MADE?   11
ARE THERE MORE SUPPLIES TO BE ORDERED?
IF THERE ARE, TYPE IN A Y AND HIT THE RETURN KEY.
IF YOU ARE DONE, JUST HIT THE RETURN KEY.


THE FOLLOWING ART SUPPLIES WILL BE NEEDED:

-------------------------------------------------

    7.00 POUNDS OF CLAY
   70.00 OUNCES OF GLAZE
       9 SETS OF WATERCOLORS
       9 CANVASES
      44 PIECES OF CHARCOAL
      88 SHEETS OF NEWSPRINT
      23 BRUSHES
```

Figure 9-10 PROGRAM ART (continued)

passed back to the main program. Notice that the variable BRUSH is used by both PROCEDURE PROJECT1 and PROJECT2. Since in both cases BRUSH is a variable parameter, the main program is able to keep a running total of the number of brushes needed.

LEARNING CHECK 9-2

1. Which of the following procedure headings are correctly formatted?
   a. PROCEDURE GRADE (EX, GOOD, AVE, POOR : CHAR) : CHAR;
   b. PROCEDURE GAME (LIFE, RISK : BOOLEAN);
   c. PROCEDURE TOOLS (WRENCH, HAMMER : CHAR; NUM1, NUM2, : INTEGER);
   d. ANIMAL (DOG, CAT, FROG, BEAR) : STRING;
2. Write a valid procedure call for each of the following procedure headings.
   a. PROCEDURE MONEY (NET, GROSS : REAL);
   b. PROCEDURE SIZE (TALL, SHORT, MEDIUM : CHAR);
   c. PROCEDURE PRESIDENT (ADAMS, NIXON, FORD : STRING);
3. After a procedure or function has been executed, the local variables become _____.
4. The formal parameter list must have the same number of variables as the _____.
5. Each actual parameter that corresponds to a variable formal parameter must be a _____.
6. Changes made to _____ parameters return their values to the calling program.

SCOPE OF A VARIABLE

Not every variable can be referenced in all of the subprograms of a given program. A variable may be referenced only by the program or subprogram in which it is declared and any procedures that are nested within this program or subprogram. The **scope** of a variable determines which procedures may reference a given variable.

Global and Local Variables

Since all subprograms are nested within the main program, any variable that is declared in the main program may be referenced anywhere in the main program and in any subprogram called by the main program. Such variables are called **global variables**. Variables that are declared in a subprogram are local variables and may be referenced anywhere within that subprogram.

The next program clarifies the difference between global and local variables. The program will add all of the odd integers together and all of the even integers together. These two sums will be printed at the end of the program. This complete program, shown in Figure 9-11, uses function FIND to determine whether a number is odd or even. After the function heading there is a variable declaration:

```
VAR
    REM : INTEGER;
```

This is a local variable declaration statement and REM is a local variable. After control is passed back to the main program REM becomes undefined and any reference made to this variable in the main program will cause an error. In program SUMS, the global variables are E_SUM, O_SUM, NUM, TOTAL, I, EVEN. These variables should never be changed in a function but may be changed in procedure.

Scope Blocks

A **scope block** is the portion of a program in which the scope of a variable is defined. A scope block is often specified by a box around a subprogram. These nested boxes will identify the scope of variables in a particular subprogram. In Figure 9-12, the outline of a program is

187

```
PROGRAM SUMS;
(* THIS PROGRAM READS A LIST OF INTEGERS TYPED AT THE KEYBOARD ONE AT
A TIME.  FOR EACH INTEGER READ, FUNCTION FIND IS CALLED TO DETERMINE IF
THE NUMBER IS ODD OR EVEN.  THEN ALL OF THE ODD NUMBERS ARE ADDED
TOGETHER AND ALL OF THE EVEN NUMBERS ARE ADDED TOGETHER.  THESE
TWO SUMS ARE PRINTED TO THE MONITOR. *)

VAR
    E_SUM, O_SUM, NUM, TOTAL, I : INTEGER;
    EVEN : BOOLEAN;

(*********************************************************************)
FUNCTION FIND (X : INTEGER) : BOOLEAN;
(* DETERMINE IF THE INTEGER IS ODD OR EVEN. *)

    VAR
        REM : INTEGER;

    BEGIN    (* FIND *)

        REM := X MOD 2;
        IF REM = 0 THEN
            FIND := TRUE
        ELSE
            FIND := FALSE

    END;    (* FIND *)
(*********************************************************************)

BEGIN    (* SUMS *)

    E_SUM := 0;
    O_SUM := 0;

    WRITELN ('HOW MANY NUMBERS ARE THERE?');
    READLN (TOTAL);
    WRITELN ('ENTER THE NUMBERS.');

    (* LOOP TO READ IN EACH NUMBER AND ASSIGN IT TO THE APPROPRIATE SUM *)
    FOR I := 1 TO TOTAL DO
        BEGIN
            READ (NUM);
            EVEN := FIND (NUM);
            IF EVEN THEN
                E_SUM := E_SUM + NUM
            ELSE
                O_SUM := O_SUM + NUM
        END;    (* FOR *)

        (* PRINT TOTALS OF ODD AND EVEN INTEGERS *)
    WRITELN;
    WRITELN ('THE SUM OF THE EVEN NUMBERS IS ', E_SUM);
    WRITELN ('THE SUM OF THE ODD NUMBERS IS ', O_SUM)

END.  (* SUMS *)




Running . . .
HOW MANY NUMBERS ARE THERE?
8
ENTER THE NUMBERS.
 15 44 33 55 67 99  0 78
THE SUM OF THE EVEN NUMBERS IS 122
THE SUM OF THE ODD NUMBERS IS 269
```

Figure 9-11 GLOBAL AND LOCAL VARIABLES

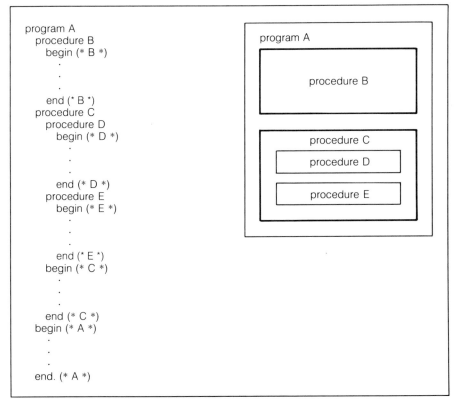

```
program A
   procedure B
      begin (* B *)
         .
         .
         .
      end (* B *)
   procedure C
      procedure D
         begin (* D *)
            .
            .
            .
         end (* D *)
      procedure E
         begin (* E *)
            .
            .
            .
         end (* E *)
      begin (* C *)
         .
         .
         .
      end (* C *)
   begin (* A *)
      .
      .
      .
   end. (* A *)
```

Figure 9-12 A SCOPE BLOCK

given with its corresponding scope block structure. The effect of scope on variables is shown below.

Variables Defined in Subprogram	Their Scope is Blocks
program A	A, B, C, D, E
procedure B	B
procedure C	C, D, E
procedure D	D
procedure E	E

This indicates that any reference to a variable defined in program A by program A or procedures B, C, D, or E can change the value of that variable. Also, any reference to a variable defined in procedure C by procedures D, C, or E can change the value of that variable. Notice that a block may only reference variables from a larger block in which it is nested.

In the above example, suppose the same identifier was declared as a local variable in procedure D and in the main program. If an assignment was made to that variable in procedure D, which variable would be changed? The solution is a rule that decides which variable takes **precedence** in such situations. The most local variable always takes precedence. Therefore, the variable in procedure D would be changed.

189

```
PROGRAM SCOPE;
(* THIS PROGRAM ILLUSTRATES PASCAL'S SCOPE RULES *)

    VAR
       X, Y, Z : INTEGER;

    PROCEDURE P1;

       VAR
          X, Y : INTEGER;

       BEGIN (* P1 *)
          X := Z;
          Y := Z * X;
          Z := 64
       END; (* P1 *)

    PROCEDURE P2;

       VAR
          X, Z : INTEGER;

       PROCEDURE Q1;

          VAR
             Z : INTEGER;

          BEGIN (* Q1 *)
             Z := X;
             Y := 10
          END; (* Q1 *)

       BEGIN (* P2 *)
          X := 12;
          Y := 5 * X;
          Z := 43;
          WRITELN (X : 5, Y : 5, Z : 5);
          Q1;
          WRITELN (X : 5, Y : 5, Z : 5);
          P1;
          WRITELN (X : 5, Y : 5, Z : 5)
       END; (* P2 *)

  BEGIN (* SCOPE *)

     X := 2;
     Y := 10;
     Z := 20;
     P1;
     WRITELN (X : 5, Y : 5, Z : 5);
     P2;
     WRITELN (X : 5, Y : 5, Z : 5)

  END. (* SCOPE *)
```

Running . . .

```
  2    10    64
 12    60    43
 12    10    43
 12    10    43
  2    10    64
```

Figure 9-13 PROGRAM SCOPE

Now, if the same identifier were only declared in procedure D and the main program and an assignment to that variable were made in procedure E, then the variable to be changed would be in program A. As shown by Figure 9-12, the variable in procedure D would not change because procedure E is not nested within procedure D.

As a final example of scope, program SCOPE is presented in Figure 9-13. The first step in tracing this example is to draw a scope block structure. The nested blocks are shown below in Figure 9-14. The local variables for each subprogram are shown in the corresponding scope block. Tracing through this program will help explain the results. Some kind of ordered variable value listing is needed. A suggested method is as follows. If one procedure calls another procedure that is nested within the calling procedure, the new local variable list is placed underneath the old variable list. Otherwise, the new variable list should be placed to the right of the old variable list. During the trace, only variables in and above the local variable list may be changed. Remember, the rule of precedence is in effect and the local variables become undefined after a subprogram has been completed.

Program SCOPE initializes X, Y, and Z and then calls procedure P1. At this point, the listing looks like this:

$$
\begin{array}{ccc}
 & X & 2 \\
\text{SCOPE} & Y & 10 \\
 & Z & 20 \\
\end{array}
$$

Procedure P1 locally declares X and Y and performs a few arithmetic operations. The listing now looks like this:

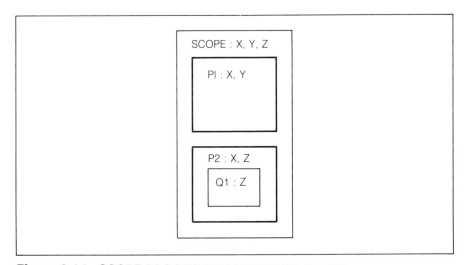

Figure 9-14 SCOPE BLOCKS FOR PROGRAM SCOPE

```
                  X    2
          SCOPE   Y    10
                  Z    64
                  _____

          P1  X    20
              Y    400
```

Note that variable Z in the main program is changed, since Z is not declared locally in procedure P1. Next, control is passed back to the main program and the local variables of P1 become undefined. The main program prints the variables and calls P2. The printed numbers will be 2, 10, and 64. Procedure P2 locally declares X and Z and also performs a few arithmetic operations. The new listing is shown below.

```
                  X    2
          SCOPE   Y    60
                  Z    64
                  _____

          P1
                  _____

          P2  X    12
              Z    43
```

The variables are printed by procedure P2, so the most local variable values are printed. These values will be 12, 60, and 43. Procedure Q1 is then called; since Q1 is nested within P2, it is placed underneath P2. The variables for P2 are still defined, since the procedure was not completed. Procedure Q1 declares Z and makes two assignments that create this listing:

```
                  X    2
          SCOPE   Y    10
                  Z    64
                  _____

          P1
                  _____

          P2  X    12
              Z    43
                  _____

          Q1  Z    12
```

Control is passed back to P2 to print the variables that have precedence. The printed values will be 12, 10, and 43. Procedure P1 is called by procedure P2 and is set to the right, since it is not nested within procedure P2. Any variable alterations will affect P1 or the main program. Again, arithmetic operations are performed to create the list below:

```
              X    2
    SCOPE  Y  10
              Z  64
              _____

      P1

              _____              _____

      P2  X  12        P1  X      64
             Z  43             Y  4096
             _____              _____

      Q1

             _____
```

Procedure P1 returns control to P2 and its variables become undefined.
Procedure P2 executes its final print statement before passing control
back to the calling main program. These printed values will be 12, 10,
and 43. Before passing control this last time, the list looks like this:

```
              X    2
    SCOPE  Y  10
              Z  64
              _____

      P1

             _____              _____

      P2  X  12        P1
             Z  43
             _____              _____

      Q1

             _____
```

After control is passed to the main program, the variables in procedure
P2 are undefined and the final print is executed. These final values will
be 2, 10, and 64. The variables in the final list contain the values of the
last print: This list is shown below:

```
              X    2
    SCOPE  Y  10
              Z  64
              _____

      P1

             _____              _____

      P2               P1
             _____              _____

      Q1  _____
```

The Importance of Parameters

Program SCOPE shows that global variables can be used anywhere in a
program. Although the example changed the value of these global

variables through the use of a procedure, this is not recommended. The use of parameters is suggested to change global variables, because of the following two reasons:

1. Using parameters enables the procedure or function to handle different data each time it is executed. This is done by simply changing the actual parameters.
2. Parameters protect against harmful side effects.

When procedures or functions change the values of nonlocal variables, this is called a side effect. This can make following a program's logic difficult and make error detection more time-consuming.

DOCUMENTING FUNCTIONS AND PROCEDURES

The functions and procedures written in this chapter have been short and easy to understand. In large programs, functions and procedures may become more complex and may contain many parameters. Because of this, subprograms should be documented in the same way as a main program. There should be a general statement of the purpose of the subprogram after the heading, including a description of the parameters passed to the subprogram. The documentation should also describe any values that are returned to the calling program.

LEARNING CHECK 9-3

1. A variable in the main program is a _____ variable and may be referenced by any _____.
2. After a subprogram has been completed, the local variables become _____.
3. In the following function heading, which formal parameter has the ability to change the value of its corresponding actual parameter?

```
FUNCTION COLOR (VAR BLUE : CHAR;   RED : CHAR) : PIGMENT;
```

Why is this statement considered to be bad programming practice?
4. When there are multiple declarations of the same identifier in different subprograms, the rule of _____ decides which of these variables will have its value changed.
5. A scope block is a _____ set of boxes that indicate the scope of a particular variable that is declared within one or more of the boxes.

Answers:

1. global, subprogram   2. undefined   3. blue; functions should not use variable parameters   4. precedence   5. nested

SUMMARY POINTS

- Functions and procedures are the two types of Pascal subprograms. Subprograms are useful for two basic reasons: 1. They may be called any number of times. 2. They help to break programs down into smaller units.
- Functions are used to return a single value to the calling program. Procedures are used to perform a specific task.
- Global variables are variables that are declared in the declaration section of a main program. They may be referred to anywhere in that program. Local variables may only be referred to in the subprogram in which they are declared or any subprogram nested within that subprogram.
- Value parameters are not affected by changes made to them in subprograms. Their value remains unchanged in the calling program. Variable parameters return their value to the calling program.
- The scope of a variable determines which subprograms may reference a given variable. When the value of this variable is changed, the rule of precedence states that the value of the most local variable with the same name is changed.
- The use of parameters is suggested to change nonlocal variables for two principal reasons: (1) to enable the procedure or function to process different data each time it is executed; (2) to protect against harmful side effects that can make program logic difficult to follow.
- Subprograms should be thoroughly documented, as though they were main programs.

VOCABULARY LIST

Actual parameter   The value that will replace the formal parameter when a subprogram is executed.

Formal parameter   A variable that represents a value to be passed to a function or procedure.

Function   A subprogram that can be used to determine a single value.

Function call   An expression that causes a function to be executed.

Function heading   The first line in a function. It contains three parts: (1) the reserved word FUNCTION followed by the name of the function, (2) the formal parameter list, and (3) the data type of the function.

Global variable   A variable that is declared in the declaration section of a main program. It may be referred to anywhere in that program.

Local variable   A variable that is declared in a subprogram. It is undefined outside of that subprogram.

Parameter   A value that is passed from a calling program to a subprogram. The value may or may not be passed back to the main program.

Precedence   A rule that determines which variable value will be changed when there is a multiple declaration of a variable.

Procedure   A subprogram that performs a specific task. Procedures allow a program to be broken down into smaller subprograms.

Procedure call   A statement that causes a procedure to be executed.

Procedure heading   The first line of a procedure. It contains two parts: (1) the reserved word PROCEDURE followed by the name of the procedure and (2) the formal parameter list.

Scope   The system that determines which subprogram may reference a given variable.

Scope block   The portion of a program in which the scope of a variable is defined.

Value parameter   A parameter whose value is passed to a subprogram, but whose value is not passed back to the calling program.

Variable parameter   A two-way parameter that returns its value to the calling program; preceded by VAR in the formal parameter list.

CHAPTER TEST

VOCABULARY

Match each term from the numbered column with the best description from the lettered column.

1. Formal parameter

2. Actual parameter

3. Function

4. Procedure

5. Value parameter

6. Variable parameter

7. Scope

8. Global variable

9. Scope Block

10. Local variable

11. Precedence

a. A variable that is declared in the main program.

b. A subprogram that must contain at least one assignment statement.

c. Determines which subprogram may reference a given variable.

d. A variable in a function or procedure heading.

e. A variable in a function or procedure call.

f. A subprogram that was designed to perform a specific task.

g. Changes to this type of parameter in a subprogram will not be reflected in the calling program.

h. A rule which decides which variable value will be changed when there is a multiple declaration of this variable.

i. The portion of a program in which the scope of a variable is defined.

j. Variables that are preceded by VAR in the formal parameter list.

k. A variable that will become undefined after a subprogram has been completed.

QUESTIONS

1. Explain the difference between a procedure and a function.
2. Tell whether each of the underlined sections of code is a function call or a procedure call.
   a. IF EVEN (NUM) THEN
   b. COST := TOTBILL (BILL, TAX, TIP);
   c. IF GRADE = 'A' THEN HONOROLL (NAME, GPA);
   d. PR_TABLE;
3. Give two reasons why subprograms are useful in Pascal programs.
4. What is the difference between a value parameter and a variable parameter? What are the advantages of each?
5. Why must the actual parameter for a variable parameter be a variable and not an expression or a constant?

6. Give two reasons why the use of parameters is suggested to change global variables.

7. Why are side effects considered harmful?

8. What features should be documented inside a subprogram?

9. What is the relationship between the scope block and global and local variables?

10. A function body must contain at least one assignment statement that assigns a value to the function name. How is it possible that a procedure may be written with no assignment statements?

11. Look at the program below. What will the values be of these variables after the program is run:

NAME , BIRTH , AGE , GRADE , HEIGHT , WEIGHT ?

```
PROGRAM EXAMPLE;

VAR
    NAME, BIRTH : STRING;
    AGE, GRADE  : INTEGER;
    HEIGHT, WEIGHT : REAL;

PROCEDURE CHANGE (VAR NEW_H : REAL; NEW_W : REAL; VAR NEW_BD : STRING;
NEW_AGE, NEW_GR : INTEGER);

BEGIN   (* CHANGE *)
    NEW_BD := '8/5/66';
    NEW_W := 108;
    NEW_GR := NEW_GR + 1;
    NEW_AGE := 18
END;   (* CHANGE *)

BEGIN   (* EXAMPLE *)

    NAME := 'KATHLEEN O''HARA';
    AGE := 17;
    HEIGHT := 62;
    GRADE := 10;
    CHANGE (HEIGHT, WEIGHT, BIRTH, AGE, GRADE);
    WRITELN('NAME':10,'BIRTH DATE':23,'AGE':6,'GRADE':8,'HEIGHT':8,'WEIGHT':8);
    WRITELN (NAME:18, BIRTH:15, AGE:6, GRADE:8, HEIGHT:8:2, WEIGHT:8:2)

END.   (* EXAMPLE *)
```

12. A logic error exists in this program segment. Identify the error and change the segment to work correctly.

```
FUNCTION WALL (LENGTH, HEIGHT : INTEGER) : INTEGER;
(* THIS FUNCTION CALCULATES THE NUMBER OF BRICKS NECESSARY TO CONSTRUCT
A WALL, EACH BRICK IS 1 FOOT LONG AND 4 INCHES HIGH.              *)

CONST
    BLEN = 12;
    BHIGH = 0.3;

VAR
    NUML, NUMH : INTEGER;

BEGIN

    NUMH := HEIGHT DIV BHIGH;
    NUML := LENGTH DIV BLEN;
    WALL := NUMH + NUML

END;
```

197

PROGRAMMING PROBLEMS

1. Write a program that reads a person's weight in pounds and then converts the weight to kilograms. This result is then printed to the monitor. Use a function to perform the actual conversion. The main program should consist of the necessary READ and WRITE statements and the function call. There are approximately 2.2 pounds in a kilogram.

2. Write a program to determine whether or not a positive integer is prime. A prime number is a number that can be divided evenly (that is, with no remainder) only by itself and one. For example, 13 is a prime number. Call a BOOLEAN function to determine if the number is prime.

3. Write a program to compute gas mileage for a car. Read the number of city miles traveled and the number of highway miles traveled from the monitor. Also read the number of gallons of gasoline used. Call a procedure to determine these three things:

   a. The miles per gallon in the city.

   b. The miles per gallon on the highway.

   c. The overall miles per gallon.

   Use variable parameters for these three items. Print the results to the monitor from the main program.

4. Two bicyclists are racing. The first can average 32 miles per hour. The second can average 25 miles per hour. If the second cyclist starts a half an hour before the first, how long will it take the first one to catch up to the second? How far will they have traveled at this point? Use a procedure to determine these two values. Print the results to the monitor.

CHAPTER 10

Predefined Functions and User-Defined Data Types

CHAPTER OUTLINE

LEARNING OBJECTIVES

INTRODUCTION

PREDEFINED FUNCTIONS

LEARNING CHECK 10-1

USER-DEFINED SCALAR DATA TYPES

SUBRANGE DATA TYPES

LEARNING CHECK 10-2

SUMMARY POINTS

VOCABULARY LIST

CHAPTER TEST
    Vocabulary • Questions

PROGRAMMING PROBLEMS

LEARNING OBJECTIVES

After studying this chapter, you should be able to:

1. Use predefined functions in programs.
2. Explain how the ordering functions SUCC, PRED, ORD, and CHR work.
3. Use user-defined data types in programs.
4. List the advantages and disadvantages of user-defined data types.
5. Write programs using subrange data types.

ADVANCED PLACEMENT CHAPTER HIGHLIGHTS

The following topics from the Advanced Placement Computer Science Exam are covered in this chapter:

predefined functions
user-defined data types

INTRODUCTION

Chapter 9 covered functions that were written by the programmer. These are called user-defined functions. Many tasks that need to be done by programmers are very common. An example of a common task would be finding the square root of a number. Because of this, the UCSD Pascal compiler has a number of built-in functions. Since these functions are built in, the programmer may call them at any time without having to write them. These are called predefined (or library) functions. Predefined functions will be studied in this chapter.

In Pascal it is possible to define original data types. The ability to define new data types is a useful feature of Pascal. It is also possible to define a subrange of an existing data type. How subranges and original data types are defined and used in programs will be explained in this chapter.

PREDEFINED FUNCTIONS

There are many predefined functions available in UCSD Pascal. This chapter will discuss some that are commonly used. For a complete list of predefined functions refer to the documentation that came with your UCSD Pascal compiler.

FUNCTION	DATA TYPE OF X	RESULT
ABS (X)	INTEGER OR REAL	Absolute value of X
TRUNC (X)	REAL	The integral part of X (X will be truncated at the decimal point)
ROUND (X)	REAL	X will be rounded to the closest integer value
ODD (X)	INTEGER	BOOLEAN value of true is returned if integer is odd
SQR (X)	INTEGER OR REAL	The square of X
SQRT (X)	INTEGER OR REAL	The square root of X
EXP (X)	INTEGER OR REAL	The value of e (2.718282) raised to the power of X
SIN (X)	INTEGER OR REAL (X must be in radians)	The sine of X
COS (X)	INTEGER OR REAL (X must be in radians)	The cosine of X

Figure 10-1   COMMON PREDEFINED FUNCTIONS

The chart in Figure 10-1 shows some commonly used predefined functions. These functions are called in the same way as user-defined functions. This statement calls for the square root function:

```
ROOT := SQRT (18);
```

The actual parameter of this function is 18. The actual parameter of a function may also be called the function **argument**. This function call will return the square root of 18 to the variable ROOT. ROOT must be declared to be of data type REAL. Figure 10-2 shows a short program that finds the absolute value of a number and then truncates this result. This number is then squared. This simple program demonstrates how easy it is to call predefined functions in programs.

Notice the ODD function. Remember the program in Chapter 9, Figure 9-11? It had a user-defined function named FIND to determine whether or not a number was even. The predefined function ODD could have been used in this program. It would have saved the effort of writing function FIND. ODD is a BOOLEAN function. It returns a result of true or false. After this statement is executed

```
NUM := ODD (235);
```

the value of NUM will be true.

```
PROGRAM DEMO;
(* THIS PROGRAM DEMONSTRATES THE USE OF THREE PREDEFINED FUNCTIONS:
ABS, TRUNC, AND SQUARE *)

VAR
    NUM, ABSOLUTE, SQUARE : REAL;
    TRUNCATE : INTEGER;

BEGIN    (* DEMO *)

    WRITELN ('ENTER A NUMBER.');
    READLN (NUM);
    ABSOLUTE := ABS (NUM);
    WRITELN (ABSOLUTE:7:2);
    TRUNCATE := TRUNC (ABSOLUTE);
    WRITELN (TRUNCATE);
    SQUARE := SQR (TRUNCATE);
    WRITELN (SQUARE:7:2)

END.    (* DEMO *)



Running . . .

ENTER A NUMBER.
-147.68
 147.68
147
 21609.0
```

Figure 10-2 USING PREDEFINED FUNCTIONS

FOR THE APPLE USER
When you are using the functions listed below
(called transcendental functions), the statement

   USES TRANSCEND;

must be placed immediately after the program
heading. The functions are:

    SIN
    COS
    EXP
    ATAN
    LN
    LOG
    SQRT

Computers assign an order to everything. The computer knows
that 2 + 5 is less than 10 and that the character N is greater than the
character A. It is such ordering that allows the computer to make

comparisons. There are some predefined functions that use this ordering ability. These functions are SUCC, PRED, ORD, and CHR. These functions may only be used with the scalar data types: INTEGER, CHAR, BOOLEAN, and user-defined (user-defined data types will be explained later in this chapter.) A table of these functions is shown in Figure 10-3. SUCC returns to scalar value following the argument.

For example:

```
AFTER := SUCC ('C');
```

will assign D to AFTER.

PRED returns the scalar value preceding the argument. In the statement:

```
BEFORE := PRED ('C');
```

BEFORE will be assigned B.

The function ORD will return the position of a scalar value:

```
PLACE := ORD ('C');
```

will assign 67 to the variable PLACE. This number represents the internal number code that the computer assigns to each character. A complete listing of these codes is available in your compiler documentation.

The CHR function will return the character value of a given integer. In this statement:

```
VALUE := CHR (PLACE);
```

VALUE will be assigned the value C. When ORD and CHR are used with character data, they are opposite to each other. Figure 10-4 demonstrates these four ordering functions.

FUNCTION	RESULT
SUCC	Successor—the next scalar value
PRED	Predecessor—the previous scalar value
ORD	Ordinal—integer corresponding to position of a scalar value
CHR	CHAR value corresponding to a given integer

Figure 10-3   FUNCTIONS THAT DETERMINE ORDER

```
PROGRAM ORDER;    (* THIS PROGRAM DEMONSTRATES FOUR ORDERING
FUNCTIONS:   SUCC, PRED, ORD, CHR *)

VAR
    LETTER, AFTER, BEFORE, VALUE : CHAR;
    PLACE : INTEGER;

BEGIN    (* ORDER *)

    WRITELN ('TYPE IN A LETTER.');
    READLN (LETTER);
    AFTER := SUCC (LETTER);
    WRITELN (AFTER);
    BEFORE := PRED (LETTER);
    WRITELN (BEFORE);
    PLACE := ORD (LETTER);
    WRITELN (PLACE);
    VALUE := CHR (PLACE);
    WRITELN (VALUE)

END.   (* ORDER *)


Running . . .
TYPE IN A LETTER.
S
T
R
83
S
```

Figure 10-4   USING ORDERING FUNCTIONS

LEARNING CHECK 10-1

1. What is a predefined function?
2. Write function calls to perform the following tasks. Use predefined functions.
   a. Find the square of X.
   b. Find the square root of 18.75.
   c. Truncate -168.753.
   d. Find the absolute value of the variable TOTAL.
   e. Round 174.73.
3. Tell what the value of the following expressions will be:
   a. PRED ('N')
   b. SUCC (1)
   c. SUCC ('X')
   d. PRED (2468)

USER-DEFINED SCALAR DATA TYPES

One of the useful features of Pascal is that it allows the programmer to define new data types. These are called **user-defined scalar data types**. This is done by using a TYPE definition. The format of the TYPE definition is shown in Figure 10-5. TYPE definitions come after any constant definitions but before the variable declarations.

These user-defined data types must always be scalar. This means that all possible values of the data type must be listed in the definition. Here is an example of a TYPE definition:

```
TYPE
    COLOR = (RED, YELLOW, GREEN, BLUE);
```

Now variables may be declared of type COLOR:

```
VAR
    TINT  : COLOR;
    SHADE : COLOR;
```

TINT and SHADE are now variables of type COLOR. They may have the value of RED, YELLOW, GREEN, or BLUE.

The computer assigns an order to these values. This is dependent on the order in which the values were listed in the TYPE declaration. In this case, RED will be assigned the ordinal number zero, YELLOW the number one, and so forth. Because these values have an order, the following expressions are true:

```
RED < GREEN
BLUE <> YELLOW
PRED (GREEN) = YELLOW
SUCC (GREEN) = BLUE
```

```
TYPE
    type_name = (list of values);
```

Figure 10-5   FORMAT FOR DEFINING USER-DEFINED DATA TYPES

205

```
PROGRAM DAYS_MONTH;
(* THIS PROGRAM PRINTS THE NUMBER OF DAYS IN A GIVEN MONTH.  *)

TYPE
   MONTHS = (JAN, FEB, MARCH, APRIL, MAY, JUNE, JULY, AUG, SEPT,
   OCT, NOV, DEC);

VAR
   NUM_MONTH, LENGTH : INTEGER;
   LEAP_Y : CHAR;
   MONTH : MONTHS;

BEGIN   (* DAYS_MONTH *)

   WRITE ('ENTER THE NUMBER CORRESPONDING TO THE MONTH: ');
   READLN (NUM_MONTH);

   (* CASE STATEMENT TO ASSIGN CORRESPONDING NAME OF MONTH *)
   CASE NUM_MONTH OF
      1 : MONTH := JAN;
      2 : MONTH := FEB;
      3 : MONTH := MARCH;
      4 : MONTH := APRIL;
      5 : MONTH := MAY;
      6 : MONTH := JUNE;
      7 : MONTH := JULY;
      8 : MONTH := AUG;
      9 : MONTH := SEPT;
      10: MONTH := OCT;
      11: MONTH := NOV;
      12: MONTH := DEC
   END;   (* CASE *)

   (* ASSIGN CORRECT NUMBER OF DAYS *)
   IF MONTH = FEB THEN
      BEGIN
         WRITELN ('IF THIS IS A LEAP YEAR, ENTER A ''Y'' AND HIT THE ');
         WRITELN ('RETURN KEY.  OTHERWISE, JUST HIT THE RETURN KEY.');
         READLN (LEAP_Y);
         IF LEAP_Y = 'Y' THEN
            LENGTH := 29
         ELSE
            LENGTH := 28
      END
   ELSE IF (MONTH=SEPT) OR (MONTH=APRIL) OR (MONTH=JUNE) OR (MONTH=NOV) THEN
      LENGTH := 30
   ELSE
      LENGTH := 31;

   WRITELN ('THIS MONTH HAS ', LENGTH, ' DAYS. ')

END.   (* DAYS_MONTH *)
```

Running . . .

```
ENTER THE NUMBER CORRESPONDING TO THE MONTH: 9
THIS MONTH HAS 30 DAYS.
```

Figure 10-6 PROGRAM DAYS_MONTH

The function ORD may also be used with user-defined data types. ORD will return the ordinal position of each value. If POS has been declared to be of data type INTEGER, the value of POS in this statement:

```
POS := ORD (BLUE);
```

will be three.

Figure 10-6 shows how a user-defined data type MONTHS could be useful in a program. This program prints the number of days in a given month. The name of the month is entered by using an integer representing that month. Using data type MONTHS makes the logic of the program easier to follow.

User-defined scalar data types are useful because they make programs more meaningful. The programmer can define data types specifically for a particular program. Unfortunately, these data types may not be read or written. For example, in program DAYS_MONTH, the statement

```
WRITELN (MONTH);
```

would not be allowed. But other than this, user-defined data types may be used just like any other scalar data type.

SUBRANGE DATA TYPES

A **subrange data type** is a data type that contains a portion of a predefined or user-defined scalar type. Subranges can be defined under the TYPE definitions. The format for subrange definitions is shown in Figure 10-7. Here is an example of a subrange definition:

```
TYPE
    PASSING = 'A' .. 'D';
```

The variable PASSING is a subrange of type CHAR. CHAR is the **base type** of subrange PASSING. Every subrange has a base type. The base type is the data type from which the subrange is taken.

```
TYPE
    AGE = 1 .. 20;
```

```
TYPE
    subrange_name = minvalue . . maxvalue;
```

Figure 10-7 FORMAT FOR DEFINING SUBRANGE DATA TYPE

The base type of AGE is INTEGER. The base type of a subrange must be a scalar data type. Here is an example of a subrange of a user-defined data type:

```
TYPE
    MONTHS = (JAN, FEB, MARCH, APRIL, MAY, JUNE, JULY, AUG, SEPT, OCT,
    NOV, DEC);
    SUMMER = JULY .. SEPT;
```

SUMMER is a subrange of MONTHS. SUMMER may have the values JULY, AUG, or SEPT.

Subranges are useful in checking for correct data. If a program asks for a person's age to be input, AGE could be defined this way:

```
TYPE
    AGE = 0 .. 110;
```

Any value entered for AGE would have to be an integer between 0 and 110. Entering values outside this range results in a run-time error.

Subranges are also important in declaring arrays, which will be discussed in Chapter 11.

LEARNING CHECK 10-2

1. What is meant by a user-defined scalar data type?
2. Name an advantage of user-defined scalar data types. Name two disadvantages.
3. Given the following TYPE definition, determine whether the expressions below evaluate as true or false.

```
TYPE
    JELLO = (STRAWBERRY, LIME, ORANGE, CHERRY, GRAPE);
```

a. PRED (CHERRY) = ORANGE
b. LIME <> SUCC (STRAWBERRY)
c. CHERRY < STRAWBERRY
d. ORD (LIME) = 1
e. ORD (STRAWBERRY + ORD (GRAPE) = 4

4. Define a subrange of data type JELLO (used in problem 3) that contains the values ORANGE, CHERRY, and GRAPE.

Answers:

SUMMARY POINTS

- Predefined functions are functions that are already written for the programmer and therefore can save time. They may be called at any point in a program by using a function call.
- User-defined data types are original data types that can be defined to meet the needs of a specific program. All possible values of the data type must be listed in the definition. Variables of this data type may not be read or written in a program. Other than this, they may be used as any other scalar type. User-defined data types make programs more meaningful.
- Subranges are defined as being a portion of a particular scalar data type. Subranges are useful when a value should fall within a given range.

VOCABULARY LIST

Argument   The value manipulated by a function; another term for actual parameter.

Base type   The data type from which a subrange is defined. The base type must be a scalar data type.

Subrange data type   A data type that contains a portion of a predefined or user-defined scalar data type.

User-defined scalar data type   A data type defined by the programmer in a TYPE definition. Every value of the data type must be listed in the definition.

CHAPTER TEST

VOCABULARY

Match each term from the numbered column with the best description from the lettered column.

1. Argument

2. Subrange data type

3. User-defined scalar data type

4. Base type

a. A data type defined by the programmer in a TYPE definition. Every value of the data type must be listed in the definition.

b. The data type from which a subrange is defined.

c. A data type that contains a portion of a predefined or user-defined scalar data type.

d. Another name for the actual parameter of a function.

QUESTIONS

1. Explain the difference between a predefined function and a user-defined function.
2. How could program SUMS in Figure 9-11 be changed to use the predefined function ODD? Would this make the program longer or shorter?
3. Explain what each of the ordering functions SUCC, PRED, ORD, and CHR do.
4. What is a subrange data type?
5. Use a TYPE definition to define a subrange of the characters J through O. List all the values this subrange includes.
6. Look at the program below. After execution, what will the values be of variables A, B, C, D, E, F, and G?

```
PROGRAM RESULT;

TYPE
    FLAVOR = (GRAPE, ORANGE, STRAWBERRY);

VAR
    I, A, C, D, E, F : INTEGER;
    LET1, B : CHAR;
    X : REAL;
    POP, G : FLAVOR;

BEGIN

    I := 5;
    LET1 := SUCC ('J');
    X := -173.55;
    POP := GRAPE;

    A := SUCC (SUCC (I+1));
    B := PRED (LET1);
    C := ABS (SQR (I));
    D := ABS (TRUNC (X));
    E := ABS (ROUND (X));
    F := ORD (POP);
    G := SUCC (POP)

END.    (* RESULT *)
```

PROGRAMMING PROBLEMS

1. Write a program that will accomplish the following tasks:
   a. Read two positive real numbers that have been entered at the keyboard.
   b. Add the numbers in (a) together.
   c. Find the absolute value of the sum in (b).
   d. Find the square root of the result in (c).
   e. Round off the result of (d) to two decimal places.
   f. Print the result of (e) to the monitor.

Use as many predefined functions as possible in this problem.

2. Write a program that will decode a word. The following code is used:

CODE: A B C D E F G H I J K L M N O P Q R S T U V W X Y Z
ACTUAL
LETTER: B C D E F G H I J K L M N O P Q R S T U V W X Y Z A

Use the SUCC function to do the decoding. Print the decoded word to the monitor. The output should be formatted like this:

```
WORD TO BE DECODED:                              RESULT

            Z                                       A
            O                                       P
            O                                       P
            K                                       L
            D                                       E
```

3. Write a program that will read a student's name and then a number representing the class of the student:

1—Freshman
2—Sophomore
3—Junior
4—Senior

Define a user-defined scalar data type called CLASS that looks like this:

```
TYPE
    CLASS = (FRESHMAN, SOPHOMORE, JUNIOR, SENIOR);
```

A CASE statement may be used to assign the appropriate class to its corresponding number. Then use this user-defined data type to:

a. Determine if the student is an underclassman or an upperclassman.
b. Determine what year the student will graduate. The output should be similar to this:

```
SARAH WILLIAMS IS AN UPPERCLASSMAN
AND WILL GRADUATE IN 1986.
```

4. In Montana there are four types of trout. Each type has a different daily limit on how many may be caught.

Type	Limit
brookie	8
brown	4
rainbow	6
cutthroat	4

Use a CASE statement to read a code number representing the type of trout. Then use a user-defined scalar data type to assign the correct type of trout to the corresponding number.

Print a WRITE statement telling the user how many of a particular type of trout may be caught in a day.

For example, if 2 was typed at the keyboard (representing brown trout), the following statement could be printed:

```
THE DAILY LIMIT ON THIS TYPE OF TROUT IS 4.
```

CHAPTER 11

Arrays

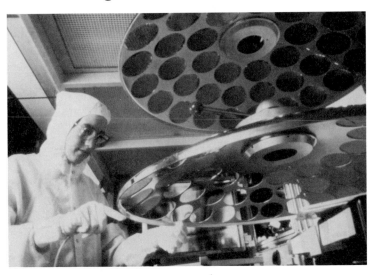

CHAPTER OUTLINE

LEARNING OBJECTIVES

After studying this chapter, you should be able to:

1. Explain what an array is.
2. Declare and use one-dimensional arrays in programs.
3. Explain how array subscripts are used and list the data types they may be.
4. Assign values to a one-dimensional array.
5. Enter data to a one-dimensional array and print the array.
6. Copy an entire array.
7. Explain what is meant by a two-dimensional array.
8. Declare and use simple two-dimensional arrays in programs.
9. Enter data to a two-dimensional array.
10. Print two-dimensional arrays in table form.

ADVANCED PLACEMENT CHAPTER HIGHLIGHTS

The following topics from the Advanced Placement Computer Science Exam are covered in this chapter:

arrays

INTRODUCTION

In the programming problems done so far in this book, values have been read to a variable one at a time and any processing has been done before another value was read. If a number is read to the variable SCORE:

```
READLN (SCORE);
```

and then another number is read to SCORE:

```
READLN (SCORE);
```

the value that was read the first time is lost. It is impossible to go back and process this first value; the second value has replaced the first. To avoid this problem, a variable could be declared for each of the scores:

```
VAR
    SCORE1, SCORE2 : REAL;

BEGIN
    READLN (SCORE1);
    READLN (SCORE2);
```

This way SCORE1 and SCORE2 can be referenced anywhere in the program.

But suppose it was necessary to read and process 50 scores. It would be very time-consuming to declare 50 variables. It would be necessary to have 50 READ statements to read them all.

Variables with multiple values can be handled much more easily by using **arrays**. An array is an ordered set of related data items. This chapter will explain how to declare arrays and use them in programs.

DECLARING ARRAYS

An array may be thought of as a table of values, all of the same data type. Figure 11-1 shows how arrays are declared. Arrays may be declared in two ways. First, array types may be declared under the TYPE definitions. Here is an example of an array type declaration:

```
TYPE
    CORRECT = ARRAY[1..10] OF REAL;
```

Then one or more variables may be declared of this type under the variable declarations:

```
VAR
    SCORE : CORRECT;
```

The second method of declaring an array is to declare it under the variable declarations with no TYPE declaration:

```
VAR
    SCORE : ARRAY[1..10] OF REAL;
```

The first method will be used in this book. This method makes it simple to declare as many variables of the same array type as are needed. For example, there could be a number of variables of type CORRECT:

FIRST METHOD

TYPE
    Array_type_name = ARRAY[subscript1 . . last_subscript] OF data_type;
 	
VAR
    Array_name : Array_type_name;

SECOND METHOD
VAR   Array_name : ARRAY[subscript1 . . last_subscript] OF data_type;

Figure 11-1 TWO METHODS FOR DECLARING ARRAYS

```
VAR
    SCORE    : CORRECT;
    HI_SCORE : CORRECT;
    LO_SCORE : CORRECT;
```

Arrays may be of any data type, including user-defined data types. The array SCORE shown above is of data type REAL. This is because each of the array's **elements** is of data type REAL. The individual values in an array are the array's elements. Figure 11-2 shows how SCORE could be represented in storage. There are ten storage locations, each of which may have a real number assigned to it.

ARRAY SUBSCRIPTS

Subscripts are used to refer to a particular array element. In an array declaration, the subscripts are always placed in brackets and establish the dimensions of the array. The first value is the smallest subscript for this array, while the last value is the largest subscript. In this example

[1..10]

determines that array SCORE may have up to ten elements. Array subscripts may be of the data types CHAR, BOOLEAN, user-defined, or subrange. The subscripts for the array SCORE are a subrange of INTEGER. The subrange is one to ten. This array could not be declared this way:

```
TYPE
    SCORE = ARRAY[INTEGER] OF REAL;
```

There are an infinite number of integers. The computer would not know how much storage to set aside for this array.

An individual array element may be referred to by using the array name with a subscript. For example, the third element of the array SCORE could be referred to this way:

```
SCORE[3] := 104.23;
```

This would assign 104.23 to the third element of array SCORE. Array subscripts may be any valid expression that evaluates as the data type of the subscript. For example:

SCORE[1] SCORE[2] SCORE[3] SCORE[4] SCORE[5] SCORE[6] SCORE[7] SCORE[9] SCORE[9] SCORE[10]

Figure 11-2 TABLE REPRESENTING ARRAY SCORE

would place 133.18 in the seventh array element. Likewise,

```
SCORE[2*4] := 74.18 + 29.20;
```

would place 103.38 in the eighth array element. Figure 11-3 shows how these values could be represented in storage.

READING AND WRITING ARRAYS

Values may be read to an array by using a loop:

```
FOR I := 1 TO 10 DO
    READ (SCORE[I]);
```

This statement would read ten scores entered at the keyboard to array SCORE. The first number read would go to SCORE[1], the second to SCORE[2], and so on. The array does not have to be filled.

```
FOR I := 1 TO 8 DO
    READ (SCORE[I]);
```

would read values to array elements one through eight. The values of array elements SCORE[9] and SCORE[10] would remain undefined.
   Arrays may be written in the same way they are read:

```
COUNT := 1;
WHILE COUNT <= 10 DO
BEGIN
    WRITELN (SCORE[COUNT]);
    COUNT := COUNT + 1
END;
```

would print each value of the array on a separate line.

PROGRAM MAGAZINES

In this section, we will write a program that prints a sales report for the band's magazine sale. The program prints each band member's name and amount sold in a table. After the table, summary information is

		104.23				133.18	103.38		
SCORE[1]	SCORE[2]	SCORE[3]	SCORE[4]	SCORE[5]	SCORE[6]	SCORE[7]	SCORE[9]	SCORE[9]	SCORE[10]

Figure 11-3 ARRAY SCORE PARTIALLY FILLED WITH VALUES   **217**

```
PROGRAM MAGAZINES;
(*  THIS PROGRAM READS MAGAZINE SALES FOR A HIGH SCHOOL BAND.
IT DETERMINES WHICH STUDENT MADE THE MOST MONEY IN SALES, THE
AVERAGE AMOUNT OF SALES BY ALL STUDENTS, AND THE TOTAL AMOUNT
OF SALES.  A TABLE IS PRINTED TO THE MONITOR GIVING EACH
STUDENT'S NAME AND SALES.  SUMMARY INFORMATION IS GIVEN AT THE
END OF THE PROGRAM. *)

CONST
   NUM = 13;

TYPE
   STUDENT = ARRAY[1..NUM] OF STRING;
   AMOUNT = ARRAY[1..NUM] OF REAL;

VAR
   NAME : STUDENT;
   SALES : AMOUNT;
   TOT_SALES, AVE_SALES, HIGHEST : REAL;
   COUNT, HIGH : INTEGER;

(*********************************************************************)

PROCEDURE READ_DATA (VAR NAME_IN : STRING; VAR SALES_IN, TOT_SALES_IN :
                   REAL);
(* THIS PROCEDURE READS THE DATA AND ACCUMULATES TOTAL AMOUNT OF SALES *)

BEGIN   (* READ_DATA *)

   WRITE ('ENTER NAME OF THE STUDENT: ');
   READLN (NAME_IN);
   WRITE ('ENTER AMOUNT SOLD BY THE STUDENT IN DOLLARS: ');
   READLN (SALES_IN);
   TOT_SALES_IN := TOT_SALES_IN + SALES_IN

END;   (* READ_DATA *)

(*********************************************************************)

PROCEDURE FIND_HIGH (F_SALES : REAL; VAR F_HIGHEST : REAL; VAR F_HIGH :
                   INTEGER; COUNT : INTEGER);
(* THIS PROCEDURE FINDS THE CURRENT TOP SALESPERSON *)

BEGIN   (* FIND_HIGH *)

   IF F_SALES > F_HIGHEST THEN
      BEGIN
         HIGHEST := SALES[COUNT];
         F_HIGH := COUNT
      END

END;   (* FIND_HIGH *)
```

Figure 11-4 PROGRAM MAGAZINES   *(continued next page)*

printed. This information includes total sales, average sales per student, and the name of the student selling the most magazines along with how much that student sold. Figure 11-4 contains this program. Notice that the number of salespeople is declared in a CONST declaration:

```
CONST
   NUM = 13;
```

```
(******************************************************************)
PROCEDURE PRINT_REPORT (PR_NAME : STUDENT; PR_SALES : AMOUNT; PR_TOT_SALES,
                        PR_AVE_SALES : REAL; PR_HIGH : INTEGER);
(* THIS PROCEDURE PRINTS THE SALES REPORT TO THE MONITOR *)

VAR
   I : INTEGER;

BEGIN   (* PRINT_REPORT *)

   WRITELN;
   WRITELN ('SALES REPORT':25);
   WRITELN ('_____');
   WRITELN;
   FOR I := 1 TO NUM DO
      WRITELN (PR_NAME[I]:25, PR_SALES[I]:8:2);
   WRITELN ('_____');
   WRITELN;
   WRITELN ('THE TOTAL SALES ARE: ', PR_TOT_SALES:7:2);
   WRITELN ('THE AVERAGE SALES PER STUDENT ARE: ', PR_AVE_SALES:7:2);
   WRITELN ('THE HIGHEST SALES WERE MADE BY: ', PR_NAME[PR_HIGH]);
   WRITELN ('THE HIGHEST AMOUNT SOLD WAS: ', PR_SALES[PR_HIGH]:7:2)

END;   (* PRINT_REPORT *)

(******************************************************************)

BEGIN   (* MAGAZINES *)

   COUNT := 1;
   HIGHEST := 0.0;
   TOT_SALES := 0.0;

   (* LOOP TO READ EACH STUDENT'S NAME AND SALES.  DETERMINE STUDENT
   WITH HIGHEST SALES AND TOTAL SALES BY ALL STUDENTS. *)
   WHILE COUNT <= NUM DO
      BEGIN
         (* CALL PROCEDURE READ DATA TO READ DATA *)
         READ_DATA (NAME[COUNT], SALES[COUNT], TOT_SALES);

         (* CALL PROCEDURE FIND_HIGH TO DETERMINE CURRENT HIGH SALESPERSON *)
         FIND_HIGH (SALES[COUNT], HIGHEST, HIGH, COUNT);

         COUNT := COUNT + 1
      END;   (* WHILE *)

   (* CALCULATE AVERAGE SALES PER STUDENT *)
   AVE_SALES := TOT_SALES / NUM;

   (* CALL PROCEDURE PRINT_REPORT TO PRINT SALES REPORT *)
   PRINT_REPORT (NAME, SALES, TOT_SALES, AVE_SALES, HIGH)

END.   (* MAGAZINES *)
```

Figure 11-4 PROGRAM MAGAZINES   *(continued next page)*

```
Running...
ENTER NAME OF THE STUDENT: MAURICE
ENTER AMOUNT SOLD BY THE STUDENT IN DOLLARS: 19.95
ENTER NAME OF THE STUDENT: GEORGIA
ENTER AMOUNT SOLD BY THE STUDENT IN DOLLARS: 56.60
ENTER NAME OF THE STUDENT: PATRICK
ENTER AMOUNT SOLD BY THE STUDENT IN DOLLARS: 40.00
ENTER NAME OF THE STUDENT: MARY
ENTER AMOUNT SOLD BY THE STUDENT IN DOLLARS: 0.00
ENTER NAME OF THE STUDENT: BERNICE
ENTER AMOUNT SOLD BY THE STUDENT IN DOLLARS: 89.90
ENTER NAME OF THE STUDENT: PAUL
ENTER AMOUNT SOLD BY THE STUDENT IN DOLLARS: 104.56
ENTER NAME OF THE STUDENT: MATTHEW
ENTER AMOUNT SOLD BY THE STUDENT IN DOLLARS: 10.75
ENTER NAME OF THE STUDENT: JONATHAN
ENTER AMOUNT SOLD BY THE STUDENT IN DOLLARS: 42.25
ENTER NAME OF THE STUDENT: NAOMI
ENTER AMOUNT SOLD BY THE STUDENT IN DOLLARS: 35.50
ENTER NAME OF THE STUDENT: VAL
ENTER AMOUNT SOLD BY THE STUDENT IN DOLLARS: 18.85
ENTER NAME OF THE STUDENT: ERIC
ENTER AMOUNT SOLD BY THE STUDENT IN DOLLARS: 0.00

ENTER NAME OF THE STUDENT: PETER
ENTER AMOUNT SOLD BY THE STUDENT IN DOLLARS: 25.99
ENTER NAME OF THE STUDENT: MEREDITH
ENTER AMOUNT SOLD BY THE STUDENT IN DOLLARS: 68.20

                  SALES REPORT
       _____

                  MAURICE    19.95
                  GEORGIA    56.60
                  PATRICK    40.00
                     MARY     0.00
                  BERNICE    89.90
                     PAUL   104.56
                  MATTHEW    10.75
                 JONATHAN    42.25
                    NAOMI    35.50
                      VAL    18.85
                     ERIC     0.00
                    PETER    25.99
                 MEREDITH    68.20

       _____

THE TOTAL SALES ARE:   512.55
THE AVERAGE SALES PER STUDENT ARE:    39.43
THE HIGHEST SALES WERE MADE BY: PAUL
THE HIGHEST AMOUNT SOLD WAS:   104.56
```

Figure 11-4   PROGRAM MAGAZINES (continued)

This program has two arrays, one containing the salesperson's name and the other the amount sold by each person. The values in these two arrays correspond to one another, that is, AMOUNT[3] contains the amount sold by NAME[3]. Notice that only the subscript of the array element containing the largest amount sold is saved. This makes it simple to print this person's name and sales at the end of the program.

Suppose the number of students and sales to be entered was not known when program MAGAZINES was written. The programmer

could then allow the user to enter a number to the monitor that would
indicate the amount of data to be entered. A variable would have to be
declared to hold this number:

```
VAR
  HOW_MANY  :  INTEGER;
```

The user could be asked to enter the number when the program was
run:

```
WRITE('SALES INFORMATION ON HOW MANY STUDENTS IS TO BE ENTERED?');
READLN(HOW_MANY);
```

The variable HOW_MANY would now be used to control the number
of repetitions of the WHILE loop:

```
WHILE COUNT <= HOW_MANY DO
```

It is important to remember that the constant NUM will still control the
maximum size of the arrays. If it is possible that the value for
HOW_MANY will ever be greater than 13, the value of NUM should be
increased.

COPYING AN ENTIRE ARRAY

An entire array may be copied to another array if both have been
declared to be of the same type. The following program segment
declares two arrays of type ANIMAL : DOG and PET. Several values have
been assigned to array elements of DOG.

```
TYPE
  ANIMAL = ARRAY['B'..'G'] OF STRING;

VAR
  DOG  : ANIMAL;
  PET  : ANIMAL;

BEGIN
  DOG[SUCC('D')] := 'COCKER';
  DOG['G'] := 'COLLIE';
  DOG[PRED ('D')] := 'BEAGLE';
  DOG['B'] := 'SPANIEL';
```

The following statement will copy DOG into PET:

```
PET := DOG;
```

Array PET could now be represented like this in storage:

SPANIEL	BEAGLE		COCKER		COLLIE
PET['B']	PET['C']	PET['D']	PET['E']	PET['F']	PET['G']

221

1. What is an array?
2. Why are arrays useful in programming?
3. Fill in the table below using the following program segment.

```
PROGRAM COST;

TYPE
    ALL = ARRAY[1..5] OF REAL;

VAR
    TOTAL : ALL;
```

a. TOTAL[3] := 31.89;
b. TOTAL[5-4] := 21.85;
c. TOTAL[4] := 45 / 6;
d. TOTAL[PRED(3)] := 14.67;

  TOTAL[1]   TOTAL[2]   TOTAL[3]   TOTAL[4]   TOTAL[5]

4. Write a FOR Loop that will read data from the monitor to the array declared below. Write another FOR loop that will print the data to the monitor. Print each value on a separate line.

```
TYPE
    SIZE = ARRAY['B'..'F'] OF CHAR;
VAR
    CODE : SIZE;
```

Answers:

4.
```
FOR LETTER := 'B' TO 'F' DO
    READ (CODE);

FOR LETTER := 'B' TO 'F' DO
    WRITELN (CODE);
```

3.

TOTAL[1]	TOTAL[2]	TOTAL[3]	TOTAL[4]	TOTAL[5]
21.85	14.67	31.89	7.5	*

TOTAL[5] is undefined.

1. An array is an ordered set of related data items.   2. Arrays are useful because they allow related data items to be stored together. The individual values may be referred to simply by using a subscript with the array name.

TWO-DIMENSIONAL ARRAYS

So far, the arrays discussed in this chapter have been one-dimensional arrays. One-dimensional arrays can be represented by a single row of values, as shown below:

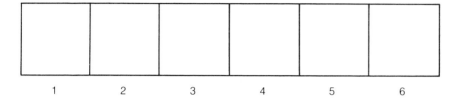

This one-dimensional array could contain up to six values.

An array may have more than one dimension. A two-dimensional array may be thought of as a table with both rows and columns. Here is a table with five rows and four columns:

COLUMNS

ROWS	1	2	3	4
A				
B				
C				
D				
E				

The subscripts in this array are subranges of data type CHAR and data type INTEGER. The subscripts could be of any scalar data type, just as they can be with a one-dimensional array. This two-dimensional array could be declared this way:

```
TYPE
   FEET = ARRAY['A'..'E',1..4] OF REAL;

VAR
   SIZE : FEET;
```

The first dimension listed gives the number of the rows. The subscripts for the rows will be A through E. The second dimension is for the columns. The subscripts for the columns will be 1 through 4. The statement below:

```
SIZE['B',3] := 10.35;
```

Assignment Statements:

```
SIZE[PRED('B'),2] := 12.23;
SIZE['D',1+2] := 10.85;
SIZE[SUCC('D'),2*2] := 15.25;
SIZE['A',4] := 23.15;
```

ROWS	COLUMNS			
	1	2	3	4
A		12.23		23.15
B				
C				
D			10.85	
E				15.25

Figure 11-5 ARRAY SIZE

will assign the value 10.35 to the second row, third column of array SIZE. Look at the assignment statements and the table in Figure 11-5. Make certain you understand how these assignment statements work.

PROGRAM PRICE_TABLE

Program PRICE_TABLE is used to print a table of prices for items. The program is illustrated in Figure 11-6. Each item is assigned a number, one to ten. A price is entered at the keyboard for each item. Discounts are given for buying items in quantity as follows:

1-4	no discount
5-9	8.5 percent discount
10-19	12.7 percent discount
20 or more	15.0 percent discount

At the end of the program, a table is printed that gives the cost per item purchased, depending on the item and the quantity bought. Notice the use of nested FOR loops to print the table. The inside FOR loop prints each row of prices. The outside FOR loop prints the correct number of rows.

```
PROGRAM PRICE_TABLE;
(* THIS PROGRAM WILL PRINT A TABLE GIVING THE PRICE OF AN ITEM DEPENDING
ON THE QUANTITY BEING BOUGHT.  EACH ITEM IS ASSIGNED A NUMBER, 1-10.
THE PRICE FOR A PARTICULAR ITEM IS ENTERED AT THE KEYBOARD.
QUANTITY DISCOUNTS ARE GIVEN AS FOLLOWS:
      1-4          - NO DISCOUNT
      5-9          - 8.5% DISCOUNT
      10-19        - 12.7% DISCOUNT
      20 OR MORE - 15% DISCOUNT     *)

CONST
   NUM = 10;

TYPE
   AMOUNT = ARRAY[1..NUM,1..4] OF REAL;

VAR
   PRICE : AMOUNT;
   I, J, K : INTEGER;
   COST : REAL;

BEGIN   (* PRICE_TABLE *)

   (*  LOOP TO READ IN PRICE AND CALCULATE COST PER ITEM DEPENDING
   ON THE QUANTITY *)
   FOR I := 1 TO NUM DO
      BEGIN
         WRITELN ('TYPE IN REGULAR PRICE OF ITEM NUMBER ', I);
         READLN (COST);
         PRICE[I,1] := COST;
         PRICE[I,2] := COST - (COST * 0.085);
         PRICE[I,3] := COST - (COST * 0.127);
         PRICE[I,4] := COST - (COST * 0.15);
      END;   (* FOR *)

   (* PRINT TABLE HEADINGS *)
   WRITELN ('PRICE TABLE':30);
   WRITELN ('_____');
   WRITELN;
   WRITELN ('1-4':16, '5-9':10,'10-19':12, '20 OR MORE':14);
   WRITELN ('_____');
   WRITELN ('ITEM NUMBER');

   (* PRINT TABLE *)
   FOR J := 1 TO NUM DO
      BEGIN
         WRITE (J:7);
         FOR K := 1 TO 4 DO
            WRITE (PRICE[J,K]:10:2);
         WRITELN
      END   (* FOR *)

   END.   (* PRICE_TABLE *)
```

Figure 11-6   PROGRAM PRICE_TABLE

(continued next page)

```
Running . . .
TYPE IN REGULAR PRICE OF ITEM NUMBER 1
    18.75
TYPE IN REGULAR PRICE OF ITEM NUMBER 2
     4.50
TYPE IN REGULAR PRICE OF ITEM NUMBER 3
    76.00
TYPE IN REGULAR PRICE OF ITEM NUMBER 4
    19.99
TYPE IN REGULAR PRICE OF ITEM NUMBER 5
    63.25
TYPE IN REGULAR PRICE OF ITEM NUMBER 6
    25.45
TYPE IN REGULAR PRICE OF ITEM NUMBER 7
   183.00
TYPE IN REGULAR PRICE OF ITEM NUMBER 8
   104.59
TYPE IN REGULAR PRICE OF ITEM NUMBER 9
    23.45
TYPE IN REGULAR PRICE OF ITEM NUMBER 10
    89.99
                    PRICE TABLE
```

	1-4	5-9	10-19	20 OR MORE
ITEM NUMBER				
1	18.75	17.16	16.37	15.94
2	4.50	4.12	3.93	3.83
3	76.00	69.54	66.35	64.60
4	19.99	18.29	17.45	16.99
5	63.25	57.87	55.22	53.76
6	25.45	23.29	22.22	21.63
7	183.00	167.44	159.76	155.55
8	104.59	95.70	91.31	88.90
9	23.45	21.46	20.47	19.93
10	89.99	82.34	78.56	76.49

Figure 11-6   PROGRAM PRICE_TABLE (continued)

LEARNING CHECK 11-2

1. What is the difference between a one-dimensional and a two-dimensional array?
2. How many elements do the following arrays have?
   a. POSITION = ARRAY['D'..'N'] OF INTEGER;
   b. CLASS = ARRAY[1..6,5..10] OF CHAR;
   c. TAX = ARRAY ['A'..'E',1..9] OF REAL;
   d. MINUTES = ARRAY[1..5,1..8] OF REAL;
3. Use the TYPE and VAR declarations below to write the code that follows:

```
TYPE
    INCHES = ARRAY[1..12,1..10] OF REAL;
VAR
    HEIGHT : INCHES;
```

   a. Assign − 172.04 to HEIGHT[6,4].
   b. Assign 14.82 to the second column, fifth row of ARRAY HEIGHT.

c. Assign 189.90 to the third row, tenth column of ARRAY HEIGHT.

d. Assign the value of HEIGHT[6,4] to HEIGHT[7,10].

Answers:

3. a. HEIGHT[6,4] := -172.04;
   b. HEIGHT[5,2] := 14.82;
   c. HEIGHT[3,10] := 189.90;
   d. HEIGHT[7,10] := HEIGHT[6,4];

1. A one-dimensional array has only one subscript. It can be thought of as a row of items. A two-dimensional array has subscripts for both the rows and the columns. It can be thought of as a table with both rows and columns.   2. a. 11 elements   b. 36 elements   c. 45 elements   d. 40 elements

SUMMARY POINTS

- This chapter has discussed declaring arrays and using them in programs. Arrays are useful when the programmer must deal with a number of related data items.
- All of the elements of an array must be of the same data type. Using arrays is an easy way to read and write these items.
- Individual array values are array elements. Array elements can be referred to by using an array subscript. The subscript makes it possible to locate a particular element in an array.
- Entire arrays may be copied to other arrays of the same type.
- Two-dimensional arrays contain two subscripts. The first subscript refers to the rows, and the second one refers to the columns.

VOCABULARY LIST

Array   An ordered set of related data items, all of the same data type.

Element   An individual value in an array. An array element must have a subscript.

Subscript   A value enclosed in brackets that is used to refer to a particular array element. For example, NAME[3] is the third element of array NAME.

CHAPTER TEST

VOCABULARY

Match each term from the numbered column with the best description from the lettered column.

1. Subscript

a. An ordered set of related data items, all of the same data type.

2. Array

    b. A value enclosed in brackets that is used to refer to a particular array element.

3. Element

    c. An individual value of an array.

QUESTIONS

1. Write type declarations and variable declarations for the arrays listed below.

    a. An array called PERCENT of type REAL that may contain up to 15 values.

    b. An array called WEEKDAYS of data type STRING that can contain up to seven values.

    c. A two-dimensional array called GRADE of data type CHAR that contains six rows and five columns.

2. Use the following program segment to fill in the table below.

```
PROGRAM ASSIGN;

TYPE
    EMPLOYEE = ARRAY[1..5,1..4] OF STRING;

VAR
    I, J : INTEGER;
    WORKER: EMPLOYEE;

BEGIN

    I := 2;
    J := 3;
    WORKER[I,J] := 'SAMPSON';
    WORKER[I*2,4] := 'MOSES';
    WORKER[1,1+1] := 'AARON';
    WORKER[I+3,J] := 'MICAH';
    WORKER[4,J-1] := 'JONATHAN';
    WORKER[3*1,1] := 'SOLOMON'

END.
```

COLUMNS

ROWS	1	2	3	4
1				
2				
3				
4				
5				

3. The program below contains several run-time errors. Type the program on your computer and run it once. Then use the program-tracing techniques discussed in Chapter 8 to find and correct the run-time errors.

```
PROGRAM P_DIET;
(* THIS PROGRAM WILL READ IN THE MEALS FOR A 7 DAY DIET AND
   PRINT THE DAYS AND MEALS IN A TABLE FORMAT *)

    VAR
        DAY   : ARRAY[1..7] OF STRING[10];
        I     : INTEGER;
        J     : INTEGER;
        MEALS : ARRAY[1..7] OF STRING[15];

    BEGIN

        WRITELN ('YOU''VE BEEN CONTACTED BY A PUBLISHING COMPANY TO');
        WRITELN ('CREATE YOUR OWN DIET FOR A NEW BOOK. TYPE IN THE');
        WRITELN ('MAIN MEAL FOR EACH DAY OF YOUR DIET.');
        WRITELN;
        WHILE I <= 7 DO
            BEGIN
                I := I + 1;
                WRITE ('DAY ', I, ' OF THE DIET IS: ');
                READLN (DAY[I]);
                WRITE ('THE MEAL FOR ', DAY[I], ' IS: ');
                READLN (MEALS[I]);
                WRITELN
            END;
        WRITELN ('            YOUR DIET PLAN');
        WRITELN;
        WRITELN ('    DAY', '                ', 'MEAL');
        REPEAT
            WRITELN (DAY[J], '              ', MEALS[J]);
            WRITELN;
            J := J + 1
        UNTIL J = 8

    END.    (* OF PROGRAM P_DIET *)
```

4. The following program contains several logic errors. Type the program on your computer and run it once. Then use the program tracing and hand-simulation techniques discussed in Chapter 8 to find and correct the logic errors.

```
PROGRAM VACATION;
(* THIS PROGRAM READS THE NAMES OF CITIES OR VACATION SPOTS AND THE
   DISTANCES BETWEEN EACH CITY.  A LIST OF THE VACATION PLAN IS PRINTED
   WITH NAME, DISTANCE, AND TRAVEL TIME LISTED *)

    VAR
        CITIES  : ARRAY[1..4] OF STRING[20];    (* ARRAY OF VACATION SPOTS *)
        CITY    : STRING[20];                   (* NAME OF VACATION SPOT *)
        HOUR    : REAL;                         (* TRAVEL TIME *)
        HOURS   : ARRAY[1..4] OF REAL;          (* ARRAY OF TRAVEL TIMES *)
        I       : INTEGER;                      (* LOOP AND ARRAY COUNTERS *)
        MILES   : REAL;                         (* NUMBER OF MILES TRAVELED *)
        TMILES  : ARRAY[1..4] OF REAL;          (* LOG OF MILES TRAVELED *)
```

```
BEGIN
    WRITELN ('THIS PROGRAM WILL HELP YOU PLAN A TRIP TO 4 CITIES OR ');
    WRITELN ('VACATION SPOTS.  THINK OF 4 PLACES YOU WOULD LIKE TO VISIT,');
    WRITELN ('THE ORDER IN WHICH YOU WANT TO VISIT THEM, AND THE ');
    WRITELN ('DISTANCE BETWEEN EACH PLACE.');
    WRITELN;

    (* CITIES AND DISTANCES READ *)
    FOR I := 1 TO 4 DO
        BEGIN
            WRITE ('CITY OR PLACE ', I, ' IS: ');
            READLN (CITY);
            CITIES[I] := CITY;

            IF I = 1 THEN                               (* FIRST CITY READ *)
                BEGIN
                    WRITE ('DISTANCE TO ', CITIES[I], ' :');
                    READLN (MILES);
                    TMILES[I] := MILES          (* DISTANCE CALCULATED *)
                END
            ELSE                                        (* OTHERS CITIES READ *)
                BEGIN
                    WRITE ('DISTANCE TO ', CITIES[1], ' FROM ', CITIES[I],
                            ' : ');
                    READLN (MILES);
                    TMILES[I] := MILES                  (* DISTANCE CALCULATED *)
                END;

            HOURS[I] := MILES * 55                      (* TRAVEL TIME CALCULATED *)
        END;    (* FOR *)

    (* VACATION PLAN PRINTED - PLACE, DISTANCE BETWEEN SPOTS, TIME *)
    WRITELN;
    WRITELN ('                   YOUR VACATION PLAN');
    WRITELN ('        PLACE           DISTANCE        TRAVEL TIME');
    WRITELN;

    FOR I := 1 TO 4 DO
        WRITELN (CITIES[I]:12,   TMILES[I]:13:2, HOURS[I]:20:2)

END.    (* VACATION *)
```

PROGRAMMING PROBLEMS

1. Read 15 numbers to array A and 15 numbers to array B. Compute the product of these two numbers and place this result in array PROD. Print a table similar to the one below at the end of your program.

A	B	PRODUCT
5	6	30
2	8	16

2. Write a program that will read your last name and print it backwards to the monitor. Example:

Input	Output
SCHWARTZ	ZTRAWHCS

3. Below is a list of schools and the number of wins each team had in four different sports. Write a program to read the name of the school and its wins in each of the four sports. Use a two-dimensional array. Put the results in a table. Set the table up as shown below:

```
SCHOOL                    SPORT

              BASEBALL  BASKETBALL  FOOTBALL  GOLF
   LAKEVIEW      2           8          5       4
   CITY          9           3          4       1
```

Then print the name of the school with the most wins in each sport like this:

THE SCHOOL WHICH WON THE MOST BASEBALL GAMES IS:
    CITY

Here are the data to be entered for this program:

	Baseball	*Basketball*	*Football*	*Golf*
Lakeview	2	8	5	4
City	9	3	4	1
Western	7	1	3	8
Washington	0	10	4	2
Scott	3	0	9	5
Central	6	5	2	4
Elmwood	7	6	6	0

4. Write a program to read the dimensions, in inches, of ten triangles. Call the triangles A, B, C, D, E, F, G, H, I, and J. Determine whether each triangle is scalene (no equal sides), isosceles (two equal sides), or equilateral (all sides are equal). At the end of the program, print the names of all the triangles of the same type together with an appropriate heading. Make up your own input. Depending on your input, the output might be formatted something like this:

```
THE SCALENE TRIANGLES ARE:
    A
    D
    E
    F
    J
THE ISOSCELES TRIANGLES ARE:
    B
    G
    H
THE EQUILATERAL TRIANGLES ARE:
    C
    I
```

5. The following program contains a single run-time error. Use program testing and debugging techniques to locate and correct the error.

231

```
PROGRAM JUKEBOX;
(* THIS PROGRAM PRINTS THE SELECTIONS ON A  JUKEBOX AND ACCEPTS A SELECTION *)

VAR
    I, SELECT : INTEGER;
    TUNES : ARRAY[1..5] OF STRING;

BEGIN   (* JUKEBOX *)

    TUNES[1] := 'BEATLES / LET IT BE';
    TUNES[2] := 'ROLLING STONES / WAITING FOR  A FRIEND';
    TUNES[3] := 'DUKE ELLINGTON / THE A TRAIN';
    TUNES[4] := 'FRANK SINATRA / NEW YORK, NEW YORK';
    TUNES[5] := 'NEIL YOUNG / OHIO';

    WRITELN ('PLEASE SELECT A SONG FROM THE FOLLOWING LIST');
    WRITELN;
    WRITELN('_____');
    FOR I := 1 TO 6 DO
        WRITELN (I, ' ', TUNES[I]);
    WRITE ('YOUR SELECTION IS (1, 2, 3, 4, 5): ');
    READLN (SELECT);
    CASE SELECT OF
        1 : WRITELN ('LET IT BE');
        2 : WRITELN ('WAITING FOR A FRIEND');
        3 : WRITELN ('THE A TRAIN');
        4 : WRITELN ('NEW YORK, NEW YORK');
        5 : WRITELN ('OHIO')
    END   (* CASE *)

END. (* JUKEBOX *)
```

CHAPTER 12

Records and Sets

CHAPTER OUTLINE

LEARNING OBJECTIVES

After studying this chapter, you should be able to:

1. Explain what is meant by a structured data type.
2. Declare and use records in programs.
3. Refer to individual fields of a record.
4. Use the WITH statement in working with records.
5. Copy entire records.
6. Use sets in programs when appropriate.
7. Be able to use the following set operators: $+, *, -$.
8. Be able to use the following set relational operators: $=, >=, <=, <>$.

ADVANCED PLACEMENT CHAPTER HIGHLIGHTS

The following topics from the Advanced Placement Computer Science Exam are covered in this chapter:

data structures
   records
   arrays of records
   sets

INTRODUCTION

In Chapter 11, one **structured data type,** arrays, was discussed. In this chapter, two more structured data types will be covered: **records** and **sets.** These are called structured data types because they can be used to store many individual values. These individual values can then be referred to as a single unit. The format of each structured data type has strict rules that must be followed and each has situations in which it is useful. Arrays, records, and sets are all linear data types; the individual elements can be thought of as being arranged in a straight line in the data structure.

    The values in an array must all be of the same data type. An array cannot be declared that has some elements of data type STRING and others of data type INTEGER. There are many situations where it might be desirable to keep data of different types in a single unit. For example, think of the data an employer might want to keep on an employee. It might include the following information:

- name
- age

- sex
- Social Security number
- hourly pay rate

A record would be ideal to contain this information. A record is a group of related data items, not necessarily of the same data type, that are gathered together as a single unit. Sets can also contain related data items. A set consists of a collection of items that are classed together. All of the items in a set must be of the same base type.

RECORDS

Declaring Records

The format for declaring records is shown in Figure 12-1. A record for employees in a company could look like this:

```
TYPE
   WORKER = RECORD
     NAME : STRING;
     AGE : INTEGER;
     SEX : CHAR;
     SS_NO : STRING;
     PAY_RATE : REAL
   END;
```

The name of this record is WORKER. All records are made up of **fields**. A field is a data item that is part of a record. Record WORKER is made up of five fields. The fields may be of any data type. Notice that the first line of the record

```
WORKER = RECORD
```

is not followed by a semicolon. The record declaration is concluded with the reserved word END.

To use this record in a program, one or more variables must be

```
TYPE
   record_name = RECORD
     field_name1 : data_type;
     field_name2 : data_type;
              •
              •
              •
     last field_name : data_type
   END;
```

Figure 12-1   RECORD DECLARATION FORMAT

235

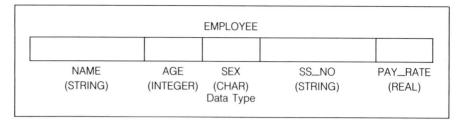

Figure 12-2 RECORD REPRESENTED IN STORAGE

declared to be of type WORKER. For example, the variable EMPLOYEE can be declared to be of type WORKER.

```
VAR
     EMPLOYEE : WORKER;
```

EMPLOYEE can now be used to refer to the record for each worker. Figure 12-2 shows how this record could be represented in storage.

Referring to Individual Fields

A field can be referred to in two ways. First, a period can be placed between the name of the record and the field name. The general format for this is:

record_name.field_name;

The NAME field of record EMPLOYEE could be assigned a value this way:

```
EMPLOYEE.NAME := 'JONES, VIOLA';
```

Even if there are other records with a NAME field, the compiler knows that the statement above refers to the NAME field of EMPLOYEE. The other fields in this record could also be assigned values in the same way:

```
EMPLOYEE.AGE := 47;
EMPLOYEE.SEX := 'F';
EMPLOYEE.SS_NO := '379-50-5244';
EMPLOYEE.PAY_RATE := 7.58;
```

JONES, VIOLA	47	F	379-50-5244	7.58
NAME	AGE	SEX	SS _ NO	PAY _ RATE

Figure 12-3 EMPLOYEE RECORD IN STORAGE

```
WITH record_variable do
    BEGIN
        •
        •
        •
    END;
```

In the body of the WITH statement, individual fields in
a record may be referenced by simply using the name
of the field.

Figure 12-4 WITH STATEMENT FORMAT

Figure 12-3 demonstrates how this record could now be represented in storage. A second and usually simpler way of referring to the fields of a record is to use the WITH statement. The general format of the WITH statement is shown in Figure 12-4. The WITH statement could be used to assign values to record EMPLOYEE this way:

```
WITH EMPLOYEE DO
    BEGIN
        NAME := 'JONES, VIOLA';
        AGE := 47;
        SEX := 'F'
        SS_NO := '379-50-5244';
        PAY_RATE := 7.58
    END;
```

Notice that the word WITH is followed by the record name. The WITH statement must start with a BEGIN and conclude with an END if it contains more than one statement within it.

Copying an Entire Record

A complete record may be copied to another record if both records are of the same record type. In the previous example, EMPLOYEE is a record of type WORKER. Suppose two variables had been declared to be of this type:

```
VAR
    EMPLOYEE : WORKER;
    TEACHER  : WORKER;
```

In the previous section, the fields of EMPLOYEE were given values individually. Suppose it was necessary to copy this entire record to TEACHER. This could be done by the statement.

```
TEACHER := EMPLOYEE;
```

Now every field of these two records will be identical. The general format for copying records is shown in Figure 12-5.

237

```
record_variable1 := record_variable2;
```

Record_variable1 and record_variable2 must be of the same record type

Figure 12-5 FORMAT FOR COPYING RECORDS

Arrays of Records

Records are most commonly used in groups. For example, an employer would want to place all of the WORKER records in the previous section together. This can be done by declaring an array of records. An array could be declared of EMPLOYEES:

```
EMPLOYEES : ARRAY[1..10] OF WORKER;
```

Figure 12-6 illustrates how each array element contains a complete record. This declaration statement will set up an array that could hold up to ten records. The fourth record in this array could be referred to by using a subscript:

```
EMPLOYEES[4]
```

Individual fields in this record can be referred to in the same way as fields in individual records. The only difference is an array subscript must be used to determine which array element is being referenced. The age field of the fourth record in the array EMPLOYEES could be assigned a value this way:

```
EMPLOYEES[4].AGE := 47;
```

This field could be referred to by using a WITH statement:

```
WITH EMPLOYEES[4] DO
   BEGIN
      AGE := 47
   END;
```

Program ODD_JOBS

Eric needs a program to keep track of odd jobs he does in the neighborhood. He would like a record for each job that contains the following information:

- name of person job was done for
- job (Eric does four jobs: rake, mow, garden, and babysit)
- time spent on the job
- cost of the job

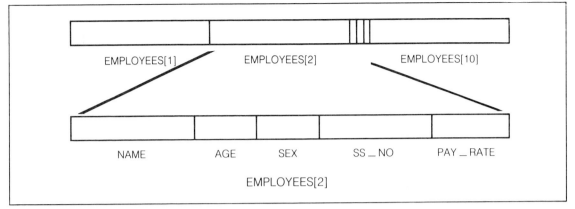

Figure 12-6 ARRAY OF RECORDS

The program will be written so that Eric can enter the first three items at the keyboard. The amount to be charged for the job will be computed by the program. Look at the program in Figure 12-7. BILL is the name of the record. An array of these records is declared:

```
VAR
    CUSTOMER : ARRAY[1..20] OF BILL;
```

CUSTOMER may contain up to 20 records. After Eric is done entering information, the program prints a table containing the contents of each record. If Eric decides to change the amount he charges per hour for a particular job, he can easily change the program.

LEARNING CHECK 12-1

1. What is a record?
2. Declare a record named PLAYER. This record will be for baseball players on a team. The record should have the following fields:

NAME	(name of the player)
AGE	(age of the player)
BAT_AVE	(batting average of the player)
POS	(position played by the player)

   Declare each field to be of an appropriate data type.
3. Study the program segment below.

```
PROGRAM GOLF;

TYPE
    PLAYER = RECORD
        NAME : STRING;
        AVERAGE : REAL
    END;
```

```
PROGRAM ODD_JOBS;
(*   THIS PROGRAM READ A CUSTOMER'S NAME, THE TYPE OF JOB DONE
FOR THE CUSTOMER, AND THE NUMBER OF HOURS SPENT ON THIS JOB.
THE AMOUNT OWED BY THE CUSTOMER IS THEN COMPUTED.   UP TO
TWENTY JOBS MAY BE ENTERED AT A TIME.   THE FOLLOWING JOBS
MAY BE ENTERED:
    MOW
    RAKE
    GARDEN
    BABYSIT
AT THE END OF THE PROGRAM A TABLE IS PRINTED TO THE MONITOR *)

TYPE
    BILL   = RECORD
      NAME : STRING[25];
      JOB  : STRING[10];
      TIME : REAL;
      COST : REAL
    END; (* BILL *)

VAR
    CUSTOMER : ARRAY[1..20] OF BILL;
    ANSWER : CHAR;
    I, COUNT : INTEGER;

BEGIN    (* ODD_JOBS *)

    COUNT := 0;

    (* SEE IF MORE DATA IS TO BE ENTERED *)
    WRITELN ('DO YOU WANT TO ENTER A JOB?');
    WRITELN ('IF YES, TYPE IN Y AND HIT RETURN KEY.');
    WRITELN ('IF NO, TYPE JUST HIT RETURN KEY.');
    READLN (ANSWER);

    WHILE ANSWER = 'Y' DO
       BEGIN
          COUNT := COUNT + 1;

          WITH CUSTOMER[COUNT] DO
             BEGIN
                WRITE ('ENTER CUSTOMER''S NAME: ');
                READLN (NAME);
                WRITE ('ENTER THE JOB: ');
                READLN (JOB);
                WRITE ('ENTER THE TIME SPENT ON THE JOB: ');
                READLN (TIME);

                (* COMPUTE AMOUNT OF BILL *)
                IF JOB = 'MOW' THEN
                   COST := 3.50 * TIME
                ELSE IF JOB = 'RAKE' THEN
                   COST := 3.00 * TIME
                ELSE IF JOB = 'GARDEN' THEN
                   COST := 3.25 * TIME
                ELSE IF JOB = 'BABYSIT' THEN
                   COST := 2.00 * TIME
             END;   (* WITH *)
```

Figure 12-7   PROGRAM ODD_JOBS

(continued next page)

```
                  WRITELN ('DO YOU WANT TO ENTER A JOB?');
                  WRITELN ('IF YES, TYPE IN Y AND HIT RETURN KEY');
                  WRITELN ('IF NO, JUST HIT RETURN KEY');
                  READLN (ANSWER)
            END;   (* WHILE *)

            (* PRINT TABLE TO MONITOR *)
            WRITELN ('NAME':20,'JOB':20,'TIME':10,'AMOUNT DUE':12);
            FOR I := 1 TO COUNT DO
                  WITH CUSTOMER[I] DO
                        WRITELN (NAME:20, JOB :20, TIME:10:2, COST:10:2)

      END.   (* ODD_JOBS *)
```

Running . . .
```
DO YOU WANT TO ENTER A JOB?
IF YES, TYPE IN Y AND HIT RETURN KEY.
IF NO, TYPE JUST HIT RETURN KEY.
Y
ENTER CUSTOMER'S NAME: ALBERTSON
ENTER THE JOB: RAKE
ENTER THE TIME SPENT ON THE JOB:    2.50
DO YOU WANT TO ENTER A JOB?
IF YES, TYPE IN Y AND HIT RETURN KEY
IF NO, JUST HIT RETURN KEY
Y
ENTER CUSTOMER'S NAME: JACKMAN
ENTER THE JOB: BABYSIT
ENTER THE TIME SPENT ON THE JOB:    4.00
DO YOU WANT TO ENTER A JOB?
IF YES, TYPE IN Y AND HIT RETURN KEY
IF NO, JUST HIT RETURN KEY
Y
ENTER CUSTOMER'S NAME: HALL
ENTER THE JOB: MOW
ENTER THE TIME SPENT ON THE JOB:    3.75
DO YOU WANT TO ENTER A JOB?
IF YES, TYPE IN Y AND HIT RETURN KEY
IF NO, JUST HIT RETURN KEY
                        NAME                 JOB      TIME   AMOUNT DUE
                   ALBERTSON                RAKE      2.50        7.50
                     JACKMAN             BABYSIT      4.00        8.00
                        HALL                 MOW      3.75       13.12
```

Figure 12-7   PROGRAM ODD_JOBS (continued)

a. Declare an array of type GOLFERS that can hold up to six records.

b. Write a loop to read six names and assign the names to the NAME field of each of the records in the array declared above. Be sure to write a prompt to tell the user when the name should be entered.

Answers:

```
1. A record is a group of related data items, not necessarily of the same data type, that are gathered together as a single
   unit.

2. PLAYER = RECORD
            NAME : STRING;
            AGE : INTEGER;
            BAT_AVE : REAL;
            POS : STRING
            END;   (* PLAYER *)

3. a. VAR
      GOLFERS : ARRAY[1..6] OF PLAYER;

   b. FOR I := 1 TO 6 DO
      WITH GOLFERS DO
      BEGIN
      WRITELN ('ENTER GOLFER''S NAME');
      READLN (NAME[I])
      END
```

SETS

Pascal is the first general-purpose programming language to include the set as a structured data type. A set is a collection of items that are classed together. Sets can be very useful in writing Pascal programs.

Declaring Sets

In mathematics a set containing the integers 1 through 7 would be written this way:

$$\{1, 2, 3, 4, 5, 6, 7\}$$

In Pascal, a SET is declared under the TYPE declarations:

```
TYPE
    SMALLNUM : SET OF 1..7;
```

A variable may then be declared of type SMALLNUM:

```
VAR
    LITTLE : SMALLNUM;
```

LITTLE is now a set containing any of the integers between 1 and 7. Here are a few examples of how the set LITTLE might look:

[2, 6, 7]
[5, 3, 1] (Set elements do not have to be in order.)
[ ]

The last example above is called the empty set. It is useful when a set needs to be initialized to nothing. The following would *not* be sets of LITTLE:

[1, 8] (No number may be larger than seven)
[−2, 3, 6] (No number may be smaller than one)

The elements of a set must all be of the same base type. In the set LITTLE above, the values are all of data type INTEGER. The base type of a set may be any scalar data type.

Assigning Values to Sets

Values may be assigned to a set by using the assignment operator (:=) :

```
LITTLE := [1, 3, 4];
LITTLE := [6];
LITTLE := [ ];
```

All of the values to be assigned to a set must be separated by commas and enclosed in brackets.

Set Operators

Three operators can be used with a set. They are:

- union (+)
- intersection (*)
- difference (−)

Each will be discussed individually.

Union

The plus sign (+) is the operator that indicates the union of two sets. The union of two sets is a set of all of the elements that are in either or both of the sets. Here are a few examples:

['A', 'B', 'Z'] + ['A', 'D', 'M'] results in ['A', 'B', 'D', 'M', 'Z']
[2, 4, 12] + [6, 4, 8, 10, 12] results in [2, 4, 6, 8, 10, 12]

Intersection

The intersection of two sets consists of a set containing only those values that are in both sets. The asterisk (*) is the operator for set intersection. Below are several examples of set intersection:

243

['A', 'B', 'Z'] * ['A', 'D', 'M'] results in ['A']
[2, 4, 12] * [6, 4, 8, 10, 12] results in [4, 12]

Difference

The difference between two sets consists of all of the values that are in the first set, but not the second. The minus sign (−) is used to represent set difference. These two examples would have the following results:

['A', 'B', 'Z'] − ['A', 'B', 'M'] results in ['Z']
[2, 4, 1] − [6, 4, 8, 10, 12] results in [2, 1]

Notice that in determining the difference between two sets, the order of the sets (but not the order of the set elements) affects the results. If the order of the first example above was changed, the result would be different.

['A', 'B', 'M'] − ['A', 'B', 'C'] results in ['M']

In set union and intersection, the order of the sets does not make a difference. The table in Figure 12-8 gives some more examples of using set operators.

Using Relational Operators with Sets

The following relational operators can be used with sets:

=	(equal to)
>=	(greater than or equal to)
<=	(less than or equal to)
<>	(not equal to)

Given these two assignment statements:

```
VALUE1 := [2, 4, 8, 16, 32];
VALUE2 := [8, 32];
```

EXPRESSION	RESULTS
[2, 3, 8] + [1,3]	[1, 2, 3, 8]
[2, 3, 8] * [1, 3]	[3]
[2, 3, 8] − [1, 3]	[2, 8]
['A', 'D'] − ['C']	['A', 'D']
['B', 'E', 'F'] + ['D']	['B', 'E', 'F', 'D']

Figure 12-8 EXAMPLES OF SET OPERATORS

the following expressions would evaluate as true:

```
VALUE1 >= VALUE2
VALUE1 <> [2, 4, 8, 16, 40]
VALUE2 <= [8, 12, 32]
[ ]     <= VALUE1
```

More examples of how relational operators are used with sets appear in Figure 12-9.

Program ACTIVITIES

Sets are useful when a program needs to determine whether or not a given item is present. For example, program ACTIVITIES (Figure 12-10) reads an individual's name and three of that person's hobbies. The hobbies are entered by using an integer code. This list of hobbies is placed in a set. It is then easy to determine whether or not a person is interested in a given hobby. In the program this expression:

```
IF HOBBIES >= [1, 4] THEN
```

checks to see which people are interested in basketball and tennis. Only those people who list both basketball and tennis as hobbies will have their names printed. The expression:

```
IF HOBBIES * [7] <> [7] THEN
```

will evaluate as true only if jogging is not listed as a hobby. It would be easy to add more statements to this program to check for other hobbies. This is an example of a good use for a set in a program.

Sets allow the programmer to declare a set of related data items under one variable name. This saves the programmer time in separately declaring the data items. Also, a value can be compared to the entire set with only one statement. By contrast, *n* separately declared data items would require *n* comparisons. Sets can help the programmer create more readable, compact programs.

EXPRESSION	EVALUATES AS
[7, 3, 4] = [4, 3, 7]	TRUE
[1, 2, 4] >= [1,4]	TRUE
['D', 'F', 'H'] <= ['D', 'H']	FALSE
['A', 'G', 'I', 'M'] >= ['I']	TRUE

Figure 12-9 EXAMPLES OF SET RELATIONAL OPERATORS

```
PROGRAM ACTIVITIES;
(* THIS PROGRAM READS 10 INDIVIDUAL'S NAMES AND A LIST OF EACH
PERSON'S HOBBIES.  EACH PERSON SHOULD PICK THEIR THREE FAVORITE
HOBBIES FROM THE 8 LISTED BELOW.  THE HOBBIES ARE ENTERED USING
THE CORRESPONDING CODE NUMBER:
   1.   BASKETBALL
   2.   RACKETBALL
   3.   READING
   4.   TENNIS
   5.   BASEBALL
   6.   FOOTBALL
   7.   JOGGING
   8.   SEWING
AFTER ALL OF THE DATA ARE ENTERED, THE NAMES OF PEOPLE WHO ENJOY
BASKETBALL AND TENNIS ARE PRINTED TO THE MONITOR.  ALSO
PRINTED ARE THE NAMES OF THE PEOPLE WHO DID NOT PICK JOGGING *)

TYPE
   ACTIVITY = SET OF 1..8;

   PERSON = RECORD
     NAME     : STRING[20];
     HOBBIES : ACTIVITY
   END;   (* PERSON *)


VAR
   PEOPLE : ARRAY[1..10] OF PERSON;
   I : INTEGER;
   A, B, C : INTEGER;

BEGIN

   (* ENTER THE DATA ON THE 10 PEOPLE *)
   FOR I := 1 TO 10 DO
      BEGIN
         WITH PEOPLE[I] DO
            BEGIN
               WRITE ('ENTER NAME: ');
               READLN (NAME);
               WRITE ('ENTER HOBBIES USING INTEGER CODE: ');
               READLN ( A, B, C);
               HOBBIES := [A, B, C];
            END   (* WITH *)
      END;   (* FOR *)


   WRITELN;

   (* PRINT THE NAMES OF PEOPLE WHO ENJOY BASKETBALL AND TENNIS *)
   WRITELN ('THE FOLLOWING PEOPLE ENJOY BASKETBALL AND TENNIS:');

   FOR I := 1 TO 10 DO
      WITH PEOPLE[I] DO
      IF HOBBIES >= [1, 4] THEN
         WRITELN (NAME);

   (* PRINT THE NAMES OF THE PEOPLE WHO DID NOT PICK JOGGING *)
   WRITELN;
   WRITELN ('THE FOLLOWING PEOPLE DID NOT PICK JOGGING:');
   FOR I := 1 TO 10 DO
      WITH PEOPLE[I] DO
      IF HOBBIES * [7] <> [7] THEN
         WRITELN (NAME)

END.   (* ACTIVITIES *)
```

Figure 12-10 PROGRAM ACTIVITIES

(continued next page)

```
Running . . .
ENTER NAME: JACKSON
ENTER HOBBIES USING INTEGER CODE:   2 4 5
ENTER NAME: SCHWARTZ
ENTER HOBBIES USING INTEGER CODE:   1 4 7
ENTER NAME: FORSE
ENTER HOBBIES USING INTEGER CODE:   2 7 3
ENTER NAME: LING
ENTER HOBBIES USING INTEGER CODE:   2 5 6
ENTER NAME: PATTERSON
ENTER HOBBIES USING INTEGER CODE:   6 1 4
ENTER NAME: FRIEDRICK
ENTER HOBBIES USING INTEGER CODE:   1 3 6
ENTER NAME: HALL
ENTER HOBBIES USING INTEGER CODE:   2 5 6
ENTER NAME: TRIGGER
ENTER HOBBIES USING INTEGER CODE:   4 5 7
ENTER NAME: SAMPSON
ENTER HOBBIES USING INTEGER CODE:   3 4 5
ENTER NAME: APPLEBAUM
ENTER HOBBIES USING INTEGER CODE:   3 6 5

THE FOLLOWING PEOPLE ENJOY BASKETBALL AND TENNIS:
SCHWARTZ
PATTERSON

THE FOLLOWING PEOPLE DID NOT PICK JOGGING:
JACKSON
LING
PATTERSON
FRIEDRICK
HALL
SAMPSON
APPLEBAUM
```

Figure 12-10 PROGRAM ACTIVITIES (continued)

LEARNING CHECK 12-2

1. What is a set?
2. What are the three operations that may be performed on sets? Explain what each operation does.
3. Answer the questions below using the following TYPE declarations:

```
TYPE
    DAYS = SET OF 1..7;
    WHOLE = SET OF 1..20;
```

a. Declare a variable WEEKDAYS to be of type DAYS. Assign the values 1, 2, 3, 4, and 5 to variable WEEKDAYS.
b. Declare a variable ODD of type WHOLE and assign all of the odd values that are contained in set WHOLE to this variable.
c. Declare a variable MULTTWO of type WHOLE. Assign to it all the multiples of 2 up to 20 (2, 4, 6, . . .)

1. A set is a structured data type consisting of a collection of values that are classed together. All of these values must be of the same base type. 2. The operations are: a. Union (+): results in a set containing all of the elements that are in one or both of the sets. b. Intersection (*): results in a set containing those values which are in both sets. c. Difference (−): results in a set consisting of all the values that are in the first set but not the second.

3. a. VAR
     WEEKDAYS : DAYS;
   WEEKDAYS := [1, 2, 3, 4, 5];

   b. VAR
     ODD : WHOLE;
   ODD := [1, 3, 5, 7, 9, 11, 13, 15, 17, 19];

   c. VAR
     MULTTWO : WHOLE;
   MULTTWO := [2, 4, 6, 8, 10, 12, 14, 16, 18, 20];

SUMMARY POINTS

- This chapter has discussed two structured data types: records and sets. A record is a group of related data items that are gathered together as a single unit. These items do not have to be of the same data type. Records are very useful in business, where a number of facts need to be kept together. An example would be a record containing information about a student in a school. The record could contain a variety of information about the student. Each item is contained in a field of the record. Records can have any number of fields. Records are often placed in arrays. An array can contain a large number of records.

- A set is a collection of items that are classed together. All of the values in a set must be of the same base type. Three set operators may be used in Pascal:

  union
  intersection
  difference

  The following relational operators may be used with sets:

  =
  > =
  < =
  <>

  Records and sets can both be useful in handling data in Pascal programs.

VOCABULARY LIST

Field   A data item that is part of a record.

Record   A structured data type that contains a group of related data items, not necessarily of the same data type, that are gathered together in a single unit.

Set   A structured data type consisting of a collection of values that are classed together. All of the values must be of the same base type.

Structured data type   A data type that can store many individual values that may then be referred to as a single unit. Each structured data type has strict rules concerning how it is to be declared and used in programs. The structured data types in Pascal are arrays, records, sets, and files.

CHAPTER TEST

VOCABULARY

Match each term from the numbered column with the best description from the lettered column.

1. Set

2. Structured data type

3. Record
4. Field

5. Scalar data type

a. A data type where all of the values of that data type may be listed.

b. A structured data type that contains a group of related data items, not necessarily of the same data type, that are gathered together in a single unit.

c. A data item that is part of a record.

d. A structured data type consisting of a collection of values that are classed together. All of the values must be of the same base type.

e. A data type that can store many individual values that may then be referred to as a single unit.

QUESTIONS

1. What are the two ways of referring to an individual field in a record? Give an example of each.

2. Use the following program segment to write the code requested below.

```
TYPE
    AUTO = RECORD
    MAKE : STRING;
    YEAR : INTEGER;
    COLOR : STRING
END;

VAR
    CAR : AUTO;
    CLUNKER : AUTO;
```

a. Use the WITH statement to assign these values to the following fields of record CAR:

```
MAKE = CHEVROLET
YEAR = 1982
COLOR = BLUE
```

b. Assign the values listed above to record CAR using this format:

record_name.field

c. Copy record CAR into record CLUNKER.

3. Given the following program segment, answer the questions below.

```
TYPE
    ALPHA = SET OF 'A'..'Z';

VAR
    VOWELS  : ALPHA;
    SMALPHA : ALPHA;

BEGIN
    VOWELS := ['A', 'E', 'I', 'O', 'U'];
    SMALPHA := ['A', 'B', 'C', 'D', 'E'];
```

a. What is the value of COMBINE?

```
COMBINE := VOWELS + ['Y', 'W'];
```

b. What is the value of TOG?

```
TOG := VOWELS * SMALPHA;
```

c. What is the value of DIFF?

```
DIFF := ['B', 'C', 'F', 'G'] - SMALPHA;
```

d. What is the value of FINAL?

```
FINAL := ['B', 'C', 'F', 'G'] * SMALPHA;
```

4. Look at the program segment below. Determine if the expressions that follow evaluate as TRUE or FALSE.

```
TYPE
    NUM = SET OF 1..20;
VAR
    POINTS1 : NUM;
    POINTS2 : NUM;

BEGIN
    POINTS1 := [2, 4, 10, 18];
    POINTS2 := [4, 8, 11, 20];
```

a. POINTS1 >= POINTS2;

b. [ ] <= POINTS1;

c. POINTS2 >= [4, 8, 11, 19, 20];

d. POINTS2 <> [4, 8, 11, 19, 20];

e. [4, 10, 18] >= POINTS1;

PROGRAMMING PROBLEMS

1. Survey your class to see which of the following toppings people like on their hamburgers. Have each student pick their three favorite toppings. Use the following list:

> cheese —1
> catsup —2
> mustard —3
> onions —4
> pickles —5
> tomatoes—6
> lettuce —7
> bananas —8

Use a set to hold the code numbers of the toppings. Enter each student's name and the set of toppings to a record. After all the data are entered, print the following headings along with the names of the students who fit into each category:

a. THE FOLLOWING STUDENTS DIDN'T CHOOSE CATSUP AS A FAVORITE TOPPING:

b. THE FOLLOWING STUDENTS LIKE ONIONS AND TOMATOES:

c. THE FOLLOWING STUDENTS CHOSE CHEESE AS ONE OF THEIR FAVORITE TOPPINGS:

2. Write a program that will print a list of the students who are eligible for driver's education. In order to be eligible for driver's education at City High a student must be at least 15 years old and have at least a 2.5 grade point average. Each student's record looks like this:

```
STUD_REC = RECORD
    NAME : STRING[20];
    AGE : INTEGER;
    GPA : REAL
END;
```

Use the following data to test this program:

NAME	AGE	GPA
MORRISON, SAM	17	2.0
JEFFERSON, JANE	15	3.6
ADAMS, SARAH	14	3.2
ROSS, BETSY	16	3.0
PAINE, TOM	15	2.5

3. Mrs. Walsh needs a program to calculate the average score on two physics tests. An array of records should be used to hold the information. Each student's record should hold the following information:

NAME   (student's name)
TEST1   (score on the first test)
TEST2   (score on the second test)
AVE   (student's average on the two tests)
DIFF   (student's difference from the class average)

The first three items will be entered at the keyboard. The student's average can then be figured at this point. After all the records have been entered, the class average can then be calculated. The program should then go back to the beginning of the array and calculate the difference between each student's average and the class average. The output should be similar to that below:

NAME	TEST1	TEST2	AVERAGE	DIFFERENCE FROM THE CLASS AVERAGE
MORRIS	77.0	83.0	80.0	3.5
STEPHENS	72.0	70.0	71.0	-5.5

The class size will not be greater than 20. You may write your own input to test this program.

4. Charlie's Used Cars would like a program to print a table that contains all the cars they currently have for sale. The program should use an array of records. There will never be more than 40 cars for sale at one time. Each record should contain the following information:

```
MAKE
YEAR
CONDITION (EXCELLENT, GOOD, FAIR, POOR)
COST
TOT_COST
```

TOT_COST includes the sales tax which is 6 percent. After all the data are entered and the TOT_COST is calculated for each car, print the information in table form. Make up your own data to test the program.

CHAPTER 13

Sorting and Searching Algorithms

CHAPTER OUTLINE

LEARNING OBJECTIVES

INTRODUCTION

RECURSION
    Recursive Definitions • Function FACTORIAL • The Towers-of-Hanoi
    Problem

SORTING ALGORITHMS
    Bubble Sort • Insertion Sort • Quicksort

LEARNING CHECK 13-1

Merge Sort • Efficiency of Sorting Techniques

LEARNING CHECK 13-2

SEARCHING ALGORITHMS
    Sequential Search • Binary Search

LEARNING CHECK 13-3

Efficiency of Sequential and Binary Searches • Hash-Coded Search   **253**

LEARNING CHECK 13-4

SUMMARY POINTS

VOCABULARY LIST

CHAPTER TEST
Vocabulary • Questions

PROGRAMMING PROBLEMS

LEARNING OBJECTIVES

After studying this chapter, you should be able to:

1. Explain how recursive algorithms work.
2. Use recursion when writing programs.
3. Explain what sorting means.
4. Explain how the insertion, bubble, quick-, and merge sorts work.
5. Use these sorts when writing programs.
6. Compare the efficiency of the bubble sort, insertion sort, and quicksort.
7. Explain what searching means.
8. Explain how the sequential, binary, and hash-coded searches work.
9. Use sequential and binary searches in programs.
10. Discuss the relative efficiency of the sequential and binary searches.

ADVANCED PLACEMENT CHAPTER HIGHLIGHTS

The following topics from the Advanced Placement Computer Science Exam are covered in this chapter:

algorithms
   recursive algorithms
   sequential search
   binary search
   hash-coded search
   linear versus logarithmic searching times
   insertion sort
   bubble sort
   merge sort
   quicksort
   quadratic versus $N * \log(N)$ sorting times

INTRODUCTION

SORTING AND
SEARCHING
ALGORITHMS

This chapter will cover two tasks often performed by computers: **sorting** and **searching**. Sorting refers to the process of putting a list of items in a particular order, such as arranging a list of names alphabetically. Searching means to locate a given item in a list of items. For example, it might be necessary to search an array of employee records to locate the record containing a specific Social Security number.

Sorting and searching are both tasks that are well suited to computers. Computers can do these jobs quickly and accurately. Many algorithms have been developed for sorting and searching. Searching and sorting algorithms often use recursion to simplify their tasks. This chapter will cover some of the most frequently used searching and sorting algorithms. Also, there will be a comparison of the efficiency of these algorithms.

RECURSION

Recursive functions and procedures are often used to search and sort. **Recursion** occurs when a function or procedure calls itself. It can be used to simplify many programming problems. This section will introduce recursion and two simple recursive algorithms. Several of the searching and sorting algorithms described in this chapter use recursion to simplify their tasks.

Recursive Definitions

Recursive definitions are often used in mathematics. They allow recursive algorithms to be described in only a few statements. The recursive definition is the process of defining sets and proofs inductively. For example, the inductive (or recursive) definition of sets has three clauses:

1. Base clause: enumerates various items within the set.
2. Inductive or recursive clause: specifies that if some entity X satisfies the definition, then so does some entity Y if and only if entity Y is related to entity X in some specified way.
3. Closure clause: specifies that nothing satisfies the definition except on the basis of clauses 1 and 2.

In most cases, the base and recursive clauses can completely describe a recursive algorithm.

Function FACTORIAL

Recursion is used in problem solving to reduce a problem to a new problem that is simpler than the original one. In this example, the factorial (written N!) of a nonnegative integer is computed. The inductive definition is:

1. Base clause: if N is zero, the factorial is one.
2. Recursive clause: for $N \geq 1$, $N! = N[(N - 1)!]$ is true.
3. Closure clause: nothing else.

The recursive clause reduces the problem to finding the factorial of the next smaller number and multiplying this value by N. The given inductive definition is illustrated with the following statements, where FACT is used as an abbreviation for "factorial."

```
FACT (0) = 1
FACT (1) = 1                        = 1 * FACT (0)
FACT (2) = 2 * 1                    = 2 * FACT (1)
FACT (3) = 3 * 2 * 1                = 3 * FACT (2)
FACT (4) = 4 * 3 * 2 * 1            = 4 * FACT (3)
FACT (5) = 5 * 4 * 3 * 2 * 1        = 5 * FACT (4)
```

A recursive factorial function would look like this:

```
FUNCTION FACT (NUMBER : INTEGER) : INTEGER;
    BEGIN
        IF NUMBER = 0 THEN
            FACT := 1
        ELSE
            FACT := NUMBER * FACT (NUMBER - 1)
    END;
```

The identifier FACT occurs in two places in the statement

```
FACT := NUMBER * FACT (NUMBER - 1)
```

and each occurrence has a distinct role. When FACT appears on the left-hand side of the assignment operator it stores the result returned by the function in a memory location. When FACT appears on the right-hand of an assignment operator it causes a recursive call to the FACT function. Function FACT is called recursively until the trivial case of NUMBER equals zero is reached.

The diagram in Figure 13-1 shows how the recursive calls will calculate 5!. After the last recursive call, the function returns a value to the previous recursive call. This returned value is computed by multiplying the result from the previous level and the value of the parameter, NUMBER at the current level. Each returned value is indicated with an upward arrow.

The Towers-of-Hanoi Problem

Recursion can be used to solve a variety of problems. One example is the Towers-of-Hanoi problem. Figure 13-2 shows three posts, labeled

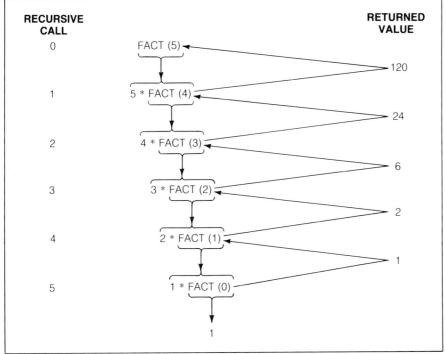

Figure 13-1   A RECURSIVE FUNCTION

1, 2, and 3. The goal of the problem is to move the three disks from post
1 to post 3 following these two rules:

1. Only one disk may be moved at a time.
2. A larger disk may never rest on a smaller disk.

The recursive solution is:

1. Move the top two disks from post 1 to post 2.
2. Move the bottom disk to post 3.
3. Move the top two disks from post 2 to post 3.

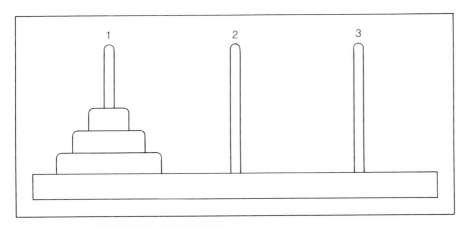

Figure 13-2   TOWERS-OF-HANOI

The problem is reduced from one involving three disks to two simpler problems involving two disks, and a problem involving one disk. This series of steps is repeated until the problem is solved.

In Figure 13-3, Program HANOI is presented to solve the Towers-of-Hanoi problem. Note that when N is zero the trivial problem of moving zero disks is realized and no recursive calls are required. When N is not zero, MOVE is called recursively to move NUMBER − 1 disks from the original source post to the original temporary post. The original destination post serves as the temporary post for this move. Next, instructions are printed to move one disk, whose number is the current value of NUMBER, from the source post to the destination post. Finally, MOVE is recursively called again to move NUMBER − 1 disks from the original temporary post to the original destination post. The original source post serves as the temporary post for this move.

Recursion is not always the most efficient way to solve a problem. For each recursive call of a function or procedure, a separate memory area must be set aside to hold the values of parameters and local variables. A more recent recursive call must not change the contents of any memory locations that an old recursive call is using. Thus the implementation of a recursive algorithm uses a large amount of memory space. Also, for each recursive call the compiler must use a certain amount of time passing parameters to the function or procedure, establishing a new memory area for it, and returning its result after it has finished executing.

Recursion is a powerful tool for solving problems. Some problems are more suitable for solution by recursion than others. Searching and sorting lists are problems well suited to solutions by recursion. Note in the following sections of this chapter how recursion can significantly reduce the size of searching and sorting algorithms.

SORTING ALGORITHMS

This chapter will discuss four sorting techniques: the bubble sort, the insertion sort, the quicksort, and the merge sort. Although the difference in the degree of efficiency among these sorts is quite large, the sorts are presented together here to show that there are many approaches to the solution of the problem of sorting. Many other sorting routines exist, but these examples represent fundamental and distinct sorting algorithms that may be combined or used in part to develop other sorting routines.

Bubble Sort

Bubble sorts are easily understood and written but have the disadvantage of requiring a great deal of computer time. When a small amount of data are to be sorted, added computer time is not critical. However,

```
PROGRAM HANOI;
(* THIS PROGRAM SOLVES THE TOWERS OF HANOI PROBLEM.  THE USER IS ASKED TO
INPUT THE NUMBER OF DISKS TO BE MOVED FROM POST 1 TO POST 3.  MOVES OF
THE DISKS ARE SUBJECT TO THE FOLLOWING RESTRICTIONS:
     1) ONLY ONE DISK CAN BE MOVED AT A TIME.
     2) A LARGER DISK CAN NEVER BE PLACED ON A SMALLER DISK.
EACH TIME A MOVE IS MADE, THE DISK NUMBER, THE SOURCE OF THE DISK, AND
THE DESTINATION OF THE DISK IS PRINTED TO THE MONITOR.                 *)

VAR
   N : INTEGER;

(*****************************************************************)

PROCEDURE MOVE (NUMBER : INTEGER; SOURCE, DEST, TEMP : CHAR);
(* THIS PROCEDURE MOVES THE SPECIFIED NUMBER OF DISKS FROM THE SOURCE
POST TO THE DESTINATION POST WITH THE AID OF THE TEMPORARY POST. *)

BEGIN   (* MOVE *)

   IF NUMBER > 0 THEN
      BEGIN
         MOVE (NUMBER - 1, SOURCE, TEMP, DEST);
         WRITELN ('MOVE DISK ', NUMBER, ' FROM POST ', SOURCE, ' TO POST ',
         DEST);
         MOVE (NUMBER - 1, TEMP, DEST, SOURCE)
      END   (* IF *)

END;   (* MOVE *)

(*****************************************************************)

BEGIN   (* HANOI *)

   (* ENTER NUMBER OF DISKS *)
   WRITE ('HOW MANY DISKS? ');
   READLN (N);
   WRITELN;
   MOVE (N, '1', '2', '3')

END.   (* HANOI *)
```

Running . . .

```
HOW MANY DISKS? 4

MOVE DISK 1 FROM POST 1 TO POST 3
MOVE DISK 2 FROM POST 1 TO POST 2
MOVE DISK 1 FROM POST 3 TO POST 2
MOVE DISK 3 FROM POST 1 TO POST 3
MOVE DISK 1 FROM POST 2 TO POST 1
MOVE DISK 2 FROM POST 2 TO POST 3
MOVE DISK 1 FROM POST 1 TO POST 3
MOVE DISK 4 FROM POST 1 TO POST 2
MOVE DISK 1 FROM POST 3 TO POST 2
MOVE DISK 2 FROM POST 3 TO POST 1
MOVE DISK 1 FROM POST 2 TO POST 1
MOVE DISK 3 FROM POST 3 TO POST 2
MOVE DISK 1 FROM POST 1 TO POST 3
MOVE DISK 2 FROM POST 1 TO POST 2
MOVE DISK 1 FROM POST 3 TO POST 2
```

Figure 13-3   PROGRAM HANOI

when dealing with large amounts of data, the cost of CPU time for the bubble sort will be high.

When arranging a list in ascending order, the bubble sort works by "bubbling" the smallest items to the top of a list. The values of adjacent array elements are compared and switched if the value of the first element is larger than the value of the second. Then the next pair of adjacent elements is compared and switched if necessary. This process continues to the end of the array. This sequence of comparisons (called a pass) is repeated, from the beginning of the array, until an entire pass is made without any elements being switched. This condition signifies a sorted array.

To illustrate the above procedure, an integer array consisting of five elements is sorted as shown in Figure 13-4. Column 1 shows how the array looks before sorting begins and the subsequent columns represent all of the exchanges that are made during each pass. During execution of the first pass, the smaller numbers are "bubbled" upward while the largest number moves to the bottom of the list. The remaining passes also move the smaller numbers upward while positioning the larger numbers toward the bottom. The array is actually sorted by the end of pass 3, but one more pass is made to make certain all of the elements are in order.

The program in Figure 13-5 shows how the bubble sort algorithm can be used to sort a list of names. Notice that after pass 1, the largest value is in its correct position. Therefore, it is only necessary to examine the elements with indices less than NUMPASS + 1 during the next pass. In addition, observe that the BOOLEAN variable EXCH determines whether the loop will be repeated. If exchanges are made, the REPEAT/ UNTIL loop is reentered. However, if no exchanges are made in the last FOR loop execution, EXCH is false and the sort is completed.

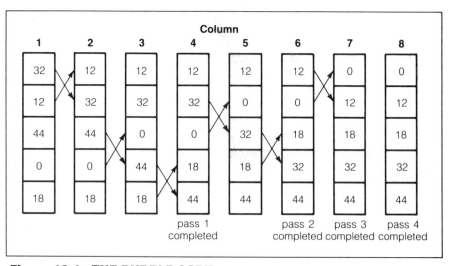

Figure 13-4 **THE BUBBLE SORT**

```
PROGRAM SORT_NAMES;
(* THIS PROGRAM USES A BUBBLE SORT TO SORT A LIST OF 10 NAMES IN ALPHABETICAL
ORDER *)

CONST
   NUM = 10;

TYPE
   PERSON = ARRAY[1..NUM] OF STRING;

VAR
   NAME : PERSON;
   EXCH : BOOLEAN;
   I    : INTEGER;

(******************************************************************************)

PROCEDURE SORT (VAR SORT_NAME : PERSON);

VAR
   J, NUMPASS : INTEGER;
   TEMP : STRING;

BEGIN    (* SORT *)

   (* SORT UNTIL NO MORE CHANGES NEED TO BE MADE *)
   REPEAT
      EXCH := FALSE;
      NUMPASS := NUM - 1;

      FOR J := 1 TO NUMPASS DO
         BEGIN
            (* IF FIRST NAME SHOULD COME AFTER SECOND NAME, SWITCH THEM *)
            IF NAME[J] > NAME[J+1] THEN
               BEGIN
                  TEMP := NAME[J];
                  NAME[J] := NAME[J+1];
                  NAME[J+1] := TEMP;
                  EXCH := TRUE
               END    (* IF *)
         END;    (* FOR *)

         NUMPASS := NUMPASS - 1
      UNTIL EXCH = FALSE

END;    (* SORT *)

(******************************************************************************)

BEGIN    (* SORT_NAMES *)

   (* ENTER 10 NAMES TO BE SORTED *)
   WRITELN ('ENTER ', NUM, ' NAMES, EACH ON A SEPARATE LINE: ');
   FOR I := 1 TO NUM DO
      READLN (NAME[I]);

   (* CALL PROCEDURE SORT TO SORT THE NAMES ALPHABETICALLY *)
   SORT (NAME);

   (* PRINT SORTED LIST TO THE MONITOR *)
   WRITELN ;
   WRITELN ('SORTED LIST OF NAMES');
   WRITELN('_____.            );

   FOR I := 1 TO NUM DO
      WRITELN (NAME[I]:15)

END.    (* SORT_NAMES *)
```

Figure 13-5 PROGRAM SORT_NAMES *(continued next page)*

```
Running ...
ENTER 10 NAMES, EACH ON A SEPARATE LINE:
SANCHEZ
MICHAELSON
BAUMANN
LING
DAHL
SANHOLTZ
LUOMA
PATRICKS
AMICON
SZYMANSKI

SORTED LIST OF NAMES
_____
        AMICON
       BAUMANN
         DAHL
         LING
        LUOMA
     MICHAELSON
      PATRICKS
       SANCHEZ
      SANHOLTZ
     SZYMANSKI
```

Figure 13-5   PROGRAM SORT_NAMES (continued)

Insertion Sort

The insertion sort is similar to the bubble sort. The insertion sort uses a loop to go through a list, placing the items in order, one at a time. To illustrate how this works, the following list is used:

$$18 \quad 12 \quad 3 \quad 77 \quad 40 \quad 44$$

The first time only the first element is checked to see if it is in order. Obviously, no change can be made here. The second time through, 12 is compared with 18, and the two will be exchanged since they are out of order. The list now looks like this:

$$12 \quad 18 \quad 3 \quad 77 \quad 40 \quad 44$$

Each time through the loop, another list item is placed in its correct position. Below is shown how the list looks at the end of each loop repetition:

List						Repetition
3	12	18	77	40	44	3
3	12	18	77	40	44	4
3	12	18	40	77	44	5
3	12	18	40	44	77	6

The loop needs to be repeated the same number of times as there are items in the list. Then the list is in order.

Quicksort

Among the fastest sorting routines is the quicksort. Although the quicksort is more complicated than the bubble sort and uses recursion, the idea behind the quicksort is simple.

The first step of the quicksort divides and rearranges the list into sublists so that the values in the first sublist are less than or equal to those values in the second sublist. At this point neither the first half nor the second half of the list is in order. The second step of this sorting process is to consider each of these sublists separately. A sublist may then be considered as a separate list by itself and may be partitioned like the original list. If this process is continued on each separate new list created, shorter and shorter lists are created until there is only one element in each list. At this point the entire original list is in order.

The heart of the quicksort is the partitioning process which was introduced above. The given list is partitioned into two smaller lists which, in turn, are partitioned separately by using a recursive call. The process of partitioning is shown in the following examples.

Assume that the original list looks like this:

2   7   8   17   22   18   29   30   14   3   5   29

After partitioning the list into halves so that the left half contains the smaller numbers and the right half the larger numbers, the list looks like this:

2   7   8   5   3   14   29   30   18   22   17   29

Note that neither half is sorted but the values in the left half are all smaller than those values in the right half. If the partitioning process is repeated on each of these new halves the result will resemble:

2   3   5   8   7   14   17   22   18   30   29   29

The partitioning process still works, even if there are an odd number of elements in a sublist:

2   3   5   7   8   14   17   22   18   29   29   30

One more recursive call and the list is sorted:

2   3   5   7   8   14   17   18   22   29   29   30

This partitioning process should have raised a couple of questions.

How is a list which contains only a single element quicksorted? The answer is that there is no way (and no need) to partition just one element. Hence, a simple check for the length of the list must be made before the partitioning process is started. The second question deals with the major deficiency of the quicksort. How is the median value of a list determined? The answer to this dilemma is that there is no practical solution. For the present, the first element in the sublist shall be used as the median value. This topic will be further discussed later in this chapter.

Figure 13-6 illustrates program QUICKSORT. To further clarify the operation of procedure QSORT, a trace of steps is presented. A small list of numbers is used to make tracing the sort easier.

Original List

```
6   4   2   7   5   1   9
↑                       ↑
LB                      UB
```

LB represents the lower bound and UB represents the upper bound of the list that will be partitioned. The QSORT procedure call in the main program passes the value of LOWER and UPPER to the formal parameters LB and UB. At the start, LB has the value of 1 and UB receives the value of 7, the number of data items to be sorted. In procedure QSORT, the PARTITION procedure is immediately called to partition the original list. L and R are now the formal value parameters which represent LB and UB respectively. FIRST gets the value 6, the assumed value of the median. The right pointer is moved left until an element is found which is smaller than FIRST (assumed median value) or the pointers are at the same position. When R equals 6, a swap is needed.

```
6   4   2   7   5   1   9
↑                   ↑
L                   R

1   4   2   7   5   1   9
↑                   ↑
L                   R
```

Notice that the value 6 is no longer in the list. This value is still stored in the variable FIRST. Next, the left pointer is moved right until an element that is greater than FIRST is found or the positions of the pointers are the same. At L = 4, a swap is needed.

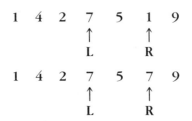

```
1   4   2   7   5   1   9
            ↑       ↑
            L       R

1   4   2   7   5   7   9
            ↑       ↑
            L       R
```

```
PROGRAM QUICKSORT;
(* THIS PROGRAM WILL SORT 20 POSITIVE INTEGERS WHICH ARE INPUT
AT THE KEYBOARD. THE NUMBER OF INTEGERS MUST BE EVENLY DIVISIBLE
BY FIVE TO BE PRINTED FIVE PER LINE BEFORE AND AFTER THE SORT *)

CONST
   LOWER = 1;
   UPPER = 20;

TYPE
   LIST = ARRAY[LOWER..UPPER] OF INTEGER;

VAR
   STR : LIST;
   I   : INTEGER;

(***********************************************************************)

PROCEDURE PRINT (STR : LIST);
(* THIS PROCEDURE PRINTS THE SORTED LIST *)

VAR
  I, J : INTEGER;

BEGIN   (* PRINT *)

   WRITELN;
   I := 0;
   WHILE I < UPPER DO
      BEGIN
        FOR J := LOWER TO (LOWER + 4) DO
           WRITE (STR[I+J]:10);
        WRITELN;
        I := I + 5
      END   (* WHILE *)

END;   (* PRINT *)

(***********************************************************************)

PROCEDURE PARTITION (VAR STR: LIST; L, R : INTEGER; VAR PIVOT: INTEGER);
(* THIS PROCEDURE PARTITIONS THE LIST *)

VAR
   DONE : BOOLEAN;
   FIRST: INTEGER;

BEGIN   (* PARTITION *)

   FIRST := STR[L];
   DONE := FALSE;
   WHILE NOT DONE DO
      BEGIN
           WHILE (R > L) AND (STR[R] >= FIRST) DO
              R := R - 1;   (* MOVE RIGHT POINTER TO THE LEFT *)
           IF R = L THEN   (* POINTERS AT THE SAME PLACE *)
              DONE := TRUE
           ELSE
              BEGIN
                 STR[L] := STR[R];
                 WHILE (L < R) AND (STR[L] <= FIRST) DO
                    L := L + 1;   (* MOVE POINTER RIGHT *)
                 IF L = R THEN (* POINTERS AT THE SAME PLACE *)
                    DONE := TRUE
                 ELSE
                    STR[R] := STR[L];
              END;   (* OUTER ELSE *)
      END;   (* WHILE *)
```

Figure 13-6 PROGRAM QUICKSORT   *(continued next page)*

```
        PIVOT := L;
        STR[PIVOT] := FIRST; (* FINISH SWAP WHEN POINTERS CROSS *)

END; (* PARTITION *)

(*******************************************************************)

PROCEDURE QSORT (VAR STR: LIST; LB, UB : INTEGER);
(* THIS PROCEDURE PERFORMS THE SORTING *)

VAR
    PIVOT : INTEGER;

BEGIN    (* QSORT *)

    IF LB < UB THEN (* MORE THAN 1 ELEMENT IN SUBLIST *)
        BEGIN
            PARTITION (STR, LB, UB, PIVOT);
            QSORT (STR, LB, PIVOT - 1);
            QSORT (STR, PIVOT + 1, UB)
        END

END;    (* QSORT *)

(*******************************************************************)

BEGIN    (* QUICKSORT *)

    WRITELN ('PLEASE ENTER ', UPPER, ' INTEGERS ON THE BELOW LINE');
    FOR I := LOWER TO UPPER DO
        READ (STR[I]);
    WRITELN;
    WRITELN;
    WRITELN ('UNSORTED LIST');
    PRINT (STR);
    QSORT (STR, LOWER, UPPER);
    WRITELN;
    WRITELN;
    WRITELN ('SORTED LIST');
    PRINT (STR)

END.    (* QUICKSORT *)
```

Running . . .

```
PLEASE ENTER 20  INTEGERS ON THE BELOW LINE
   4 50 62 12 18   0 93 24 17 30 35 82 61 47 13 30 48 40 26 21

UNSORTED LIST

            4         50         62         12         18
            0         93         24         17         30
           35         82         61         47         13
           30         48         40         26         21


SORTED LIST

            0          4         12         13         17
           18         21         24         26         30
           30         35         40         47         48
           50         61         62         82         93
```

Figure 13-6 PROGRAM QUICKSORT (continued)

At this point, the value 6 is still not in the list but it is still stored in FIRST. Since DONE equals false and more swaps are needed, the main WHILE loop is reentered. When R equals 5, a swap is needed.

```
1   2   4   7   5   7   9
            ↑   ↑
            L   R

1   4   2   5   5   7   9
            ↑   ↑
            L   R
```

FIRST still contains the value 6. The left pointer is now moved right until the conditions are met. At L equals 5, L is no longer less than R.

```
1   4   2   5   5   7   9
                ↑
                R
                L
```

Since L equals R, DONE is set to true and the main WHILE loop is exited. PIVOT, which is the break point for the two new lists, gets the value of the pointer position where L equals R. This pivot position gets the value of FIRST. Now, the list looks like this:

```
1   4   2   5   6   7   9
                ↑
                L
                R
```

Since procedure PARTITION has been completed, control is returned to QSORT with PIVOT having a value of 5. QSORT now makes two recursive calls

```
QSORT (STR, LB, PIVOT - 1);
QSORT (STR, PIVOT + 1, UB);
```

which are now equivalent to

```
QSORT (STR, 1, 4);
QSORT (STR, 6, 7);
```

This causes the PARTITION procedure to be applied to the two separate parts of the list, which in turn causes other recursive calls to QSORT. PARTITION is applied to smaller and smaller sublists until all the partitions of length one are processed. At this time, the entire array is in order.

1. What is indicated when a bubble sort makes an entire pass without making an exchange?
2. The quicksort recursively _____ each sublist into smaller sublists.
3. What is the "heart" of program QUICKSORT?
4. What is the major deficiency of program QUICKSORT?

Answers:

1. a sorted array   2. partitions   3. the partitioning process   4. the determination of a median value in a sublist

Merge Sort

The purpose of the merge sort is to combine two sorted lists into one larger sorted list. It operates in the following manner. Suppose that there are two sorted integer arrays, array A and array B, that need to be merged into array C.

Originally, the first elements in each array are compared to each other. The smaller integer is placed into array C. Since 1 is smaller than 2, array C looks like this:

C

1				

The integer that was placed into array C is not considered again. Next, the integer 2 in array A is compared to the integer 2 in array B. Since they are of equal value, the B array is chosen to supply the next element of array C. The 2 in array B is no longer considered. Array C now contains:

C

1	2			

Integers 3 and 2 are now compared. Since 2 is less than 3, 2 is moved into array C.

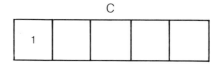

The 2 in array A is no longer considered. Now 3 and 4 are considered, and since 3 is smaller than 4, it is moved into array C.

C

1	2	2	3	

At this point, all of array B has been transferred into array C. The remaining element of array A is now moved to array C.

C

1	2	2	3	4

In this case, only one element remains in array A. However, if array A was larger, many integers may have needed moving.

Figure 13-7 presents procedure MERGE. Notice that arrays A and B are passed as value parameters and array C is a variable parameter. Originally, array C is likely to be empty. As indicated in the traced example above, if two compared integers are equal, the integer from array B is placed in array C. When one array is completely used, the remaining integers in the other array are added to array C. The new sorted array is then passed back to the calling statement.

Efficiency of Sorting Techniques

As previously mentioned, a bubble sort requires a great deal of CPU time. To bubble sort a list of length N, the maximum number of comparisons that are needed is

$$(N - 1) + (N - 2) + (N - 3) + \ldots + 1$$

This expression is derived by considering that for each pass, one data item is placed into its correct position. For instance, if there are 15 data items and the sixth pass was just completed, then there would only be 15 − 6 data items remaining to be sorted.

The above expression reduces to

$$N(N - 1)/2$$

which is

$$N^2/2 - N/2$$

```
PROCEDURE MERGE (A, B : NUMARRAY1; SIZE1, SIZE2 : INTEGER;
                 VAR C : NUMARRAY1);
(* THIS PROCEDURE MERGES TWO SORTED ARRAYS *)

    VAR I, J, K : INTEGER;

    BEGIN

        I := 1;
        J := 1;
        K := 1;

        (* MERGE UNTIL ALL OF ONE FILE IS READ *)
        WHILE (I <= SIZE1) AND (J <= SIZE2) DO
            BEGIN
                IF A[I] < B[J] THEN
                    BEGIN
                        C[K] := A[I];
                        I := I + 1
                    END
                ELSE
                    BEGIN
                        C[K] := B[J];
                        J := J + 1
                    END;

                K := K + 1

            END;   (* WHILE *)

        (* ADD REMAINING ITEMS TO END OF NEW ARRAY *)
        WHILE I <= SIZE1 DO
            BEGIN
                C[K] := A[I];
                I := I + 1;
                K := K + 1
            END;

        WHILE J <= SIZE2 DO
            BEGIN
                C[K] := B[J];
                J := J + 1;
                K := K + 1
            END    (* WHILE *)

    END;   (* MERGE *)
```

Figure 13-7 A MERGE SORT

When N is very large, N/2 is very small in comparison with $N^2/2$. Therefore the expression reduces to

$$N^2/2$$

Hence, the execution time of the bubble sort algorithm varies as N^2, the square of the number of data items. The insertion sort algorithm also varies as N^2.

The major deficiency of the quicksort is the selection of the median. The quicksort is even faster when the selection of the median is near the actual median. The median can be accurately determined, but the large amount of added execution time is not economical.

Which element should be chosen to be the median value? The choice is arbitrary if the values in the list are in random order. However, there are certain advantages in choosing a value near the middle of the list. First, if the list is almost in order, then a value near the middle of a list has a good chance of being close to the median. Secondly, if a list is supposed to be in order and only confirmation is needed, a middle list median choice also has a good chance of being close to the median.

As shown in Figure 13-8, each time quicksort is called, PARTITION divides the list (or sublist) into two parts. How many times can N be divided by two until the result is one?

The result is given by the function

$$\log_2 N$$

To ultimately find the order of the execution time of the quicksort, the generation time of successive lists must be determined. When a sublist is divided into halves, each element in that sublist is examined once by the procedure PARTITION. Each call to procedure PARTITION examines all N elements. Since all N elements are examined for each $\log_2 N$ line, the total number of examinations is $N * \log_2 N$. Hence the execution time of the quicksort algorithm varies $N * \log_2 N$.

In the formal parameter list of procedure MERGESORT in Figure 13-7, arrays A and B are declared as value parameters. If A and B are very long, it may be wise to declare these parameters as variable parameters. This will save the computer some time because it will not have to create a "dummy" copy of these arrays.

The two lists that are merged with the merge sort must be previously sorted. Suppose a file of N items needs to be sorted. A bubble sort

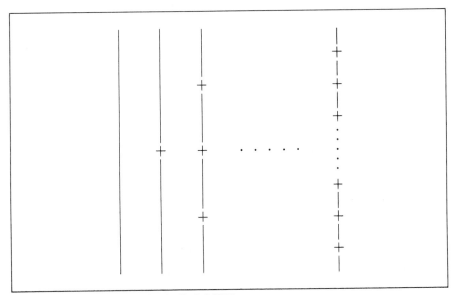

Figure 13-8 PARTITIONING A LIST

may be used on two files, which means N/2 − N/4 comparisons for the bubble sort and N for the merge. The combined total of this operation is $N^2/4 + N/2$ comparisons. By comparing this estimate to the estimate for the bubble sort alone, it may be seen that for a large N, the bubble-merge method is almost twice as fast as the straight bubble sort.

✎ LEARNING CHECK 13-2

1. If two lists are to be merged, which of the following must be true?
   a. The two lists must be the same length.
   b. They must be sorted.
   c. They can have no repeating elements.
   d. The two lists must of a different length.
2. How does the execution time of a bubble sort vary?
3. A merge sort combines two arrays into another array. Does this third array have to be originally empty?
4. Why would it be a bad idea to add an extra routine to QUICKSORT that will accurately determine the actual median of a sublist?

Answers:

1. b 2. N^2 3. no 4. A large amount of execution time will be added to procedure PARTITION.

SEARCHING ALGORITHMS

Computer programs often need to search lists. Sorting and searching are frequently used together in programs. It is much easier to find a given value in a list if that list has already been sorted. Think of how long it would take to find a name in the Chicago phonebook if the names were not listed alphabetically. It would be quite a job, even for a computer. The sorting algorithms covered in the first part of this chapter will come in handy for certain types of searches.

Many different algorithms have been developed for searching. Three of these will be covered here: sequential, binary, and hash-coded searching.

Sequential Search

Probably the simplest search to write is the sequential search. Sequential searching refers to the process of going through a list of items, starting at the beginning, until the desired value is found. People make a sequential search when they look down a list of names one at a time until they find the one they are looking for. The search is performed in the sequence in which the items are listed. Sequential searching is also called linear searching. This is because the searching is carried out in a straight line, one item after the other.

Figure 13-9 shows a procedure called FIND. This procedure searches an array of records until it locates the record in which the field NUMBER equals the value being looked for. The array subscript of this record is then passed back to the main program.

If there is more than one record with the same value in the field ACCOUNTS NUMBER, the first record that matches the value being searched for causes the search to end. If the record with the correct account number is not found, the user will be given an appropriate message. Sequential searches are very easy to use and there is no need

```
PROGRAM SEQUEN;
(* THIS PROGRAM READS THE NAME, ADDRESS, AND ACCOUNT NUMBER OF A LIST
OF COMPANIES.  THEN PROCEDURE FIND IS USED TO SEQUENTIALLY LOCATE THE
NAME AND ADDRESS OF A PARTICULAR COMPANY WHEN THE ACCOUNT NUMBER IS
GIVEN.                                                             *)

TYPE
   ACCREC = RECORD
      NAME : STRING[20];
      ADDRESS : STRING[35];
      NUMBER : INTEGER
   END;  (* RECORD *)

VAR
   SIZE, VALUE, I, LOC : INTEGER;
   FOUND : BOOLEAN;
   ACCOUNTS : ARRAY[1..40] OF ACCREC;

(***************************************************************************)

PROCEDURE FIND ( SIZE, VALUE : INTEGER; VAR FOUND : BOOLEAN;
                 VAR LOC : INTEGER);
(* THIS PROCEDURE DETERMINES AND RETURNS TO THE CALLING PROGRAM THE
SUBSCRIPT OF THE COMPANY WITH THE DESIRED ACCOUNT NUMBER. *)

VAR
   J : INTEGER;

BEGIN   (* FIND *)

   FOUND := FALSE;
   J := 0;

   WHILE (J <= SIZE) AND (NOT FOUND) DO
      BEGIN
         J := J + 1;
         IF ACCOUNTS[J].NUMBER = VALUE THEN
            BEGIN
               FOUND := TRUE;
               LOC := J
            END   (* IF *)

      END   (* WHILE *)

END;   (* FIND *)

(***************************************************************************)
```

Figure 13-9 PROGRAM SEQUEN *(continued next page)*

```
BEGIN    (* SEQUEN *)

   (* DETERMINE HOW MANY COMPANIES ARE TO BE ENTERED *)
   WRITE ('HOW MANY COMPANIES ARE TO BE ENTERED? ');
   READLN (SIZE);

   (* READ INFORMATION FOR EACH COMPANY *)
   FOR I := 1 TO SIZE DO
      BEGIN
         WITH ACCOUNTS[I] DO
            BEGIN
               WRITELN ('ENTER COMPANY NAME:');
               READLN (NAME);
               WRITELN ('ENTER COMPANY''S ADDRESS:');
               READLN (ADDRESS);
               WRITELN ('ENTER ACCOUNT NUMBER:');
               READLN (NUMBER);
            END    (* WITH *)
      END;    (* FOR *)

   (* READ NUMBER OF THE ACCOUNT TO BE LOCATED. *)
   WRITELN;
   WRITE ('ENTER NUMBER OF ACCOUNT TO BE FOUND: ');
   READLN (VALUE);

   (* CALL PROCEDURE FIND TO LOCATE CORRECT COMPANY RECORD *)
   FIND (SIZE, VALUE, FOUND, LOC);
   IF FOUND THEN
      BEGIN
         WRITELN ('THE COMPANY WITH ACCOUNT NUMBER ', ACCOUNTS[LOC].NUMBER);
         WRITELN ('IS: ', ACCOUNTS[LOC].NAME, ' AND THE ADDRESS IS: ');
         WRITELN (ACCOUNTS[LOC].ADDRESS)
      END    (* IF *)
   ELSE
         WRITELN ('ACCOUNT NUMBER ', VALUE, ' WAS NOT LOCATED.');

END.    (* SEQUEN *)
```

Figure 13-9 PROGRAM SEQUEN

(continued next page)

for the list to be in alphabetical order. But they can use up a great deal of CPU time, particularly if large amounts of data are to be searched.

Binary Search

Often the data to be searched are already in order or can be placed in order by sorting. This makes searching the list much easier. For example, a dictionary is arranged in alphabetical order. If it is necessary to look up the word "peristyle," it would be foolish to start at "A" and go through the dictionary sequentially.

If a list of 20 names needs to be searched, it might be efficient to use a sequential search. But this obviously is not appropriate when you are searching for a word in the dictionary. The binary search is one of the most efficient methods of searching a list that is already in order. The binary search uses a method somewhat like one that a person uses in looking up a word in the dictionary. In looking up "peristyle," the searcher would probably open the dictionary to about the middle. If

```
Running...
HOW MANY COMPANIES ARE TO BE ENTERED? 5
ENTER COMPANY NAME:
RON'S TAXIDERMY
ENTER COMPANY'S ADDRESS:
188 EUCLID
ENTER ACCOUNT NUMBER:
145
ENTER COMPANY NAME:
OK WELDING
ENTER COMPANY'S ADDRESS:
1013 HASKINS
ENTER ACCOUNT NUMBER:
102
ENTER COMPANY NAME:
BUTLER JEWELRY
ENTER COMPANY'S ADDRESS:
303 MAIN
ENTER ACCOUNT NUMBER:
47
ENTER COMPANY NAME:
MYLE'S PIZZA
ENTER COMPANY'S ADDRESS:
918 WOOSTER
ENTER ACCOUNT NUMBER:
52
ENTER COMPANY NAME:
PUTT PUTT GOLF
ENTER COMPANY'S ADDRESS:
990 FRONT
ENTER ACCOUNT NUMBER:
80

ENTER NUMBER OF ACCOUNT TO BE FOUND: 47
THE COMPANY WITH ACCOUNT NUMBER 47
IS: BUTLER JEWELRY AND THE ADDRESS IS:
303 MAIN
```

Figure 13-9 PROGRAM SEQUEN (continued)

"peristyle" came after this point, the searcher would skip the number of pages that seemed appropriate. Gradually the search would be narrowed down to the exact page that "peristyle" appeared on.

The binary search works similarly. First, the middle of the list to be searched is found. Then, the program determines if the value to be located is above or below this middle. This half of the list is then divided in half. Then it is determined if the target value is above or below this new middle. This process continues until the exact value being searched for is located. To demonstrate this, a search is made of the following array of characters:

B   D   F   H   I   J   K   N   Q   S   T   Z

The value to be located is H. First the middle is determined by adding the first array subscript to the last subscript and dividing by two:

$$\frac{1 + 12}{2} = 6$$

```
(****************************************************************
 *   THE FOLLOWING ARE TWO VERSIONS OF THE BINARY SEARCH ALGORITHM,
 *   THE FIRST IS NON-RECURSIVE AND THE SECOND IS RECURSIVE.  IN BOTH
 *   CASES, AN ARRAY OF CHARACTERS IS SEARCHED FOR THE VALUE OF 'KEY'.
 *   IF IT IS FOUND, THEN 'FOUND' IS SET TO TRUE AND 'LOC' CONTAINS THE
 *   ARRAY SUBSCRIPT OF 'KEY' IN THE ARRAY.  OTHERWISE 'FOUND'
 *   IS SET TO FALSE AND 'LOC' IS UNDEFINED.                       *)

PROCEDURE BINARY1 (KEY : CHAR; LIST : VALUE; LB, UB : INTEGER;
VAR LOC : INTEGER; VAR FOUND : BOOLEAN);


BEGIN    (* BINARY1 *)

   FOUND := FALSE;

   WHILE (LB <= UB) AND (NOT FOUND) DO
        BEGIN
           LOC := (UB + LB) DIV 2;
           IF LIST [LOC] = KEY THEN
              FOUND := TRUE
           ELSE
              IF LIST[LOC] < KEY THEN
                 LB := LOC + 1
              ELSE
                 UB := LOC - 1
        END    (* WHILE *)

   END;    (* BINARY1 *)

(****************************************************************)

PROCEDURE BINARY2 (KEY : CHAR; LIST : VALUE; LB, UB : INTEGER;
VAR LOC : INTEGER; VAR FOUND : BOOLEAN);

BEGIN    (* BINARY2 *)

   LOC := (LB + UB) DIV 2;

   IF UB < LB THEN
      FOUND := FALSE
   ELSE
      IF LIST[LOC] .= KEY THEN
         FOUND := TRUE
      ELSE
         IF LIST[LOC] < KEY THEN
            BINARY2(KEY, LIST, LOC+1, UB, LOC, FOUND)
         ELSE
            BINARY2 (KEY, LIST, LB, LOC-1, LOC, FOUND)

   END;    (* BINARY2 *)
```

Figure 13-10 TWO PROCEDURES FOR BINARY SEARCHES

Notice that this value would actually be 6.5, but it is truncated to 6. The sixth array element is J. If the value being searched for was J, the search would stop here. Since H is less than J, the lower half of the list will now be divided. The middle is found by the same formula:

$$\frac{1 + 5}{2} = 3$$

The third array element is F, lower than H. Now there are only two elements left:

H, I

The center is now:

$$\frac{4 + 5}{2} = 4$$

The fourth element is H. In three steps the value being searched for has been found. Two procedures for binary searches are shown in Figure 13-10.

Both procedures use the DIV function to locate the center of the list. In procedure BINARY1, if this value is not the target value, the procedure determines if the value is above or below this value and then goes back to the top of the WHILE loop to split the list again. BINARY2 illustrates a recursive implementation of the binary search. Procedure BINARY2 splits the list and continues to call itself until the target value is located.

◤LEARNING CHECK 13-3

1. How does sequential searching work?
2. In a sequential search of this list:

    12   44   103   177   236   582   978   1235

    how many values will be examined before 236 is located?
3. If a binary search was made of the above list, how many values would be examined before 236 was located?
4. Must a list be in order to do a sequential search? Must a list be in order to do a binary search?

Answers:

1. It searches a list from the beginning, one item at a time, until the target value is found.   2. 5   3. 3   4. no; yes

Efficiency of Sequential and Binary Searches

As has been mentioned, sequential searches, particularly of long lists, can use a great deal of CPU time. The worst case for a sequential search would be to examine every value in the list. This would occur if the target value was the last item on the list. If there are N items in a list, the average number of items examined would be N/2. This would occur if the target value was at the middle of the list. In a sequential search, if the length of the list doubles, the search time also doubles. In the binary search, each time through the loop, the list is cut in half. If N is the number of items in the original list, the list decreases in size in the following manner until the target value is found:

$$N/2, N/4, N/8, N/16 \ldots$$

The maximum number of values that need to be examined in a binary search is:

$$\log_2 N$$

Therefore, the average number of searches will be:

$$N/2 * \log_2 N$$

Figure 13-11 compares the average number of comparisons with a binary search and a sequential search. Notice that as the size of the list grows, so does the advantage of using a binary search. This is because the number of comparisons needed in a binary search grows logarithmically while the number of searches needed in a sequential search grows linearly. Although the binary search requires lists to be already sorted, the extra time needed to do the sorting is well spent when you are dealing with large lists.

Hash-Coded Search

Hashing refers to manipulating the **primary key** of a record in such a way as to determine the location of the record itself. The primary key of a record is the record field that uniquely identifies that record. This means that in a given file, two primary keys may not be the same. An example would be a field containing an employee's Social Security number in that employee's record. No two employees would have the same Social Security number. When a primary key is hashed, a mathematical formula called a **hashing algorithm** is applied to the key. This results in a number that can then be used to locate a particular record. Often this number represents an actual physical address on a disk.

Number of Items	Average Number of Items Examined Using Sequential Search	Average Number of Items Examined Using Binary Search
10	5	4
100	50	7
1,000	500	10
1,000,000	500,000	20

Figure 13-11 COMPARISON OF EFFICIENCY OF SEQUENTIAL AND BINARY SEARCHES

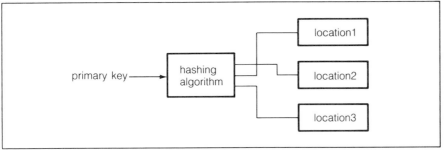

Figure 13-12   HASHING ALGORITHM

There are many different hashing algorithms. A commonly used one is the division method. This method involves dividing the primary key by a prime or an odd number and using the remainder as an address to locate a storage location for the data item. The general form of this statement is:

```
HASH := KEY MOD NUM;
```

This makes hash-coded searching an efficient way of searching large quantities of information. Figure 13-12 shows how the hashing algorithm works.

It is usually not possible to develop a hashing algorithm that will uniquely identify every record in a file. If a hashing algorithm results in the same result for two (or more) primary keys, this is called a **collision**. There are many ways of dealing with collisions. One method is to place the record to be inserted in the next empty spot on the disk. This means that when the record needs to be located later on, the result of the hashing algorithm will not lead directly to the desired record. Once the program reaches the location identified by the hashing algorithm, the list is searched sequentially by primary key. When the record with the correct primary key is located, the search stops.

LEARNING CHECK 13-4

1. If a list has 24 elements, what is the maximum number of searches necessary to locate a value using a sequential search? What is the maximum number of searches using a binary search?
2. What is meant by the term "hashing"?
3. How are hash-coded searches generally used?
4. What formula represents the average number of values that will need to be examined in a sequential search?
5. What formula represents the average number of values that will need to be examined in a binary search?
6. No two records in a file may have the same _____.

SUMMARY POINTS

- Sorting is the process of putting items in a particular order.
- Recursion is used in many searching and sorting algorithms.
- The recursive definition has two major clauses. The first clause describes various items. The second clause states that if some entity X satisfies the definition, then so does some entity Y if the entity Y is related to entity X in some specified way.
- Recursion reduces a problem to a new problem which is similar to the original but smaller in scope.
- Four sorting algorithms were covered in this chapter: the bubble sort, the insertion sort, the quicksort, and the merge sort.
- The quicksort is more efficient than the bubble sort or insertion sort unless the list is very short.
- The merge sort is used to combine or merge two previously sorted lists.
- Searching refers to locating a particular item in a list of items.
- The searching algorithms studied in this chapter were the sequential search, the binary search, and the hash-coded search.
- The sequential search involves going through a list, an item at a time, until the target item is found. In a binary search a list is repeatedly divided in half, depending on whether the target item is above or below the point at which the list has been split.
- Unless a list is very short, the binary search is more efficient than the sequential search, even though a list must be sorted before a binary search can be made.
- A hash-coded search uses a hashing algorithm to manipulate a primary key to determine the location of a record. Hash-coded searches are often used to determine the actual address of a record on a disk.

VOCABULARY LIST

Collision   The situation that occurs when a hashing algorithm results in the same record location for two different primary keys.

Hashing   Applying a mathematical formula to a primary key of a record to obtain a resulting record location.

Hashing algorithm   A mathematical formula applied to the primary key of a record to determine the location of that record.

Primary key   A field in a record that uniquely identifies that record. No two records in a file may have the same primary key.

Recursion   The situation when a procedure or function calls itself.

Search   To locate a particular item in a list of items.

Sort   To arrange a list of items in a particular order, such as to arrange names alphabetically.

CHAPTER TEST

VOCABULARY

Match each term from the numbered column with the best description from the lettered column.

1. Hashing

2. Sort

3. Collision

4. Hashing algorithm

5. Primary key

6. Search

7. Recursion

a. A field in a record that uniquely identifies that record.

b. The situation that occurs when a hashing algorithm results in the same record location for two (or more) primary keys.

c. To attempt to locate a particular item in a list of items.

d. A mathematical formula applied to the primary key of a record to determine the location of the record.

e. To arrange a list of items in a particular order, such as to arrange names alphabetically.

f. Applying a mathematical formula to the primary key of a record in order to locate the record.

g. The situation when a procedure or function calls itself.

QUESTIONS

1. The expression for the maximum number of comparisons that are needed to bubble sort a list of length N is shown below.
   $(N - 1) + (N - 2) + (N - 3) + \ldots + 1$
   How is this expression obtained?
2. A quicksort requires the median value of a list to be chosen. What are the advantages in choosing a value near the middle of the list?
3. When you are using a merge sort, would it be economical to declare two arrays to be merged as variable parameters?
4. In what order does a quicksort divide a list into two sublists?
5. The order of recursive calls to procedure QSORT is

   ```
   QSORT (STR, LB, PIVOT - 1);
   QSORT (STR, PIVOT + 1, UB);
   ```

   If this order was reversed, would the program QUICKSORT still work? Explain.
6. Look at the list of values below:
   14   77   80   99   183   277   300

281

If this list of values was used as input for the binary search procedure BINARY1 (Figure 13-10), what would the value of LOC be at the end of each WHILE loop repetition? Assume that the value being searched for is 183 and that the procedure has been modified to search integer rather than character data.

7. In the example in question 6, how many times would the WHILE loop be executed?

8. What is a collision when you are using a hashing algorithm? Name one way a collision can be dealt with.

PROGRAMMING PROBLEMS

1. Write a program using a bubble sort that will alphabetize the last names of the students in your class. Write it so that the names will be alphabetized in ascending order (A, B, C, . . .). Then change it so that the names are in descending order (Z, Y, X . . .).

2. Change program QUICKSORT so that it uses the middle element in the list as the median if there are an odd number of elements. Otherwise, use the element left of center as the median.

3. Change QUICKSORT so that it uses the last element in a list as the median.

4. Modify the program in Figure 13-5 so that the successor of the median or middle name of the final sorted array is printed if this name is LUOMA. If the successor of the median name is not LUOMA, print a message to inform the user of the situation. If the number of array elements, NUM, is even, the median should be considered to be NUM/2. If NUM is odd, the actual middle element is the median. Use function ODD to determine which element is the median element and use the SUCC function to find the successor of the median. Use the same input as used in program SORT_NAMES.

5. Ask 50 students the name of their favorite NFL team. Write a program that reads the name of each team and the number of students voting for that team. Use a bubble sort to sort the teams so that the most popular is first and the least popular is last. Print this list to the monitor. Here is an example of how the output might look:

NAME	NUMBER OF VOTES
STEELERS	12
COWBOYS	10
RAMS	7

6. Write a program for problem 5, but use an insertion sort instead of a bubble sort.

7. Write a sequential search that will search an array of records. The format for each record follows:

```
TYPE
    FISHING = RECORD
        NAME : STRING;
        BASS : REAL;
        NORTHERN : REAL;
        WALLEYE : REAL;
        PERCH : REAL
    END
```

Each record contains a person's name and the size of the largest fish caught by that person for each type of fish. If the person did not catch any of that type of fish, a zero should be entered in that field. In your program, allow the user to enter up to 20 records. Then have the program determine who caught the largest fish of each type. Format your output like this:

```
NAME        TYPE        SIZE

----        ----        ----

GEORGE      BASS        12.8  INCHES
BECKY       NORTHERN    23.5  INCHES
MARGE       WALLEYE     20.0  INCHES
FRED        PERCH        8.7  INCHES
```

Use a sequential search to locate the winner in each category. Make up your own data to test this program.

8. Write a program to allow the user to enter the names and populations of 20 cities in your state. Use a quicksort to place these names in alphabetical order. Then allow the user to enter the name of a particular city. Use a binary search to locate and print the population of that city.

CHAPTER 14

Files

CHAPTER OUTLINE

LEARNING OBJECTIVES

After studying this chapter, you should be able to:

1. Define the terms file, sequential file, and random-access file.
2. Describe why files are important.
3. Describe what text and interactive files are.
4. Declare sequential files.
5. Describe and use the REWRITE and RESET procedures.
6. Describe and use a file pointer and a buffer variable.
7. Describe and use the PUT and GET procedures.
8. Describe and use the end-of-file and end-of-line markers and functions.
9. Describe and use the CLOSE and LOCK procedures.
10. Read from and write to sequential files.
11. Describe the primary difference between text and interactive files.

ADVANCED PLACEMENT CHAPTER HIGHLIGHTS

The following topics from the Advanced Placement Computer Science Exam are covered in this chapter:

file input and output

INTRODUCTION

Disk files are commonly used to store program output. Up to this point, program output could only be saved by sending it to a printer. By using a disk file, data can be stored and reused by a program. Data stored on a diskette are not lost when the computer is turned off.

A Pascal disk file is an ordered collection of data items, of the same data type, that are stored on a disk. Disk files can contain data of type ARRAY, CHARACTER, INTEGER, REAL, RECORD, or STRING. Disk files must be declared in the VAR section of a program. The format for declaring a file is:

Filename : FILE OF type;

Figure 14-1 illustrates a few examples of file declaration. Example A shows the declaration of file COUNT in the VAR section. Example B shows the declaration of the files CLIENT and SALESPEOPLE in the VAR section. Notice that CLIENT and SALESPEOPLE are files of type PEOPLE. PEOPLE is declared in the TYPE section. If several files of the same type are used in a program, this type of format should be used.

```
A.                  VAR
                        COUNT : FILE OF REAL;

B.                  TYPE
                        PEOPLE = FILE OF STRING[10];

                    VAR
                        CLIENT : PEOPLE;
                        SALESPEOPLE : PEOPLE;

C.                  TYPE
                        STUDENT = RECORD
                            NAME : STRING[20];
                            YEAR : INTEGER;
                            GRADE : CHAR
                        END;

                    VAR
                        CLASS : FILE OF STUDENT;
```

Figure 14-1 FILE DECLARATION

Example C shows the declaration of the file CLASS. CLASS is a file of records. Because CLASS has been declared as a file of records, it can store data of many types. Notice that CLASS contains characters, integers, and strings. Many businesses, schools, and government organizations use files of records. These files normally contain names, Social Security numbers, addresses, and other related information. Though the data are of different types, one file can store all these data if they are organized into records.

TYPES OF PASCAL FILES

Sequential and **random-access files** are the two main types of files in UCSD Pascal. In a sequential file, data items are stored one right after another. Data items must be accessed in sequence. For example, to access the tenth item in a sequential file, a program must read through the first nine items. This process can be very slow if a file is large. Sequential files are most often used to store data that are rarely changed.

Random-access files allow data items to be stored anywhere within a file. Data items can be directly accessed. For example, a program could directly access the tenth item in a random-access file. Random-access files require the computer to keep track of the locations of all the data within a file. This often makes a program using a random-access file more complex than a program using a sequential file.

Text and interactive files are special types of sequential files. They are found in most versions of UCSD Pascal. Text files are used when data are in the form of lines or strings. Text files are often used to send data to a printer. Interactive files allow the computer to communicate

287

with other devices besides the disk drive. Two frequently used interactive files are INPUT and OUTPUT. These files are automatically opened when any UCSD Pascal program executes. The INPUT file allows commands to be sent to the computer by using the keyboard. The OUTPUT file allows the computer to send results to the monitor screen. Files are an important part of the Pascal language.

◥LEARNING CHECK 14-1

1. What do disk files allow programs to do?
2. Define the following terms:
   disk file
   sequential file
   random-access file
   text file
   interactive file
3. Where are Pascal files normally declared?

Answers:

3. Files are normally declared in the VAR section.
   drive.
Interactive file: a sequential file used when a programmer wants to read or store data from devices other than the disk
   Text file: a sequential file used with string data or data in the form of lines.
Random-access file: a file that allows data items to be stored anywhere. Data items can then be directly accessed.
Sequential file: a file that stores data items one right after another. Data items must also be accessed in sequence.
data can be retrieved so that they can be reused.   2. Disk file: an ordered collection of data items of the same data type.
1. Disk files allow programs to store output on a diskette. The data will not be lost when the computer is turned off. Also, the

CREATING AND WRITING TO A FILE

Disk files are used in two ways. Data can be written to a file or data can be read from a file. Pascal requires programs to specify how a disk file will be used. This section describes how to create and write to a file.

To use a disk file, it must first be created. Creating a file is a two-step process. First, a file must be declared in the VAR section of a program. Second, a disk file must be opened and assigned space on a diskette. The REWRITE procedure opens a disk file and allows data to be written to the file. The format of the REWRITE statement is:

REWRITE (program filename, 'directory name'):

The program filename is the name of the disk file as declared in the program. The directory name is the name of the disk file in the directory of the diskette. Figure 14-2 illustrates the program name and directory name of a file in a REWRITE statement. In this example, the

```
VAR
    CUSTOMER : FILE OF STRING[20];
    Program file name

        REWRITE (CUSTOMER, 'APPLE0: CUSTFILE' );
```

Figure 14-2 USING THE REWRITE STATEMENT

program file CUSTOMER will be stored on the diskette named APPLE0: under the directory file name CUSTFILE.

Once a file is created, data can be written to the disk file. Data are written to a file by using a file pointer, a buffer variable, and a PUT procedure. When a file is opened by REWRITE, the computer automatically creates a file pointer and a buffer variable. Imagine the file pointer as an arrow in the computer's memory that points to data items in a file. The file pointer points to the beginning of a file when the file is first opened. The buffer variable is a window through which a program can write and read data to and from a file. The buffer variable is referenced by typing the program filename and the character ^. For example, the buffer variable for the file STUDENT is STUDENT^. Some computers use the up arrow symbol (↑) instead of the caret (^) to represent the buffer variable. Buffer variables can be used like any variable. Data are assigned to the buffer by using an assignment statement in the following format:

program filename^ := variable;

The PUT procedure actually writes the data to the file. PUT will first make a copy of the current contents of the buffer variable. It will then insert the copy into the file location marked by the file pointer. The format of the PUT statement is:

PUT (program filename);

Figure 14-3 illustrates the relationship between the file pointer, buffer variable, and program.

Let's try writing some data to the file STUDENT. First, the file STUDENT must be opened by using the REWRITE statement. Second, the data to be sent to the file are assigned to the buffer variable. Figure 14-4 illustrates a program segment that writes names to the file STUDENT. Notice that the variable NAME is of the same type—STRING—as the file STUDENT. Any data assigned to the buffer variable must be of the same type as the file. The third step in writing data to a file is the PUT statement. The PUT statement inserts a copy of the contents of the buffer variable into the file.

289

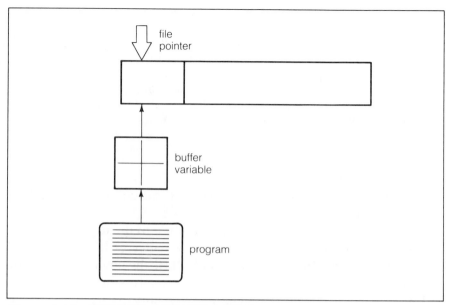

Figure 14-3 WRITING DATA TO A FILE

CLOSING A FILE: 1

A file must be closed to save its contents. The data in the file can then be used again. Any file that is opened in a UCSD Pascal program must be closed before the end of the program. A program error will occur if a file is not closed. UCSD Pascal files are closed with the CLOSE and LOCK statements. The format of the CLOSE and LOCK statements are:

CLOSE (program filename, LOCK);

The CLOSE command alone will satisfy the compiler. However, if the LOCK statement is not used, the file will be lost after it is closed. The

```
PROGRAM FILE_WRITE;

TYPE
   NAMES = STRING[20];

VAR
   NAME : NAMES;
   STUDENT : FILE OF NAMES;

BEGIN

   REWRITE ('STUDENT, 'APPLE0: STUDFILE');
   WRITELN ('ENTER STUDENT NAME:');
   READLN (NAME);
   STUDENT^ := NAME;
   PUT (STUDENT);
```

Figure 14-4 WRITING DATA TO A FILE BY USING PUT

LOCK statement tells the compiler to make the file permanent.
The file's directory name will then be placed in the diskette's directory.

Now you can create, write to, and save a disk file. Learning to use disk files is not always easy. But with a little practice, you can learn to use disk files in useful ways. The exercises in this chapter will help you learn how to use disk files in your programs. Once you understand the ideas in this chapter, you can learn even more complex and interesting ways to use disk files.

✏️ LEARNING CHECK 14-2

1. What are the two steps necessary to create a disk file?
2. Describe the file pointer and buffer variable. How do they work together?
3. Use a buffer variable and a PUT statement to write:
   a. the contents of variable TEAM to the file TEAMS.
   b. the contents of variable FRIEND to the file FRIENDS.
   c. the contents of variable HOURS to the file WORK.
4. Close and save the contents of the files TEAMS, FRIENDS, and WORK.

Answers:

CLOSE (WORK, LOCK);
CLOSE (FRIENDS, LOCK);
4. CLOSE (TEAMS, LOCK);

PUT (WORK);
c. WORK↑ := HOURS;

PUT (FRIENDS);
b. FRIENDS↑ := FRIEND;

PUT (TEAMS);
3. a. TEAMS↑ := TEAM;
used to send data from the program to the file location marked by the file pointer.
pointer points to a file location. The buffer variable is a window that can send data to a file location. The buffer variable is
file. The two steps necessary to create a disk file are (a) declaring the disk file and (b) opening the disk file. 2. The file

READING A FILE

Disk files are often used to store data for later use. To use data in a disk file, the disk file is read. Then, the data can be used or changed within a program.

In order to access a saved file, the file must be opened. First, the file must be declared in the VAR section of the program. Second, the computer must be told how the file is to be used. The RESET procedure opens a file so that it can be read. The format of the RESET statement is:

RESET (program filename, 'directory name');

The RESET statement must appear before the program tries to use data from the file. The RESET command causes the computer to look for a file in a diskette's directory that matches the declared directory name. If the file is found, a file pointer is assigned to the first data item of the file. Then, the first data item is read into the file's buffer variable and the file pointer is moved to the second data item.

Data are read from a file with the buffer variable and GET procedure. The GET procedure copies the file contents marked by the file pointer, moves the copy into the buffer variable, and moves the file pointer to the next data item. The RESET procedure performs an automatic GET after it has located a file. The format of the GET statement is:

$$GET\ (program\ filename);$$

The buffer variable acts as a window to read or write data. Once a GET procedure is executed, the contents of the buffer variable can be assigned to a program variable. Then, the data can be used within a program. Figure 14-5 illustrates the relationship among the file pointer, buffer variable, and the GET procedure.

Files must be read in a specific way since the RESET statement automatically performs a GET. Figure 14-6 illustrates a program that reads all the data in the file HOURS. Notice that the file is declared in the VAR section and opened with a RESET statement. Next, a WHILE loop is used to read all the data from HOURS. Notice that the tested condition of the WHILE loop is NOT EOF. EOF is a function that returns the BOOLEAN value true when the file pointer has reached the end-of-

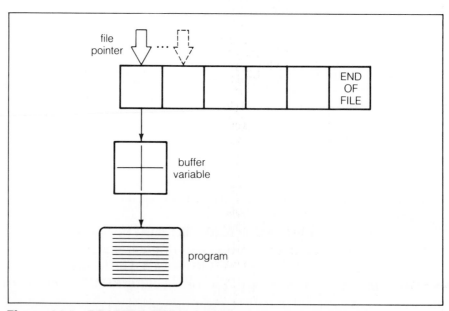

Figure 14-5 READING FROM A FILE

```
                PROGRAM READ_HOURS;

                VAR
                    HOUR  : REAL;
                    HOURS : FILE OF REAL;
                    I     : INTEGER;

                BEGIN

                    RESET (HOURS, 'APPLEO: HOURSFILE');
                    WHILE NOT EOF (HOURS) DO
                        BEGIN
                            HOUR := HOURS^;
                            GET (HOURS)
                        END;
                    CLOSE (HOURS)

                END.
```

Figure 14-6   USING EOF TO READ A FILE

file marker. The end-of-file marker is automatically assigned to the end of a file when it is closed. The WHILE loop in Figure 14-6 repeats until the end-of-file marker is reached.

Next, notice the position of the GET and buffer variable within the WHILE loop. The contents of the buffer variable are first assigned to the program variable HOUR. Then, a GET statement is executed. What would happen if the GET statement was executed first? The first data item would be lost if a GET statement was executed first. Since the RESET statement automatically performs a GET, the buffer variable automatically holds the value of the first data item in the file HOUR. If the GET was performed first, it would erase the first data item. The WHILE loop is the easiest and safest way to read the contents of a file.

One of the advantages of UCSD Pascal is the way in which records can be handled. Reading a file of records is the same as reading any file. Figure 14-7 illustrates a program that reads all the records in the file CLASS. Notice that the variable STUDENT is assigned the value of the buffer variable CLASS. The variable STUDENT is a record that contains the name and address of students. Once a record is read to the program, the record's information can be used. In Figure 14-7, the names and addresses of the students are printed on the monitor screen.

CLOSING A FILE: 2

All disk files opened in a program must be closed before the end of a program. Reading a file does not change the contents or organization of a disk file. The rules, or syntax, of Pascal still require opened disk files to be closed. Disk files that are opened by a RESET statement can be closed by a CLOSE statement. The LOCK statement, however, is not necessary. For example, the file STUDENT is closed by the statement CLOSE (STUDENT);.

```
PROGRAM CLASS_READ;

TYPE
    STUD_REC = RECORD
        NAME     : STRING[20];
        ADDRESS  : STRING[30]
    END;

VAR
    CLASS    : FILE OF STUD_REC;
    STUDENT  : STUD_REC;

BEGIN

    RESET (CLASS, 'APPLE1: CLASSFILE');
    WHILE NOT EOF (CLASS) DO
        BEGIN
            STUDENT := CLASS^;
            WRITELN ('NAME OF STUDENT: ', STUDENT.NAME);
            WRITELN ('ADDRESS OF STUDENT: ', STUDENT.ADDRESS);
            GET (CLASS)
        END;
    CLOSE (CLASS)

END.  (* CLASS_READ *)
```

Figure 14-7 READING A FILE OF RECORDS

✏️LEARNING CHECK 14-3

1. Open the following disk files so that they can be read. Use your own program file names.
   a. JOG
   b. BASEBALL
   c. PHONEBOOK
2. Read one data item from the files below. You can assume that the files have been opened with RESET and no GET statements have been executed.
   JOG, a file of real numbers
   BASEBALL, a file of records
   PHONEBOOK, a file of records
3. Why must a file be closed if it is opened within a program?

Answers:

3. The syntax or rules of UCSD Pascal require that all files opened in a program must be closed before the end of a program.

```
        GET (PHONEBOOK);
c. NUMBER := PHONEBOOK^;

        GET (BASEBALL);
b. HITS := BASEBALL^;

        GET (JOG);
2. a. MILES := JOG^;

c. RESET (NUMBERS, 'PHONEBOOK');

b. RESET (HOMERUNS, 'BASEBALL');

1. a. RESET (JOGGING, 'JOG');
```

Files of records are a compact and useful method of storing and accessing data. The record data type allows different types of information to be stored and accessed together. Files of records are often used in database programs because of this characteristic. The following example demonstrates how a file of records can be used to store and access related data in a small database.

Several procedures are necessary to store and access records in a file. First, the file must be created and the original records written to the file. Second, records may need to be inserted or deleted. Third, records may need to be accessed and changed. These three procedures perform most of the operations needed to store and access files of records.

The first procedure creates a file and allows the user to write original data to the file. The file used in this procedure stores records of the day, hours worked, and tips of a waiter or waitress. In order to keep the database small, the files will store up to seven records, one for each day of a week. Figure 14-8 illustrates the declarations of the file WORK-WEEK in the main program. Figure 14-9 illustrates procedure STORE, which creates the original database. A REWRITE statement opens the file WORKWEEK. Next, data are read into the record TODAY and assigned to the buffer variable WORKWEEK^. Finally, a PUT statement writes the record to the file. Notice that the CLOSE and LOCK statements are used to permanently add the file to the diskette's directory.

The second procedure inserts or deletes records in the file. Sequential files are static data structures. Once a file has been created, records cannot be inserted or deleted from it. To avoid this problem, the file WORKWEEK is opened and its records read into the array TEMP. Next, the file is closed and then reopened with a REWRITE statement. Now, new records can be written to the new version of WORKWEEK or records can be skipped over so that they do not appear

```
PROGRAM MAIN;

TYPE
   WORKDAY = RECORD
      DAY : STRING;
      HOURS : REAL;
      TIPS : REAL
   END;
   WORKDAYS = FILE OF WORKDAY;

VAR
   TODAY    : WORKDAY;
   WORKWEEK : WORKDAYS;
   CONT     : CHAR;
   FUNC     : INTEGER;
```

Figure 14-8 DECLARATION SECTION FOR PROGRAM MAIN   **295**

```
          PROCEDURE STORE (TODAY : WORKDAY; VAR WORKWEEK : WORKDAYS);
          (* THIS PROCEDURE CREATES AND STORES A FILE OF RECORDS *)

          VAR
             CONTINUE : CHAR;
             I, MAX    : INTEGER;

          BEGIN   (* STORE *)

             REWRITE (WORKWEEK, 'APPLE2: WORKWEEK');
             I := 1;
             MAX := 7;

             WHILE I < MAX DO
                BEGIN

                   WITH TODAY DO
                      BEGIN
                         WRITE ('ENTER DAY OF WEEK: ');
                         READLN (DAY);
                         WRITE ('ENTER HOURS WORKED: ');
                         READLN (HOURS);
                         WRITE ('ENTER TOTAL TIPS: ');
                         READLN (TIPS)
                      END;    (* WITH *)

                   WORKWEEK^ := TODAY;
                   PUT (WORKWEEK);
                   WRITE ('DO YOU HAVE ANOTHER DAY TO RECORD (Y OR N): ');
                   READLN (CONTINUE);
                   IF CONTINUE = 'Y' THEN
                      I := I + 1
                   ELSE
                      I := MAX
                END;    (* WHILE *)

             CLOSE (WORKWEEK, LOCK)

          END;   (* STORE *)
```

Figure 14-9 PROCEDURE STORE

in the new WORKWEEK. Figure 14-10 illustrates the procedure INOUT, which inserts and deletes records. This procedure is long since the file WORKWEEK must be opened and closed twice. This method is awkward but necessary when using sequential files.

The third procedure updates or changes records within the file. Unfortunately, a sequential file cannot be changed once it is created. To avoid this problem, the file WORKWEEK is opened and read into an array until a target record is reached. This record is then changed and read to the array. WORKWEEK is then closed, reopened, and the new records written to the file. Figure 14-11 illustrates the procedure UPDATE, which changes records within the file WORKWEEK. Again, the length and complexity of the procedure is due to the inability of Pascal to modify components within a sequential file.

The three procedures described above create a file of records and allow it to be manipulated. Since all of the procedures use variable parameters to access the file WORKWEEK, the contents of the file are actually changed by the procedures. The procedures could be used in a

```
PROCEDURE INOUT (VAR WORKWEEK : WORKDAYS);
(* THIS PROCEDURE INSERTS OR DELETES AN ENTIRE RECORD IN A FILE *)

VAR
   I, J, FUNC : INTEGER;
   TARGET     : STRING;
   TEMP       : ARRAY[1..7] OF WORKDAY;

(***************************************************************************)

PROCEDURE INSERTREC (VAR WORKWEEK : WORKDAYS);
(* THIS PROCEDURE INSERTS A RECORD IN A FILE *)

BEGIN   (* INSERTREC *)

   WITH TODAY DO
      BEGIN
         WRITE ('WHICH DAY DO YOU WISH TO INSERT: ');
         READLN (DAY);
         WRITE ('ENTER HOURS WORKED: ');
         READLN (HOURS);
         WRITE ('ENTER TOTAL TIPS: ');
         READLN (TIPS)
      END;   (* WITH *)

   I := 1;

   WHILE NOT EOF (WORKWEEK) DO
      BEGIN
         TEMP[I] := WORKWEEK^;
         I := I + 1;
         GET (WORKWEEK)
      END;   (* WHILE *)

   CLOSE (WORKWEEK);
   REWRITE (WORKWEEK, 'APPLE2:WORKWEEK');
   J := I - 1;

   FOR I := 1 TO J DO
      BEGIN
         WORKWEEK^ := TEMP[I];
         PUT (WORKWEEK)
      END;   (* FOR *)

   WORKWEEK^ := TODAY;
   PUT (WORKWEEK);
   CLOSE (WORKWEEK, LOCK)

END;   (* INSERTREC *)

(***************************************************************************)

PROCEDURE DELETEREC (VAR WORKWEEK : WORKDAYS);
(* THIS PROCEDURE DELETES A RECORD FROM A FILE *)

BEGIN (* DELETEREC *)

   WRITE ('WHICH DAY DO YOU WISH TO DELETE: ');
   READLN (TARGET);
   I := 1;

   WHILE (WORKWEEK^.DAY <> TARGET) AND (NOT EOF (WORKWEEK)) DO
      BEGIN
         TEMP[I] := WORKWEEK^;
         I := I + 1;
         GET (WORKWEEK)
      END;   (* WHILE *)
```

Figure 14-10 PROCEDURE INOUT   *(continued next page)*

```
        IF EOF (WORKWEEK) THEN
            WRITELN (TARGET, ' IS NOT IN FILE')
        ELSE
            BEGIN
                GET (WORKWEEK);
                WHILE NOT EOF (WORKWEEK) DO
                    BEGIN
                        TEMP[I] := WORKWEEK^;
                        I := I + 1;
                        GET (WORKWEEK)
                    END   (* WHILE *)
            END;   (* ELSE *)

        CLOSE (WORKWEEK);
        REWRITE (WORKWEEK, 'APPLE2: WORKWEEK');
        J := I - 1;

        FOR I := 1 TO J DO
            BEGIN
                WORKWEEK^ := TEMP[I];
                PUT (WORKWEEK)
            END;   (* FOR *)

      CLOSE (WORKWEEK, LOCK)

   END;   (* DELETEREC *)

   (****************************************************************************)

   BEGIN   (* INOUT *)

      RESET (WORKWEEK, 'APPLE2: WORKWEEK');
      WRITELN ('DO YOU WISH TO INSERT (PRESS1)');
      WRITE ('OR DELETE (PRESS2) A RECORD: ');
      READLN (FUNC);

      WHILE (FUNC < 1) OR (FUNC > 2) DO
          BEGIN
              WRITE ('PLEASE PRESS 1 TO INSERT, 2 TO DELETE: ');
              READLN (FUNC)
          END;   (* WHILE *)

      CASE FUNC OF
          1 : INSERTREC (WORKWEEK);
          2 : DELETEREC (WORKWEEK)
      END   (* CASE *)

   END;   (* INOUT *)
```

Figure 14-10 PROCEDURE INOUT (continued)

number of different main programs. Figure 14-12 illustrates a main program that uses STORE, INOUT, and UPDATE. This main program allows the user to execute any of the procedures.

Files of records can be very useful. However, creating programs that manipulate files can be time-consuming. Do not be discouraged by the length of the procedures in this section. STORE, INOUT, and UPDATE use simple Pascal commands and algorithms. Use these procedures as the basis for your own programs. You will discover that manipulating files can be a time-consuming but simple programming task.

```
        PROCEDURE UPDATE (VAR WORKWEEK : WORKDAYS);
        (* THIS PROCEDURE UPDATES ANY RECORD IN THE FILE WORKWEEK *)

        VAR
            I, J   : INTEGER;
            TARGET : STRING;
            TEMP   : ARRAY[1..7] OF WORKDAY;
            TDAY   : STRING;
            THOURS : REAL;
            TTIPS  : REAL;

        BEGIN   (* UPDATE *)

            RESET (WORKWEEK, 'APPLE2: WORKWEEK');
            WRITE ('WHICH DAY DO YOU WANT TO UPDATE? ');
            READLN (TARGET);
            I := 1;

            WHILE (WORKWEEK^.DAY <> TARGET) AND (NOT EOF (WORKWEEK)) DO
                BEGIN
                    TEMP[I] := WORKWEEK^;
                    I := I + 1;
                    GET (WORKWEEK)
                END;   (* WHILE *)

            IF EOF (WORKWEEK) THEN
                BEGIN
                    WRITELN (TARGET, ' IS NOT IN FILE');
                    CLOSE (WORKWEEK)
                END   (* IF *)
            ELSE
                BEGIN
                    WRITELN ('PRESS THE RETURN KEY TO DISPLAY');
                    WRITELN ('EACH ITEM OF THE RECORD');
                    WRITELN ('IF YOU WISH TO CHANGE THE ITEM,');
                    WRITELN ('TYPE THE CHANGE ON THE LINE PROVIDED');
                    WRITELN ('IF NO CHANGE IS DESIRED, TYPE 0');
                    WRITELN ('AND PRESS THE RETURN KEY');
                    WRITELN;
                    WRITELN ('DAY IS', WORKWEEK^.DAY);
                    WRITE ('DAY: ');
                    READLN (TDAY);
                    IF (TDAY = '0') THEN
                        TODAY.DAY := WORKWEEK^.DAY
                    ELSE
                        TODAY.DAY := TDAY;
                    WRITELN ('HOURS ARE ', WORKWEEK^.HOURS);
                    WRITE ('HOURS: ');
                    READLN (THOURS);
                    IF (THOURS = 0) THEN
                        TODAY.HOURS := WORKWEEK^.HOURS
                    ELSE
                        TODAY.HOURS := THOURS;
                    WRITELN ('TIPS ARE ', WORKWEEK^.TIPS);
                    WRITE ('TIPS: ');
                    READLN (TTIPS);
                    IF (TTIPS = 0) THEN
                        TODAY.TIPS := WORKWEEK^.TIPS
                    ELSE
                        TODAY.TIPS := TTIPS;
                    TEMP[I] := TODAY;
                    I := I + 1;
                    GET (WORKWEEK);
```

Figure 14-11 PROCEDURE UPDATE   *(continued next page)*

```
                    WHILE NOT EOF (WORKWEEK) DO
                        BEGIN
                            TEMP[I] := WORKWEEK^;
                            I := I + 1;
                            GET (WORKWEEK)
                        END;   (* WHILE *)

                    CLOSE (WORKWEEK);
                    REWRITE (WORKWEEK, 'APPLE2:WORKWEEK');
                    J := I - 1;

                    FOR I := 1 TO J DO
                        BEGIN
                            WORKWEEK^ := TEMP[I];
                            PUT (WORKWEEK)
                        END;   (* FOR *)

                    CLOSE (WORKWEEK, LOCK);
                END   (* ELSE *)

        END;   (* UPDATE *)
```

Figure 14-11   PROCEDURE UPDATE (continued)

TEXT AND INTERACTIVE FILES

Up to this point, disk files have only been used to store data on a diskette and to read data from a diskette. Text and interactive files allow programs to output to the printer and to use the keyboard for input. Text and interactive files are an easy way to add to the variety of UCSD Pascal programs.

Text files are very useful when a program reads or writes strings. It is the structure of text files that makes them so useful. Text files are made up of lines terminated with end-of-line (EOLN) markers. Figure 14-13 illustrates the structure of a typical text file. Like the end-of-file marker, the end-of-line (EOLN) marker can be used to test for the end of a line of data. The EOLN function returns the BOOLEAN value true when the file pointer reaches an end-of-line marker. The BOOLEAN value false is returned if the file pointer is not positioned at an end-of-line marker.

Text files must be declared in the VAR section of a program. The format for declaring a text file is:

filename: TEXT;

Text files must also be opened for reading or writing with either the RESET or REWRITE statements. So far, text files are very similar to the sequential files already discussed. Reading and writing to text files, though, is much easier than reading or writing to normal sequential files. Text files are read with a modified version of the READLN statement. The format of the modified READLN statement is:

READLN (program filename, program variable);

```
PROGRAM MAIN;

TYPE
   WORKDAY = RECORD
       DAY   : STRING;
       HOURS : REAL;
       TIPS  : REAL
   END;

   WORKDAYS = FILE OF WORKDAY;

VAR
   TODAY    : WORKDAY;
   WORKWEEK : WORKDAYS;
   CONT     : CHAR;
   FUNC     : INTEGER;


BEGIN   (* MAIN *)

   CONT := 'Y';

   WHILE (CONT = 'Y') DO
      BEGIN
          WRITELN ('PRESS 1 TO CREATE A FILE');
          WRITELN ('PRESS 2 TO INSERT OR DELETE A RECORD');
          WRITELN ('PRESS 3 TO UPDATE A RECORD');
          WRITE ('FUNCTION (1, 2, OR 3): ');
          READLN (FUNC);
          WHILE (FUNC < 1) AND (FUNC > 3) DO
             BEGIN
                 WRITE ('PLEASE PRESS 1, 2, OR 3');
                 READLN (FUNC)
             END;   (* WHILE *)
          WRITELN;
          CASE FUNC OF
             1 : STORE (TODAY, WORKWEEK);
             2 : INOUT (WORKWEEK);
             3 : UPDATE (WORKWEEK)
          END;   (* CASE *)

          WRITELN;
          RESET (WORKWEEK, 'APPLE2: WORKWEEK');
          WHILE NOT EOF (WORKWEEK) DO
             BEGIN
                 WRITELN (WORKWEEK^.DAY);
                 WRITELN (WORKWEEK^.HOURS);
                 WRITELN (WORKWEEK^.TIPS);
                 WRITELN;
                 GET (WORKWEEK)
             END;
          CLOSE (WORKWEEK);
          WRITE ('DO YOU WISH TO CONTINUE (Y OR N): ');
          READLN (CONT)
      END

END.   (* MAIN *)
```

Figure 14-12 PROGRAM MAIN

String	EOLN	String	EOLN	String	EOLN	String	EOLN	EOF

Figure 14-13 STRUCTURE OF A TEXT FILE

```
READLN (CONCERTS, SHOW);          SHOW := CONCERTS^;
                                  GET (CONCERTS);

READLN (CAR, GAS);                GAS := CAR^;
                                  GET (CAR);
```

Figure 14-14   COMPARISON OF THE TWO METHODS OF READING A FILE

Do you remember how the buffer variable and GET statement were used to read data? The modified READLN statement performs the entire reading process in one statement. Figure 14-14 compares the two file reading methods. Remember, both methods do the same thing.

Text files are written with a modified version of the WRITELN statement. The format of the WRITELN statement is:

WRITELN (program filename, program variable);

The modified WRITELN statement performs the functions of the buffer variable and PUT statement. Figure 14-15 compares the two methods of file writing.

A common use for text files is to print the contents of a file. Text files can be sent to the printer. The program in Figure 14-16 reads data from the disk file PAPERFILE and writes them to the file PRINTER:. PRINTER: is a system-defined file that allows communication with the printer. Notice that the REWRITE statement opens communication to the printer by opening the file PRINTER:. Instead of data being sent to a diskette, they are sent to a printer. Next, look at the READLN and WRITELN statements. The READLN statement copies the current lines' contents into the variable LINE and moves the file pointer past the EOLN marker to the next line. The WRITELN statement copies data from the variable LINE, sends the data to the printer, and adds an EOLN marker. When the printer receives the EOLN marker, it performs a carriage return and moves the printer paper up a line. The WHILE loop that encloses the READLN and WRITELN statements uses the EOF function. The EOF function stops the execution of the WHILE loop when the end-of-file marker is reached. Finally, the program uses CLOSE statements to close both files. Since the file PRINT is not a disk file, the LOCK statement is not necessary.

```
WRITELN (CONCERTS, SHOW);         CONCERTS^ := SHOW;
                                  PUT (CONCERTS);

WRITELN (CAR, GAS);               CAR^ := GAS;
                                  PUT (CAR);
```

Figure 14-15   COMPARISON OF THE TWO METHODS OF WRITING A FILE

```
          PROGRAM PRINT_OUT;

          VAR
              LINE      : STRING[80];
              PAPER     : TEXT;
              PRINT     : TEXT;

          BEGIN

              RESET (PAPER, 'PAPERFILE');
              REWRITE (PRINT, 'PRINTER:');
              WHILE NOT EOF (PAPER) DO
                 BEGIN
                     READLN (PAPER, LINE);
                     WRITELN (PRINT, LINE)
                 END;
              CLOSE (PAPER);
              CLOSE (PRINT)

          END.
```

Figure 14-16 USING A TEXT FILE TO PRINT A FILE

Interactive files are used when devices other than the disk drive are used to input or output data. The **predefined files** INPUT and OUTPUT are interactive files. The predefined file KEYBOARD is also an interactive file. KEYBOARD represents data sent from the keyboard.

Interactive files can use all the file commands described for text files. Interactive files must be declared, except for INPUT, OUTPUT, and KEYBOARD, in the VAR section. The format for declaring an interactive file is:

filename: INTERACTIVE;

The biggest difference between interactive files and other sequential files lies in reading a file. Remember that the RESET statement automatically executes a GET command. The buffer variable then contains a copy of the contents of the first file location. The RESET statement, however, does not execute an automatic GET statement on interactive files. The reason is simple. Since interactive files often represent the keyboard, the file has no contents until a key is pressed. If an automatic GET were performed before a key was pressed, the program would find nothing in the file. Figure 14-17 illustrates the difference beween the

Interactive READLN	*Text READLN*
GET (KEY); GRADE := KEY^;	GRADE := KEY^; GET (KEY);

Figure 14-17 COMPARISON OF THE INTERACTIVE AND TEXT READLN STATEMENTS

interactive READLN and the text READLN. Notice that the statements are identical, though they appear in reverse order. In fact, the interactive and text READLN statements can be used in the same way. Be aware, though, that they perform the GET and the buffer variable assignment statements in reverse order.

Disk files are useful and often necessary in many programs. To handle disk files well, you must practice using them in different programs. The problems at the end of this chapter should only be a beginning. Think of how you could use disk files to store information and try to write your own programs. You will soon realize the usefulness of disk files.

⩗LEARNING CHECK 14-4

1. Describe the structure of a text file.
2. When does the EOLN function return the BOOLEAN value true?
3. Open the files below. Include the variable declarations and RESET or REWRITE statements.
   a. SENTENCES, a disk file, to read text.
   b. WORK, a file to write text to the printer.
   c. WROTE, disk file, to write text.

Answers:

1. Text files are made up of lines or strings of text terminated by end-of-line markers. The entire file ends with an end-of-file marker. 2. The EOLN function returns the BOOLEAN value true when the file pointer is located at an end-of-line marker. 3. a. SENTENCES : TEXT;
   RESET (SENTENCES, 'SENTENFILE');
   b. WORK : TEXT;
   REWRITE (WORK, 'PRINTER:');
   c. WROTE : TEXT;
   REWRITE (WROTE, 'WROTEFILE');

SUMMARY POINTS

- UCSD Pascal can use sequential and random-access files. With sequential files, data must be accessed one item after another. With random-access files, data can be accessed directly.
- To create a sequential file, the file must be declared in the VAR section and it must be opened with a REWRITE statement. Data are written to a sequential file with a buffer variable and a PUT statement. Any files opened within a program must be closed before the end of the program. New files are usually closed with the CLOSE and LOCK statements. The LOCK statement permanently adds a file to a diskette.
- To read a sequential file, the file must be declared in the VAR section of a program and the file must be opened with a RESET statement. Data are read from a sequential file with a buffer variable and a GET statement.

- Text and interactive files are special forms of the sequential file. Text files are made up of lines of strings which end with end-of-line markers. Text files are often used to write a file on a printer. Interactive files are used to access devices other than the disk drive or printer. Data are read from and written to text and interactive files using modified versions of the READLN and WRITELN statements.

VOCABULARY LIST

Predefined file A file that is declared and opened automatically by the UCSD Pascal system.

Random-access file A file that allows data items to be stored anywhere. Data items can then be directly accessed.

Sequential file A file that stores data items one right after another. Data items must also be accessed in sequence.

CHAPTER TEST

VOCABULARY

Match each term from the numbered column with the best description from the lettered column.

1. Predefined file

2. Sequential file

3. Random-access file

a. A file that stores data items one right after another. Data items must also be accessed in sequence.

b. A file that is declared and opened automatically by the UCSD Pascal system.

c. A file that allows data items to be stored anywhere. Data items can then be directly accessed.

QUESTIONS

1. Declare the following files in the VAR section of a program.
   a. ORDERS, a file of real numbers.
   b. DELIVERIES, a file of records that contains the variables: DRIVER: STRING[20], CASES: INTEGER, TIME: REAL, and NEXT_DEL: STRING [8].
   c. CUSTOMERS, a file of STRING[20].
2. What is the difference between sequential and random-access files?

3. Create the files listed below. Write a VAR section and REWRITE statement. Use your own directory names.
   a. TEAMS, a file of STRING[20].
   b. FRIENDS, a file of records that contains the variables: NAME: STRING[20], ADDRESS: STRING[30], CITY: STRING[15], STATE: STRING[15], and ZIP: INTEGER.
   c. WORK, a file of real numbers.
4. Why must a file that is opened in a program be closed and locked before the end of the program?
5. Write a program segment that opens the file PHONEBOOK, reads all of the records it contains (i.e. reaches the end-of-file marker), and stores the contents of the file in an array of records. The layout of the file is illustrated below. Include your variable declarations. Use your own directory name.
   PHONEBOOK: a file of records
        NAME: STRING[20]
     ADDRESS: STRING[30]
     NUMBER: INTEGER[10]
6. Describe how the file pointer, buffer variable, and GET statement work to read a file.
7. Explain the difference between reading text files and reading interactive files.

PROGRAMMING PROBLEMS

1. Write a program that stores the following strings in a text file:

   - UCSD Pascal is a structured
   - programming language that allows
   - you to write clear, organized
   - programs

2. Write two programs, one that writes the contents of the above text file to the monitor, and one that writes to the printer.
3. Write a program that stores the miles jogged by a person Sunday through Saturday. The program should prompt the user to enter the number of miles jogged each day. For example, the program could prompt, MILES JOGGED ON SATURDAY:, and the user would enter the number of miles jogged that day.
4. Write a program that creates an electronic phonebook. The program should prompt a user to enter the name, address, and phone number of at least two people. Treat each person's name, address, and number as a record.
5. Write a program that writes to the screen or printer the contents of the electronic phonebook created above.

CHAPTER 15

Pointer Variables and Linked Lists

LEARNING OBJECTIVES

After studying this chapter, you should be able to:

1. Define and use dynamic variables and pointer variables.
2. Create a node in a linked list.
3. Distinguish the correct uses of pointers.
4. Manipulate the contents of a node at any defined storage location.
5. Create a linked list.
6. Delete any node (except the dummy element) in a linked list.
7. Use procedure DISPOSE to free space.
8. Insert a node anywhere in a linked list (except before the dummy element).

ADVANCED PLACEMENT CHAPTER HIGHLIGHTS

The following topics from the Advanced Placement Computer Science Exam are covered in this chapter:

pointer variables
linked lists

INTRODUCTION

This chapter will introduce pointer variables and their operations and **dynamic data structures**. Dynamic data structures change in size as a program executes. A dynamic data structure is a group of items (called **nodes**) that can grow or shrink, depending on how much storage space is needed. Since the structure is flexible, the location of the beginning and end of the list of nodes is not known. Pointer variables contain the memory addresses of the nodes.

POINTER VARIABLES

In the previous chapter, all the variables were static. **Static variables** are declared at the beginning of a program or a subprogram and remain in existence throughout the execution of the blocks in which they were declared. The static variable declaration makes the computer set aside a small portion of its memory as a location. This location is an area in the computer memory that stores a value which can be changed by using an assignment statement. The Pascal language will only allow values of one particular type to be stored in a given storage location.

When you are writing a program, the amount of memory that a program will need is unknown. Suppose a situation arises where the amount of memory space available for a program is very restricted. During execution of a program, some variables are used and then are no longer needed. Disposing of these variables will leave the corresponding memory locations free to be reused when new variables are created. Variables that can be created and disposed of as a program executes are called **dynamic variables**.

Since a dynamic variable is not declared when the program is written, there is no identifier that can be used to refer to it. Instead, the procedure that creates a dynamic variable returns the address of the corresponding memory location. Such a memory address is stored in a special type of variable, called a **pointer variable** (or **pointer**). Pointers, which may be pictured as actually pointing to a particular storage location, cannot be involved in any arithmetic expressions except comparisons. The contents of a location can be inspected or changed through the pointer if special notation is used.

pointer^.field_name

The field specified by field_name, currently pointed to by pointer variable pointer, is manipulated. If this notation is not used, an assignment to a pointer-type variable changes the particular location the variable references, without affecting the contents of this location.

Pointer Type and Variable Declaration

A **pointer type** is defined as referencing or pointing to a location of a particular type called the **reference type**. An up arrow (↑) or caret (^) precedes the name of the reference type.

pointer_name = ^node_name

The identifier pointer_name is defined as the pointer type of those elements with type node_name. The declaration of a pointer type variable resembles any other variable declaration.

```
VAR
      pointer1, pointer2, pointer3 : pointer_name;
```

The pointer_name in the declaration is the same as the pointer_name in the pointer type definition. Pointer1, pointer2, and pointer3 are pointer variables of type pointer_name.

Procedure NEW

A variable declaration statement cannot be used to set aside storage for a dynamic data structure in advance because the programmer does not know how much storage space will be needed. Because of this, the storage space for each node is allocated when it is needed. Then this

309

node is joined to the rest of the data structure. Storage for a new node is allocated by using the NEW statement:

NEW (pointer1);

Pointer1 is a pointer variable that points to the new node. The type of new node allocated is determined by the type of pointer.

The following example will illustrate the ideas that were presented above. The type and variable declarations are as follows:

```
TYPE
   NODE = RECORD
      BIRD : STRING;
      CAGE : INTEGER
   END;
   POINTER = ^NODE;

VAR
   A, B, C : POINTER;
```

To allocate storage for two records that are pointed to by pointers A and B, procedure NEW must be used.

```
NEW (A);

NEW (B);
```

Since A and B are type POINTER, the new records must be type NODE.

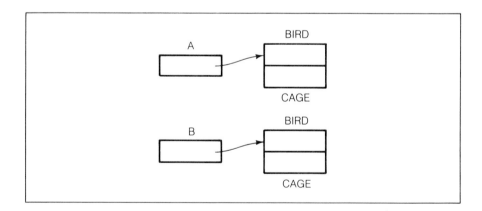

At this point, nothing is stored in these two nodes. Next, the BIRD field of the records is defined.

```
A^.BIRD := 'CANARY';
B^.BIRD := 'PARROT';
```

The nodes now resemble:

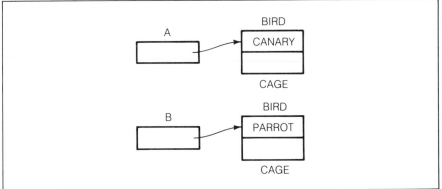

The statements

```
A^.CAGE := 1;
B^.CAGE := 4;
```

will assign values to the CAGE fields.

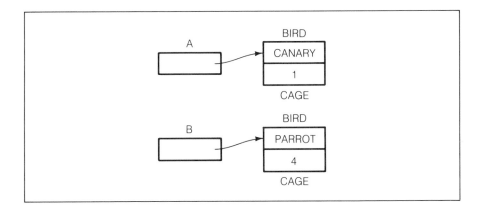

At this time the pointer assignment statement will be introduced, using the above example. The statement below causes the memory address stored in pointer2 to be copied into pointer1.

pointer1 := pointer2;

Pointer1 will now point to the same node as pointer2. Pointer1 and pointer2 must have the same pointer type. In the example, the pointer assignment statement

```
C := B;
```

copies the value of pointer variable B into pointer C. Pointers B and C are now pointing to the same node, while pointer A remains unchanged.

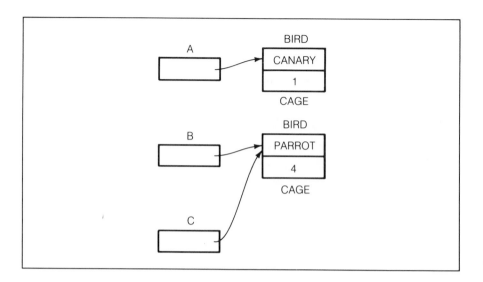

The statements

```
B := A;
A := C;
```

will result in the following:

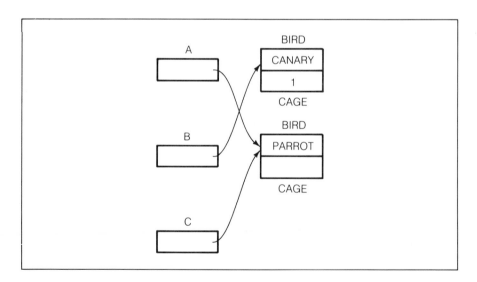

The entire sequence of statements is presented in Figure 15-1.

To print the BIRD field of the records pointed to by pointers A, B, and C, the statement

```
WRITELN (A^.BIRD, B^.BIRD, C^.BIRD);
```

could be used. The output for this expression would look like

```
PARROTCANARYPARROT
```

```
PROGRAM BIRDNUM;
(* THIS PROGRAM WILL ILLUSTRATE THE VARIOUS POINTER VARIABLE OPERATIONS *)

TYPE
   NODE = RECORD
       BIRD : STRING;
       CAGE : INTEGER
   END;
   POINTER = ^NODE;

VAR
   A, B, C : POINTER;

BEGIN

   NEW (A);
   NEW (B);
   A^.BIRD := 'CANARY';
   B^.BIRD := 'PARROT';
   A^.CAGE := 1;
   B^.CAGE := 4;
   C := B;
   B := A;
   A := C;
   WRITELN (A^.BIRD, B^.BIRD, C^.BIRD)

END.   (* BIRDNUM *)


Running . . .
PARROTCANARYPARROT
```

Figure 15-1 USING POINTER VARIABLES

Although the values stored in the fields of a node may be printed, the values of the pointer variable pointing to that node may not be printed. This is because it is the address of a storage location.

▲LEARNING CHECK 15-1

1. When the amount of memory space needed for the execution of a program is not known, a _____ structure is implemented.
2. In the above type of structure, _____ variables will be used instead of _____ variables.
3. Contents of a storage location can be referenced or changed with the use of a pointer when the pointer is _____ this storage location.
4. In the statement below, identify all the parts and their purpose.

                 POINTER = ^NODE;

What operation does this statement perform?

5. In the illustrated example above, the sequence of assignment statements

```
C := B;
B := A;
A := C;
```

was used to exchange the values of pointers A and B. Pointer A now points to the element containing PARROT and pointer B to the element containing CANARY. What would the sequence

```
C^.BIRD := B.BIRD;
B^.BIRD := A.BIRD;
A^.BIRD := C.BIRD;
```

do and what is the difference between these two sequences?

Answers:

LINKED LISTS

Linked lists are the simplest form of dynamic data structure. A linked list is a data structure containing one or more nodes that are linked or connected together. Since these connections are linear in nature, linked lists are linear data structures. New information may be added very easily to the structure by creating a new node and inserting it between two existing nodes. The structure can also be modified by deleting an existing node. This procedure has a clear advantage over modifying an array of records. For example, in an array, if the kth data item in a list of n items needed to be removed, $n - k$ data items would have to be shifted. The $k + 1$ data item would be shifted down to the k position, the $k + 2$ item would be shifted to the $k + 1$ position, and so on. The dynamic data structure only requires a reassignment of pointers.

Creating a Linked List

As stated earlier, a linked list is a group of nodes that are linked or connected together. A three-node linked list is shown below:

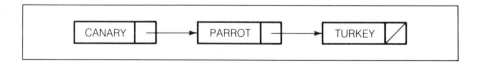

Each node in the list has two fields. The first field contains data and the second field is the link, which is a pointer to the next list element. The slash symbol (/) in the pointer field of the last node indicates the end of the list. The value **NIL** is stored in this field.

Any pointer variable can be assigned the value NIL. This kind of pointer is called a **nil pointer;** it does not reference a location. The advantage of a nil pointer over one that is just undefined is that a pointer variable's NIL/NOT NIL status may be checked with a BOOLEAN expression. The value NIL may be assigned to a pointer of any type and is a predefined identifier in UCSD Pascal. In standard Pascal, NIL is a reserved word. It may also be compared to the values of other pointer variables.

The following example will illustrate the creation of the simple linked list at the start of this section. In order to represent a linked list in memory, it is necessary to define a record type with at least one field that is a pointer.

```
TYPE
   POINTER = ^NODE;
   NODE = RECORD
      BIRD : STRING;
      LINK : POINTER
   END; (* NODE *)

VAR
   FIRST, B, C : POINTER;
```

The pointer type POINTER points to records of type NODE. Each record of type NODE contains a data field named BIRD and a link field named LINK. Since LINK is of type POINTER, the **circular definition** is completed. It is called this because the record type NODE appears in the declaration of POINTER and the pointer type POINTER appears in the declaration of NODE. Note that the pointer type must be declared before the record type. The variable declaration statement defines FIRST, B, and C to be variable pointers. FIRST will be the pointer that points to the first element of the list or the **list head.**

The list creation begins with the statements

```
NEW (FIRST);

FIRST^.BIRD := 'CANARY';
```

These statements initialize the BIRD field of the new list element that is referenced by pointer FIRST.

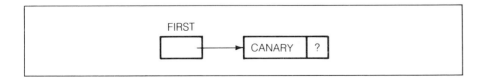

The LINK field of this new element needs to be defined so that it points to the next list element. The statements

```
NEW (B);

FIRST^.LINK := B;
```

link a new element to the list as shown below.

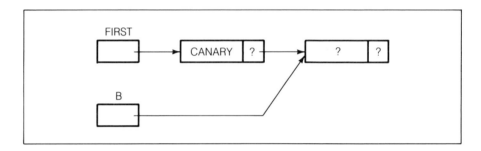

The memory cell address of the newly created node is placed into the LINK field of the previous node. The second statement links the two elements.

The following sequence of statements define the remainder of the linked list.

```
B^.BIRD := 'PARROT';

NEW (C);

B^.LINK := C;

C^.BIRD := 'TURKEY';
```

The first statement assigns PARROT to the BIRD field of the second element. The next statement creates a third element that is pointed to by C. This new element is connected to the second element by the third statement and the fourth statement assigns TURKEY to the BIRD field of the third element. The present data structure is shown below.

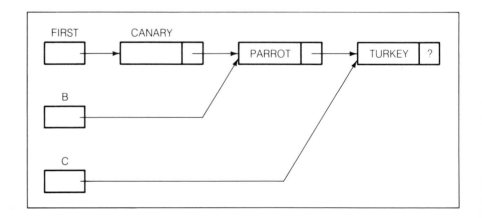

The last element in the created list is pointed to by C. Since this is the last element of the list, the pointer field must contain the value NIL. The statement

```
C^.LINK := NIL;
```

totally finishes the list creation process.

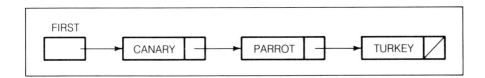

It is evident that many statements are required to create this short linked list. Therefore, the following example will implement procedure CREATE and procedure NEW_NODE to eliminate the similar statements. Procedure CREATE calls procedure NEW_NODE to create the node and enter the data to its fields. CREATE will initialize the first list element to some data of arbitrary origin. The importance of this "dummy" first element will be realized in future list operations.

Figure 15-2 shows the procedures that will read and build a list from a sequence of guest records for the Bates Motel. These records consist of a name, room number, and the number of occupants in the room. The main program will contain the following data type declarations.

```
TYPE
   GUEST = RECORD
      NAME : PERSON;
      ROOMNUM : INTEGER;
      OCCUPANTS : INTEGER
   END;
   GUESTPOINTER = ^GUESTNODE;
   GUESTNODE = RECORD
      GUESTINFO : GUEST;
      LINK : GUESTPOINTER
   END;
```

In procedure CREATE, the pointer variable FIRST is defined and used as the pointer to the first new list element. The pointer variables LAST and NEXT are declared inside the procedure. They will represent the pointer to the last list element and the pointer to the new list element, respectively. This procedure will only create five new nodes because the FOR loop will only execute five times. If the creation of more nodes is desired, the range of the FOR loop would have to be extended.

Notice that a pointer was used to specify a record name in the WITH statement. In the WITH statement header

```
WITH FIRST^, GUESTINFO DO
```

```
PROCEDURE CREATE (VAR FIRST: GUESTPOINTER);
(* THIS PROCEDURE READS THE GUEST RECORDS AND STORES THEM IN A LIST *)

  VAR
    LAST, NEXT : GUESTPOINTER;
    I          : INTEGER;

  PROCEDURE NEW_NODE (VAR NEXT : GUESTPOINTER);
  (* THIS PROCEDURE ALLOCATES MEMORY FOR A NEW NODE AND STORES THE
     INFORMATION ON THE NEW GUEST *)

    BEGIN  (* NEW_NODE *)

      NEW (NEXT);
      WITH NEXT^, GUESTINFO DO
        BEGIN
          WRITE ('NAME OF GUEST: ');
          READLN (NAME);
          WRITELN;
          WRITE ('ROOM NUMBER: ');
          READLN (ROOMNUM);
          WRITELN;
          WRITE ('NUMBER OF OCCUPANTS: ');
          READLN (OCCUPANTS);
          WRITELN;
          LINK := NIL
        END    (* WITH *)

    END; (* NEW_NODE *)

  BEGIN  (* CREATE *)

   (* CREATE THE FIRST NODE *)
   NEW (FIRST);

   WITH FIRST^, GUESTINFO DO
      BEGIN
        NAME := 'AAAAAAAAAA';
        ROOMNUM := 0;
        OCCUPANTS := 0;
        LINK := NIL
      END;  (* WITH *)

   (* READ EACH GUEST'S DATA TO NEXT. ATTACH THE NODE NEXT TO NODE LAST*)

   LAST := FIRST;

     FOR I := 1 TO 5 DO
        BEGIN
          NEW_NODE (NEXT);
          LAST^.LINK := NEXT;
          LAST := NEXT
        END

   END; (* CREATE *)
```

Figure 15-2 **CREATING A LINKED LIST**

FIRST^ is the name of a record to be manipulated. The field references inside the WITH block are abbreviations for the following:

```
FIRST^.GUESTINFO.NAME

FIRST^.GUESTINFO.ROOMNUM

FIRST^.GUESTINFO.OCCUPANTS

FIRST^.LINK
```

The link field of each new element is initialized to NIL.

CREATE joins the NEXT element to the last element with the statement

```
LAST^.LINK := NEXT;
```

The statement

```
LAST := NEXT;
```

advances LAST to point to the newest list node.

Node Deletion

Dynamic data structures are relatively easy to change. One modification is the deletion of a node from a linked list. In the linked list below, suppose the string PARROT needs to be deleted.

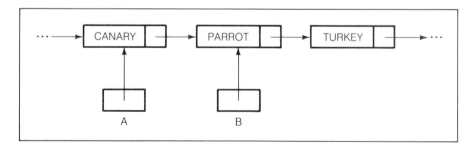

Two pointers are required to perform the deletion. One pointer must point to the node that is being deleted (B) and the other must point to the node just before it. The statement

```
A^.LINK := B^.LINK;
```

has the effect of modifying the LINK field of the node that is pointed to by A. The string CANARY will no longer be linked to PARROT but now will be linked to TURKEY. The modified data structure is shown below.

319

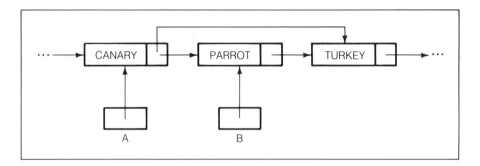

At this point, PARROT is considered to be deleted. This part of the list now only consists of two nodes with BIRD field values of CANARY and TURKEY. Note that even though the node with BIRD field value PARROT is still pointed to by B, it is no longer considered part of the list.

Now that the node has been deleted, the next objective is to free the storage that it is occupying so it may be reallocated.

The statement

DISPOSE (B);

is used to "return" the node pointed to by B to unused storage. The word "return" has special significance. B still exists but is undefined and does not reference any storage location. It is in the condition it was in before the original call of NEW (B). At first, the use of DISPOSE may be confusing because it appears that the pointer variable B is being disposed rather than the node whose address is in B. Once the difference is understood, the use of DISPOSE will not cause any problems.

The student should note that most but not all Pascal compilers include the prewritten procedure DISPOSE. Before you attempt to use procedure DISPOSE, check the compiler reference manual for your particular compiler. If your compiler does not include procedure DISPOSE, one of the following steps must be taken:

1. You must write and insert procedure DISPOSE into the program.
2. All statements that call procedure DISPOSE must be deleted.
3. A dummy procedure named DISPOSE must be inserted into the program. This dummy procedure will consist of a BEGIN and END statement.

Although the first step is not feasible for the beginning programmer, the second two steps could be easily implemented. It should be pointed out that the last two steps will not free storage.

As an example of node deletion, procedure DELETE is presented to delete a guest who is checking out of the Bates Motel. A traversal of the list is needed to find the node in the linked list that contains the record of the vacating guest. Therefore, procedure DELETE will need to call procedure TRAVERSE to sequentially search the list for the guest's name. Three parameters will have to be passed to procedure DELETE.

```
PROCEDURE DELETE (FIRST : GUESTPOINTER; FIND: STRING; VAR GONE : BOOLEAN);
(* THIS PROCEDURE FINDS A GIVEN GUEST'S NAME AND THEN DELETES THAT NODE *)

   VAR
     LAST, NEXT : GUESTPOINTER;

   PROCEDURE TRAVERSE (FIRST : GUESTPOINTER; FIND : STRING; VAR LAST,
                       NEXT : GUESTPOINTER);
   (* THIS PROCEDURE TRAVERSES THE LIST UNTIL THE NAME IS FOUND OR
      THE END OF THE LIST IS REACHED *)

     BEGIN

       NEXT := FIRST;
       WHILE (NEXT^.GUESTINFO.NAME <> FIND) AND (NEXT^.LINK <> NIL) DO
         BEGIN
           LAST := NEXT;
           NEXT := NEXT^.LINK
         END  (* WHILE *)

     END;  (* TRAVERSE *)

   BEGIN  (* DELETE *)

     TRAVERSE (FIRST, FIND, LAST, NEXT);
     (* DELETE THE NAME IF FOUND AND SET GONE TO TRUE *)

     IF NEXT^.GUESTINFO.NAME = FIND THEN
       BEGIN
         LAST^.LINK := NEXT^.LINK;
         GONE := TRUE
       END
     ELSE
         GONE := FALSE

   END;  (* DELETE *)
```

Figure 15-3 DELETING A NODE

The first is the pointer that points to the first node in the list. The second is the name of the guest to be deleted. The third is a BOOLEAN variable parameter to indicate if the deletion was completed. Two local pointer variables, LAST and NEXT, need to be declared inside the procedure. They will go through the list until the desired name is found or until the NIL value is found in a LINK field. LAST points to the previous list node and NEXT points to the current list node. Procedure DELETE is shown in Figure 15-3. In this procedure, GONE is set to true if the target was found by procedure TRAVERSE. If the end of the list was encountered before the target in procedure TRAVERSE, procedure DELETE would set GONE to false. The person whose name was entered as the target was evidently not a guest. Procedure TRAVERSE in Figure 15-3 traverses the list in search of the desired name. The above procedure has two aspects that should be considered. The first is the condition

```
(NEXT^.NAME <> FIND) AND (NEXT^.LINK <> NIL)
```

It seems that the condition

```
(NEXT^.GUESTINFO.NAME <> FIND) AND (NEXT <> NIL)
```

would be needed instead to control loop repetition. This last statement is not appropriate because the value of NEXT^.GUESTINFO.NAME is not defined when NEXT is NIL. The second item that should be noted concerns the dummy element in the list. If the first list element was not a dummy element and the first list element needed to be deleted, problems would arise. The pointer variable NEXT would point to the first list node, which is being deleted, and pointer variable LAST points to the node just before it. There is the problem: there is no node before the first node. This is the reason the dummy element was introduced to the list. If there were no dummy element, procedure DELETE would have to be written differently.

Node Insertion

This section will cover inserting a node into a list. Suppose the following list segment exists.

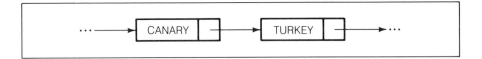

A node with PARROT in its BIRD field needs to be inserted between the two nodes shown above. Two pointers, A and B, are needed to point to the nodes that immediately precede and follow the new node.

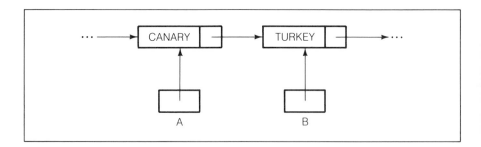

Two simple statements will produce the desired effect.

```
NEW (A^.LINK);
A^.LINK^.LINK := B;
```

The result is shown at the top of the next page.

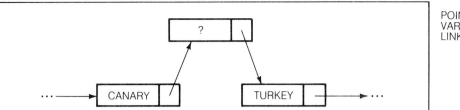

The new node that was created by the first statement is pointed to by the link field of a node A. The new node's link field, represented by A^.LINK^ .LINK, points to the same node as pointer B. To complete the problem, PARROT must be assigned to the BIRD field of the new list element. The statement

```
A^.LINK^.BIRD := 'PARROT';
```

produces the final desired effect. The new list segment with its new list element between nodes A and B is shown below.

To maintain an ordered list, a list insertion may be needed rather than simply attaching a new node on to the end of a list. In the previous example of the motel roster, suppose the names of the guests are kept in alphabetical order. When adding a new guest, it is necessary to determine where the guest's name should be inserted into the list.

Mr. Randle has just checked into the Bates Motel and his name needs to be inserted into the list. The desired location of Mr. Randle's name is shown below.

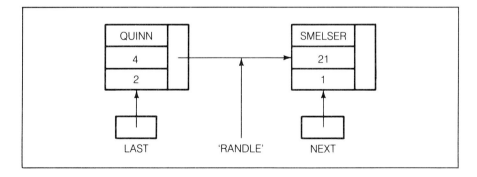

Before pointers LAST and NEXT obtained their shown position, they had to traverse the list until this desired position was found. The

```
PROCEDURE ADD_GUEST (NEWGUEST : GUEST; FIRST : GUESTPOINTER);
(* THIS PROCEDURE INSERTS A NEW GUEST INTO THE LIST *)

  VAR
    LAST, NEXT : GUESTPOINTER;

  PROCEDURE TRAVERSE2 (VAR LAST, NEXT : GUESTPOINTER; NEWGUEST : GUEST);

    BEGIN

      NEXT := FIRST;
      WHILE (NEWGUEST.NAME > NEXT^.GUESTINFO.NAME)
      AND (NEXT^.LINK <> NIL) DO
        BEGIN
          LAST := NEXT;
          NEXT := NEXT^.LINK
        END

    END;   (* TRAVERSE2 *)

  PROCEDURE CREATE_INSERT (NEWGUEST : GUEST; VAR LAST : GUESTPOINTER;
                           NEXT : GUESTPOINTER);
  (* THIS PROCEDURE INSERTS A NODE BETWEEN LAST AND NEXT OR AT THE
     END OF THE LIST *)

    BEGIN

      NEW (LAST^.LINK);

      WITH LAST^.LINK^ DO
          BEGIN
            GUESTINFO := NEWGUEST;
            LINK := NEXT
          END

    END;   (* CREATE_INSERT*)

  BEGIN  (* ADD_GUEST *)

    TRAVERSE2 (LAST, NEXT, NEWGUEST);

    IF NEWGUEST.NAME = NEXT^.GUESTINFO.NAME THEN
      NEXT^.GUESTINFO := NEWGUEST
    ELSE IF NEWGUEST.NAME < NEXT^.GUESTINFO.NAME THEN
      CREATE_INSERT (NEWGUEST, LAST, NEXT)
    ELSE
        CREATE_INSERT (NEWGUEST, NEXT, NIL)

  END;   (* ADD_GUEST *)
```

Figure 15-4 INSERTING A NODE

traversal of the list will be stopped for one of the following reasons. A
name that alphabetically follows the new guest's is found; a duplicate of
the new guest's name is found; the end of the list is reached. If the first
case is encountered, the name and the corresponding data for the new
guest will be inserted into the list. If the second case is encountered,
the room number and the number of occupants will be updated. It is
assumed that no two guests have the same name. In the last case, the
new name is added to the end of the list since it must alphabetically
follow all guest names already in the list.

In procedure ADD_GUEST, shown in Figure 15-4, the guest list is assumed to be in alphabetical order. The name of the new guest (NEWGUEST) and the pointer to the first list element (FIRST) are passed to the procedure by the calling program. Procedure CREATE_INSERT is also shown in Figure 15-4. Note that LAST is a variable parameter. The LINK field of node LAST now points to the new node.

◢◣LEARNING CHECK 15-2

1. The _____ of a node may link another node to the list.
2. A BOOLEAN expression may check the NIL/NOT NIL status of a pointer variable to determine if it is a _____.
3. What one field must be defined inside a record to create a linked list?
4. The statement DISPOSE (pointer) is used to _____ so that it may be reallocated.
5. State the three major steps in creating a linked node in a list.

Answers:

1. pointer field   2. NIL pointer   3. pointer field   4. free storage   5. (a) create node with NEW statement; (b) initialize data fields; (c) link the next element.

SUMMARY POINTS

- Dynamic, not static, variables are used in a dynamic data structure. These variables can be created and disposed of as a program executes.
- The memory address of the dynamic variable is stored in a pointer variable (or pointer).
- A pointer type is defined as referencing or pointing to a location of a particular type called the reference type. The following notation is used:
  pointer_name = ^node_name
  Pointer_name is the pointer type and node_name is its reference type.
- The dynamic allocation procedure NEW gives a pointer type variable a location in memory to reference. Procedure DISPOSE frees this space.
- A pointer may be given an address only by using NEW or by assigning it the address of another pointer of the identical type (this makes them both reference the same location). However, any pointer variable may be assigned the value NIL (NIL pointer).
- A pointer's address may not be printed or inspected. It may be compared to other pointer values or to NIL for equality or inequality.
- The contents of a location can be inspected or changed through the pointer if the following special notation is used:
  pointer^.field_name
- A pointer may be defined as referencing a type that has not yet been defined. However, it will be defined to complete the circular definition.

325

VOCABULARY LIST

Circular definition Declarations of a new pointer type that point to records involve an unusual characteristic that uses a reference type in the declarations before it has been defined as a record. The pointer type that is associated with the reference type is used inside the record declaration to complete the definition.

Dynamic data structure A collection of elements that can change in size, depending on the data storage requirements of a program.

Dynamic variables Variables that may be created or disposed of as a program executes.

Linked list The simplest form of dynamic data structure, consisting of one or more nodes that are linked or connected together.

List head The first list element in a linked list.

NIL A value of null that is placed in a link field of an element.

NIL pointer A pointer that has been assigned the value NIL.

Node An element in a dynamic data structure.

Pointer type The type of a pointer that may reference a particular type of storage location.

Pointer variables Variables that contain a memory address of a dynamic variable.

Pointers See **Pointer variables**.

Reference type A particular type of memory location that can be referenced by a pointer type.

Static variables Variables that are declared at the beginning of a program or subprogram and remain in existence throughout the execution of the blocks in which they were declared. For each variable, the computer sets aside a small portion of its memory as a location.

CHAPTER TEST

VOCABULARY

Match each term from the numbered column with the best description from the lettered column.

1. List head

2. Dynamic variables

3. Node

4. Dynamic data structure

5. Static variables

6. Pointer variables
7. Pointer type

8. Reference type

a. A pointer variable that has the null value NIL.

b. Variables that remain in existence throughout the execution of the block in which they are declared.

c. The type of a pointer that may reference a particular type of storage location.

d. Declaration of a dynamic data structure.

e. One element of a dynamic data structure.

f. The first element in a list.

g. A particular type of memory location that is pointed to by a pointer type variable.

h. A group of nodes that can change in size depending on the data storage requirements.

9. NIL pointer

10. Linked list
11. Circular definition

i. Contain the memory address of data.
j. A collection of connected nodes.
k. Variables that can be created and disposed of as a program executes.

QUESTIONS

1. Why was the name 'AAAAAAAAAA' used as the dummy element in procedure CREATE?

2. What is the advantage of a dynamic data structure over an array of records?

3. Why is the declaration of a dynamic data structure called a circular definition?

4. When nodes are disposed they are sent to free storage. What is free storage?

5. What is wrong with the following statements? Assume that the pointers A, B, and C are pointing to INTEGER storage locations.

a. `A^ := 5;`

b. `B^ := NIL;`

c. `WRITELN (C);`

d. `A^ := B + C;`

6. A small portion of memory is set aside as a location for a static variable. How much is this small portion?

7. The program segment below was written to delete the last node from a linked list. Pointer variable FIRST points to the first node in the list, if there is one, or has the value null.

```
TYPE
    POINTER = ^NODE;
    NODE = RECORD
        NUM : INTEGER;
        LINK : POINTER
    END;

VAR
    A, B, FIRST : POINTER;

BEGIN

    A := FIRST;
    B := A^.LINK;
    WHILE B^.LINK <> NIL DO
        BEGIN
            A := B;
            B := B^.LINK
        END;
    A^.LINK := NIL;
```

Which of the following choices will enable the algorithm to work properly?
a. All linked lists.
b. A linked list with one entry.
c. No linked lists.
d. All nonempty linked lists.
e. All linked lists with more than one entry.

327

PROGRAMMING PROBLEMS

1. Write a procedure that determines the length of an arbitrary list terminated by NIL.

2. Write a main program that will implement procedures CREATE, DELETE, and INSERT. The user should be able to choose among the three for an unlimited number of operations until the stopping condition is entered. (Hint: The use of a CASE statement may make the programming simpler and easier to follow.)

3. It is possible to represent a polynomial as a linked list. The coefficient and exponent of a given term would be contained in each node. The linked list representation of the polynomial $7Y^4 - 5Y + 2$ is shown below.

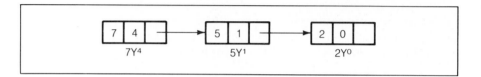

Write a program to read two polynomials and store them as linked lists. Then add them together, and print the result as a polynomial. Store this result in a third linked list. Write out all the steps in finding the solution thoroughly before starting to write the program.

4. The following declarations describe a linked list that contains an alphabetical ordering of names.

```
TYPE
    POINTER = ^NODE;
    NODE = RECORD
        NAME : STRING[10];
        LINK : POINTER
    END;
```

The first node in the list does not contain a name. Write a procedure with the header statement

```
PROCEDURE NAMEDELETE (LISTPOINTER : POINTER; BEGINLETTER,
                      ENDLETTER : CHAR; VAR DELETED :
                      POINTER);
```

that deletes from the list pointed to by LISTPOINTER all nodes with names that begin with a letter in the range from BEGINLETTER to ENDLETTER. Names that begin with BEGINLETTER and ENDLETTER are not to be deleted. DELETED should point to the list of deleted nodes.

Stacks, Queues, and Trees

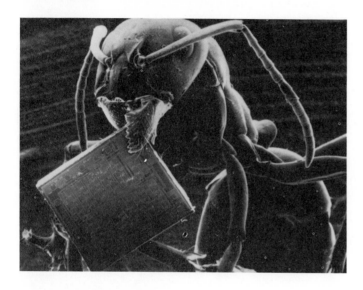

CHAPTER OUTLINE

LEARNING OBJECTIVES

After studying this chapter, you should be able to:

1. Define and implement a stack.
2. Discuss some of the uses of a stack.
3. Define and implement a queue.
4. Define and use a circular list that implements a queue.
5. Discuss some of the uses of a queue.
6. Define and implement a tree.
7. Discuss the needed steps for traversing a tree.
8. Identify a node in a tree using the correct terminology.

ADVANCED PLACEMENT CHAPTER HIGHLIGHTS

The following topics from the Advanced Placement Computer Science Exam are covered in this chapter:

linear data structures
   stacks
   queues
tree structures
   terminology
   binary trees

INTRODUCTION

In the previous chapter, the simplest form of dynamic data structure, the linked list, was discussed. Linked lists may be manipulated in different ways to perform specific tasks. Two such manipulations involve two linear structures called the stack and the queue. Another interesting data structure that can be represented by using pointer variables is the tree. Although stacks, queues, and trees involve complex forms of dynamic data structures, the general idea behind these data structures is simple if linked lists are thoroughly understood.

STACKS

In the preceding chapter we showed how to insert and delete nodes in a linked list. The insertions and deletions could be made anywhere in the list. A list that is restricted to having entries to or removals from one end only is called a **stack**. Insertions and deletions can only be made at the top of the stack. A good analogy for a stack is a pile of trays in a

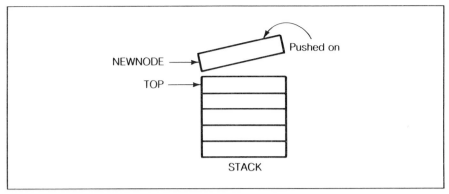

NEWNODE

TOP

Pushed on

STACK

Figure 16-1 ADDING AN ELEMENT TO A STACK

cafeteria. When you want a tray you take it off the top of the stack. When you are finished with the tray you put it back on the top. When a list is used as a stack, the pointer that points to the current top of the list is called TOP. When an element is removed from the top, the element is said to be **popped** off. TOP must be adjusted to point to the next element. When an element is added to the top, it has been **pushed** onto the stack.

Stacks can be used in many computer operations. Many kinds of reversals use stacks. A reversal is an operation that reverses the order of a list. For example, a recursive call could be used to reverse a line of input that is stored in the computer's stack. Each data item is stacked on top of the previous data item. When data items are popped off the stack, the last data item in the line of input is the first to be removed. So, the first data item in the line will be the last to be removed from the stack. Also, stacks are often used to evaluate arithmetic expressions. The order of operators and operands on a stack does away with the need for parentheses. When you are using a stack to evaluate an arithmetic expression, the order of the operators in an expression with parentheses must be rearranged. Before an operator is placed on the stack, any operators having higher priorities must be removed from the stack. Thus, the operators are reordered into the order in which they will be applied, as dictated by the priorities.

Procedure PUSH

Procedure PUSH puts a new element on top of a stack. Figure 16-1 shows an element, referenced by pointer NEWNODE, being placed on the stack.

After the new element is placed on top of the stack, pointer TOP is advanced to point to this new element.

The type of declaration of stacks needs to be understood when programming stacks. A typical type declaration of a stack appears on the next page.

331

```
TYPE
  NODEPOINTER = ^NODE;
  NODE = RECORD
    DATA : DATATYPE;
    LINK : NODEPOINTER
  END;
```

The individual elements, or nodes, of a stack are declared as records. DATA represents the data stored in the nodes of the stack. Standard or user-defined data types can be used in a stack. LINK points to the next element of the stack.

Procedure PUSH is presented in Figure 16-2 below.

Note that TOP is the only parameter that needs to be passed as a variable parameter. TOP is the only variable to be permanently changed in the procedure.

Procedure POP

Procedure POP would be called to remove the top element of a stack. In Figure 16-3, procedure POP is shown. The procedure begins by duplicating the pointer variable TOP into pointer POPNODE. Next TOP is moved down one element and the pointer field of the node that was just popped is set to NIL.

The assignment of the value NIL has the effect of isolating the popped node from the rest of the stack. This is not essential but it helps prevent inadvertent errors in another part of the program. If the LINK field was not set to NIL, POPNODE could be used to access and change the entire stack.

QUEUES

The **queue** is another specialized type of list. For this type of list, additions are made at the end of the list and deletions are made from the beginning. A good analogy is a line of people at the movie theater. As people are admitted from one end, people are added to the other. The first person in is always the first person out.

Queues are essential to time-shared computer systems. Since data cannot be relied on to arrive in an orderly fashion, queues are used to

```
PROCEDURE PUSH (NEWNODE : NODEPOINTER; VAR TOP : NODEPOINTER);
(* PUSHES NEWNODE ON TOP OF THE STACK *)

BEGIN
  TOP^.LINK := NEWNODE;
  TOP := NEWNODE
END; (* PUSH *)
```

Figure 16-2 PROCEDURE PUSH

```
PROCEDURE POP (VAR POPNODE, TOP : NODEPOINTER);
(* POPS POPNODE FROM THE STACK *)

BEGIN
  POPNODE := TOP;
  TOP := TOP^.LINK;
  POPNODE^.LINK := NIL
END;  (* POP *)
```

Figure 16-3 PROCEDURE POP

keep track of each user's input. In effect, the computer executes commands at one end of the queue while adding new commands to the other end as they come in. Also, queues are useful for simulating real-life processes. Suppose a ticket counter is operated and information is needed to decide if each window should have its own line, or if a single line should feed all the windows. The nature of the problem, customers arriving at irregular intervals and being served after varying waits, calls for a queue representation.

Figure 16-4 shows a linked list with pointers to its head and tail. The type definition for stacks is also valid for queues. However, since two pointers are used by queues, they must be declared. Therefore

```
VAR
  HEAD, TAIL  : NODEPOINTER;
```

must be included in the declaration section.

One approach to setting up a queue as a data structure would be to add new nodes to the tail, on the left, and remove them when they've worked their way up to the head of the queue at the right. The following statements could be used to add nodes.

```
NEW (TEMPPOINTER);
TEMPPOINTER^.LINK := TAIL;
TAIL := TEMPPOINTER;
```

However, removing a node from the head is pretty difficult because the HEAD pointer can't be moved backward. So, some elaborate code is required to complete the operation. It is shown on the next page.

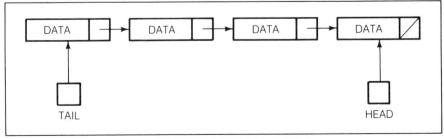

Figure 16-4 LINKED LIST WITH HEAD AND TAIL

```
(* START TEMPPOINTER AT THE TAIL OF THE LIST *)
TEMPPOINTER := TAIL;
WHILE TEMPPOINTER^.LINK <> HEAD DO
(* PUT TEMPPOINTER JUST BEFORE HEAD *)
TEMPPOINTER := TEMPPOINTER^.LINK;
(* BOTH POINTERS NOW REFERENCE THE NEXT TO LAST ELEMENT *)
HEAD := TEMPPOINTER;
(* TEMPPOINTER NOW POINTS TO THE LAST NODE AND MAY BE REMOVED *)
TEMPPOINTER := TEMPPOINTER^.LINK;
```

Although these statements perform the operation, a simpler method is desired. Actually, the solution is very simple. Reversing the pointers will transform our linked list into a convenient representation of a queue. The reversed pointers are shown in Figure 16-5.

A new node may be added with the following statements.

```
NEW (TAIL^.LINK);
TAIL := TAIL^.LINK;
TAIL^.LINK := NIL;
```

Similarly, a node may be deleted with the code below:

```
TEMPPOINTER := HEAD;
IF HEAD^.LINK <> NIL THEN
    HEAD := HEAD^.LINK;
```

Nothing in the definition of LISTNODE says that we have to create lists with heads or tails. A **circular list** has no beginning or end—the last element points to the first. An interesting case of a circular list is one with only one element.

```
NEW (LISTPOINTER);
LISTPOINTER^.LINK := LISTPOINTER;
```

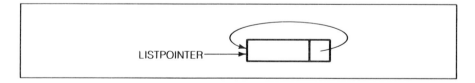

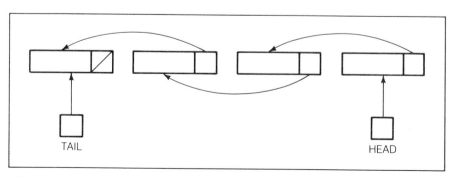

Figure 16-5 DIAGRAM OF A QUEUE

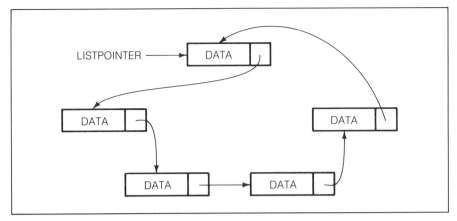

Figure 16-6 A CIRCULAR LIST

Although some applications specifically require circular data structures, many circular lists are generated because a single "current position" pointer can act as both a head and tail pointer. Figure 16-6 illustrates an example of a circular list that implements a queue.

LISTPOINTER points to the end of the queue. A new node is put on the queue with the following statements:

```
NEW (TEMPPOINTER);
TEMPPOINTER^.LINK := LISTPOINTER^.LINK;
LISTPOINTER^.LINK := TEMPPOINTER;
LISTPOINTER := LISTPOINTER^.LINK;
```

The node that has been on the queue the longest is removed. The code below performs this operation.

```
(* POINT TEMPPOINTER AT THE OLDEST ELEMENT *)
TEMPPOINTER := LISTPOINTER^.LINK;
(* RELINK THE LIST AROUND IT *)
LISTPOINTER^.LINK := LISTPOINTER^.LINK^.LINK;
```

⩗LEARNING CHECK 16-1

1. Pointer variable TOP in procedure PUSH must be passed as a _____ so that the location of the new top stack element is known by the main program.
2. What has the effect of isolating a popped node from the rest of the stack?
3. What is the purpose of isolating a popped node?
4. Which structure, stack or queue, is referred to as first in–first out?
5. Why is removing a node from the head of a queue difficult?

Answers:

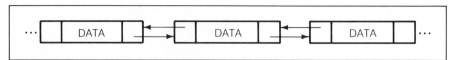

Figure 16-7   A DOUBLY-LINKED LIST

TREES

Nodes in a list may have more than one pointer field. This is known as a **multiply-linked list**. In Figure 16-7, a doubly (or two-way) linked list is shown.

Each node in the list has a forward pointer that points to the next node and a backward pointer that points to the previous node. The statements below declare a node with two link fields.

```
TYPE
    LINK = ^MULTINODE;
    MULTINODE = RECORD
        DATA : (DATATYPE);
        FORWARD : LINK;
        BACKWARD : LINK
    END;
```

A **tree** is one special type of multiply-linked list that is used in computer science. The tree is a nonlinear data structure. A **binary tree** is a special kind of tree that has no more than two branches from each node. An illustration of a binary tree is presented in Figure 16-8.

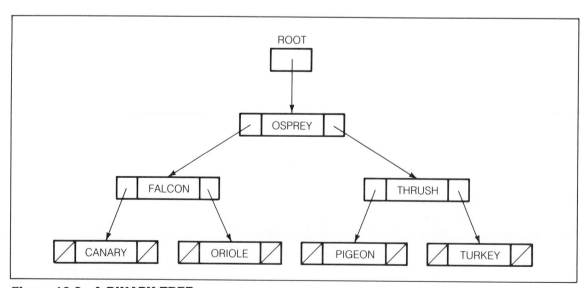

Figure 16-8   A BINARY TREE

Notice that instead of growing from the bottom up, this tree grows from the top down. The topmost element is called the **root** of the tree. As shown in Figure 16-8, pointer ROOT points to the root of the tree. Each node has one data field and two pointer fields, called the left branch and the right branch. A **branch** is a pointer field of a node in a tree. The NIL pointer is indicated by a slash (/). Any node with both pointer fields equal to NIL is called a **leaf**.

The **parent** of the nodes containing CANARY and ORIOLE is the node containing the string FALCON. The nodes CANARY and ORIOLE are the **children** of node FALCON. The node CANARY is the **sibling** of node ORIOLE. The **descendants** of a node are the node's children, it's children's children, and so forth. The **ancestors** of a node are its parent, its parent's parents, and so on until the root of the tree is reached.

Every node in a tree may be thought of as the root node of its own **subtree**. In a binary tree each node has no more than two branches so it may have up to two subtrees, a left subtree and a right subtree.

The statements below declare a node of the form in Figure 16-8.

```
TYPE
    BRANCH = ^TREE;
    TREE = RECORD
        BIRD : STRING;
        LEFT, RIGHT : BRANCH
    END;
```

Figure 16-9 shows another example of a binary tree. This tree represents an expression that is stored in memory.

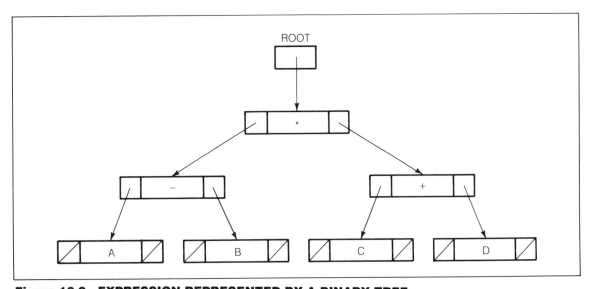

Figure 16-9 EXPRESSION REPRESENTED BY A BINARY TREE

The left subtree contains the expression $(A - B)$ and the right subtree contains $(C + D)$.

The entire expression that the tree represents is

$$(A - B) * (C + D)$$

In order to efficiently locate a given item in a tree, a tree must be organized to keep related data items together. The tree in Figure 16-8 is ordered so that the left descendant of each node alphabetically precedes its parent and the right descendant alphabetically follows its parent. Because of this ordering, the path taken when searching for a given value depends on the value of the current node. If the given value is less than the current node value, the left branch is taken. If the given value is greater than the value of the current node, the right branch is taken.

Building a Tree

This section will create the tree that was illustrated in Figure 16-8. The creation will be performed by procedure TREECREATE. The root of the tree is defined by a pointer named ROOT. The first string will be stored in this node. The following strings are read to NEXTBIRD and positioned in the tree by comparing each one to the string stored in each ancestor node (starting with the root). The left branch is followed if NEXTBIRD alphabetically precedes the string in the ancestor node. If the opposite is true, the right branch is followed. When a NIL pointer is reached, it is replaced by a pointer to a new node that contains NEXTBIRD.

This process is obviously affected by the order in which character strings are read. The first string input will become the permanent root. Therefore, OSPREY must begin the input of strings. Next, either FALCON or THRUSH must be placed in position before their corresponding children are entered. It should be noted that a subtree (down to the leaves) could be entirely completed before another branch is even started.

Below, an input ordering is given. Before proceeding, see if you can determine how the tree is created?

1. OSPREY.
2. THRUSH.
3. TURKEY.
4. PIGEON.
5. FALCON.
6. CANARY.
7. ORIOLE.

This ordering completely finishes the right subtree beginning at the root. After the fourth character string is read, the tree looks like this:

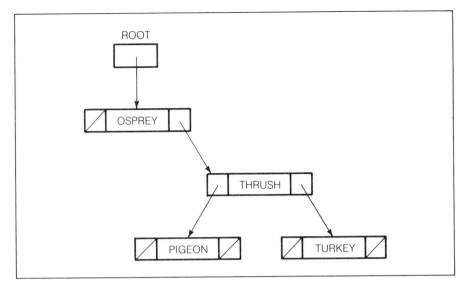

Procedure TREECREATE requires the following type declarations in the main program.

```
TYPE
    BRANCH = ^TREE;
    TREE = RECORD
        BIRD : STRING;
        LEFT, RIGHT : BRANCH
    END;
```

The only variation from the singly-linked list declarations is the extra pointer field variable. Additionally, procedure TREECREATE has one parameter. In fact, it is the pointer parameter (ROOT) that references the root node of the new tree.

In Figure 16-10 procedure TREECREATE is shown. Nested within this procedure are procedures ATTACH and TREESEARCH. Procedure ATTACH allocates a new node for NEXTBIRD, pointed to by PARENT, and attaches this new node to the tree. Procedure TREESEARCH searches for NEXTBIRD and inserts it into the tree by calling ATTACH if NEXTBIRD isn't found.

It should be evident that TREESEARCH is the heart of the solution to the problem. It locates the correct position to place the new node. Two program variables are needed to communicate with TREE-SEARCH. The first is a pointer called PARENT. Originally, it is initialized to the starting point of the search (ROOT). After the return from TREESEARCH, it points to the node that contains NEXTBIRD. The second is a BOOLEAN variable called FOUND. It indicates whether NEXTBIRD was in the tree (true) or not (false).

As the search progresses, pointer PARENT, which corresponds to an update parameter of TREESEARCH, may be modified. Since every search begins at the root node, PARENT must be initialized to ROOT before TREESEARCH is called. If NEXTBIRD is already in the tree,

339

```
PROCEDURE TREECREATE (VAR ROOT : BRANCH);
(* CREATES AN ORDERED TREE *)

VAR
   I          : INTEGER;
   NEXTBIRD : STRING;
   PARENT    : BRANCH;
   FOUND     : BOOLEAN;
   FLOCK     : TEXT;

(*********************************************************************)

PROCEDURE ATTACH (NEXTBIRD : STRING; VAR PARENT : BRANCH);
(* CREATES A NEW NODE POINTED TO BY PARENT *)

BEGIN    (* ATTACH *)

   NEW (PARENT);

   WITH PARENT^ DO
      BEGIN
          BIRD := NEXTBIRD;
          LEFT := NIL;
          RIGHT := NIL
      END    (* WITH *)

END;    (* ATTACH *)

(*********************************************************************)

PROCEDURE TREESEARCH (VAR PARENT : BRANCH; NEXTBIRD : STRING; VAR
                      FOUND : BOOLEAN);

BEGIN    (* TREESEARCH *)

   IF PARENT = NIL THEN
      BEGIN
          FOUND := FALSE;
          ATTACH (NEXTBIRD, PARENT)
      END    (* IF *)
```

Figure 16-10 PROCEDURE TREECREATE   *(continued next page)*

procedure TREESEARCH finds it by tracing through the tree until
PARENT points to the node containing NEXTBIRD. This situation
causes a message to be printed that indicates the duplicate entry. If
NEXTBIRD is not in the tree, PARENT eventually reaches the node
where NEXTBIRD is attached. The pointer from this node has a value of
NIL.

Procedure TREESEARCH starts at the root node and follows left or
right pointers until it finds NEXTBIRD or reaches the node where
NEXTBIRD will be attached (indicated by the pointer value NIL). As
with many operations on trees, it is easier to implement TREESEARCH
as a recursive algorithm. When a stopping state for the recursion is
reached, procedure ATTACH is called to create and assign the correct
values to a new node that is pointed to by PARENT.

```
        ELSE IF NEXTBIRD = PARENT^.BIRD THEN
            FOUND := TRUE
        ELSE IF NEXTBIRD < PARENT^.BIRD THEN
            TREESEARCH (PARENT^.LEFT, NEXTBIRD, FOUND)
        ELSE
            TREESEARCH (PARENT^.RIGHT, NEXTBIRD, FOUND)

    END;   (* TREESEARCH *)

    (***************************************************************)

BEGIN   (* TREECREATE *)
(* INSERT THE FIRST STRING IN THE ROOT NODE *)

    RESET (FLOCK, 'APPLE2: FLOCK');

    IF NOT EOF (FLOCK) THEN
        BEGIN
            READLN (FLOCK, NEXTBIRD);
            ATTACH (NEXTBIRD, ROOT)
        END   (* IF *)
    ELSE
        ROOT := NIL;

    (* READ EACH STRING TO NEXTBIRD AND ATTACH TO ITS PARENT *)
    WHILE NOT EOF (FLOCK) DO
        BEGIN
            READLN (FLOCK, NEXTBIRD);
            PARENT := ROOT;
            TREESEARCH (PARENT, NEXTBIRD, FOUND);
            IF FOUND THEN
                WRITELN (NEXTBIRD, ' IS ALREADY A TREE ELEMENT.')
        END;   (* WHILE *)

        CLOSE (FLOCK)

    END;   (* TREECREATE *)
```

Figure 16-10   PROCEDURE TREECREATE (continued)

Tree Traversal

It is necessary to traverse an ordered tree in a systematic way in order
to efficiently scan the data in each node. The three types of tree
traversals are inorder, preorder, and postorder. Of these three, only the
inorder traversal will be discussed. This particular approach involves
three steps. They are described recursively as follows:

1. Traverse the left subtree.
2. Visit the current node.
3. Traverse the right subtree.

To visit the current node implies performing some type of operation on
that node. An inorder traversal of the tree in Figure 16-8 is shown in

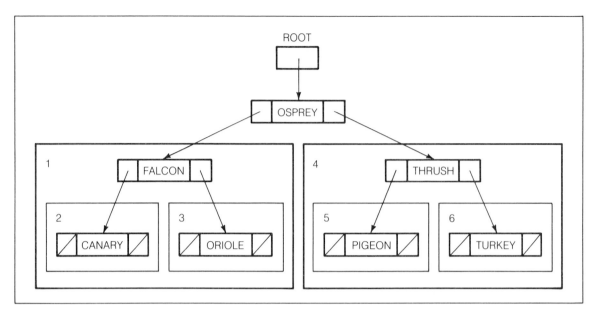

Figure 16-11 TRAVERSING A TREE

Figure 16-11. If the above three steps are followed, the resulting alphabetical sequence is generated.

```
CANARY   FALCON   ORIOLE   OSPREY   PIGEON   THRUSH   TURKEY
```

Figure 16-11 shows the tree with boxes drawn around each subtree. The steps in doing an inorder traversal of this tree are:

a. Traverse the left subtree of OSPREY (1).
b. Traverse the left subtree of FALCON (2) and print CANARY since it has no left child.
c. Since CANARY has no right child either, go back to FALCON and print it.
d. Traverse the right subtree of FALCON (3), printing ORIOLE since it has no left child.
e. Go back up to the root and print OSPREY.
f. Traverse the right subtree of OSPREY (4) in the same way, printing PIGEON, THRUSH, and TURKEY.

The recursive procedure TRAVERSE, shown below in Figure 16-12, performs the three-part traversal of an ordered tree. The parameter ROOT represents the pointer to the root node of the tree being traversed. Procedure VISIT is used to print all the data values stored in each node.

```
PROCEDURE TRAVERSE (ROOT : BRANCH);
(* THIS PROCEDURE PERFORMS AN INORDER TRAVERSAL OF A TREE *)

(*********************************************************************)

PROCEDURE VISIT (ROOT : BRANCH);

BEGIN   (* VISIT *)
   WRITELN (ROOT^.BIRD);
   WRITELN
END;   (* VISIT *)

(*********************************************************************)

BEGIN   (* TRAVERSE *)

   (* IF THERE IS ANOTHER NODE, VISIT IT *)
   IF ROOT <> NIL THEN
      BEGIN
         TRAVERSE (ROOT^.LIFT);
         VISIT (ROOT);
         TRAVERSE (ROOT^.RIGHT)
      END   (* IF *)

END;   (* TRAVERSE *)
```

Figure 16-12 PROCEDURE INORDER

LEARNING CHECK 16-2

1. A binary tree is one special kind of _____.
2. A child is a _____ of another child of the same parent.
3. All nodes below the root of a tree are _____ of the root node.
4. Every node in a tree may be thought of as the _____ of its own subtree.
5. _____ of a tree contain the value NIL in all of their pointer fields.

Answers:

1. tree   2. sibling   3. descendants   4. root node   5. Leaves

SUMMARY POINTS

- A stack is a list in which all insertions, deletions, and accesses to the list are from one end, known as the top of the stack.
- A stack may be used to reverse a line of input or eliminate the need for parentheses in an arithmetic expression.
- A queue is a list in which all insertions are made to the end of the list and deletions are made from the beginning.

- A queue keeps track of each user's input on a time-shared computer and simulates such real-life processes as a ticket counter.
- A circular list may be implemented as a queue to eliminate the need for one extra pointer. Since the head and the tail of the list are connected, one pointer may reference the beginning and end of the list.
- In multiply-linked lists, the individual nodes have more than one link.
- Trees are non-linear data structures with a root that points to zero or more subtrees.
- In binary trees, each parent may not have more than two children.
- The use of an ordered binary tree instead of a linked list decreases the traversal time needed to locate a particular element.
- The three recursive steps needed to inorder traverse a tree are:

1. Traverse the left subtree.
2. Visit the current node.
3. Traverse the right subtree.

VOCABULARY LIST

Ancestor   A node from which other nodes have descended in a tree.

Binary tree   A dynamic data structure that may connect a maximum of two nodes to a single node via two different pointers. In turn, two more nodes may be connected to each of these two added nodes. This process continues until leaves are formed.

Branch   Pointer field of a node in a tree.

Child   The node immediately below a parent node in a tree.

Circular list   A queue that has its head and tail connected by a pointer.

Descendant   Any node that comes below a given node in a tree.

Leaf   A node in a tree that has no children.

Multiply-linked list   A list of elements with more than one link.

Parent   A node in a tree that has a branch or branches to other nodes.

Pop   To delete the topmost node on a stack.

Push   To insert a node at the top of a stack.

Queue   A list in which all insertions are made at the end of the list and deletions are made from the beginning.

Root   The topmost element in a tree; the ancestor to all other nodes.

Siblings   Children of the same parent node.

Stack   A list in which all insertions, deletions, and accesses to the list are from one end, known as the top of the stack.

Subtree   Any node in a tree that has or may have at least one branch.

Tree   A dynamic data structure that has one or more nodes where one node is designated as the root which points to zero or more distinct subtrees.

CHAPTER TEST

VOCABULARY

Match each term from the numbered column with the best description from the lettered column.

1. Stack

    a. A list of elements with more than one link.

2. Queue

    b. A list such that all insertions, deletions, and accesses to the list are from one end, called the top.

3. Pop

    c. A dynamic data structure that has one node designated as the root, which may then point to zero or more subtrees.

4. Push

    d. The topmost element in a tree; the ancestor to all other nodes.

5. Circular list

    e. Pointer field of a node in a tree.

6. Multiply-linked list

    f. A node that has at least one child.

7. Tree

    g. Children of the same parent node.

8. Branch

    h. A list in which all insertions are made at the end of the list and deletions are made from the beginning.

9. Leaf

    i. A node in a tree with no descendants.

10. Root

    j. A node from which others have descended.

11. Parent

    k. To insert a node at the top of a stack.

12. Siblings

    l. To delete the topmost node on a stack.

13. Ancestor

    m. A queue that has its head and tail connected by a pointer.

QUESTIONS

1. Give two reasons why a stack might be implemented.
2. Give two reasons why a queue might be implemented.
3. How is a linked list transformed into a representation of a queue?
4. In creating a tree, what must be considered?
5. Why is ordering the input so important in procedure TREECREATE?
6. What are the three recursive steps involved in the inorder traversal of a binary tree?

7. Draw the binary tree representations of the following two expressions. The tree must be subject to an inorder traversal.

A * B MOD (A + B) DIV C

A * B MOD A + B DIV C

8. Give at least two input orderings of strings that would create the tree shown in Figure 16-8.

9. What would be printed by the inorder traversal of the tree below?

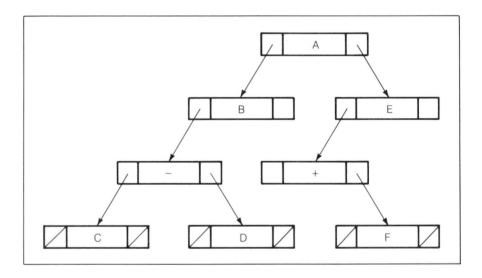

10. What can be said about the inorder traversal of any tree created by procedure TREECREATE in Figure 16-10?

PROGRAMMING PROBLEMS

1. In the previous chapter procedure CREATE was given to store the data of guests at the Bates Motel in a linked list. Rewrite procedure CREATE so that the data on the guests are stored in a binary tree. Also write a short driver program with the needed data type declarations.

2. Write a program to represent the Morse code as a binary tree. Use your library to find out about Morse code. The dot symbol (•) should cause a branch to the left and the dash symbol (–) a branch to the right. The data field of each node should be the letter represented by the corresponding code. The top part of the tree will look like this:

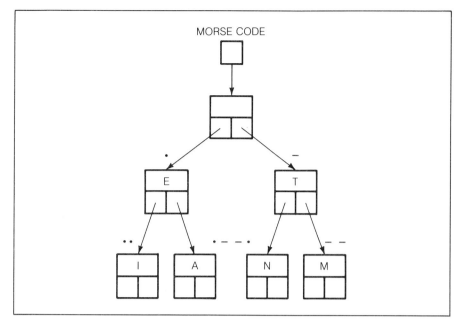

The input of the program should consist of a letter, the code string length, and the code string. After the complete tree has been built, allow a message in Morse code to be entered. Then print the message in English.

3. Use three arrays to implement two stacks which store operands and operators that make up a fully parenthesized expression, and one circular queue that is used as an output buffer, storing a "trace" of its evaluation. Since the expression is fully parenthesized, no operator precedence rules are necessary. When designing the program, assume that A, B, C, and D will be the only operands which appear in the expressions. Addition and multiplication will be the only operations which appear in the expression and all of the expressions may be assumed to be syntactically correct, containing exactly one pair of parentheses for each operation to be performed. The output should include a "trace" of how the expression was evaluated. For example, the output for ((A + B) * (C + D)) might look like this:

$$2 + 3 = 5 \qquad 6 + 4 = 10 \qquad 5 * 10 = 50$$

The expressions are evaluated by storing the values of the variables on the operand stack and the operators on the operator stack. Every time a right parenthesis is encountered, two values are popped off the operand stack and an operator is popped off the operator stack and the calculation is performed. The result is stored on the operand stack. After each operation is performed, a copy of it is sent to the output queue to provide a trace of the expression's evaluation.

347

CHAPTER 17

Numerical Algorithms

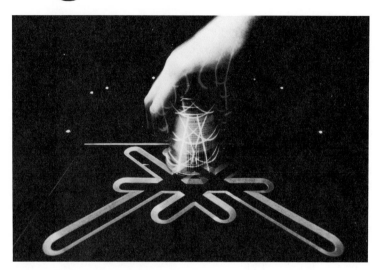

CHAPTER OUTLINE

LEARNING OBJECTIVES

INTRODUCTION

APPROXIMATIONS
  Zeros of Functions by Bisection • The Monte Carlo Technique
      LEARNING CHECK 17-1

STATISTICAL ALGORITHMS
  Measures of Central Tendency • Measures of Dispersion
      LEARNING CHECK 17-2

NUMERICAL ACCURACY
  Truncation Error • Round-Off Error • Error in Original
  Data • Blunders • Propagated Error
      LEARNING CHECK 17-3

SUMMARY POINTS

VOCABULARY LIST

CHAPTER TEST
  Vocabulary • Questions

PROGRAMMING PROBLEMS

LEARNING OBJECTIVES

After studying this chapter, you should be able to:

1. Use the bisection method to find the zeros of a function.
2. Explain the operation that the Monte Carlo technique performs.
3. Discuss three ways of producing random values.
4. List and describe two characteristics of an ungrouped set of random values.
5. Identify two measures of central tendency.
6. Identify two measures of dispersion.
7. Explain and identify the types of errors that may be present in a calculation.

ADVANCED PLACEMENT CHAPTER HIGHLIGHTS

The following topics from the Advanced Placement Computer Science Exam are covered in this chapter:

numerical algorithms
    approximations
    statistical algorithms
    numerical accuracy

INTRODUCTION

In this chapter numerical algorithms will be introduced. The three major topics covered in this chapter—approximations, statistical algorithms, and numerical accuracy—are diverse but interrelated. The section on statistical algorithms identifies and describes the characteristics of the random values created by the Monte Carlo technique. Since all calculations involve some type of error, numerical accuracy is covered so that the type of error can be identified and possibly reduced.

APPROXIMATIONS

There are many methods of approximately solving various mathematical and physical problems. Two methods are bisection and the Monte Carlo technique. The **bisection method** determines the zeros of a function. Graphically, the *x*-intercepts of a function (x) are found. The **Monte Carlo technique** utilizes the simulation of random data to find a nonrandom result.

Zeros of Functions by Bisection

The bisection method is the simplest method for finding the real zeros of a continuous function $f(x)$ on an interval $a \leq x \leq b$ and is probably the safest if a computer routine is to be depended upon completely. The heart of the bisection method is the assumption that an interval $x_1 \leq x \leq x_2$ has been found such that

$$f(x_1) \leq 0 \leq f(x_2)$$

The method proceeds to decrease the size of the interval. This decrease is accomplished by evaluating the function $f(x)$ at the midpoint of the interval; that is, by computing

$$f\left(\frac{x_1 + x_2}{2}\right)$$

In Figure 17-1 the halved interval is shown.

If the function does not evaluate as zero at the interval midpoint, then one of the interval bounds is changed to the midpoint value. If the sign of the function evaluation at the first interval bound is the opposite sign of the function evaluation at the midpoint, the midpoint value becomes the new second interval bound. Thus $\frac{1}{2}(x_1 + x_2)$ replaces either x_1 or x_2 (most of the time) and the process may be repeatedly continued. Each repetition halves the length of the interval, and ten repetitions, for example, reduce the length of the original interval by a factor of

$$2^{10} = 1024 > 1000 = 10^3$$

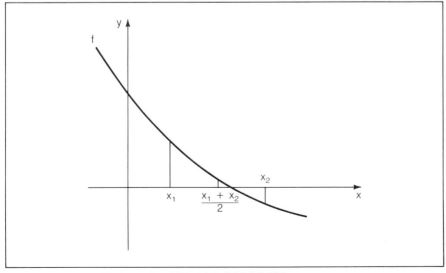

Figure 17-1 BISECTION METHOD DIAGRAM

Thus, from 10 to 20 repetitions may be required to find the zero of a given continuous function.

To further illustrate the bisection method, the cubic

$$f(x) = x^3 + x^2 - 3x - 3 = 0$$

is considered. At $x_1 = 1$, $f(x_1)$ has the value -4. At $x_2 = 2$, $f(x_2)$ has the value $+3$. Note that $f(x_1) \leq 0 \leq f(x_2)$. Since the function is continuous, it is obvious that the change in sign of the function between $x = 1$ and $x = 2$ guarantees at least one root, or solution, in the interval $(1, 2)$. Figure 17-2 illustrates the above function.

Suppose the function at $x = 1.5$ is now evaluated and the result is compared to the function values at $x = 1$ and $x = 2$. Since the function changes sign between $x = 1.5$ and $x = 2$, a root lies between these values. The process is continued to determine a smaller and smaller interval within which a solution must lie. For this example, continuation of the process yields an approximation to the root at $x = \sqrt{3} = 1.7320508075$. This process is illustrated in Figure 17-3.

While a graphic method, as illustrated in Figure 17-3, may be suitable if an approximate answer is desired, to obtain more accuracy, an algorithm that can be implemented as a computer program is needed. An algorithm is represented in Figure 17-4.

The presented algorithm requires the user to specify a tolerance value. Since a root must lie between the x-values where the function changes sign, the error in the last approximation can be no more than

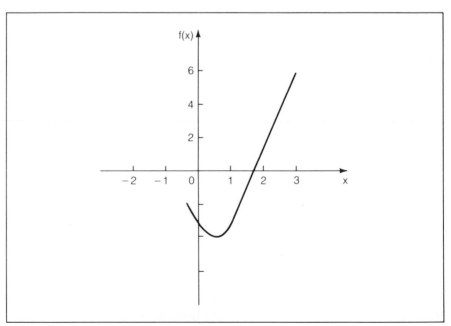

Figure 17-2   A CUBIC FUNCTION

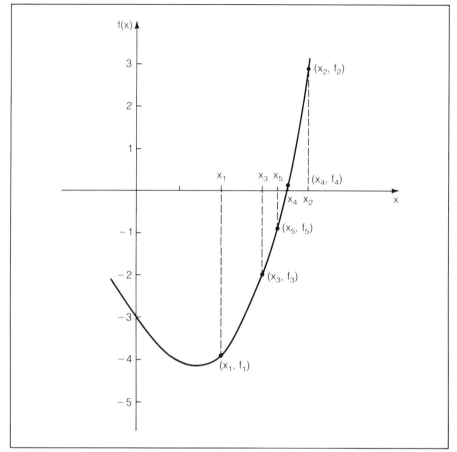

Figure 17-3 BISECTION OF A CUBIC FUNCTION

one-half the last interval of which it is the midpoint. This interval is known exactly since the original difference, $[x_1 - x_2]$, is halved at each **iteration**. The repetition of an algorithm is called iteration and successive approximations are termed the **iterates**.

The bisection method requires starting values to be obtained before the method can begin. This is true of most methods of root finding. Obtaining the starting values can be done by making a rough graph, by trial calculations, or by writing a search program on a computer or programmable calculator. In the previous illustrated example, the starting values, $x = 1$ and $x = 2$, which straddle the x-axis, could have been found by any of the above methods. The bisection method's solution based on these starting values is shown by the iterations listed in Table 17-1. Two different starting values could be chosen, which would produce a completely new set of data.

The Monte Carlo Technique

Random selection occurs when every number in a given set has an equal probability of being selected. In the 19th and early 20th cen-

To determine a root of $f(x) = 0$, accurate within a specified tolerance value, given values x_1 and x_2 such that $f(x_1)$ and $f(x_2)$ are of opposite sign,

WHILE ½ $|x_1 - x_2| \geq$ tolerance value   DO
  BEGIN
      Set $x_3 = (x_1 + x_2) / 2$
      IF $f(x_3)$ of opposite sign to $f(x_1)$
        Set $x_2 = x_3$
      ELSE   Set $x_1 = x_3$;
  END (*WHILE*)

The final value of x_3 approximates the root.
   Note: The method may give a false root if $f(x)$ is discontinuous on $[x_1, x_2]$.

Figure 17-4   BISECTION METHOD

turies, statistical problems were sometimes solved with the help of random selections, that is, by the Monte Carlo method. Before the appearance of electronic computers, this method has not widely applicable, since the simulation of random quantities by hand is a time-consuming process. Thus the development of the Monte Carlo method into a widespread numerical technique only became possible with the appearance of computers.

Monte Carlo is a city in the principality of Monaco, famous for its gambling houses. One of the simplest mechanical devices for generating random quantities is the roulette wheel. Thus the Monte Carlo method derived its name from a simple random number generator.

Example: Finding an Area

Although this example is very simple, it should clarify the idea behind the Monte Carlo technique. Suppose that the area of the figure S in

METHOD OF HALVING THE INTERVAL FOR $f(x) = x^3 + x^2 - 3x - 3 = 0$ **TABLE 17-1**

ITERATION NUMBER	x_1	x_2	x_3	$f(x_1)$	$f(x_2)$	$f(x_3)$	MAXIMUM ERROR IN x_3
1	1	2	1.5	−4.0	3.0	−1.875	0.5
2	1.5	2	1.75	−1.875	3.0	0.17187	0.25
3	1.5	1.75	1.625	−1.875	0.17187...	−0.94335...	0.125
4	1.625	1.75	1.6875	−0.94335...	0.17187	0.40942	0.0625
5	1.6875	1.75	1.71875	−0.40942...	0.17187...	−0.12478	0.03125
6	1.71875	1.75	1.73437...	−0.12478...	0.17187...	−0.02198	0.015625*
7	1.71875	1.73437...	1.72656...				0.0078125
	⋮	⋮	⋮				
∞			1.73205...			−0.00000...	

*Actual error in x_3 after 5 iterations is 0.01330.

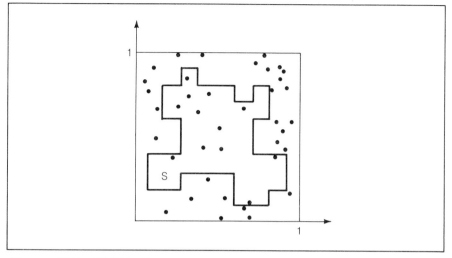

Figure 17-5   USING THE MONTE CARLO TECHNIQUE

Figure 17-5 needs to be computed. For this example, it should be assumed that S is contained completely within the unit square.

Now, if N points are randomly chosen in the square and N' designates the number of points lying inside S, the area of S is approximately equal to the ratio N'/N. In this example, $N = 40$ points were selected. Of these, $N' = 12$ points appeared inside S. The ratio $N'/N = 12/40 = 0.30$, while the true area of S is 0.35.

The above example required the random selection of points inside the unit square for the calculation. How are the random points chosen? Let us imagine that Figure 17-5 (on an increased scale) is hanging on a wall as a target. The experiment proceeds by aiming and throwing N darts at the center of the square. If we assume that the darts are not in the hands of the world champion and that they are thrown from a sufficiently great distance from the target, it is obvious that not all the darts will fall exactly in the center. They will strike the target at N random points.

The result of such an experiment is shown in Figure 17-6. In this experiment $N = 40$, $N' = 24$, and the ratio $N'/N = 0.60$ is almost double the true value of the area (0.35). It is clear that when the darts are thrown with great skill, the result of the experiment will be very bad, as almost all of the darts will fall near the center and thus in S. This method of computing area will be valid only when the random points are not simply random but, in addition, uniformly distributed over the whole square.

Generating Random Numbers on a Computer

If everything the computer does must be programmed beforehand, where can randomness come from? Several difficulties are associated with this question and their solution belongs more to philosophy than to mathematics. The use of random variables should be regarded not as providing a perfect description of natural phenomena, but as a tool in

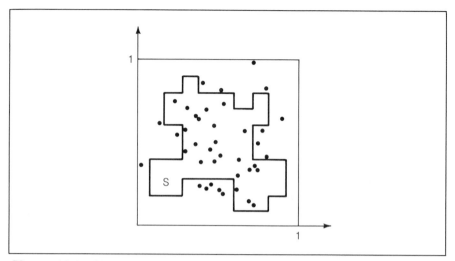

Figure 17-6 N'/N = 0.60

solving particular problems. Ordinarily, three ways of obtaining random values can be distinguished. **Tables of random numbers, random number generators**, and the **pseudorandom number** method can be used to obtain random numbers.

Tables of random numbers may be compiled in many different ways. For example, suppose ten identical slips of paper are marked with the digits 0, 1, 2 . . . 9. These slips of paper are placed in a hat, mixed together, and then drawn out, returned, and mixed again. The digits obtained in this way are written down in a table form. Such a table is called a table of random digits. It is possible to put such a table into a computer's memory.

Obviously this method would be tedious and time-consuming if a large number table was needed. Therefore, a special roulette wheel can be constructed that operates electronically. Figure 17-7 shows an elementary version of such a wheel.

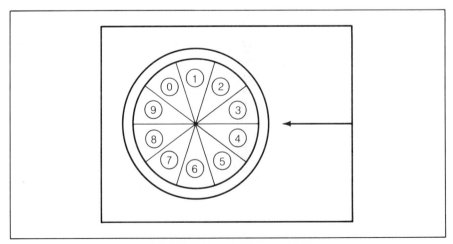

Figure 17-7 AN ELECTRONIC ROULETTE WHEEL

The roulette wheel is rotated and then stopped. The number indicated by the stationary arrow is then selected.

Compiling a good table of random numbers is not an easy task. A real physical device produces random variables with a distribution differing slightly from the ideal distribution. During an experiment such as the paper-and-hat experiment, accidents may occur. One of the slips of paper in the hat might stick to the lining for some time. Therefore, the compiled tables are carefully checked by special statistical tests to verify a good distribution.

Tables of random numbers are usually used for Monte Carlo technique calculations performed by hand. Most computers have comparatively small internal memories, and so a large table will not fit into them.

A second way to produce random values is by using a random-number generator. It would seem that the electronically operated roulette wheel could be attached to a calculating machine and be made to produce random numbers as needed. However, any mechanical device would be too slow for a computer. Therefore, noise from some type of noise maker is used as a random-number generator. The noise level of the noise maker is monitored, and if, within some fixed interval of time, the noise exceeds a set threshold an even number of times, a zero is recorded; if an odd number of times, a one. These random zeros and ones are placed into all the binary places of a particular memory location. At any point in its calculations the computer can go to this location and take from it the random value.

This method is also not free from defects. It is necessary to make periodic tests, since a distribution drift may occur. The zeros and ones in one of the places may begin to appear in unequal frequencies. Also, it is often desirable to be able to repeat a calculation on the computer. But it is impossible to duplicate a sequence of random numbers if they are not held in the memory throughout the calculation. However, if they are held in the memory, we are back to random-number tables.

The last method for random-number generation is pseudorandom numbers. Numbers obtained by a formula that imitate the values of a random variable are called pseudorandom numbers. The values will imitate randomness as long as the calculations performed with them remain unrelated to the particular formula by which they were produced. One algorithm for obtaining pseudorandom numbers is called the middle-of-squares method. It is illustrated with the following example.

Suppose a four-digit integer $n_1 = 9876$ is obtained. It is squared. Usually an eight-digit number $n_1^2 = 97535376$ will result. The middle four digits of this number are removed and designate the result $n_2 = 5353$. Then n_2 is squared ($n_2^2 = 28654609$) and the middle four digits are once more removed, obtaining $n_3 = 6546$. Then $n_3^2 = 42850116$, $n_4 = 8501$, $n_4^2 = 72267001$, $n_5 = 2670$, $n_5^2 = 07128900$, $n_6 = 1289$, and so forth. The proposed values for the random variable are 9876, 5353, 6546, 8501, 2670, and 1289.

This particular algorithm is unfortunately not suitable since it tends to produce smaller numbers than it should. It is also prone to falling into traps such as the sequence 0000,0000 . . . , and 6100, 2100, 4100, 8100, 6100 . . . .

The problem of generating true random numbers with a computer has not been solved. Random number generators and pseudorandom numbers can be used to approximate the selection of random numbers. The systematic nature of electronic computers makes the creation of computer-generated random numbers a formidable task.

LEARNING CHECK 17-1

1. Give two reasons for wanting to find the zeros of a function.
2. What will indicate the general vicinity of a polynomial's root?
3. What must be obtained before the bisection method may be implemented?
4. What technique produces random numbers?
5. Name three ways to generate random numbers.

Answers:

1. To make the polynomial as small as required at the chosen values of X; reconstruct the polynomial by using the zeros. 2. Two polynomial evaluations with different signs. 3. Two root estimates that straddle the x-axis. 4. Monte Carlo 5. tables, random number generator, pseudo-random numbers

STATISTICAL ALGORITHMS

The purpose of this section is to display some characteristics exhibited by a distribution of random values. Two such characteristics generally associated with the distribution of a random variable are **central tendency** and **dispersion**. Although these characteristics do not totally describe a random variable distribution, they are the most useful ones. To describe these characteristics, a smooth curve is used to graphically represent the distribution. A smooth frequency curve of a distribution of an observable random variable is shown on the next page in Figure 17-8.

Measures of Central Tendency

The first characteristic relates to the tendency of some observations to center or group around a central value. Thus, a measure that reflects the point about which the values center is desired. One measure of central tendency is sometimes called an average. The average, or mean, is the sum of a set of observations divided by the total number of observations.

Different sets of observations often exhibit different central tendencies. For example, a study was conducted that compared the reading times of 20 year-old males newly hired by an organization and 50-

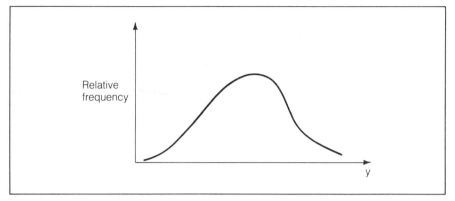

Figure 17-8 FREQUENCY CURVE

year-old males who had been with the organization for 15 or more years. Figure 17-9 illustrates the curves, or distributions, of the reading times of the two groups.

By looking at these two distributions it can be seen that they differ as to the point about which they center. Therefore, measures of central tendency should indicate the location of the point about which the distribution is centered.

The Mode

In many observed distributions, the frequency of occurrence increases as the center of the distribution is approached. Thus it is reasonable to use the value of the variable that occurs most frequently as a measure of central tendency. This measure is called the **mode**.

To determine the mode for ungrouped data, the single value that occurs most frequently is chosen, although for a particular set of ungrouped data it is possible that the mode does not exist (all values occur at an equal frequency) or that several modes might exist (several values occur at the highest frequency).

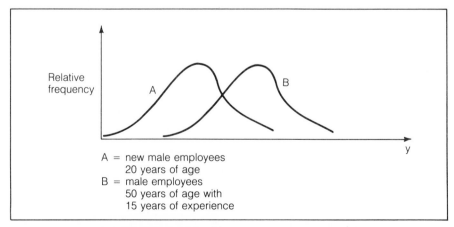

Figure 17-9 DISTRIBUTIONS WITH DIFFERENT CENTRAL TENDENCIES

The Median

The **median** is defined as the value which 50 percent of the observations fall below and 50 percent fall above. For ungrouped data, the values of the observations are first ranked in ascending or descending order. The median M_d is then found by the following rule:

1. If the number of observations n is odd, then M_d is equal to the middle value or

$$M_d = Y_{(n + 1)/2}$$

2. If n is even, then the median is the average of the two middle values, or

$$M_d = \frac{Y_{(n/2)} + Y_{(n/2+1)}}{2}$$

Measures of Dispersion

In Figure 17-10, two distributions are shown that are very different, even though they have essentially the same central tendency. Notice that distribution A shows less variation around the central point than does distribution B. Thus, the observations from distribution A cluster closer around the center of the distribution than the observations from distribution B. This characteristic is referred to as dispersion or variability. Several measures of the variability of a distribution can be used.

The Range

The **range** R is defined as the difference between the largest and smallest observation. Thus for ungrouped data, the range is

$$R = Y_{\max} - Y_{\min}$$

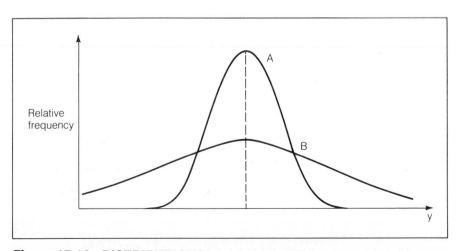

Figure 17-10 DISTRIBUTIONS WITH DIFFERENT DISPERSIONS

In the above equation, Y_{max} represents the largest observation and Y_{min} represents the smallest observation.

The Average Absolute Deviation

The **average absolute deviation** $\overline{D}$ is defined as the average of the absolute deviations from the mean. For ungrouped data, it is given by

$$\overline{D} = \frac{\sum_{i=1}^{n} |Y_i - \overline{Y}|}{n}$$

In the above equation, n represents the number of values in the table. Y_i represents the individual data elements that will be incremented one by one and the $\overline{Y}$ is the mean of the data list.

✎ LEARNING CHECK 17-2

1. What characteristic of a distribution is sometimes called an average?
2. What is indicated by a measure of central tendency?
3. A measure of central tendency that identifies a variable that occurs most frequently is called the _____ .
4. The separation between the leftmost and rightmost points on a smooth distribution curve is called the _____ .

Answers:

1. mean   2. The location of the point about which the distribution is centered.   3. mode   4. range

NUMERICAL ACCURACY

Several sources of error can interact to affect the accuracy of a result. Five different sources of error are discussed below. They include truncation error, round-off error, original data error, blunders, and propagated error. It should be noted that no experiment or calculation may be completed without error. Some, but not all, of these errors may be eliminated and different types of errors may be present at the same time.

Truncation Error

When you are dealing with a large and complex polynomial with a high degree, it is sometimes worthwhile to truncate the smaller terms. For iterative methods, the error produced by the truncation can usually be reduced by repeated iterations, but since life is finite and computer time is expensive, approximations to the exact analytical answer must be accepted.

Round-Off Error

All computing devices represent numbers with some imprecision. Digital computers, which are the normal devices for implementing numerical algorithms, frequently use floating point numbers with a fixed word length. The true values are not exactly expressed by such representations. This error is called round-off error, whether the decimal function is rounded or chopped after the final digit.

Error in Original Data

Real-world problems, in which an existing or proposed physical situation is modeled by a mathematical equation, frequently have coefficients that are imperfectly known. The model itself may not perfectly reflect the behavior of the real world. The numerical analyst can do nothing to overcome such errors. Tests can be performed to determine how sensitive the results are to changes in the input information and how realistically the equation models real-world phenomena.

Blunders

It is anticipated that the student will use a digital computer or an electronic calculator to solve numerical problems. Such machines infrequently make mistakes, but since humans are involved in programming, operation, preparing input, and interpreting output, blunders or gross errors do occur. The solution to this error is care and a careful examination of the results for reasonableness.

Propagated Error

This error is more subtle than the other errors. Propagated error is an error in the succeeding steps of a process that results from the occurrence of an earlier error. This is in addition to the local error made at that step.

⩗LEARNING CHECK 17-3

1. How may truncation errors be reduced?
2. Give two reasons why errors in original data may be present in calculations.
3. What kind of error can be detected by close observation of the results?
4. An earlier error may cause added errors in the succeeding steps of a process. What is the name of this type of error?

Answers:

1. By increasing the number of iterations that an iterative method makes.   2. Imperfect model equation coefficients; the model does not perfectly reflect the behavior of the situation.   3. blunder   4. propagated

- An iterative method called bisection reduces an interval that contains the zero of a function by half each time until a tolerance value is reached.
- The Monte Carlo technique produces random numbers between a given range that can represent the data of a given result.
- Three methods for producing random numbers have been discussed. They are tables of random numbers, random-number generators, the pseudo-random number generators. Although all three can be used, the easiest and best is the pseudorandom number generator.
- The mode and median are two measures of central tendency. Central tendency is a characteristic of a distribution of random values that have a tendency to center or group themselves around a central value.
- Two measures of a dispersion are the range and average absolute deviation. Dispersion is a characteristic of a distribution of random values in which two distributions may have the same central tendency but one may cluster more closely around the center of the distribution than the other.
- Numerical accuracy can be affected by many types of error. Some types are truncation, round-off, original data, blunder, and propagated error. Not all error can be eliminated from a calculation. Some types of errors may be totally eliminated but others can only be reduced. More than one type of error may occur in a single calculation.

VOCABULARY LIST

Average absolute deviation The average of the absolute deviations from the mean.

Bisection method An iterative method that reduces an interval that contains the zero of a function by half each time until a tolerance value is reached.

Central tendency The tendency of randomly generated values to center or group themselves around a central value.

Dispersion A characteristic of a distribution of random values in which two distributions may have the same central tendency but one may cluster more closely around the center of the distribution than the other.

Iterates Successive approximations of a function.

Iteration The repetition of an algorithm.

Median The value that half the observations fall above and half fall below.

Mode The value of a variable that occurs most frequently.

Monte Carlo technique A method that uses randomly produced values that can represent the data of a given result.

Pseudorandom numbers Numbers obtained by a formula that imitate the values of a random variable.

Random number generators A method of generating random values by monitoring discrete changes in noise.

Range The difference between the largest and smallest observation.

Tables of random numbers A list of random values that were produced by a simple repetitive experiment.

CHAPTER TEST

VOCABULARY

Match each term from the numbered column with the best description from the lettered column.

1. Bisection method

    a. A method that uses randomly produced values within a given range that can represent the data of a given result.

2. Iterates

    b. An iterative method that reduces an interval that contains the zero of a function by half each time until a tolerance value is reached.

3. Iteration

    c. Successive approximations of a function.

4. Pseudorandom numbers

5. Dispersion

    d. The repetition of an algorithm.

    e. A list of random values that were produced by a simple repetitive experiment.

6. Mode

    f. A method of generating random values by monitoring discrete changes in noise.

7. Average absolute deviation

    g. Numbers obtained by a formula that imitate the values of a random variable.

8. Monte Carlo technique

    h. The tendency of randomly generated values to center or group themselves around a central value.

9. Tables of random numbers

    i. The value of the variable that occurs most frequently.

10. Random number generators

    j. The value that half the observations fall above and half fall below.

11. Central tendency

    k. A characteristic of a distribution of random values in which two distributions may have the same central tendency but one may cluster more closely around the center of the distribution than the other.

12. Median

    l. The difference between the largest and smallest observation.

13. Range

    m. The average of the absolute deviations from the mean.

1. What must occur if the sign of the function evaluation at the first interval bound in the bisection method is opposite to the function evaluation at the midpoint?
2. What is essential for numbers to be considered truly random?
3. What are the drawbacks of each of the following methods that produce random numbers?

   a. Tables of random numbers.
   b. Random-number generator.
   c. Pseudorandom numbers.

4. Suppose that two distinct distributions have essentially the same central tendency. What must be the difference between the two distributions if the characteristic of dispersion is identified?
5. What is found when the differences between the mean and each point are calculated and summed and then divided by the total number of differences? Assume that each difference subtracts the smaller number from the larger.
6. What kind of error is produced because a computer cannot hold all of the digits of a calculated result?
7. Which errors may be totally eliminated from a calculation, sometimes eliminated, or never eliminated but only reduced?

PROGRAMMING PROBLEMS

1. Use the algorithm in Figure 17-4 to write a program that will find a zero of the cubic equation $f(x) = x^3 + x^2 - 3x - 3 = 0$. Since this cubic equation was used in the chapter as an illustration, a good start has already been given. Use 1 and 2 as the initial root estimates and iterate until a tolerance value of .005 is reached. Print the root estimate and the error in the term.
2. Use a hat containing numbers 1 through 35 and create a table of 20 random values. Create a roulette game that a user can play by betting on numbers 1 through 35 or even and odd numbers. The table of random numbers should be on a piece of paper next to the user. Be sure that the user does not see the sheet before the bets are made.
3. Use the table of random values from Problem 2 and find the mode, the median, the range, and the average absolute deviation.

CHAPTER 18

Applications of Computing

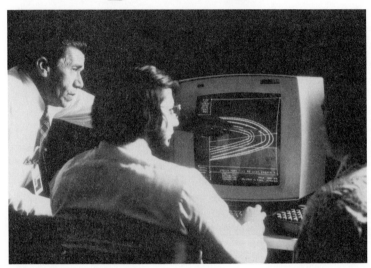

CHAPTER OUTLINE

LEARNING OBJECTIVES

INTRODUCTION

COMPUTERS IN BUSINESS

LEARNING CHECK 18-1

COMPUTERS IN SCIENCE

LEARNING CHECK 18-2

COMPUTERS IN EDUCATION

LEARNING CHECK 18-3

COMPUTERS IN THE HOME

FUTURE TRENDS IN COMPUTING

SUMMARY POINTS

VOCABULARY LIST

CHAPTER TEST
Vocabulary • Questions

LEARNING OBJECTIVES

After studying this chapter, you should be able to:

1. Describe four broad categories of computer application.
2. Explain how computers are used in business.
3. Explain how computers are used in the sciences.
4. Explain how computers are used in education.
5. Understand the controversies on computer literacy and computer-assisted instruction.
6. Explain how computers are used in the home.
7. Explain how telecommunications can expand the capabilities of home computers.
8. Describe some future trends in computing.

ADVANCED PLACEMENT CHAPTER HIGHLIGHTS

The following topics from the Advanced Placement Computer Science Exam are covered in this chapter:

applications of computing

INTRODUCTION

Computers and computer-based technologies have become increasingly important in our everyday lives. Computers are used in a variety of applications. These applications can be grouped into four broad categories. First, computers are used for administrative purposes. The administration of small and large organizations requires mass storage and retrieval of information with some ability to manipulate the information. A second application of computers is to help humans solve problems. People often use computers to help compose and write documents, to solve mathematical problems, and to make important decisions. A third computer application is to control other machines. Computers are used in industry to manufacture different products and in the sciences to control complex measurement machines. A final application of computers is to entertain. Video games, televisions, motion pictures and other sources of entertainment rely on computers. These four application categories provide a framework to group many uses of computers.

Computers are used in business, government, the sciences, education, and the home. Computer users have varying needs. Large organizations, such as corporations, government agencies, and universities, use mainframe and minicomputers, primarily for administrative and problem-solving purposes. Smaller organizations often use minicomputers and microcomputers for a variety of purposes. It is imporant to realize that specific computer applications require certain hardware and software combinations.

COMPUTERS IN BUSINESS

Computers are able to rapidly process large amounts of information. The business world increasingly depends on computer-based technology to perform many business activities. Computers can reduce paperwork, speed up the processing of routine transactions, help people solve problems, and control the manufacturing of many products. Because many organizations require mass storage of information, businesses often use mainframes or minicomputers. Microcomputers are becoming increasingly important to small businesses for problem solving and record keeping.

As consumers, most people are familiar with business applications of computers. Many retail stores use **point-of-sale** (POS) **terminals** and the **Universal Product Code** (UPC) to increase productivity. The UPC is a standardized bar code now found on most products in retail outlets. The UPC code is used to identify the product and its manufacturer (see Figure 18-1), while the POS terminal (see Figure 18-2) is used to record product sales, much like a cash register. Salespeople can use **optical scanners** to read the codes and speed up the sales process. Computer systems based on POS terminals are used to control inventory levels, calculate sales figures, and determine a customer's credit status.

The banking industry makes extensive use of computer-based technology. Banks rely heavily on computers to process huge amounts of paperwork in the form of checks, loan records, deposits, investment

Figure 18-1   UNIVERSAL PRODUCT CODE

Figure 18-2   POS TERMINAL

Figure 18-3   A CUSTOMER USING A 24-HOUR TELLING MACHINE

information, and the like. New innovations such as 24-hour banking (see Figure 18-3) and bank-by-phone systems are based on the use of computers and telecommunication. **Electronic funds transfer** (EFT) is the automatic recording of account transactions and money transfers. EFT is based on computers transferring funds electronically, without actual paper money or checks changing hands. Computers have become a familiar and important part of the banking industry.

Businesses often use computers to help solve problems. Managers can use electronic spreadsheet programs to help them make decisions. **Spreadsheet programs**, such as *Lotus 1-2-3* and *VisiCalc,* allow users to analyze financial data, to make predictions based on the data, and to illustrate the data in various graphic formats. Engineers and technicians also use computers to help make decisions. **Computer-assisted design** (CAD) programs allow the user to specify the requirements of a product or design and then generate a graphic image of the product (see Figure 18-4). The automobile and aircraft industries have used

Figure 18-4   CAD/CAM COMPUTER SCREEN (TOP) LOCATES WHERE ROBOTS SPOT WELD AN AUTOMOBILE (BOTTOM)

Figure 18-5   INDUSTRIAL ROBOTS PAINTING CARS

CAD technology to design and test products for years. Business and industry use computers to help solve problems.

Computers are often used in businesses to control other machines. The most advanced applications of this technology are in manufacturing. Computer-aided manufacturing (CAM) is a growing area of computer application. Robots are essentially machines controlled by one or several computers. Industrial robots are used to paint cars, assemble appliances, and mine coal (see Figure 18-5). Computers are also used to help manufacturers in quality control of their products. Quality control is the identification of flaws or weaknesses in a product. Computers are used to control machines that perform **nondestructive testing** (NDT) of products. NDT uses X-rays, high-frequency sound waves, or laser beams to allow inspection of products.

Computers have become an integral part of the business world. The applications of computers to business problems are varied. From automobile manufacturing to the prediction of sales trends, computers assist, and sometimes replace, people at work.

LEARNING CHECK 18-1

1. Describe four users of computer applications mentioned in this section.
2. How are POS terminals and the UPC used in retail stores?
3. How are computers used in manufacturing?

Answers:

1. The four users of computer applications are business, the sciences, education, and entertainment.   2. POS terminals are used in retail stores to read the UPC on products. The POS terminal searches for the price of the product indexed by the UPC and adds the price to the present sub-total.   3. Computers are used in manufacturing to aid in design (CAD) and to control industrial robots (CAM).

COMPUTERS IN SCIENCE

The sciences use computers and computer-based technologies in a variety of applications. While business applications stress the storage and retrieval abilities of computers, the sciences more often use computers to help solve problems. Computers are frequently used to monitor and control scientific equipment. This section will provide a brief overview of scientific applications of computers.

Scientists are often problem solvers, though the magnitude of the problems vary greatly. The rapid processing abilities of computers allow scientists to quickly and easily solve problems. Social scientists often use computer packages, such as the Statistical Analysis System (SAS), to perform statistical analyses of data. Many statistical packages have advanced graphics abilities, so data can be displayed in a variety of formats.

Simulation and modeling are widely used techniques in science and industry. During simulations, computers analyze data and the results are used to generate models or make projections. Weather forecasting is often based on projections made by computers. Computers are also used by military planners to simulate wars and to train personnel. Flight simulators are frequently used to test the abilities of new aircraft, instrumentation, and pilots.

Computers can more directly influence the problem-solving process. The field of medicine provides some examples. Computer-aided diagnosis uses computers to perform tests, store results of tests, ask patients questions, provide diagnoses, and suggest methods of treatment. **Multiphasic health testing** (MPHT) **centers** provide reasonable alternatives to visits to a private physician for preventive health care. The MPHT center will administer all the standard tests included in a complete physical exam. Routine tests, such as hearing and eye exams, chest X-rays, pain tolerance tests, and blood tests are administered by nurses and technicians. The computer evaluates the results by comparing them to established normal results and a patient's family history. Physicians can then examine the computer-generated results and evaluation and make a diagnosis.

Physicians also use computers to control X-ray machines and produce **computerized axial tomographies** (CAT). CAT scans allow physicans to see three-dimensional composites of organs or bones (see Figure 18-6). Physicians can use CAT scans to make more informed and accurate diagnoses.

Computers have become important tools for scientists. Statistical packages and graphic displays allow many scientists to analyze and examine data in new ways. Simulation and modeling programs help scientists design new products and test new and old theories. Computer-controlled devices perform a variety of tasks that previously were impossible or time-consuming. For example, psychologists use computers to control experiments and record subjects' responses; seismologists use computers to monitor seismographs to measure earthquakes.

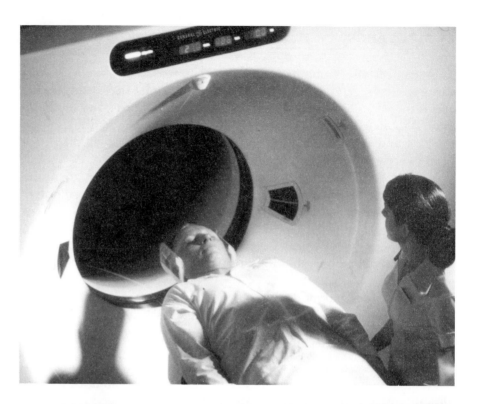

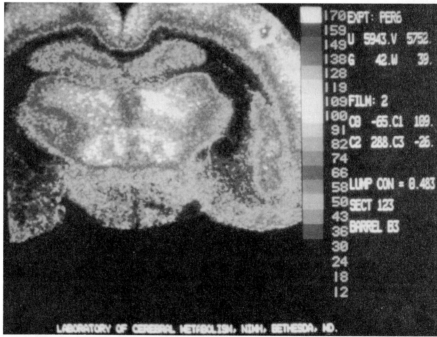

Figure 18-6 MEDICAL X-RAY SCANNING DEVICE (TOP) AND COMPUTER-GENERATED SCAN OF A NORMAL BRAIN (BOTTOM)

The advent of computer-controlled devices in the sciences let scientists research new areas. The sciences are an expanding area of computer applications.

LEARNING CHECK 18-2

1. What is a frequent scientific application of computers?
2. Describe an MPHT center.
3. List an example of how computers are used to control scientific equipment.

Answers:

1. Computers are frequently used in the sciences to help solve problems. 2. An MPHT center administers all the standard tests included in a complete physical exam. Computers aid in performing tests and diagnosing test results. 3. Computers are used to control experiments, record responses, monitor seismographs, and control X-ray machines.

COMPUTERS IN EDUCATION

Computers have had a significant impact on education during the past decade. Computers were first used in classrooms during the 1960s; however, at that time they were utilized as little more than automated flash cards. A recent survey by the Market Data Retrieval Company found that 68 percent of the 15,275 schools polled had computers. Computers are used in three broad areas in education. First, computers are used to help in the administration of schools. Second, computers are used to teach students about computers and computer programming. Third, computers are used to help teach students other topics through drill and practice, simulations, games, and exploration. Computers can be effective tools for administrators, educators, and students.

Computer literacy is a frequently used term in education. Many different definitions of computer literacy exist. Computer literacy can be generally defined as a basic knowledge of computers. Basic knowledge of a computer can include knowing what a computer can and cannot do, the etiquette of computer usage, basic (not BASIC) programming skills, how to use application packages (i.e., word processors, spreadsheets, data-base managers), and basic hardware-related knowledge.

Is computer literacy necessary? Scientists, educators, and students disagree on the answer to this question. The increased use of computers in business and the sciences suggests that some level of familiarity with computers is necessary. Critics, however, point out that most students will use applications packages in the future. Knowledge of a programming language may not be necessary or useful to most students. No clear answer to the question of how to teach computer literacy exists at present. Research in this area may produce a clear

375

definition of computer literacy and discover the knowledges and skills necessary for people to function in a computerized world.

Computer-assisted instruction (CAI) is used to help teach a wide variety of topics. CAI uses computers to control a learning situation (see Figure 18-7). A common application of CAI is in drill and practice exercises. Multiple choice questions appear on a screen for students to answer. If the student answers a question correctly, the computer responds appropriately and asks another question. If the student's response is incorrect, the computer presents material and new questions to steer the student to the correct answer. CAI can also be used to supplement the teacher by providing remedial or enrichment material, tests, or the opportunity to explore new topics.

Some scientists and educators oppose the use of CAI in drill and practice exercises. They argue that drill and practice exercises promote memorization, rather than understanding, of material. While memorization is important in some areas—for example, learning to type—under-

Figure 18-7 COMPUTER-ASSISTED INSTRUCTION (CAI) IS GAINING IN POPULARITY AMONG U.S. SCHOOL SYSTEMS

standing is far more important in topics that require problem-solving skills.

Seymour Papert, a primary developer of the **Logo** programming language, suggests that people learn best by exploration of a topic. Logo is designed to allow easy control of a **turtle**. A Logo turtle is a screen figure, or sprite, that can move across a monitor screen and draw lines. Papert has shown that students who learn to move the turtle also gain knowledge about geometry, mathematics, and computers. By allowing students to explore with the computer, CAI can be an effective way of increasing students' understanding of many topics.

The use of computers in education is increasing. However, there are controversies over how computers should be used and what students should learn about them. Through computer literacy courses, students can learn about computers and their effect on society. Computer-assisted instruction (CAI) can be used to teach students a variety of topics. The impact of computers in education is important, since the ability to interact with computers at some level is becoming important in many areas of society.

✎ LEARNING CHECK 18-3

1. Describe three applications of computers in education.
2. What are a few facts, skills, or abilities important to a basic knowledge of computers?
3. Why is computer literacy considered important?
4. What is CAI?
5. Why do some scientists and educators oppose the use of CAI in drill and practice exercises?

Answers:

1. Computers are used in education to help in the administration of schools, to teach students about computers and computer programming, and to help teach students other topics.   2. Basic knowledge of a computer can include knowing what a computer can and cannot do, the etiquette of computer usage, basic programming skills, how to use application packages, and hardware-related knowledge.   3. Computer literacy is considered important since using computers is becoming an important part of our society.   4. CAI is computer-assisted instruction.   5. CAI, as used in drill and practice exercises, promotes rote memorization rather than understanding. In many tasks, understanding is more important than memorization.

COMPUTERS IN THE HOME

With the introduction of inexpensive microcomputers, computers are being purchased and used in homes. The personal computer industry has grown from zero to nearly $1 billion in annual sales. The number of general-purpose microcomputers in the United States is increasing by 40 percent per year. Computers are used in the home to maintain records, help solve problems, control devices in the home, and entertain.

A large body of software exists for personal computers. Data-base

377

management programs, such as *Pfs:File,* allow users to create series of linked records. The records can be stored, accessed, sorted and printed with the data-base management system. Word processor and spreadsheet programs can help people solve problems and increase their productivity. Word processing software is popular and useful. The majority of word processors allow the user to perform simple operations, such as changing margins, and complex operations, such as moving blocks of text between text files. Spreadsheet programs, such as Lotus' *Symphony,* help users analyze, display, and store data.

Microcomputers are also used to control a wide range of devices around the home. By adding sensors, motors, and switches to a microcomputer, security systems, heating and air-conditioning, ovens, lights, and the like can be controlled.

Entertainment is a popular use of home computers. The design and marketing of video games is a big business. Computer games range from the conventional, such as chess and backgammon, to the fantastic, such as three-dimensional space games (see Figure 18-8). Graphics are an integral part of many computer games. Recent flight simulator games

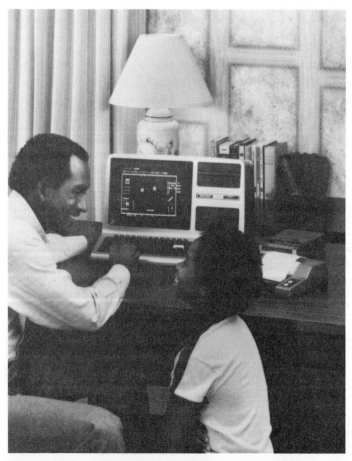

Figure 18-8 COMPUTER GAMES IN THE HOME

Figure 18-9 A MODEM

provide realistic action through the use of complex graphics programs that generate three-dimensional screen effects.

Telecommunications is a relatively new application of home computers. Through the use of modems and terminal communications software, home computers can communicate with mainframe computers, other home computers, and data-base services such as Compu-Serve or The Source. **Modems** are electronic devices that convert a computer's signals to a format that can be sent across normal telephone lines. **Terminal communications packages** allow home computers to transfer data from another computer to its disk drive (downloading), to send data to another computer's disk drive (uploading), and to simply use a home computer as a terminal to a larger mainframe system. By using a modem and terminal communications software, a home computer can become part of a network of mainframe, minicomputers, and microcomputers (see Figure 18-9).

Home computers can be used in many different ways. The capabilities of most home computers are barely used by the majority of users. However, the growing availability of applications software is introducing home computer owners to new uses for their computers. The development of home computer hardware and software is one of the most exciting and innovative areas of the computer industry.

FUTURE TRENDS IN COMPUTING

In many areas, the true utility of computers is just being discovered. While many people are able to use computers, most are unfamiliar with the more complex and useful computer applications. User-friendly software and hardware may help introduce more people to computers.

Apple Corporation's Lisa and Macintosh microcomputers are good examples of user-friendly computers (see Figure 18-10). Future trends in hardware and software development should increase the number of computer users.

Hardware developments, such as the miniaturization of integrated circuit (IC) chips and bubble memory, promise to bring considerably more computing power to computer users. Bubble memory consists of magnetized spots (or bubbles) resting on a thin film of semiconductor material. The bubbles have the opposite polarity of their supporting semiconductor material. A bubble memory module the size of a quarter can store more than 20,000 characters of data. The size of computers used in business, the sciences, education, and the home should decrease. The introduction of portable computers, such as the Apple IIc and Hewlett-Packard's HLP-100, provides users with light (7-10 pound) but powerful microcomputers (see Figure 18-11).

Future hardware and software developments may change the work habits of many people. Increased use of robots in manufacturing should automate many assembly lines. The displacement of workers in these areas is a serious problem. Telecommunications is a rapidly developing area. In the near future, many workers may do their work at home on microcomputers and communicate with the home office through the telephone lines and mainframe computers. These are just a few examples of future computing. The development of new hardware and software will certainly increase the number of computer applications and the effects of computer technologies on our lives.

Figure 18-10 STUDENTS USING AN APPLE MACINTOSH MICRO-COMPUTER

Figure 18-11   PORTABLE COMPUTER

SUMMARY POINTS

- Computer applications can be grouped into four categories: administration, problem solving, control of machines, and entertainment.
- Business applications of computers include administration, problem solving, and control. Office automation uses computers to help maintain records and process paperwork. Managers often use spreadsheet programs and simulations to aid in decision-making. Computers are used to automate assembly lines to increase productivity and decrease costs.
- Scientific applications of computers also include administration, problem solving, and control. Computers are used to collect and analyze data for experiments. Simulations are used to predict weather, plan strategies, and test abilities. Computers are used in medicine to control complex machines and aid in making diagnoses.
- Like the other areas, educational applications of computers include administration, problem solving, and control. Computers are often the topic of computer literacy courses. Computers are also used to teach other topics.

381

Considerable controversy exists about the teaching and use of computers in education.

- Home applications of computers include entertainment as well as administration, problem solving, and control. Word processors, data-base management, and spreadsheet programs help home users maintain and organize records and solve problems. Microcomputers can be used to control a wide range of devices in the home. Graphics and games are a popular use of home computers.

VOCABULARY LIST

Computer-assisted instruction (CAI) The use of computers to control a learning situation.

Computer-assisted design The use of computers to simulate the design and stress points of a product.

Computerized axial tomography A form of X-rays that are interpreted by a computer to form a three-dimensional picture of an object.

Computer literacy A basic knowledge of computers.

Electronic funds transfer The automatic, electronic recording of account transactions and money transfers.

Logo An educational programming language.

Modems Electronic devices that convert computer signals to a format that can be sent across telephone lines.

Multiphasic health testing center A medical center that uses computers to maintain records, control tests, and aid in diagnoses.

Nondestructive testing The use of computer-controlled X-rays, high-frequency sound waves, or laser beams to inspect a product.

Optical scanners Devices used to read Universal Product Codes.

Papert, Seymour The creator of the Logo programming language.

Point-of-sale terminals Terminals used in retail stores to maintain sales records, control optical scanners, and perform the normal functions of a cash register.

Simulations Computer-generated models based on analyses of data.

Spreadsheet programs Computer packages used to make calculations on rows and columns of data.

Telecommunications The transfer of data across telephone lines, televisions, or other similar media.

Terminal communications packages Software that allows different computers to communicate, usually across telephone lines.

Turtle A small screen object that is used in the Logo language to draw figures.

Universal Product Code A standardized bar code used to identify products.

CHAPTER TEST

VOCABULARY

Match each term from the numbered column with the best description from the lettered column.

1. Terminal communications packages

a. Computer-generated models based on analyses of data.

2. Turtle

    b. Computer packages used to make calculations on rows and columns of data.

3. Universal Product Code

    c. The automatic electronic recording of account transactions and money transfers.

4. Seymour Papert

    d. The use of computer-controlled X-rays, high frequency sound waves, or laser beams to inspect a product.

5. Point-of-sale terminals

    e. A standardized bar code used to identify retail products.

6. Simulations

    f. Terminals used in retail stores to maintain sales records, control optical scanners, and perform the normal functions of a cash register.

7. Telecommunications

    g. The use of computers to control a learning situation.

8. Spreadsheet programs

    h. The creator of the Logo programming language.

9. Computer-assisted instruction

    i. Software that allows different computers to communicate, usually across telephone lines.

10. Electronic funds transfer

    j. The transfer of data through telephone lines, televisions, or other similar media.

11. Nondestructive testing

    k. A small screen object that is used in the Logo language to draw figures.

QUESTIONS

1. What types of business activities can computers perform?
2. How are computers used in the banking industry?
3. Describe how simulations can be used in the sciences.
4. How can a spreadsheet program be used?
5. What can modems and terminal communications packages allow a home computer to do?
6. Describe some future hardware developments in computing.
7. How might future hardware and software developments affect future trends in computing?

CHAPTER 19

Social Implications of Computing

CHAPTER OUTLINE

LEARNING OBJECTIVES

INTRODUCTION

PRIVACY
Fair Credit Reporting Act • Privacy Act of 1974 • Financial
Laws • Objectives of Privacy Legislation

LEARNING CHECK 19-1

SECURITY
Common Security Problems • Controls

LEARNING CHECK 19-2

ETHICS

SUMMARY POINTS

VOCABULARY LIST

CHAPTER TEST
Vocabulary • Questions

LEARNING OBJECTIVES

After reading this chapter, you should be able to:

1. Describe the development of privacy-of-information laws.
2. Understand how to use privacy-of-information laws.
3. Understand the problems with privacy-of-information legislation.
4. Describe common security problems.
5. Describe controls or solutions for some common security problems.
6. Describe and understand why computer ethics are necessary to reduce computer crime.

ADVANCED PLACEMENT CHAPTER HIGHLIGHTS

The following topics from the Advanced Placement Computer Science Exam are covered in this chapter:

ethical and social implications of computer use

INTRODUCTION

The preceding chapter described some of the many areas in which computers are beneficial. The use of computers makes possible significant savings in time and costs. As computers have been more widely used in business, science, education, and the home, several problems have arisen. The rapid growth in computer usage during the past decade is partially responsible for these problems.

Developments in the computer industry have brought about social changes as well as technological advances. In some instances, computer developments have been responsible for the enactment of new laws. These new laws, however, have not fully resolved the problems caused by computer usage. Problems resulting from computer use can be grouped into the following three categories: privacy, ethics, and security.

PRIVACY

An important and useful feature of computers is their ability to store and retrieve large amounts of data very quickly. Since the development of storage devices such as magnetic disk and tape, it has become economical to store large amounts of data that are used infrequently. For example, government agencies can now compactly store data on magnetic tapes and then maintain a tape library for future reference.

The collection, storage, and use of data became an important issue during the late 1960s. At the time, no guidelines existed to specify what data could legally be collected about individuals and for what purposes the data could be used. Also, no guidelines existed for how data should be maintained to ensure accuracy. Individuals and organizations became concerned with how collected information was used, especially if the information was personal.

These concerns of individuals and organizations led to the passing of several laws safeguarding the privacy of information. Restrictions now exist on what type of data can be collected, how data can be used, and how data must be maintained. These laws were passed to protect the individual's right to privacy.

Fair Credit Reporting Act

The **Fair Credit Reporting Act of 1970** was one of the first major legislative efforts to attempt to safeguard privacy. This law was aimed at dealing with problems associated with the collection, maintenance, and reporting of credit, insurance, and employment information. The act enabled consumers to protect themselves against erroneous credit information that may be collected and used by consumer credit reporting agencies. The act gives individuals the right to know what information is maintained about them. This provision helps eliminate secret information. Consumer credit reporting agencies are required to reveal the contents of their files to those who are refused credit. Information that is challenged must be investigated and changed if necessary.

The Fair Credit Reporting Act restricts the use of obsolete or out-of-date information. For example, if information on a bankruptcy is more than fourteen years old, it is considered obsolete and must be deleted from an individual's record. Information pertaining to legal suits and judgments, debts placed in the hands of collection agencies, and records of arrest, conviction, or imprisonment must be deleted if it is more than seven years old.

The act also restricts who may have access to an individual's credit file. Only those who have a valid court order or who have written permission from the concerned individual may look at a person's credit file. The act also limits access of information to only those who need the information for a defined relevant purpose, such as to process a valid credit or business transaction or to investigate an employment or insurance claim.

Privacy Act of 1974

Except for the Fair Credit Reporting Act of 1970, most privacy legislation applies to the federal government. The **Privacy Act of 1974** was passed to limit the information practices of the government. It restricts the manner in which personal data can be used by federal agencies. The main provisions of the law are as follows:

- Individuals must be permitted access to information stored on them in data banks.
- Individuals may correct their own records and the federal agency must investigate each claim promptly. In the case of a disputed record, an individual may insert his or her own perception of the facts.
- Information collected for one purpose should not be used or made available for any other purpose without the consent of the individual. For example, information relating to an individual's credit history could not be sent to an employer without the consent of the individual.
- Federal agencies must establish appropriate administrative, technical, and physical safeguards to ensure the security and confidentiality of sensitive information.
- Any government agency or employee who willfully discloses or maintains a record in violation of the law is considered to be guilty of a misdemeanor and subject to fine of up to $5000.

The Privacy Act of 1974 has been criticized because it only applies to federal agencies. Although state and local governments along with private industry were originally included when the act was first proposed, the final version of the act only restricts federal agencies. Legislators believed the regulation of state and local governments and private industry would be difficult, since the concept of what is adequate privacy seems to vary from state to state and industry to industry. Also, the cost of implementing privacy laws in these areas could be extremely high. The cost of implementing the Privacy Act within the federal government was initially $200 million and requires $100 million dollars yearly.

Several states, however, have chosen to adopt the principles included in the Privacy Act of 1974. Most state laws specify what information can be collected and stored and how it can be used. The laws outline policies and procedures regarding data storage. They also provide safeguards to ensure that data stored about individuals are accurate, complete, and correct.

Financial Laws

The **Financial Privacy Act of 1978** states that no government authority may have access to or obtain copies of the information contained in an individual's financial records, except through an administrative subpoena, summons, or search warrant. If an individual's financial records are released, the financial institution must notify the individual that his or her records have been transferred and the identity of the recipient of the records.

The **Electronic Transfer Act of 1978** prohibits financial institutions from engaging in any transaction with a customer through an electronic terminal without clearly disclosing to the customer all terms and conditions governing such a transfer. The financial institution's disclosure must include the following:

- The types of transfers a customer can make.
- The circumstances in which the financial institution will release information concerning the customer's account to others.
- The customer's right to receive electronic fund transfer (EFT) receipts and account statements.

The Electronic Funds Transfer Act also outlines the consequences for the unauthorized transfer of customer's funds and for the financial institution's improper transfer of funds. Failure to comply with any provision of the act can result in fines up to $5000 or imprisonment up to one year.

Objectives of Privacy Legislation

Laws like the Fair Credit Reporting Act of 1970 and the Privacy Act of 1974 are designed to protect the individual's right to privacy. This body of legislation also attempts to ensure that information that is collected and maintained on individuals is "fair" and accurate. An individual has the right to expect that certain records maintained about him or her will be treated as confidential and will not be used for purposes other than those for which they were intended.

The implementation of privacy laws has resulted in several problems. First, the cost of implementing privacy laws is high. Since costs are ultimately passed on to citizens, the content of privacy laws will be dependent on their support from citizens. Second, excessive restrictions imposed by privacy laws could have negative effects on research, planning, and other activities. The goal of ensuring privacy of information is both legitimate and desirable. However, a balance between the individual's need for privacy and society's need for information should be a major consideration in future privacy legislation.

ᐯᐱLEARNING CHECK 19-1

1. List two provisions of the Fair Credit Reporting Act of 1970.
2. List three provisions of the Privacy Act of 1974.
3. Why does the Privacy Act of 1974 only apply to federal agencies?
4. Under the Financial Privacy Act of 1978, what must financial institutions do if they release an individual's records?
5. What does the Electronic Funds Transfer Act of 1978 prohibit?

SECURITY

Security focuses on the protection of hardware, software, and data from destruction, illegal access, or unauthorized modification. Security applies to the technical and administrative aspects of collecting and storing data. This differs from privacy, which attempts to maximize the fairness of how the information or data are used.

Common Security Problems

The largest number of security problems are unintentionally caused by omissions, errors, and accidental destruction. Computer systems and data are vulnerable to several hazards including fire, natural disasters, environmental problems, and computer crime. Some of the most common security problems are listed below.

- *Omission and errors.* Many security precautions are designed to prevent simple machine and human errors and omissions from occurring. For example, batches of data that were submitted to the computer might never be processed, or information could be sent from the computer to the wrong terminal. Large amounts of output have been lost because a printer ran out of paper and no one noticed that more paper needed to be added. Once information has been printed, listings have been known to be lost, misplaced, or inadvertently picked up by persons other than those intended to receive the output.
- *Accidental destruction.* Data or equipment have been destroyed in a variety of ways. Typically, output is thrown out by mistake, or data on a storage device are accidently erased.
- *Fire, flood, and natural disasters.* Devastating fires, floods, and natural disasters can occur at any computer installation. If a fire occurs, water cannot be used to extinguish flames since magnetic media and hardware will be damaged. Floods pose a serious threat to computer hardware and wiring. Natural disasters such as cyclones, hurricanes, and earthquakes have destroyed entire computer centers.

- *Computer crime.* Every organization, regardless of how large or small, is a potential victim of computer crime. Both hardware and software can be purposefully vandalized by outsiders or even dissatisfied employees. Software can be illegally copied and resold to competitors or others for personal gain. Home computers and electronic funds transfer systems pose a threat to the billions of dollars in data banks accessible through telephone lines. Many crimes go undetected and unpunished, but it is estimated that losses range from at least $2 billion to more than $40 billion a year.

Controls

Proper controls can eliminate or reduce the frequency of many of the problems listed above. Some problems can be entirely avoided through careful planning, sufficient personnel training, and an efficiently run computer installation. Other problems, such as computer crime, have been difficult to control. Some examples of common security measures are listed below.

- Back-up copies of data are stored outside the organization's location, and recovery procedures are established.
- Authorized users are given special passwords that change on a periodic basis.
- The sites for computers are carefully chosen so that water or steam pipes that could potentially burst are not located nearby. Ideally, sites limit the number of people who can access the equipment.
- Data are **encrypted**, or translated into a secret code, through the use of special software. The most popular encryption software is called **DES (Data Encryption Standard)** and is sold by IBM. When data are transmitted to or from remote terminals, they are encrypted (or scrambled) at one end and then decrypted (or unscrambled) at the other.
- Hiring and training standards for personnel are one of the most important ways to attempt to ensure that employees are responsible, capable, and honest. Although personnel may have been screened carefully, it is still possible that incidents of dishonest or unethical behavior could occur. In such cases, it is important that proper corrective action be taken.

There are numerous other security measures that can be taken to protect computer systems. The determination of how much security a computer system should have is basically dependent on four factors:

- The value of hardware.
- The value of software (including programs and data stored on various storage devices).
- The cost of replacing either hardware or software.
- The cost of controls.

The primary objective of security precautions is to reduce the risk of destruction, damage, or theft of computer hardware and software while keeping costs within reach.

⋈ LEARNING CHECK 19-2

1. Briefly distinguish between privacy and security.
2. List three common security measures that can be implemented to protect a computer installation.
3. What is data encryption?

Answers:

1. Security is concerned with the protection of hardware, software, and data against destruction, illegal access, or unauthorized modification. Privacy, on the other hand, attempts to maximize the fairness of how information or data are used. 2. Backup copies of data are made and stored in another location; authorized users are assigned passwords which are changed periodically; data are encrypted, or translated into a secret code. 3. Translation of data into a secret code through the use of special software.

ETHICS

While efforts can be made to resolve the problems of privacy of information and the security of computer installations, the ethics behind these issues are difficult to resolve. Illegal copying of software or unauthorized access to data files can be accomplished despite the implementation of strict policies, standards, or even technical controls. It is important for people to realize the importance of adhering to ethical behavior. While policies and guidelines can be outlined that distinguish between right and wrong behavior, the final decision of what is right or wrong is up to the individual.

Computer crime has many forms. Individuals or organizations can access confidential information stored about others within personnel records. Computer time and equipment may be used by employees for their own personal use, which can cost a company thousands of dollars. Software can be illegally copied (**computer piracy**) and sold for personal use. This causes the original developers to lose large amounts of money in potential sales.

Computer crime is sometimes considered a victimless crime. Unfortunately, this idea is not true. Computer piracy robs programmers and other employees of software development companies of salaries and consumers of the development of new software. Tampering with data is equivalent to forgery or fraud. Computer ethics is a personal issue. Individuals need to assume responsibility for their own behavior and to consider the rights of others when using computer software and hardware.

- Privacy legislation is intended to protect the individual's need for privacy by ensuring that data are accurate, complete, and up-to-date.
- One of the first privacy laws passed was the Fair Credit Reporting Act of 1970. The main purpose of the act was to enable consumers to protect themselves against erroneous credit information being collected and used by consumer credit reporting agencies. The act stipulates that data cannot be used after a certain number of years since they are then considered to be obsolete.
- The Privacy Act of 1974 applies only to federal agencies. The various guidelines are intended to limit the information practices of the government by placing restrictions on how federal agencies can use personal data.
- Concerns relating to privacy legislation center on the costs of implementing and enforcing privacy laws, in addition to the possibility that excessive restrictions could severely limit research, planning, and other important activities. It is important, therefore, to achieve a balance between the individual's need for privacy and society's need for information.
- Security focuses on the protection of hardware, software, and data from illegal access, destruction, or unauthorized modification.
- Some of the most common security problems are omissions and errors; accidental destruction; fire, flood, and natural disasters; and computer crime.
- Many security problems can be avoided through careful planning, sufficient personnel training, and an efficiently run computer installation.
- Ethics relating to the use of computer hardware and software can be specified to a certain extent in policies and procedures, but it is ultimately the responsibility of the individual to assume ethical behavior.

VOCABULARY LIST

Computer piracy   The illegal copying of copyrighted software.

(DES) Data encryption standard   Software that translates data into a secret code.

Encryption   The translation of information into a secret code.

Electronic Transfer Act of 1978   Law restricting when and how financial institutions can electronically transfer customer's funds.

Fair Credit Reporting Act of 1970   Law out-lining collection, maintenance, and access practices for consumer credit information.

Financial Privacy Act of 1978   Law restricting agencies' access to individuals' financial information and outlining procedures for legally obtaining such information.

Privacy Act of 1974   Law limiting the manner in which personal data can be used by federal agencies.

CHAPTER TEST

VOCABULARY

Match each term from the numbered column with the best description from the lettered column.

1. Electronic Funds Transfer Act of 1978

2. Computer piracy

3. Financial Privacy Act of 1978

4. Encryption

5. Privacy Act of 1974

6. Fair Credit Reporting Act of 1970

7. Data encryption standard

a. Restricts agencies' access to individuals' financial information and outlines procedures for legally obtaining such information.

b. Software that translates data into a secret code.

c. The illegal copying of copyrighted software.

d. Outlines the collection, maintenance, and access of consumer credit information.

e. The translation of information into a secret code.

f. Limits the manner in which personal data can be used by federal agencies.

g. Restricts when and how financial institutions can electronically transfer customers' funds.

QUESTIONS

1. Imagine you are applying for a position at a private company. What credit and financial information could be obtained about you without and with your permission?
2. You are rejected for credit. What can you do to challenge the finding by the credit company? Cite what law you are basing your argument on.
3. List some problems with privacy-of-information legislature.
4. Why are good security measures not enough to ensure untampered data, hardware, and software?

APPENDIX A

Identifiers

UCSD Pascal identifiers must follow these rules:

- Begin with a letter
- Contain only letters or numbers or the underscore character (__)
- Uppercase and lowercase are seen by the compiler as being the same
- The underscore character is ignored by the compiler
- The compiler looks at only the first 8 characters of an identifier

Syntax Diagrams

SYNTAX FIGURES

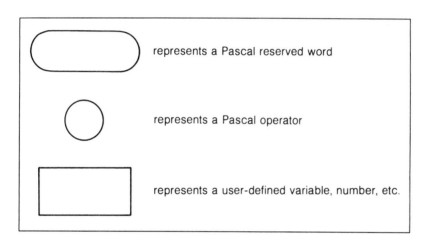

represents a Pascal reserved word

represents a Pascal operator

represents a user-defined variable, number, etc.

PROGRAM

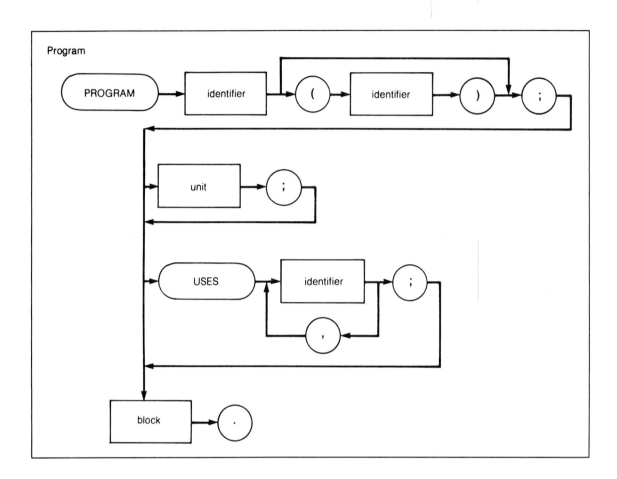

DECLARATIONS

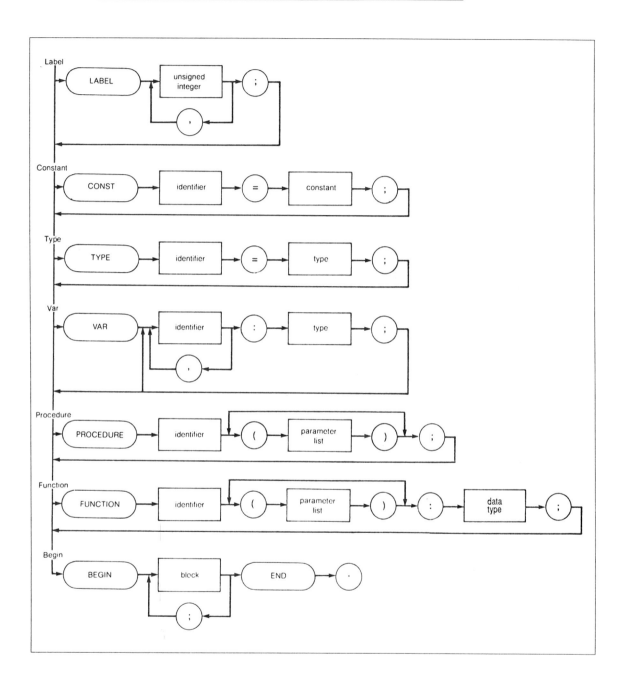

CONDITIONAL STATEMENTS

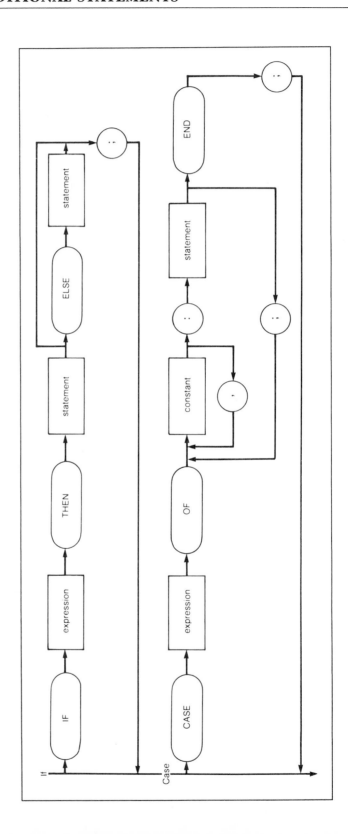

LOOPING STATEMENTS

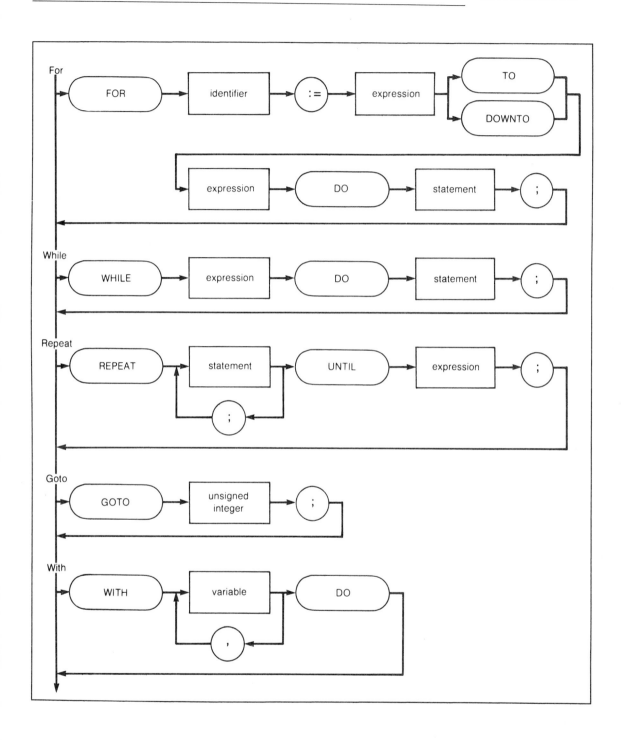

Pascal Reserved Words

AND	FILE	#NIL	THEN
ARRAY	FOR	NOT	TO
BEGIN	FORWARD	OF	TYPE
CASE	FUNCTION	OR	* UNIT
CONST	GOTO	PACKED	UNTIL
DIV	IF	PROCEDURE	*USES
DO	IN	PROGRAM	VAR
DOWNTO	*IMPLEMENTATION	RECORD	WHILE
ELSE	*INTERFACE	REPEAT	WITH
END	LABEL	* SEGMENT	
*EXTERNAL	MOD	SET	

* UCSD Pascal only
\# Standard Pascal only

APPENDIX D

Pascal Standard Identifiers

ABS
*APPLESTUFF
BOOLEAN
*BUTTON
CHAR
*CLOSE
*CONCAT
*COPY
COS
*DELETE
*EOF
EDLN
EXIT
*EXP
FALSE
*FILLSCREEN
GET

*GOTOXY
*INITTURTLE
INPUT
INTEGER
*INTERACTIVE
KEYBOARD
KEYPRESS
LENGTH
LOG
MAXINT
MOVE
MOVETO
ODD
ORD
OUTPUT
PACK
*PADDLE

*PENCOLOR
POS
PRED
PUT
*RANDOM
READ
READLN
REAL
RESET
REWRITE
ROUND
*SCREENBIT
*SEEK
SIN
SQR
SQRT

STRING
SUCC
TEXT
TRUE
TRUNC
TURN
TURNTO
TURTLEANG
TURTLEGRAPHICS
TURTLEX
TURTLEY
UNPACK
VIEWPORT
WRITE
WRITELN

* UCSD Pascal Only

Pascal Operators

RELATIONAL

=	equal to
<>	not equal to
>	greater than
>=	greater than or equal to
<	less than
<=	less than or equal to

ARITHMETIC

( )	parentheses
**	exponentiation
DIV MOD	integer division, remainder of integer
/ *	division and/or real division, multiplication
+ −	addition, subtraction

BOOLEAN

NOT	Evaluates to the opposite (or the negation) of the operand
AND	Evaluates to true only if both operands are true
OR	Evaluates to true if one or both operands are true

Order of Operations

```
NOT
AND, *, /, DIV, MOD
OR, +, −
<, <=, =, <>, >=, >
```

Operators on the same level are evaluated
from left to right

APPENDIX G

Packed Arrays

Packed arrays must be used to handle character strings when using Pascal compilers that do not include data type STRING. In order to use packed arrays, the programmer must be familiar with the structured data type array that is covered in Chapter 11. Packed arrays are not part of the original definition of Pascal.

Packed arrays are declared under the TYPE declaration:

```
TYPE
    STR15 = PACKED ARRAY [1 . . SIZE] OF CHAR;
```

Then one or more variables may be declared of this type:

```
VAR
    VEGGIE : STR15;
```

VEGGIE may now contain a character string consisting of 15 characters. The reserved word PACKED tells the compiler to store the array in such a way as to save space, that is, to pack it. Also, the compiler will now allow certain operations to be done with this array that are not allowed on unpacked arrays. These operations are:

1. Relational operators can be used to compare two entire packed arrays alphabetically.
2. The packed array can be written all at once, rather than a character at a time, as would have to be done with an unpacked array.
3. A character string can be assigned to a packed array using a single assignment statement.

PROGRAM VEGETABLES demonstrates operations that can be done on packed arrays. A character string must be read to a packed array one character at a time. This is done in the same way as with a packed array. But a character string may be assigned to the packed array with a single assignment statement. The entire value of the array may then be printed with a single WRITE statement.

```
PROGRAM VEGETABLES;
(* THIS PROGRAM DEMONSTRATES SEVERAL OPERATIONS THAT CAN BE DONE ON
PACKED ARRAYS *)

CONST
   SIZE = 15;

TYPE
   STR15 = PACKED ARRAY[1..SIZE] OF CHAR;

VAR
   VEGGIE1 : STR15;
   VEGGIE2 : STR15;
   NUM     : INTEGER;

BEGIN   (* VEGETABLES *)

   NUM := 1;
   WRITELN ('ENTER THE FIRST VEGETABLE:');

   (* READ FIRST VEGETABLE TO PACKED ARRAY *)
   WHILE NOT EOLN AND (NUM <= SIZE) DO
      BEGIN
         READ (VEGGIE1[NUM]);
         NUM := NUM + 1
      END;    (* WHILE *)

   READLN;

   (* ASSIGN CAULIFLOWER TO SECOND PACKED ARRAY *)
   VEGGIE2 := 'CAULIFLOWER    ';

   (* PRINT CONTENTS OF THE TWO PACKED ARRAYS TO THE MONITOR *)
   WRITELN (VEGGIE1);
   WRITELN (VEGGIE2)

END.   (* VEGETABLES *)



Running . . .
ENTER THE FIRST VEGETABLE:
CELERY
CELERY
CAULIFLOWER
```

APPENDIX H

Taking Care of a Floppy Disk

Much hard work went into writing the programs on a floppy disk. To make sure these programs are not destroyed, the disks must be cared for properly.

- Handle the disk only by the protective jacket and label. Do not touch the disk itself.
- Use only a felt-tip pen to write on a disk label already attached to the disk. Remember not to press hard. (It is best to write on the label before attaching it to the disk.)
- Do not bend the disk.
- Store disks in their envelopes and then in an upright position. Disk storage boxes might be available for use.
- Direct sunlight, moisture, and extremes of cold and heat are bad for disks. Store disks away from any of these conditions.
- Magnets or other electrical devices (like television sets and telephones) can destroy programs stored on the disk.
- Do not place the disk on top of the computer or on top of the disk drive. Remember, these are electrical devices and the programs stored on the disk can be destroyed.

APPENDIX I

Filer and Editor Basics

The Filer and Editor of the p-system are frequently used in the creation, editing, and storage of UCSD Pascal programs. To program in the UCSD Pascal system, the programmer must learn at least a few basics about the Filer and Editor. This section will outline a few simple ways to use the Filer and Editor to create, edit, save, and run UCSD Pascal programs with the Apple or IBM versions of UCSD Pascal. For a detailed explanation of the capabilities of the Filer and Editor, take a look at the User's Manual for your version of UCSD Pascal.

CREATING A PROGRAM

To create a UCSD Pascal program, you must first boot the p-system on a microcomputer. The main menu of UCSD Pascal (see Figure I-1) should now be on the screen. If you are in another menu, type Q. This should bring up the main menu. Follow these steps to enter the Editor:

1. Type E
2. a. If the next message says NO WORKFILE PRESENT, press the RETURN key.
   b. If a program appears, you must delete it from the p-system's workfile. To do this type Q. Then, type E. You should now be at the main menu again. Now, you must enter the Filer. To do this, type F. Then, type N for the new command. When the message THROW AWAY CURRENT WORKFILE? appears, type Y. Now,

```
COMMAND: E(DIT, R(UN, F(ILE, C(OMP, L(INK, X(ECUTE, A(SSEM
```

Figure I-1   THE MAIN MENU OF UCSD PASCAL

```
>EDIT: A(DJUST C(PY D(LETE F(ND I(NSRT J(MP
R(PLACE Q(UIT X(CHNGE Z(PP
```

Figure I-2 THE EDITOR SCREEN

return to the main menu by typing Q. Follow steps 1 and 2a to re-enter the Editor.

You should now be in the p-system Editor. Figure I-2 illustrates the Editor screen. To begin entering a program, simply press I and begin typing your program. Press the RETURN key at the end of each line.

At the end of your program, press the CTRL and C keys. Notice that you can now move the cursor across the Editor screen. If you are satisfied with your program, type Q. Then, type U to store the current version of your program in the p-system's workfile. You should now see the main menu. If you need to make corrections to your program, see the Editing program section.

SAVING A PROGRAM

To save the workfile, first enter the p-system's main menu. Next, enter the Filer by typing F. Then, type S for the Save command. The message SAVE AS Volume name: File name ? may appear. At this point, you must make a decision. On what diskette do you want to store your program? You should insert that diskette into drive #5 (for 2-drive users) or drive #4 (for 1-drive users). In most cases, you will type N to the above message. Another message will appear that asks SAVE AS? or SAVE AS WHAT FILE? Type in the volume name of your diskette (or #4 for 1-drive users, #5 for 2-drive users), a colon (:), and a file name. Then press the RETURN key. Your program should now be saved.
EXAMPLE:

Prompt:　　SAVE AS SYSTEM.WORK.TEST?
Response:　N
Prompt:　　SAVE AS WHAT FILE?
Response:　MYDISK:PROGRAM1 and PRESS RETURN

RUNNING A PROGRAM

In order to run a program, the program should be in the workfile. If the program is not in the p-system's workfile, read the 'Editing a Program' section now. It will show you how to move a program into the p-system's workfile. If the program is in the workfile, enter the p-system's main menu. Next, if you have a 2-drive system, insert the

APPLE2: or PASCAL: diskette into the second drive (#5). Finally, type R. The p-system will then compile the program in the workfile. Program errors will be noted by the p-system's compiler. If the program does not have any syntax errors, the program will be executed.

EDITING A PROGRAM

Program errors are part of the programming process. Everyone makes errors at some time. The USCD p-system allows you to edit program files easily. This section will show you how to edit files that are already in the p-system's workfile and how to edit files that are stored on a diskette.

To edit a program file, you must move the program file into the p-system's editor. If your program is currently in the p-system's workfile, follow these steps to enter the Editor:

1. Enter the p-system's main menu. In most cases, pressing Q will move you to the main menu.
2. Type E. You should now be in the Editor. You should see your program.

If your program is currently *not* in the p-system's workfile *and* is on a diskette, follow these steps:

1. If you have a program in the p-system's workfile and you want to keep that program, save the program. Follow the instructions in the "Saving a Program" section. Then, go to step 4 in these instructions.
2. Enter the p-system's main menu.
3. Type F to enter the Filer.
4. Type N to clear the p-system's workfile.
5. When the message "THROW AWAY CURRENT WORKFILE?" appears, type Y.
6. If you have a One-Drive system,
   a. Type T.
   b. Remove the system diskette (APPLE1: or SYSTEM2:) and insert the diskette with the program.
   c. When the message "TRANSFER?" appears, type the name of the diskette, a colon, and the name of the program file. Then, press the RETURN key.
   d. When the message "TO WHERE?" appears, type: APPLE1: SYSTEM.WRK.TEXT and press the RETURN key.
   e. Insert the APPLE1: or SYSTEM2: diskette and press the space bar.
7. If you have a Two-drive system,
   a. Insert the diskette with the program in drive #5.
   b. Type G.
   c. When the message "GET?" appears, type #5: and the name of the program file. Then, press the RETURN key.

411

8. Type Q to exit the Filer.

9. Type E to enter the Editor. You should now be in the Editor. You should see your program.

Now that you have the program in the Editor, you can edit the program. The p-system's Editor is very powerful. This section will cover how to insert and delete lines and characters. The Editor can do much more. Refer to your User's Manual for more information on the Editor.

To insert and/or delete part of a program, you must move the cursor. The four basic keys that move the cursor in Apple's version of USCD Pascal are: ---->, to move right one character, <----, to move left one character; or CTRL-O to move up one line; or CTRL-L, to move down one line. Try moving the cursor with these keys. You can move the cursor quickly to most parts of a program.

To delete characters, move the cursor directly on top of the first character to be deleted. Then, type D. Notice that the line DELETE: <> <MOVING COMMANDS> [<ETX> TO DELETE, <ESC> TO ABORT] appears at the top of the screen. If you press the ----> key, the character under the cursor is deleted. If you press the <---- key, the character to the left of the cursor disappears. Press CTRL and C when you are done deleting characters on a line to make the deletions permanent. Press the <ESC> key to cancel the deletions. To delete lines, move the cursor to the beginning of a line. Type D. Press the <RETURN> key, Press CTRL and C to delete the line permanently. Press the <ESC> key to cancel the deletion.

To insert characters, move the cursor to the character left of the position where you want to add characters. For example, if you had this line in a program WRITE ('THIS IS AN EXAMPLE'); and you wanted to add LN to the WRITE, you would move the cursor on top of the E. Then, you must type I. Notice that the line INSERT: TEXT [<BS> A CHAR, <DEL> A LINE] [<EXT> ACCEPTS, <ESC> ABORTS] appears at the top of the screen. Now just type the necessary characters onto the line. To make an insertion permanent, press the CTRL and C keys. To cancel an insertion, press the <ESC> key. To insert a line, move the cursor to the end of the line above the position you want to insert the new line. For example, if you had the program segment below and wanted to insert an

```
FOR 1 := 1 to 10 DO
   BEGIN
      WRITELN ('THIS IS AN EXAMPLE')
      WRITELN ('FOR INSERTING LINES')
```

END statement, you would move the cursor to the end of the WRITELN ('FOR INSERTING LINES') line. Then, press the I and <RETURN> keys. You can then type in the new line and, if necessary, add more lines. Don't forget to press the CTRL and C keys to make the insertions permanent or to press the ESC key to cancel the insertions.

Now your program is corrected or changed. To exit the Editor, type Q. You have a number of options at this point. The most commonly used option is to update the workfile. This tells the Editor to save your corrections and to *erase* the old version of the program in the workfile.

This section has only covered the basics of the p-system's Editor and filer. As you use the p-system more often, you may need to use more of UCSD's abilities. The UCSD User's Manuals are good sources of information. With a little effort, you can find the Editor and Filer functions that best fit your needs.

Glossary

Acronym A word whose letters each stand for another word.

Actual parameter The value that will replace the formal parameter when a subprogram is executed.

Algorithm A sequence of steps used to solve a problem.

Ancestor A node from which others have descended in a binary tree.

Application program A program designed to meet a particular user need.

Argument The value manipulated by a function; another term for actual parameter.

Arithmetic/logic unit The part of the CPU which performs arithmetic and does logical operations.

Arithmetic operator A symbol that stands for an arithmetic process, such as addition or subtraction.

Array An ordered set of related data items, all of the same data type.

Assembler language A symbolic programming language that uses abbreviations rather than zeros and ones; an assembler program translates assembler language into machine language.

Assignment statement A statement that allows a value to be stored in a variable.

Average absolute deviation The average of the absolute deviations from the mean.

Base type The data type from which a subrange is defined. The base type must be a scalar data type.

Batch processing A method of processing data using programs in which items are collected and forwarded to the computer in a group and processed in a continuous stream.

Binary tree A dynamic data structure that may connect two nodes to a single node via two different pointers. In turn, two more nodes may be connected to each of these two added nodes. This process continues until leaves are formed.

Bisection method An iterative method that reduces an interval that contains the zero of a function by half each time until a tolerance value is reached.

Bit The smallest unit of information that can be represented in binary notation; a zero or one for off or on as an electrical impulse; short for *bi*nary digi*t*.

Bottom-up program design A method of designing a program where the programmer works from the specific to the general.

Boundary case The data that fall at the very extremes of the legal range.

Branch Pointer field of a node in a tree.

Bug An error in a program that causes a program to behave incorrectly.

Central processing unit (CPU) The part of the computer that does the work. The CPU also directs the order in which operations are done and has a memory.

Central tendency The tendency of randomly generated values to center or group themselves around a central value.

Child The node immediately below a parent node in a tree.

Circular definition Declarations of a new pointer type that point to records involve an unusual characteristic that uses a reference type in the declarations before it has been defined as a record. The pointer type that is associated with the reference type is used inside the record declaration to complete the definition.

Circular list A queue that has its head and tail connected by a pointer.

Collision The situation that occurs when a hashing algorithm results in the same record location for two different primary keys.

Comments Statements in a computer program that explain to users what is being done in the program. They are ignored by the computer.

Compiler A program that translates an entire source program into machine language. The resulting program is the object program.

Compile-time error See **Syntax error.**

Complete testing approach A method of program testing that tests all paths of logic in a program.

Compound statement A series of statements that starts with BEGIN and concludes with END.

Computer-assisted design The use of computers to simulate the design and stress points of a product.

Computer-assisted instruction The use of computers to control a learning situation.

Computerized axial tomography A form of X-rays that are interpreted by a computer to form a three-dimensional picture of an object.

Computer literacy A basic knowledge of computers.

Computer piracy The illegal copying of copyrighted software.

Constant An identifier whose value may not change during program execution.

Constant declaration statement The statement that tells the compiler the specified value to be associated with a constant.

Control statement A statement that allows the programmer to determine whether or not a statement (or a group of statements) will be executed and how many times.

Control unit The part of the CPU which determines the order in which computer operations will be performed.

Cursor A box that indicates where printing will next appear on the screen.

Data Facts that the computer uses as input.

(DES) Data encryption standard Software that translates data into a secret code.

Debugging The process of locating and correcting program errors.

Decision step A step in solving a problem where a comparison is made. The step that will be done next depends on the results of the comparison.

Decision structure A control statement used to determine whether or not a statement or statements in a program will be executed.

Defensive programming A method of programming that stresses the anticipation of input errors and the protection of a program from possible errors.

Descendant Any node that comes below a given node in a tree.

Descriptive variable name A variable name that explains what the variable represents. For example, the variable AVE could be used to represent the average of a group of numbers.

Dispersion A characteristic of a distribution of random values in which two distributions may have the same central tendency but one may cluster more closely around the center of the distribution than the other.

Double-alternative decision step A decision step in which the step follows if the comparison made in the decision step is true and another if it is false.

Dynamic data structure A collection of elements that can change in size, depending on the data storage requirements of a program.

Dynamic variables Variables that may be created or disposed of as a program executes.

Electronic funds transfer The automatic, electronic recording of account transactions and money transfers.

Electronic Transfer Act of 1978 Law restricting when and how financial institutions can electronically transfer customers' funds.

Element An individual value of an array. An array element must have a subscript.

Encryption The translation of information into a secret code.

Execute To read and carry out the instructions in a program.

Exponential notation The representation of a real number with only one digit to the left of the decimal point, multiplied by a power of ten. For example, in Pascal 153.25 would be represented in exponential notation as 1.5325OE2.

Expression Any valid combination of variable(s), constant(s), operator(s), and parentheses.

Fair Credit Reporting Act of 1970 Law outlining the collection, maintenance, and access practices for consumer credit information.

Field A data item that is part of a record.

Financial Privacy Act of 1978 Law restricting agencies' access to individuals' financial information and outlining procedures for legally obtaining such information.

Flowchart A method of visually representing the steps in solving a problem.

Formal parameter A variable that represents a value to be passed to a function or procedure.

Format To control the way in which output will be printed.

Function A subprogram that can be used to determine a single value.

Function call An expression that causes a function to be executed.

Function heading The first line in a function. It contains three parts: (1) the reserved word FUNCTION followed by the name of the function, (2) the formal parameter list, and (3) the data type of the function.

Global variable A variable that is declared in the declaration section of a main program. It may be referred to anywhere in that program.

Hand simulation The process of the programmer performing all operations in a program normally performed by the computer.

Hard copy Output that is printed on paper.

Hardware The actual physical components of a computer system.

Hashing Applying a mathematical formula to a primary key of a record to obtain a resulting record location.

Hashing algorithm A mathematical formula applied to the primary key of a record to determine the location of that record.

High-level language An English-like programming language that must be translated into machine code before execution.

Identifier A name chosen by the programmer to represent a storage location.

Illegal case Data that violate the specifications or logic of a program.

Infinite loop A loop in which the condition controlling loop repetition will never contain the value needed to stop the loop.

Initialize To set a variable to a starting value.

Input Data that are put into a computer to be processed.

Input devices Equipment such as a keyboard, disk drive, or cassette recorder used to enter data into a computer.

Input/output (I/O) management system A part of the operating system that controls and coordinates the CPU while receiving input, executing programs in storage, and regulating output.

Input variable A value that is placed into the computer to obtain a needed result.

Integer A whole number or its opposite.

Interactive processing Processing in which the user can communicate with the computer while the program is being executed.

Interpreter A program that translates a source program into machine language one line at a time.

Iterates Successive approximations of a function.

Iteration The repetition of an algorithm.

Job control program A program that translates into machine langauge the job control statements written by a programmer to indicate what the computer should do during a program.

Language translation program The instruction: that translate the English-like programs written by pro grammers into machine-executable code.

Library program A user-written or manufacturer-supplied program or subroutine that is frequently used in other programs.

Linked list The simplest form of dynamic data structure, consisting of one or more nodes that are linked or connected together.

List head The first list element in a linked list.

Local variable A variable that is declared in a subprogram. It is undefined outside of that subprogram.

Logic error A flaw in the algorithms, formulas, or logic of a program.

Logo An educational programming language.

Loop A control statement that allows a series of instructions to be executed repeatedly as long as specified conditions are constant.

Loop control variable A variable whose value is used to control the repetition of a loop.

Low-level language A programming language, such as assembler language, that is close to machine language.

Machine language The language a program must be in for a computer to be able to execute the program. It must be written in binary code.

Mainframe A large computer, often used in business, to which many terminals can be attached.

Main memory Storage area where the computer keeps information.

Median The value that half the observations fall above and half fall below.

Microcomputer A small digital computer with most of the capabilities of larger computers; the center of the computer is the microprocessor.

Microprocessor A single silicon chip in a microcomputer, on which the CPU is located.

Minicomputer A generally lower-priced, general-purpose system that can perform many of the same functions as a mainframe.

Mnemonics A symbolic name or memory aid; used in assembly language and in high-level computer languages.

Mode The value of the variable that occurs most frequently.

Modems Electronic devices that convert computer signals to a format that can be sent across telephone lines.

Modularization The process of breaking a program down into modules.

Module A fairly independent part of a larger program that is designed to perform a specific job.

Monte Carlo technique A method that uses randomly produced values that can represent the data of a given result.

Multiphasic health testing center A medical center that uses computers to maintain records, control tests, and aid in diagnoses.

Multiply-linked list   A list of elements with more than one link.

Nested statement   A statement that is contained within another statement.

NIL   A value of null that is placed in a link field of an element.

NIL pointer   A pointer that has been assigned the value NIL.

Node   An element in a dynamic data structure.

Nondestructive testing   The use of computer-controlled X-rays, high-frequency sound waves, or laser beams to inspect a product.

Null case   Occurs when a table holds zero elements, a file is empty, or a variable contains no value.

Object program   The program that results when a compiler translates a source program into machine language.

Operand   A value on which an arithmetic operation is performed.

Operating system   A collection of programs that permit a computer to manage itself and avoid idle CPU time.

Operator   A symbol that stands for a process.

Optical scanners   Devices used to read Universal Product Codes.

Order of operations   The sequence in which expressions are evaluated.

Ordinal data type   See **Scalar data type**.

Output   Results the computer obtains after processing input.

Output devices   Equipment such as a screen, disk drive, cassette recorder, or printer used to store, display, or print out information.

Output variable   Information the computer gives as the result of processing input.

Papert, Seymour   The creator of the Logo programming language.

Parameter   A value that is passed from a program to a subprogram. The value may or may not be passed back to the main program.

Parent   A node in a tree that has a branch or branches to other nodes.

Point-of-sale terminals   Terminals used in retail stores to maintain sales records, control optical scanners, and perform the normal functions of a cash register.

Pointers   see **Pointer variables**.

Pointer type   Variables that reference or point to a location of a particular type, called the reference type.

Pointer variables   The type of a pointer that may reference a particular type of storage location. They contain a memory address of a dynamic variable.

Pop   To delete the topmost node on a stack.

Precedence   A rule that determines which variable value will be changed when there is a multiple declaration of a variable.

Predefined file   A file that is declared and opened automatically by the UCSD Pascal system.

Predefined identifiers   Words that have a specific meaning to the Pascal compiler. They may not be redefined by the programmer.

Primary key   A field in a record that uniquely identifies that record. No two records in a file may have the same primary key.

Primitive data type   See **Simple data type**.

Privacy Act of 1974   Law limiting the manner in which personal data can be used by federal agencies.

Procedure   A subprogram that performs a specific task. Procedures allow a progrm to be broken down into smaller subprograms.

Procedure call   A statement that causes a procedure to be executed.

Procedure heading   The first line of a procedure. It contains two parts: (1) the reserved word PROCEDURE followed by the name of the procedure and (2) the formal parameter list.

Program   A list of instructions that a computer uses to solve a specific problem.

Program documentation   A written description of a program and what it accomplishes.

Program error   A flaw or error in a program that causes the program not to run properly; a syntax, runtime, or logic error.

Program heading   The first statement in a Pascal program. It contains the reserved word PROGRAM, followed by the program name.

Program proof concept   A method of program testing that uses program statements to prove mathematical theorems about program behavior.

Program testing   A systematic process of testing a program to see if it contains any program errors.

Program tracing   A method of locating program errors by using WRITELN statements.

Programmer   A person who writes programs.

Programming style   The way in which a program is written and whether it is easy for people to read and understand the program.

Prompt   A statement printed to the monitor that tells the user to enter data.

Pseudocode   Program statements written briefly in English, not in a programming language; a verbal description of the programming logic.

Pseudorandom numbers Numbers obtained by a formula that imitate the values of a random variable.

Push To insert a node at the top of a stack.

Queue A list in which all insertions are made at the end of the list and deletions are made from the beginning.

Random-access file A file that allows data items to be stored anywhere. Data items can then be directly accessed.

Random number generators A method of generating random values by monitoring discrete changes in noise.

Range The difference between the largest and smallest observation.

Record A structured data type that contains a group of related data items, not necessarily of the same data type, that are gathered together in a single unit.

Recursion The situation when a procedure or function calls itself.

Reference type A particular type of location that can be referenced by a pointer type.

Relational operators Operators that compare one operand with another.

Reserved words Words that have a specific meaning to the Pascal compiler. They may not be redefined by the programmer.

Right-justified Lined up on the right side of the field, so that any blank spaces will be on the left side of the field.

Root The topmost element in a tree; the ancestor to all other nodes.

Run-time error A program error that causes abnormal program behavior during execution.

Scalar data type A data type where all of the values of that data type may be listed. INTEGER, CHAR, and BOOLEAN, are all scalar data types, as is the user-defined data type.

Scientific notation See **Exponential notation**.

Scope The system that determines which subprogram may reference a given variable.

Scope block The portion of a program in which the scope of a variable is defined.

Search To locate a particular item in a list of items.

Selective testing approach A method of program testing that tests the boundary, null, and illegal cases.

Sequential file A file that stores data items one right after another. Data items must also be accessed in sequence.

Set A structured data type consisting of a collection of values that are classed together. All of the values must be of the same base type.

Siblings Children of the same parent node.

Simple data type A data type that cannot be broken down into smaller components.

Simulations Computer-generated models based on analyses of data.

Single-alternative decision step A decision step in which a subsequent step is performed only if the comparison made in the decision step is true. If the comparison is false, no action is taken.

Soft copy Output displayed on the terminal.

Software A program or a series of programs.

Sort To arrange a list of items in a particular order, such as to arrange names alphabetically.

Source program A program that must be translated into machine language before it can be executed.

Spreadsheet programs Computer packages used to make calculations on rows and columns of numerical data.

Stack A list in which all insertions, deletions, and accesses to the list are from one end, known as the top of the stack.

Standard identifier See **Predefined identifier**.

Static variables Variables that are declared at the beginning of a program or a subprogram and remain in existence throughout the execution of the blocks in which they were declared. For each variable, the computer sets aside a small portion of its memory as a location.

Stepwise refinement The process of breaking a large program down into smaller and smaller subprograms, used in top-down programming design.

Structured data type A data type that can store many individual values that may then be referred to as a single unit. Each structured data type has strict rules concerning how it is to be declared and used in programs. The structured data types in Pascal are arrays, records, sets, and files.

Structured programming language A language that allows a large problem to be broken down methodically into smaller units. It also allows the programmer to easily control the order in which a program will be executed. This approach leads to programs that are logical and easy to understand.

Subprogram A part of a larger program that performs a specific job.

Subrange data type A data type that contains a portion of a predefined or user-defined scalar data type.

Subtree Any node in a tree that has or may have at least one branch.

Subscript A value enclosed in brackets that is used

to refer to a particular array element. For example, NAME [3] is the third element of array NAME.

Supercomputer   An extremely large, powerful computer capable of performing at least 10 million arithmetic operations per second.

Supervisor program   The major component of an operating system; it coordinates the activities of all other parts of the operating system.

Syntax error   A violation of the grammatical rules of a programming language.

Syntax rules   Conventions that explain how the parts of a language should be put together.

System program   A program written to coordinate the operation of computer circuitry and to help the computer run quickly and efficiently.

Tables of random numbers   A list of random values that were produced by a simple repetitive experiment.

Telecommunications   The transfer of data across telephone lines, televisions, or other similar mediums.

Terminal communications packages   Software that allows different computers to communicate, usually across telephone lines.

Top-down program design   A method of designing a program that works from the general to the specific by using stepwise refinement.

Tree   A dynamic data structure that has one or more nodes where one node is designated as the root which points to zero or more distinct subtrees.

Truncate   To cut off part of a value. For example, if 17.23 was truncated at the decimal point the result would be 17.

Turtle   A small screen object that is used in the Logo language to draw figures.

UCSD Pascal compiler   The compiler most widely used for Pascal on microcomputers.

Unary minus sign   A symbol ($-$) used alone with a number that gives the opposite of the number.

Unary plus sign   A symbol ($+$) used alone with a number that leaves the number unchanged.

Universal Product Code   A standardized bar code used to identify retail products.

User-defined scalar data type   A data type defined by the programmer in a TYPE definition. Every value of the data type must be listed in the definition.

Utility program   A part of the operating system that can perform functions such as sorting, merging, and transferring data from one input or output device to another.

Valid   Correct, follows the rules.

Value parameter   A parameter whose value is passed to a subprogram, but whose value is not passed back to the calling program.

Variable   A name chosen by the programmer to represent a storage location. The value in the storage location may change during program execution.

Variable declaration statement   The statement that tells the compiler the variable names that will be used to represent storage locations.

Variable name   See **Variable**.

Variable parameter   A two-way parameter that returns its value to the calling program; preceded by VAR in the formal parameter list.

INDEX